Robin Mark, Mireille Pouget &
Edward Thomas (eds)

Adults in Higher Education

Learning from Experience in the New Europe

PETER LANG
Oxford • Bern • Berlin • Bruxelles • Frankfurt am Main • New York • Wien

Bibliographic information published by Die Deutsche Bibliothek
Die Deutsche Bibliothek lists this publication in the Deutsche Nationalbibliografie; detailed bibliographic data is available on the Internet at ‹http://dnb.ddb.de›.

British Library and Library of Congress Cataloguing-in-Publication Data:
A catalogue record for this book is available from The British Library, Great Britain, and from The Library of Congress, USA

Adults Learning & Participating in Education
alpine
A Higher Education Project

Education and Culture
Programme

This project has been funded with support from the European Commission. This publication reflects the views only of the authors, and the Commission cannot be held responsible for any use which may be made of the information contained therein.

Produced within the framework of ALPINE, Adults Learning and Participating in Education, SOCRATES Nr. 87515-CP-1-2000-1-UK-GRUNDTVIG-ADU.

Alpine logo: Produced by Alan Reid
Cover design: Thomas Jaberg, Peter Lang AG

ISBN 3-03910-182-X
US-ISBN 0-8204-6992-0

Hochfeldstrasse 32, Postfach 746, CH-3000 Bern 9, Switzerland
info@peterlang.com, www.peterlang.com, www.peterlang.net

Printed in Germany

Adults in Higher Education

Contents

Preface

A Europe of knowledge is essential for economic development, for social and human growth and for consolidating and enriching European citizenship.

Since the 1990s, the emergence of a European strategy for the development of lifelong learning has raised new questions for higher education. The role of universities and other higher education institutions in developing lifelong learning raises many questions about how they might provide for the needs of adults of all age groups and from different backgrounds.

The Adults Learning and Participating in Education Project, (known as ALPINE), recognises the need to involve more adult learners in the higher education sector. The Project examines existing provision for adults in European higher education and highlights the barriers which adults face when trying to access higher education.

The Project examines how issues in increasing and widening participation are being addressed in twenty different European countries and reports on new ways in which adults can be involved. The findings from the Project are reported both in this book and in an e-manual.

The ALPINE book

This book begins by examining existing European perspectives on lifelong learning and the problems in increasing and widening adult participation in higher education institutions in Europe. It summarises key areas identified by the Project in providing ways forward across Europe. The detailed situation in each of the participating countries, as seen by national experts, is then presented. Each national chapter sets out to examine, as far as possible, how the provision for adults is organised in higher education institutions, the barriers which prevent adults participating in higher education (including the problems of particular adult groups) and the policies and practices adopted at the national and institutional levels which seek to involve more adults. Each chapter highlights examples of innovative practice, including where possible special initiatives for specific disadvantaged groups. While many of the problems faced by adults across Europe are similar, the ways of dealing with them vary considerably. The concluding chapters provide an overview of the issues and problems. They summarise problems experienced by adult students in higher education institutions across central and western Europe and seek to draw general conclusions on the ways of overcoming these barriers.

Although the focus of this book is firmly on adult students in higher education, it is hoped that much of the content will be of use and interest to managers and teachers concerned with all adult education provision.

The ALPINE e-manual of good practice

The Project has also prepared an e-manual of good practice which looks in greater detail at the practical issues associated with increasing and widening participation in higher education institutions.

Issues examined include the adult curriculum, student support and adult guidance, community outreach, information and communication technology (ICT) as a tool for reaching adults, engaging non-traditional groups, adult teaching and learning, and language and cultural learning for adults. Other key issues such as assessment, accreditation and the funding of adult learning might also have been included but were restricted by the time available. Summaries of key points and case studies of good practice can be found at the ALPINE Project Web site: http://www.qub.ac.uk/alpine (Mark, Moore and Valk, 2004).

This manual presents information on good practice for managers and teachers who have a role in developing adult provision in higher education institutions. It should also be of value to policy makers and administrators with responsibility for adult higher learning, the staffs of national agencies who have a role to play in increasing adult participation in higher education institutions, staff trainers and others with an interest in widening participation in the higher education sector.

The Project outcomes

Together, the book and manual provide a compendium of ideas for increasing and widening participation for adults in European higher education institutions. They show how countries, and their individual higher education institutions, are increasing adult provision. This includes meeting the needs of underrepresented groups of adults and highlights the many problems that have still to be overcome. It is hoped that these twin resources will help higher education institutions to manage the process of change in increasing the numbers of adult students. This, in turn, should improve the quality of provision for adult students in European higher education institutions generally.

The Project took place over a three year period and was funded by the Gruntvig strand of the European Union's Socrates Project (Project Number: 85715-CP-1-2000-UK-GRUNDTVIG-ADU (2001–2004)). It began in May 2001 and completed its work in June 2004.

The Grundtvig programme

The aims of the ALPINE Project are closely allied to the European Commission's published strategies and proposals for lifelong learning.

The European Union (EU) Socrates programme is based on Article 150 of the Maastricht Treaty. (See http://www.eurotreaties.com/maastrichtext.html). This Article requires the EU to contribute to the development of high quality education carried out in close cooperation with the Member States.

The Grundtvig action is one means used by the European Commission to promote lifelong learning both at the European level and in each participating country. This action supports all levels and sectors of adult learning (general, cultural and social). In addition to formal and non-formal learning, it also supports learning that takes place in an informal way, such as self-directed learning. The Grundtvig action attaches a great deal of importance to lifelong learning and seeks to improve its quality, to introduce the European dimension to adult education in the broadest sense, and to help make lifelong learning opportunities more widely available to Europe's citizens.

Terms used

Throughout the book, the authors of the individual chapters have been encouraged to give common educational terms in their native languages as well as in English. Choosing an appropriate English translation here is not always simple, however. Taking the term 'higher education', for example, in French this is *education supérieure* and the translation into English is straightforward. In Czech, however, the term is *terciálního vzdělávání* and the literal translation for this is 'tertiary education'. In Polish, it is *szkoły wyższe* for which the translation is 'higher school'. In each case it is the same form of education that is being referred to and, for this reason, the translation 'higher education' has been used in each case. Some of the terms will look slightly strange to some readers as a result. It is intended, however, that this should be helpful overall.

Data collection

At the first meeting of the partners of the ALPINE Project in Belfast in May 2001, a representative from each participating country was nominated to gather data and write a national report on participation in adult learning in his or her universities. Guidelines for writing these reports were drawn up and agreed at the meeting.

These asked each writer to include information on the following:

1. The current situation for adult students in universities in each country.
   The current involvement of adults in higher education in universities and how it is organized; the variation in the organisation of lifelong learning between universities in

each country; government and institutional policy on increasing access for adults to higher education; what is happening where there is no policy; the kinds of courses offered for adults in universities, e.g. vocational, general interest, personal and social development courses;

2. The kinds of problems which exist for adults wishing to go to university
   The socio-economic/cultural groups that have traditionally suffered disadvantage, e.g. the unemployed, older adults, people with disabilities, ex-offenders/prisoners, adults in rural/isolated communities, immigrants, asylum seekers or minority ethnic groups. The problems in attracting these groups of adults to universities, describing how the barriers are being overcome; the role of universities and of the learners themselves in finding solutions; and
3. Examples of good practice from each country.
   Noteworthy practices in the country or university aimed at enabling adults to enter higher education, e.g. initiatives undertaken with specific disadvantaged groups or successful outreach and community-based activities.

It was recognised from the start that the use of general guidelines might be difficult for the authors as they might not be appropriate in every national context. Each of the authors of the country chapters was therefore encouraged to make their own decision about what to include, working within the broader guidelines of the book. The extent to which they have chosen to do this can be seen in the following chapters.

The target group of the study

A common understanding of what is meant here by the term 'adult' in the context of universities is important. It was agreed to examine the provision for students who had completed their initial education followed by a period when they had not been involved in formal education. The kind of education provision examined particularly includes the non-traditional learner both in vocational courses, where the motive is to develop skills and knowledge for work, and in non-vocational provision for personal development or for social and community development. It was also felt that groups which had traditionally suffered disadvantage, such as those experiencing rural isolation or immigrants, should be a particular focus of the study, as far as possible.

Relatively little information has been previously published on this subject. Osborne and Thomas (2003) in *Lifelong learning in a changing continent* provide a base-line study of continuing education in the universities of Europe. Some of the findings reported in this book are relevant and have been integrated into the chapters when appropriate. In this way, as broad a picture as possible is presented of adults in higher education across Europe.

Learning gives people the tools and the skills to shape their own lives and fulfil their personal ambitions and it can considerably enhance a person's happiness and motivation in life. Society as a whole benefits from having more knowledgeable citizens who understand their culture and history and who become more involved in their communities. Access to lifelong learning helps adults to become more tolerant and to build a fairer and a better society. It is hoped that some of the ideas contained in this book will help to do just that.

Project Partners

The ALPINE Project was coordinated by the Institute of Lifelong Learning of the Queen's University Belfast, with the financial management being provided by the International Office of the University.

The universities which participated in the Project were:

Belgium – Université de Liége and Universiteit Gent
Bulgaria – University of Chemical Technology and Metallurgy, Sofia
Czech Republic – Masaryk University
Estonia – Tartu University

Finland – Åbo Akademi University, University of Helsinki and the University Continuing Education Network in Finland
France – Université de Haut Alsace (Mulhouse) and Université Charles de Gaulle, Lille 3
Germany – Universität Hannover
Greece – National and Kapodistrian University of Athens, University of Ioannina, University of Macedonia and the University of Patras
Hungary – University of Debrechen, University of Pecs
Ireland – University of Limerick
Italy – Universitá degli studi' G. d'Annunzio (Chieti)
Latvia – University of Latvia, (Riga)
Lithuania – Kaunas University of Technology
Poland – Marie Curie-Sklodowska University (Lublin) and the Pedagogical University, Warsaw
Portugal – Universidade de Aveiro
Romania – University of Craiova
Slovakia – Bratislava University of Economics
Slovenia – Slovenian Institute for Adult Education (Ljubljana)
Sweden – Lund University
United Kingdom:
England – City University (London), Coventry University, Goldsmith's College (University of London), University of Bristol, University of North London
Scotland – University of Stirling
Northern Ireland – Queen's University Belfast.

Robin Mark, Mireille Pouget and Edward Thomas, 2004

References

Mark, R., Moore, P.A. and Valk, A., 2004. *ALPINE Project Manual of Good Practice.* Socrates (Grundtvig) Project 85715-CP-1-2000-UK-GRUNDTVIG-ADU (2001–04). Available at: http://www.qub.ac.uk/alpine

Osborne, M. and Thomas, E., eds., 2003. *Lifelong Learning in a Changing Continent: continuing education in the universities of Europe.* Leicester: National Institute of Adult Continuing Education.

Contributors

Belgium

Anne-Marie André is an International Officer at the University of Liège, responsible for international projects in education and cooperation. Formerly a Lecturer in History and Demography, her interests in European issues led her to become the Secretary General of the Fondation Liège Université d'Europe, a think-tank covering a variety of fields, including ethics, economics, education and research.

Geneviève Cochez is currently working in the International Relations Office of Ghent University where she is responsible for the coordination and implementation of the Socrates programme. Her interests cover the broad aspects of internationalisation in higher education, linked to the general policies of the European Union (EU). She formerly worked at the EU desk of the Belgian Ministry of Foreign Affairs.

Bulgaria

Rossica Betcheva is the Dean of International Student and Foreign Language Education at the University of Chemical Technology and Metallurgy, Sofia. She is the Institutional Coordinator for European Educational Programmes and the contact person of several international projects in the field of higher education coordinated by the Bulgarian Ministry of Education. As a Professor of Textile Chemistry, she directs undergraduate and postgraduate courses for full-time and part-time students and short courses.

Czech Republic

Miloslava Chovancová is an Assistant Professor at Tomas Bata University in Zlín, teaching Marketing. She has created distance education modules on the subject and has also developed and facilitated a number of labour market and business skills development courses for unemployed women and courses on marketing skills for working managers.

Andras Chernel is a Senior Lecturer at Tomas Bata University and also works for the University Centre of Continuing Education. He has taught English for 11 years in the Czech Republic and is currently creating distance education modules for Business English and e-modules on the EU. His interests are in e-learning and nurturing 'communities of purpose'.

Estonia

Aune Valk is the Director of the Open University and the Head of the Department of Academic Affairs in the University of Tartu. Her special interests include the accreditation of prior learning and work experience, regional development and the use of information and communication technology (ICT) in adult education. She chairs the Council of the Estonian E-University and is the contact person for the Estonian Network for University Continuing Education.

Finland

Jyri Manninen is a Director of Research at the University of Helsinki, Palmenia Centre for Continuing Education. His research interests include adult learning in general and particularly the application of modern ICT in adult learning.

Tina Engblom is the Head of the Open University at Åbo Akademi University where she has been involved in the development of open university activities since 1982. She is also the Vice-Director of the Centre for Continuing Education at Åbo Akademi University and a member of the University Senate.

France

Guy Arquembourg teaches English at Charles de Gaulle University, Lille 3. He has been a researcher in the use of ICT for teaching and learning languages for the past 20 years and is responsible for the Multimedia Department of the Continuing Education Service and the development of interactive multimedia training material.

Arnaud Haeringer is the Director of the Service d'Enseignement et de Recherche en Formation d'Adultes (SERFA) in the Department of Continuing Education at the Université de Haute Alsace, Muhouse. He is involved in several e-learning and European projects in continuing education.

Germany

Martin Beyersdorf is the Head of the Central Office for Continuing Education at the University of Hanover. Since 1997 he has been a member of the Board of the German Association of University Continuing Education and Distance Learning (Deutsche Gesellschaft für Wissenschaftliche Weiterbildung und Fernstudium) and is the speaker of the Central Offices for Continuing Education (Konferenz Universitärer Zentralstellen) in Northern Germany. His academic interests cover the institutionalization of educational organisations, the teaching of adults and new social movements.

Greece

Athina Sipitanou is a Lecturer in the Department of Educational and Social Policy of the University of Macedonia and specialises in adult education. Her main teaching duties and research interests concern continuing education and lifelong learning. She was the president of the Management Council of the Greek Pedagogical Association Branch in Macedonia-Thrace and is a member of the Management Council of the Balkan Pedagogical and Educational Association.

Hungary

Anikó Kálmán is the Director of the Debrecen University Lifelong Learning Centre. She is an expert in adult education methodology, competency and comparative research and has led working groups in a number of EU-funded projects. She is the Secretary General of MELLearN, the Hungarian University Lifelong Learning Network and is a member of the Lifelong Learning Strategy Committee of the Hungarian Ministry for Education.

Ireland

Patricia-Anne Moore is the manager of the Department of Lifelong Learning at the University of Limerick. She has been the co-leader of the ALPINE project group on Student Support and Guidance and has taken an active part in the English language editing of the ALPINE manual. Currently she chairs the Higher Education Lifelong Learning Network (HELLNET), the national network of lifelong learning practitioners in higher education institutions in Ireland.

Italy

Margrit Wetter is a Senior Lecturer in the History of the German Language and German Linguistics at the University 'G. D'Annunzio' Chieti/Pescara and also teaches in the Faculty of Economics at the University of Rome 'La Sapienza'. Since 2002 she has been a board member of the Italian Association for German Studies. Her research is on foreign language acquisition, German for special purposes and sociolinguistics.

Latvia

Ineta Kristovska is an Assistant Professor at the University of Latvia. She has been the Director of the Distance Education Centre of Latvia since 1997 and is interested in adult and continuing education and open and distance learning. She has been a partner in a number of international projects and her research is on support systems for adults engaged in distance learning.

Lithuania

Daiva Dumčiuvienė is the Deputy Director of the Office of Academic Affairs of Kaunas University of Technology and an Associate Professor in the Institute of Europe and the Department of International Economics and Trade. Her academic interests are industrial economics and policy, the economics of European integration and the internationalisation of adult and higher education.

Marius Mikulėnas is a specialist in investment and EU project management and is currently the Director of the Kaunas Regional Development Agency. Before taking his present position, he was the Head of the Corporate Relations Office of Kaunas University of Technology where he was particularly concerned with the organisation of technology transfer and with providing support for the University's adult education activities.

Danguolė Rutkauskienė is the Head of the Distance Education Centre at Kaunas University of Technology. Her academic interests include the policy and management of open and distance learning (ODL) systems in Lithuania and Europe, adult literacy and tutor training. She is the President of the National Distance Education Association in

Lithuania and the coordinator of many European projects in the field of ODL.

Poland

Dimtcho Tourdanov is a Senior Lecturer and the Institutional Coordinator of the Socrates programme at the Pedagogical University, Warsaw He teaches political sciences, the institutions of the European Community and Community law. He also manages the activities concerned with continuing education in the University. His academic interests are mainly in political sciences and sociology.

Portugal

Nilza Costa is an Associate Professor in the Department of Didactics and Technology Education of the University of Aveiro. Her main academic interest is the impact of educational research, mainly on masters courses for the professional development of teachers, and she coordinates a number of national and international research projects.

Pedro Mantas was the President of the Executive Committee of the Association for Professional Development (UNAVE) in the University of Aveiro from 1998 to 2002. This is concerned with the university's interaction with society in the field of continuing education.

Luis Marques is an Associate Professor at the Department of Didactics and Technology Education in the University of Aveiro. His academic interests are based mainly on science education and the relation between science education research and science school practices and he coordinates a number of research projects.

Romania

Ion Olteanu is the Vice-Rector in charge of academic reform in the University of Craiova. He is a member of the Evaluation Commission of the National Council for Academic Evaluation and Accreditation, a member of the National University Research Council and the Commission for Diploma and Doctorate Evaluations of the Ministry of Education.

Valentin Oprea is the Director of the Vocational Guidance and Counselling Centre of the University of Craiova and is a founder member of the National Association of University Counsellors. He was the project assistant for the TEMPUS project 'Networking for student counselling management' and has also managed other international projects for the University.

Slovakia

Ján Porvazník is the Director of the Centre for Advanced Studies of the University of Economics in Bratislava. In 2001 he also became the Head of the Institute of Management at the Tomas Bata University in Zlin in the Czech Republic. His research interests centre on the management of small and medium-sized enterprises and the management of universities. He is the founder of the Club of Economics in the University of Economics and has chaired this since 1994.

Marína Hučková is the manager for international projects in the Centre for Advanced Studies of the University of Economics in Bratislava. She cooperates with foreign universities and other institutions on the organisation of international educational activities, including the international MBA programme. In addition, she organises seminars and other educational activities and works on international project proposals.

Slovenia

Margerita Zagmajster is the Deputy Director of the Slovene Institute for Adult Education and was previously the Head of the Slovenenian National Contact Point for Distance Education. She has been involved in national and international projects on distance education, e-learning and university continuing education and has written a number of papers on these topics.

Sweden

Ebba Ossiannilsson is a Project Manager and Senior Administrative Officer in the Office for Continuing and Distance Education (OCDE) at Lund University. Her academic interests include lifelong learning, distance education and e-learning. She is involved in several international and EU projects and networks and also in the Lund Net-university.

United Kingdom

Michael Osborne is the Professor of Lifelong Education and the Co-director of the Centre for Research in Lifelong Learning at the University of Stirling. He has worked on access to higher education since 1980, first as a lecturer on some of the earliest access courses for adults in the United Kingdom. He is the author of numerous papers and monographs in this and related topics and is the editor of the *Journal of Adult and Continuing Education*.

Editors

Robin Mark is a Senior Lecturer and the Assistant Director of Lifelong Learning at the Queen's University of Belfast. He served as the deputy chair of the Northern Ireland Inter-Centre Access to Higher Education Forum and has worked as an access to higher education tutor and coordinator both in universities and in adult colleges. His academic interests include adult education and disadvantage, adult literacy and adult tutor education. He is the coordinator of the ALPINE project 'Increasing Adult Education in European Universities' and has more than sixteen years' experience working in the area of adult access to universities in the UK.

Mireille Pouget is the Development Officer for Widening Access at the University of Stirling. She was previously a Senior Lecturer in Further Education with extensive experience in teaching community development and as a practitioner in adult education and guidance. She has developed a number of widening participation projects at the University of Stirling and is a member of various Scottish Wider Access committees. Her research interests are in the recognition of prior learning.

Edward Thomas is an Emeritus Professor in the University of Bristol. He is a founder member of the European Universities Continuing Education Network (EUCEN) and was its Secretary General from 1991 to 2000. His academic interests cover adult higher education in Europe and he is the joint coordinator of the ALPINE Working Group on the survey of European adult higher education.

Introduction

ROBIN MARK

1: Increasing Adult Participation in Higher Education

Lifelong learning and society's changing needs

The need for change in today's modern knowledge-driven society is generally accepted as one of the major challenges facing Europe at the start of the new millennium.

The evolution towards a knowledge-based society and its implications for cultural, social and economic life have meant that lifelong learning, including education during the adult years, has taken on a much higher profile. The role of lifelong learning in facilitating the successful transition to a knowledge-based society is now widely recognised at the local, national and European levels. Lifelong learning has become a European, and indeed a worldwide, imperative and provides a way for citizens to acquire the skills necessary for their continued participation in the economic life of their communities. As well as providing skills for work, lifelong learning can also provide knowledge and understanding of a whole range of other issues such as an awareness of shared values, the feeling of belonging to a common social and cultural community, and the skills and knowledge necessary to develop and strengthen a stable, peaceful and democratic society. Much has been written about lifelong learning and recent European Commission (EC) policy documents (2001a; 2002a) emphasise the need for member countries to move towards a shared understanding and a common system of practice and at the same time acknowledging this is far from the reality.

There is considerable diversity in the provision for adult students across Europe and much still needs to be learnt about the complexities of the current educational systems and the ways in which they need to change.

Lifelong learning and access to higher education in Europe

The meaning of lifelong learning is often linked to the vision of a learning society, which, in its most literal interpretation, stretches from the 'cradle to the grave'. Higher education, and the opportunities it affords learners, is just one part of the whole continuum of lifelong learning. In recent years, the European Union (EU) has sought to stimulate a debate on the future of higher education and the role of lifelong learning in increasing and widening access to learning.

The Sorbonne Declaration (1998) emphasised the need to move towards a Europe of knowledge which would strengthen and build upon the intellectual, cultural, social and technical heritage of the continent. It called on countries to improve and update education continuously for their citizens by developing a common frame of reference across Europe. One year later, the Bologna Declaration (1999) highlighted the need to establish a coherent, compatible and competitive European higher education area which would have high international standing. This Declaration noted that such a system would require the adoption of comparable degrees and the establishment of a European credit system which could be acquired in non-traditional educational contexts, including lifelong learning. The need to encourage cooperation in quality assurance (with a view to developing comparable criteria and methodologies and to promoting the European dimension in higher education, particularly with regard to curricular developments) was also seen to be important. The Bologna process addressed not only national governments, responsible for the education systems in each country, but also the whole higher education sector, including universities, their associations and networks.

On 30 October 2000, the EC published a 'Memorandum on Lifelong Learning' (2000). This sought to identify coherent strategies and practical measures with a view to fostering lifelong learning for all. It emphasises the need to encourage adults to take up educational opportunities and lifelong learning was confirmed as a key element of that strategy. The Memorandum defined lifelong learning as encompassing the whole spectrum of formal, non-formal and informal learning, including learning for active citizenship, personal fulfilment and social inclusion. It emphasised the centrality of the learner, the importance of equal opportunities and the quality and relevance of learning opportunities. In doing this, six key messages were highlighted: valuing learning; information, guidance and counselling; investing time and money in learning; bringing learning and learners closer together; new basic skills; and innovative pedagogy. These messages were further defined in a communication from the European Commission (2001a) 'Making a European Area of Lifelong Learning a Reality'. These reports and the key messages they contain are central to the work of the ALPINE Project.

Lifelong learning and widening participation

Raising people's educational level is seen as one essential requirement of creating a successful transition to a knowledge-based society and its achievement has major implications for the involvement of adults in universities. Lifelong learning closely links with a wide range of policy goals including economic and social advancement. These include, for example, providing skills for the labour market, reducing poverty, assisting community development, enhancing citizenship, and promoting social and cultural development.

The Lisbon European Council confirmed lifelong learning as a basic component of the European social model (EC, 2001a, p.6), which paved the way for the development of policies and actions in the Member States. The EU has acknowledged the importance of promoting lifelong learning through widening participation in education. The Memorandum on Lifelong Learning (2000, p.3) notes:

> Lifelong learning is no longer just one aspect of education and training; it must become the guiding principle for provision and participation across the full continuum of learning contexts. The coming decade must see the implementation of this vision. All those living in Europe, without exception, should have

> equal opportunities to adjust to the demands of social and economic change and to participate actively in the shaping of Europe's future.

The need to challenge the barriers that discourage adults from engaging in learning is widely acknowledged as a necessary first step to widening participation. Speaking on this problem Romano Prodi noted:

> We do not yet have a coherent strategy on lifelong learning [...] barriers that discourage people from entering the workforce or restrict their mobility should be eliminated. This requires more investment in education and lifelong learning and specific measures to address the skills gap.
>
> (Speech on the State of the Union, European Parliament, 13 February 2001)

The challenge for higher education

The emergence of lifelong learning onto the European policy agenda has undoubtedly influenced the development of access to higher education. The importance of changing higher education in order to promote greater equity through wider access was noted at the UNESCO World Conference on Higher Education. The foreword to the Conference noted:

> It is now clear that, to fulfil its mission, higher education must change radically, by becoming organically flexible, and at the same time more diverse in its institutions, its structures, its curricula, and the nature and forms of its programmes and delivery systems.
>
> (Foreword, UNESCO World Conference on Higher Education, 1998b, p.2)

The European University Association (2003, p.1) in *Trends 2003* reveals that a majority of European countries are either in the processes of developing a lifelong learning strategy or intend to do so. Data collected from 900 questionnaires (750 of which came from higher education institutions), reveal that policies and actions undertaken at the European and national levels do not currently target the higher education sector.

The survey noted that most national lifelong learning policies contain two coexisting agenda: of social inclusion (stressing flexible access and diversity of criteria for different learner profiles); and economic competitiveness (focussing on efficient updating of professional knowledge and skills). The report notes that the development of lifelong learning provision in universities currently has a clear market orientation and there is a well-developed dialogue between the universities and the other stakeholders. The market dimension is often funded by, and developed in partnership with, the other market stakeholders. It notes that the competitiveness agenda is reinforced by tight national budgets and, if not counterbalanced by government incentives, university provision of lifelong learning may well be forced to ignore the more costly social agenda.

The report notes that lifelong learning provision in Europe is still generally marginalised and is rarely integrated into the general strategies, core processes and central decision-making of the institutions and concludes:

> In order to position themselves in an expanding market and clarify the added value of their expertise, higher education institutions will have to make more of an effort to integrate lifelong learning into their core development processes and policies.
>
> (European University Association, 2003, p.2)

The survey showed that a majority of student associations in the previous three years had observed changes in attitude towards lifelong learning in higher education institutions in their countries. Nearly half the students' representatives noted changes with respect to courses offered to non-traditional students, while one-third observed a greater encouragement of a lifelong learning culture among the students. The report noted that exchanging experience in European networks of continuing education and European cooperation between institutions in lifelong learning (for example, for joint course development) was still the exception rather than the rule. It also noted that little change had been observed with respect to teaching methodologies or access policies.

Adults in European universities

Widening participation can provide universities with a wider social mix of learners, particularly from previously excluded groups. It is one of the universities' major responses both to the economic implications of globalisation and to the social exclusion of some groups in society. Osborne (2003, p.6) noted that the move to increase and widen participation in higher education is associated with a number of themes central to lifelong learning which include:

> [...] the economic imperative created by global competition, technological change and the challenge of the knowledge economy, individual responsibility and self-improvement, employability, flexibility of institutions and individuals, social inclusion and citizenships.

International bodies and national governments have called for the increasing and widening access to higher education from traditionally excluded groups. Osborne notes that these strands of thought are evident in key statements of many international organisations such as the Council of Europe (1996; 1999; 2001), UNESCO (1998a; 1998b), OECD (2001) and the European Commission (1995; 2001a; 2001b). These documents reaffirm the need for equality of opportunity irrespective of political, religious, socio-economic or cultural background (Council of Europe, 1996). At the European level, the Budapest Declaration of the Council of Europe (quoted in Rugaas, 2001, p.10) calls for the political goals of equity and social cohesion:

> [...] a new strategy for social cohesion promoting a more tolerant and just society based on solidarity, shared values and a common heritage; education for democratic citizenship as a lifelong learning experience fostering active participation of Europeans in all spheres of life; extensive use of information and communication technologies maximising their educational potential.

At the policy level, the importance of economic goals has to a large extent been matched by the acknowledgement of the need for social cohesion:

> Increased access to education therefore is seen as one means of ensuring that those most at risk for reasons including geographical location, the socio-economic situation, ethnicity and disability, are afforded greater opportunity within the 'knowledge society'.
>
> (Osborne, 2003, p.7)

The need to increase and widen participation

Findings from studies in European countries demonstrate considerable evidence that while absolute participation rates in higher education have increased for all socio-economic groupings, the relative rates for different groups have not changed substantially. Data from Germany (Schitzer 1999) show that while 33% of young people from the lowest socio-economic grouping reached the upper secondary school, only 8% managed to get to higher education. In contrast, 84% from the highest group got to upper secondary school and 72% to higher education. This picture is quite consistent across countries regardless of educational structures and policy initiatives. McGill and Morgan (2001, p.47) note that in Belgium economically disadvantaged groups are still under-represented, while in Denmark the percentage of higher education students from lower socio-economic backgrounds has not changed since the 1980s. (Nexelmann, cited by Skillbeck and Connell, 2000) A thirteen-country study by Shavit and Blosfield (1993), who studied social classes attending higher levels of education, found that the relative advantage associated with higher-class origin has increased: while in absolute terms lower socio-economic groups have done better in terms of access to higher education, the relative differences between classes have not greatly changed. The Shavit and Blosfield study showed that only two of the countries studied, Sweden and the Netherlands, had made significant progress in changing the relative positions of higher and lower socio-economic groups. Clancy and Wall (2000) quoted in McGill and Morgan (2001, p.45) analysed the social background of higher education entrants in the Republic of Ireland between 1980 and 1998. Striking differences were found between the socio-economic groups participating in higher education. In the 1998 study, 58% of higher education entrants were found to come from four socio-economic groupings (higher professional, lower professional, employers and managers, and farmers) even though these groups constituted only 37% of the relevant population. In contrast, other groups were under-represented in higher education, making up 41% of entrants even though they constituted 63% of the cohort. Those in the categories of agricultural workers and unskilled groups were found to have only a third of the places in higher education that their numbers in the population warranted.

Osborne (2003, p.5) noted that there have been significant increases in the numbers participating in higher education across Europe. He quotes Gellert (1993, p.17), who a decade earlier noted how institutions were changing to include new programmes, modes of teaching and learning and increased concern with widening access and educational opportunity. Osborne (2003, p.17) argued that much of the change is pragmatic rather than indicating a genuine commitment to providing greater equity. It can therefore be seen as a short-term response to demands from traditional groups. The goal of social justice appears to have taken second place to the twin aims of economic development and expediency. Research suggests that a great deal still needs to be done to widen participation in higher education, particularly from traditionally excluded groups.

In the United Kingdom, where policy has traditionally focussed on younger learners, up to 18 years old, there is now a shift towards providing opportunities for the 19–30 year age range. The United Kingdom government has set targets for 50% of people under the age of 30 to have experienced higher education by the year 2010.

The Race Relations (Amendment) Act 2000, makes it unlawful to discriminate against anyone on grounds of race, colour, nationality (including citizenship), ethnic or national origin. At the same time, the Special Educational Needs and Discrimination Act (2001) has focussed attention on approaches which institutions need to take to redress the systematic institutional exclusion faced by disabled people and those from the Black and Asian communities. Policy is also focussing on efforts to link higher education more closely to local communities, connecting with the wider voluntary and community sectors. Providing a clear picture of adult participation in learning activities in higher education is not an easy task. What is considered learning in higher education may differ from one university to another and adults are involved in learning in a range of departments across the university.

Problems in widening participation

Widening participation in higher education has become a key issue in many European universities and there have been many initiatives aimed at increasing adult participation, in adult education departments and through specially funded initiatives.

The barriers which adults experience when returning to learning have been well documented and a number of research projects have identified strategies for overcoming these problems. Cross (1981) classified barriers to participation in three categories: personal, situational, and institutional. McGivney (1991) later added a fourth category, informational barriers, to this list. Personal barriers are those where the individual has particular attitudes, perceptions or expectations that affect their ability to participate, e.g. low aspiration, low self-esteem, lack of a culture of study or bad previous educational experiences. Situational barriers relate to a person's actual situation, e.g. lack of time, distance from educational provision, lack of appropriate facilities (such as a crèche or disabled facilities) or the cost of study. Institutional barriers refer to the perception of educational providers as formal institutions traditionally catering for a particular type of student and not suited to the needs of non-traditional learners, e.g. ethnic minority groups or ex-prisoners. Informational barriers relate to the difficulties adult learners face in accessing information about the educational provision available.

McGivney (1999, p.73) summarises the general factors affecting non-participation as follows:

> These can be divided into factors which impede a person's readiness to engage in learning (cultural, social and psychological barriers) and factors which inhibit his or her ability to participate (practical and structural barriers). As the motivation to learn comes before the experience of barriers, it is often assumed that its absence represents the most powerful deterrent. However, adult participation is the result of a complex process. It is the interaction of a whole swathe of cultural, structural and practical factors that brings some groups an introduction and keeps others out. An understanding of these should inform any approaches designed to increase their participation.

The ALPINE study found that all these issues affected adults' opportunity to study in European universities.

Government policies influence participation in higher education, both in terms of how many participate and also, more importantly, of who do so. Educational policies have the potential both to construct barriers to participation and to help extend educational opportunities to a wider cohort of students. Policies can act as a positive influence on the participation of underrepresented groups or conversely, they can contribute to the construction of barriers to participation. There can be conflicting political agendas at all levels. For widening participation to be successful, it needs to be given a high priority in terms of resourcing if it is to succeed. Without appropriate funding, supportive institutional cultures and a commitment to include groups not traditional represented, it is unlikely to succeed.

Widening participation (in terms of class, gender, ethnicity and previous educational attainment) is costly and may conflict with the market approach which has a growing influence in shaping higher education provision. Key factors determining whether non-traditional students are able to participate include the cost of participation (i.e. course fees and other living costs), constraints associated with entry qualifications and the need for alternative admission routes. The need for appropriate and flexible learning opportunities and the extent of the additional support services available, are also factors. If universities are to succeed in widening their access, additional resources are required both to recruit the adult learners and to support them through their learning.

Strategies for involving more adults

Woodrow (2000), who examined the higher education access practices and policies in six European countries, drew attention to the importance of first and second level schools in ensuring wider access to higher education. In particular, she noted that the division of secondary education into vocational and academic strands creates obstacles which are difficult for those in the vocational stream to overcome later. Similarly, the improvement of pre-school facilities and the reduction in the age of starting school can prevent children from disadvantaged backgrounds from falling behind at the primary level. She also suggested that the period of compulsory education should be lengthened and that the choice between vocational and academic education should be postponed. Rigid admission criteria, which are often regarded as a way of treating all applicants 'equally', are in fact often a barrier to adult students.

McGill and Morgan (2001, p.47) have mentioned a number of other factors that would assist in improving access to higher education: monitoring, and ensuring compliance with, policies for access and equity; and considering these policies when determining the resources to be provided for individual institutions. This, they argue, would lead to providing additional resources for universities that have preformed well in widening their access and in retaining specific under-represented groups.

The development of new kinds of institutions, adopting more flexible forms of teaching and learning, recognising prior learning and credit transfer, providing support and guidance for students with special needs, flexible scheduling of courses and more part-time and distance education courses, are all issues which must be addressed if participation is to be widened. Locating institutions in areas where there are relatively low levels of participation can also help greatly. Different types of provision, to meet the needs of different adult learners, are a powerful way of addressing the needs of disadvantaged groups.

The improvement of access for disadvantaged groups requires different kinds of action at many levels both in education and in the wider society. Skilbeck and Connell (2000) mention the need for an 'educational equity chain' providing school teachers with opportunities and incentives for in-service education and professional development, taking steps to ensure successful learning by all at the primary level, and providing an institutional ethos in higher education that is supportive and inclusive. They also support the introduction of bridging courses, flexible assessment practices and welcoming entry arrangements in order to meet the needs of under-represented groups.

McGill and Morgan (2001, p.49) note that additional financial support for learners is the most common and sometimes the only solution available to combat the under-representation of students from disadvantaged backgrounds. Targeting resources to support travel costs for those living far away from provision who would not otherwise be able to pay the high transport costs and creating pathways within the curriculum to improve transfer and participation are also seen as important. The development of links with other educational providers, for example special units run in partnership with schools, the participation of higher education learners in mentoring, and having some third level courses in schools, are all ideas that have been proposed.

There is also evidence that special entry programmes may be of particular value in ensuring better access. Studies have shown that students who enter under special admission procedures do as well academically and in their subsequent careers as those who enter through the conventional routes to the same institution. (Bowen and Bok, 1998)

McGill and Morgan (2001, p.51) argue that to widen participation in higher education, there is a need to address the low level of performance of young people from educationally disadvantaged backgrounds, to develop new forms of assessment for entry to higher education, to develop fruitful partnerships between different educational institutions, including schools, to set targets for the numbers of under-represented groups who are admitted to courses, and to examine the factors leading to success in examinations and course completion for students from disadvantaged backgrounds.

McGivney (2001, p.162) noted that there is a need for a broader notion of learning if participation is to be widened: it should be seen as something that is conducted for social and family reasons and for personal development, as well as for vocational reasons. Diversity and creativity of provision are needed to address the social imbalances in participation and to enable providers of adult and community learning to deliver a varied, flexible and responsive programme of opportunities to attract new adult groups. Learning cannot be divorced from the overall context of people's lives. To achieve a culture of lifelong learning will require the recognition of, and support for, learning that does not involve a formal course but which is generated by and connected to people's everyday lives.

There is no single solution to under-participation in learning but research data indicate that centrally driven policies can make a significant difference. However, it will take courage to introduce major shifts in priorities and resource allocation. For example, in Sweden a number of measures, such as social benefits for adult learners, subsidies for outreach activities, group targeting and the introduction of educational leave, have been in place since the 1970s and have led to increased participation at all levels. This provides a useful model from which to move forward.

The ALPINE Manual and widening access

The need to find alternative ways for adults to participate in learning opportunities in higher education is widely recognised. Removing social, geographical and psychological barriers which prevent adults entering higher education is part of the solution.

As well as providing a comparative study across twenty different European countries, the ALPINE Project's Manual (Mark, Moore and Valk, 2004) identifies six key areas where improvements can be made and which can assist with widening participation.

The *first* of these is the adult curriculum. The manual examines how the curriculum is increasingly seen as crucial in widening participation in higher education and the ways in which it can contribute to widening access. The need for a flexible curriculum, which is not elitist and which can empower learners, is paramount.

The *second* key area is the role of student support and adult guidance in making learning more accessible to adults. The importance of information, guidance and counselling services as a key interface between learners' needs and the learning on offer, is crucial in helping adult learners to find a place in an increasingly complex learning system. Non-traditional students have different learning needs and, once they have negotiated the initial barriers, they require different types of support services. Flexible routes, providing a range of study options across the spectrum of learning environments, are essential if adult students are to succeed.

The role of community outreach using information and communications technology (ICT) is a *third* area which has much to contribute to widening access. Distance education, especially education based on the new communication technologies, is of growing importance in adult learning, as the use of the Internet and e-learning lower barriers between countries, allowing new providers to enter the market. E-learning has the potential to provide new models of learning for those where traditional classroom provision is not appropriate. It also has the ability to overcome the barriers that adults face in terms of time and space by granting a degree of flexibility in learning. It can help increase access, bringing learning opportunities to remote geographical areas and to adults who are faced with daily constraints to learning.

The *fourth* key area is the way that universities engage with adults from traditionally excluded groups. These groups vary across countries and can include ethnic minorities, the disabled and handicapped, older adults and the long-term unemployed with low educational attainment. Each group requires a special response if it is to engage most effectively in higher education.

The *fifth* area is the teaching and learning methodology used. Classroom instruction currently plays a major role in adult learning, followed by instruction in the work environment. The success of provision for adults is driven by methods which put the adult student at the centre of the learning process and which engage and motivate adult learners. Ensuring that the context of learning is relevant to adults' experience, particularly using project-based methods, is among the ways in which this can best be done.

The *sixth* and final key area is that of language and cultural learning. As the EU expands to embrace even more languages and cultures, and as more immigrants and asylum seekers are included, the policies and practices embracing the language and cultural needs of adults become paramount for promoting active citizenship, social cohesion and the general well-being of citizens.

These are not the only factors. Other equally important issues include the adaptation of entry requirements, recognising requirements to take account of non-formal and informal learning and ensuring that progression routes exist. Approaches to improving the quality of adult learning can also greatly contribute to increasing access through better monitoring and by adopting coordinated approaches to improving provision.

The ALPINE Survey of Provision

Adult learning in universities covers a wide spectrum of course subjects and forms and for this reason it can be difficult to measure. Given these problems and the wide geographical area, coupled with the limits of time and finance in this project, it was not possible for the ALPINE project to conduct a quantitative survey. Instead, the survey that was carried out focussed on providers' perceptions of provision.

The study included vocational courses and personal development courses for adults and courses aimed at widening participation for particular groups. A wide variation in provision across Europe was revealed. The main reason for participation in adult education and training was shown to be job related. Patterns and profiles of provision showed that adults who follow learning activities do so mostly for employer-related reasons and for short periods of time. This is often a response to the need to improve productivity, to assist the unemployed in finding work and to help those in low wage groups to raise their skills and wage opportunities. The kinds of programmes offered vary considerably from country to country.

In the EU, particularly in the new central European countries, there is a preponderance of courses in subjects which focus on providing skills to enable adults to become economically active or to develop knowledge and skills for work. There are also many examples of provision offering activities geared towards personal development, active citizenship and democracy. In some cases it is difficult to know what is vocational and what is not. For example, language training courses for adults can fulfil both vocational and personal development needs. As many of the courses are designed for adult groups not normally in universities, different levels of entry qualifications are required to enable them to participate and accreditation is often at the pre-degree certificate or diploma levels. In some countries there has been a noticeable growth in courses for special groups. For example, growing migration rates may have helped to raise the importance of learning for immigrants.

The picture which emerges across Europe is complex. There is a very varied system of provision and the relatively large numbers of public and private institutions can make the system appear opaque. The willingness of institutions to embrace change and respond to the differing needs of traditionally under-represented groups will to a large extent dictate their ability to succeed in attracting the new groups of learners.

Conclusion

Provision for adults in higher education is often marginalized. It rarely integrated into the general strategies, core processes and decision making of higher education institutions and is not always recognised on an equal footing with the rest of higher education teaching and research. There is a clear need to integrate the educational needs of adult students into the core development processes and policies of the institutions. Coherent strategies and practical measures need to be developed which will enable lifelong learning to become more open and flexible, so that learners can choose individual learning pathways suitable to their needs and interests. These efforts are enriched if they are supported at the European level through the sharing of ideas, experience and good practice.

Widening opportunity has many benefits: it strengthens democracy; achieves economic and social progress; advances human rights; and improves the efficiency, quality and performance of the educational system. There are no easy solutions to making the European area of lifelong learning a reality. A first step is to develop our knowledge of how adults learn and what is needed to bring these methods and adult learners closer together. This will assist universities to translate current principles into action.

References

Bologna Declaration 1999. *The European Higher Education Area Joint Declaration of European Ministers*. 19 June 1999. Available at: http://www.bologna-berlin2003.de/pdf/bologna_declaration.pdf

Bowen, W. and Bok, D., 1998. *The Shape of the River: Long-term consequences of considering race in colleges and university admissions*. New York: Cambridge University Press.

Budapest Declaration. Available at: http://iche.sas.upenn.edu/overview/budapest.htm

Clancy, P. and Wall, J., 2000. *Social background of Higher Education Entrants*. Dublin: Higher Education Authority.

Council of Europe, 1996. *Project on Access to Higher Education in Europe: working report. Part 1: Synthesis and Recommendations*. Strasbourg: Council of Europe.

Council of Europe, 1999. *Lifelong Learning for Equity and Social Cohesion: a new challenge to higher education. Working on meeting the needs of all students in a changing society.* Bornholm, 27–29 May 1999. Strasbourg: Council of Europe.

Council of Europe, 2001. *Lifelong Learning for Equity and Social Cohesion: a new challenge to Higher Education*. Final Conference, Paris, 15–17 November 2001, Strasbourg: Council of Europe.

Cross, K., 1981. *Adults as Learners: Increasing Participation and Facilitating Learning*. San Francisco: Jossey-Bass.

European Commission, 1995. *White Paper on Teaching and Learning: Towards the Learning Society.* Brussels: Commission of the European Communities.

European Commission, 2000. *Memorandum on Lifelong Learning*. Brussels: Commission of the European Communities. Available at: http://www.bologna-berlin2003.de/pdf/MemorandumEng.pdf

European Commission, 2001a. *Making a European Area of Lifelong Learning a Reality*. COM (2001) 678. Brussels: Commission of the European Communities.

European Commission, 2001b. *The European Union programmes for 2000–06.* Directorate-General for Education and Culture. Luxembourg: Office for Official Publications of the EU.

European Commission, 2002a. *Making Lifelong Learning a Reality for All.* Directorate-General for Education and Culture. Luxembourg: Office for Official Publications of the EU. Available at: http://europa.eu.int/comm/dgs/education_culture/publ/pdf/lll/making_en.pdf

European Commission, 2002b. *Socrates: European Community action programme in the field of education, 2000–06. Gateway to education.* Luxembourg: Office for Official Publications of the EU.

European University Association, 2003. Progress Towards the European Higher Education Area. In *Trends.* Available at: http://www.unige.ch/eua/En/Publications/TRENDS/Trends_111.html

Gellert, C., ed., 1993. *Higher Education in Europe.* London: Jessica Kingsley.

Mark, R., Moore, P.A. and Valk, A., 2004. *ALPINE Project Manual of Good Practice.* Socrates (Grundtvig) Project 85715-CP-1-2000-UK-GRUNDTVIG-ADU (2001–04). Available at: www.qub.ac.uk/alpine

McGill, P. and Morgan, M., 2001. *Ireland's Learning Poor: Adult Educational Disadvantage and Cross-Border Co-operation.* Armagh: Centre for Cross Border Studies, Queen's University at Armagh, Northern Ireland.

McGivney, V., 1991. *Access to Education for Non-Participant Adults.* Leicester: National Institute of Adult Continuing Education.

McGivney, V., 1999. *Excluded Men: Men who are missing from Education and Training.* Leicester: National Institute of Adult Continuing Education.

McGivney, V., 2001. *Fixing or Changing the Pattern? Reflections on widening adult participation in learning.* Leicester: National Institute of Adult Continuing Education.

OECD, 2001. *Economics and Finance of Lifelong Learning.* Paris: Organisation for Economic Cooperation and Development.

Osborne, M., 2003. *Increasing or Widening Participation in Higher Education? – A European overview.* European Journal of Education, 38(1) 5–24.

Race Relations (Amendment) Act, U.K., 2000. Available at: http://www.cre.gov.uk/legaladv/rra.html

Rugaas, B., 2001. Opening Address. In: Council of Europe. *Proceedings of Lifelong Learning for Equity and Social Cohesion: a new challenge to higher education.* Final Conference, Paris, 15–17 November 2001. Strasbourg: Council of Europe.

Schnitzer, K., 1999. *Student Life in Germany: the socio-economic picture.* Bonn: Bundesministerium für Bildung und Forschung.

Special Educational Needs and Disability Act, U.K., 2001. Available at: http://www.hmso.gov.uk/acts/acts2001/20010010.htm

Shavit, Y. and Blosfield, H., 1993. *Persistent Inequality: Changing educational attainment in thirteen countries*. Boulder: Westview Press.

Skilbeck, M. and Connell, H., 2000. *Access and Equity in Higher Education: an international perspective on issues and strategies*. Dublin: Higher Education Authority.

Sorbonne Declaration, 1998. *Joint Declaration on harmonisation of the architecture of the European higher education system.* Paris: Sorbonne. 25 May 1998. Available at: http://www.bolognaberlin2003.de/pdf/Sorbonne_declaration.pdf

Thompson, J., 2000. *Stretching the Academy. The Politics and Practice of Widening Participation in Higher Education.* Leicester: National Institute of Adult Continuing Education.

UNESCO, 1998a. *Mumbai Statement on Lifelong Learning. Citizenship and the Reform of Higher Education.* Available at: http://www.unesco.org/education/uie/online/olpub.html

UNESCO, 1998b. *The World Conference on Higher Education in the Twenty-first Century: Vision and Action.* UNESCO Headquarters, Paris, 5–9 October 1998. Available at: http://portal.unesco.org/education/ev.php?URL_ID=1935&URL_DO=DO_TOPIC&URL_SECTION=201

Woodrow, M., 2000. European experience of good practice in widening access to young people from disadvantaged backgrounds. In: R. Osborne and H. Leith, eds. *Evaluation of targeted initiative on widening access for young people from socio-economically disadvantaged backgrounds.* Dublin: Higher Education Authority.

Country Chapters

ANNE-MARIE ANDRÉ AND GENEVIÈVE COCHEZ

2: Adults in Belgian Higher Education

Introduction

Since 1970, Belgium has undertaken a number of reforms to the legislative power in the three regions of the country: Flanders, Wallonia and Brussels. These mirror the linguistic communities: the Dutch-speaking community (Flanders and Brussels); and the French-speaking community (Wallonia and Brussels). (There is also a German-speaking community in the east of Belgium but, since this does not have a university, it will not be considered further here.) This decentralisation has resulted in Flanders having a Flemish parliament (for both regional and linguistic matters) which sits in Brussels, the Brussels Region with its own bilingual parliament; and Wallonia with its parliament for regional matters sitting in Namur. In addition, the French-speaking Community has a Council which sits in Brussels. These reforms have brought a gradual transfer both of power and of financial independence from the central government to the regions in areas such as culture, education, the economy, public health, welfare and labour.

Since 1989, responsibility for all educational matters has rested with the communities. However, these Councils have legislative power only over those matters which concern their own communities; they cannot override the national laws. This chapter will consider the Flemish and French Councils' strategies and initiatives concerning the education of adults.

Flanders

Flemish continuing education and strategies for lifelong learning[1]

Four Flemish people out of every six have taken a course and one in six is planning to do so. Functional, job-oriented courses in the field of technical skills recruit 50% of all students, 12.5% take personal, general or cultural courses, 7% study languages and 6.5% informatics. 2.5% want to obtain a degree through adult education. Fewer than 0.5% are in basic or second chance education.

Social injustice is not decreased by adult education; on the contrary, it seems to be increasing it at the moment. The reason for this is that not all social classes participate in adult education in the same way. The most active learner is a male employee between 25 and 44 years. He is well educated, socially active and earns a good living. At the other end of the scale is a young single woman with children from a low social class. She is not well educated and earns little or is unemployed. Socially she is not active and it does not occur to her to participate in adult education. More highly educated people are aware of the importance of lifelong learning (LLL) but, because of the pressure of their working lives, they focus on job-oriented courses. Education as a leisure activity is more attractive for the less well-educated learner. The risk clearly exists that adult education is increasing the separation of the classes here.

The Flemish Government, local authorities, social partners, professional organisations and the higher education institutions have all put a great deal of effort into adult education in the last decade and LLL is reflected in almost every government policy. This resulted in February 2002 in the so-called '*Pact van Vilvoorde*', an agreement resulting from a number of meetings between different partners, including ministers and employers.

Adult education in Flanders is not only encouraged by the government but is also a priority for learners and teachers. The

1 For information on lifelong learning (LLL) in Flanders (in Dutch) see http://www.ivo.be

Learners' Week initiative (*Grote leerweek*) is an example of this philosophy and involves several thousand students and teachers each year.

As mentioned in its national report to the European Commission in 2003 (*Actieplan een leven lang leren in goede banen.* 7/72000), Flanders has focussed on six key messages. Each of these has its own objectives and they in turn have been translated into a variety of measures and concrete actions. Encouraging more adults, particularly those in vulnerable groups, to continue their education or to take part in LLL initiatives at the university level, is an explicit part of the strategy followed in the region. Both the Flemish regional government and the universities themselves play an active role in stimulating demand from the adult population.

The six principles for LLL in Flanders are briefly summarised here. The *first* key message guarantees universal and continuing access to learning for everyone, allowing them to gain or renew the skills that they need for sustained participation in the knowledge society. The Flemish Government focusses on offering learning opportunities to all groups in society at all levels and for all purposes. This has resulted in a number of measures, some of which are particularly relevant to universities. The Flemish strategy for LLL pays special attention to the progression routes from one level of education to another, especially the transition from secondary education to higher studies. Several initiatives have already been taken to provide more guidance for adults concerning the options available in higher education and the relevant entry levels. In the near future the Flemish Community, in close collaboration with the higher education institutions and the social partners (the trades unions and the employers' associations), intends to develop a complete and coherent educational framework which will enable further modularisation and certification of non-formal learning. The aim is to accredit informal educational processes and experiences in addition to the traditional learning, which takes place in definable environments, following traceable paths and methods and leading to recognisable outcomes. At the moment, a Law on Flexible Learning (*Flexibiliseringsdecreet*) is under discussion in the Flemish parliament which is aiming to introduce more flexible ways of learning and of accumulating credits in higher education, taking into account the formal experiences of learning and working.

The *second* key message is to raise the level of investment in human resources in order to give priority to Europe's most important asset, its people. Here, democratisation is the main issue at stake. To translate this into concrete action, the universities and the regional government are required to ensure that opportunities and choices are open to all. Study guidance, quality assurance, feedback possibilities, the recognition of skills, advice on entering the labour market and increasing graduates' employability are all especially important from the universities' perspective.

Innovation in teaching and learning for adults is the *third* key message. Here the improvement of information and communication technology (ICT) skills is seen as a key factor. This is expected to be achieved by tailor-made teaching and learning approaches in the ICT field, with all the participants (the government, universities and the social partners) sharing the responsibility for this development. Lifelong learning requires an innovative education strategy. It is of the utmost importance, therefore, for teacher training departments to change, taking into account the LLL perspective. It is also suggested that there should be a shift in focus towards LLL within the existing research programmes. In particular, research projects should identify and analyse examples of best practice to find further ways to stimulate LLL.

As far as the universities' involvement is concerned, these three key messages are likely to be the most important. The *fourth* key message advocates valuing learning, particularly of the non-formal and informal variety. The Flemish government intends to set up expert groups to establish a first blueprint for the certification of all forms of learning. Benchmarks drawn from other countries will set the example. The *fifth* key message includes a review of the guidance and counselling services to ensure that there is easy access for all to good quality information and advice about learning opportunities throughout their lives. The universities' central services will support this policy by making complete, correct and up-to-date information about their learning opportunities available to potential students and to graduates, particularly using the Internet. The *sixth* key message is that learning should be brought closer to students' homes. This can be done using libraries, museums or community learning initiatives, for example, and by supporting the learning through ICT-based facilities wherever appropriate. The universities are committed to bringing ICT facilities to all their students.

The Flemish Community has established several expert groups and organisations in order to implement these principles. These are responsible for the promotion, organisation and assessment of the different LLL opportunities in Flanders. In addition, they provide the government with the necessary data about these initiatives and take part in the preparation of policy and the strategic development of future initiatives.

Some of the most important provisions are:

- Distance Learning (*Afstandsonderwijs*), with the Flemish Government organising virtual courses, while the Flemish universities offer a limited range of courses via the Internet (but only available to their mainstream students);
- Basic Education (*Basisonderwijs*), with courses organised by the Flemish Government for vulnerable groups of adults;
- Monitored Individual Studies (*Begeleid indivueel studeren*), a selection of non-mainstream subjects taken individually and established by the Flemish Community, based on distance learning methods;
- Education for Social Promotion (*Onderwijs voor Sociale Promotie*), an organisation with three target groups: students aiming at an additional basic qualification (vertical promotion); participants specialising in particular subjects (horizontal promotion); and courses aiming at increasing the social integration or citizenship of the participants; and
- Second Chance Education (*Tweedekansonderwijs*), offering adults the opportunity to finish their secondary education. Here, the participants take examinations set by a commission established by the Flemish Community.

The Flemish Open University

The Dutch-speaking Open Universiteit (OU) has its headquarters in Heerlen in the Netherlands and has a network of 24 regional study centres throughout Belgium and the Netherlands. Of these, six are in Belgium and each is linked to a Dutch-speaking university. The Flemish centres are supported financially by the Flemish Ministry of Education with grants proportional to their numbers of students. They are also linked to the Departments of Educational Affairs of their universities from which they receive support in the form of accommodation and the use of the Department's services. Their students communicate mostly with their own study centres.

Open University centres can be found in Antwerp, Diepenbeek, Ghent, Kortrijk, Leuven and Brussels. They offer flexible university programmes starting at their students' previous levels of educational attainment and leading to complete university programmes through guided self-study. These centres operate autonomously and they are responsible for their own publicity and the recruitment of the programmes. They provide access to multimedia resources, libraries of course materials and facilities for self-study groups and student organisations. In addition, the examinations (both regular and computerised) take place here. The course materials, mainly in printed form, are delivered direct to each student's home. These are sometimes supplemented by additional educational media, such as interactive videos, computer-aided learning and Web-based courses.

In general, a qualification is not required to enter an OU course. The OU makes it possible for those who were unable to continue their education when they left school; they provide a second chance. In addition, the OU seeks to enrol school leavers who wish to combine further study with a job or other activities, or those who simply prefer the distance education system, sometimes called the 'second route' ('*tweede weg*' or '*tweede kans*'). For others, studying in the OU offers a way of enhancing their professional skills. A considerable number of the OU's students are already graduates, taking further courses either for continuing professional development (CPD) reasons or to retrain for a different occupation. The study centre tutors provide guidance and advice to prospective students and support individual students throughout their studies. This system of guided self-study allows students a great deal of freedom in choosing where and when to study.

All the OU certificates, transcripts and degrees are legally recognised and are equivalent to the qualifications from other higher education institutions. This legal validity makes it possible for OU students to transfer to other institutions of higher education and vice versa. The OU has set up an elaborate internal system to assure educational quality regarding both content and teaching.[2] Each course forms a self-contained unit ending with an examination and a certificate is issued for each examination passed.

The considerable freedom and openness that the OU's educational system offers to its students makes great demands on its educational organisation and on the production of materials. In this case, ICT offers a way of solving the problem and, at the same time, improving the quality of the education provided. For example, an Internet-based 'study net' enables students to get up-to-date information about their courses, enter into discussions with other students and tutors, and print out useful course material.

Further information on the continuing education provided by Belgium's Flemish-speaking universities has recently been provided by Gehre (2003).

Facts and figures on the Open Universiteit, 2002

Budget: 56.2 million euros
Staff members: 795
Active students: 21,182; course enrolments: 51,739
Course certificates issued: 25,255

2 The main stages of the OU's quality assurance system are: submission of course plans for formal approval by the Executive Board and the Board of Professors' Education Committee; a detailed procedure to specify and develop the course, including a pre-test of the course material by students before finalisation; the development of the course content by external subject specialists; systematic evaluation of courses and programmes; and permanent quantitative research on students' performance and examinations.

Student profile: 48% female, 52% male; age 18–25: 10%; age 26–35: 37%; age 36–45: 33%; age above 45: 20%. 65% of the students are in paid employment of 35 to 40 hours per week. 53% opt for the OU because of the time- and location-independent character of its course units. 33% follow a full academic programme (6,916 students), 39% are second-chance students, not having completed a higher professional or university-level education before (8,211 students)

Student location: 18,838 students in the Netherlands (89%), 1,934 students in Belgium (9%), 410 students in the rest of the world (2%)

Electronic learning environment: 14,813 students make use of Studienet (70%)

Bachelors programmes: 7

Masters programmes: 17

Schools: Management, Cultural Studies, Computer Sciences, Natural Sciences, Psychology, Law, Education

Academic courses: 384.

Continuing education in the University of Ghent: an example

The OU Study Centre in Ghent, like the other study centres of the Dutch-speaking OU, offers flexible university programmes, tailor-made to suit its students' educational needs. The student target groups are the same as for all the other OU centres. The Ghent Centre provides continuing education through approximately 280 courses, together with a number of separate lectures. It caters for professionals who hope that, by acquiring new knowledge and skills, they will be able to become more mobile within their employment. In this respect the Study Centre offers general in-service training and CPD for professional specialisations and is currently catering for approximately 900 students.

These courses are organised in cooperation with the University of Ghent's faculties. In addition, the University has a language centre and an institute, which offer in-service training for older adults. It also provides programmes leading to qualifications through guided self-study in cooperation with the OU. Overall, the University of Ghent enrolled 777 adult students in 2003 (34.4% of Flemish students) and the total student population increased by 2.6%. 42.2% of students are between 26 and 35 years old; 14.2% are older than 45 years; and 64.5% of them have jobs. The percentage of unemployed people is increasing slightly.

The full degree programmes of the OU are similar to mainstream higher education programmes. These require approximately 5,600–7,000 hours of study and lead to legally recognised academic degrees entitling the graduates from the academic year 2004/05 onwards to use the title 'master'. The Belgian students originally obtain a Dutch degree but it is also possible to receive an equivalent Belgian degree from the Ministry of Education.

Each programme contains an introductory package with the curriculum's two core courses. In addition, the students are offered a learning skills induction at the Study Centre, which includes training in ICT skills and preparation for taking examinations. These induction programmes were initially provided in response to student demand and they are now offered twice a year.

Belgium's French-speaking Community

The 'Contract For The Future' (*Contrat d'Avenir de la Wallonie,* 1999–2010) is a declaration of broad social policy for Belgium's French-speaking community in Wallonia, the southern part of Belgium. This policy sets out four priorities: sustainable economic development; regional development supported by Europe; the involvement of young people in Wallonia's development; and the creation of a knowledge-based society. Wallonia has made LLL, together with free access to the information society, priorities and rights for everyone, as well as key elements in a competitive economy and the struggle against social exclusion. These priorities were established after a rigorous analysis of the economic and social situation in the region: an initial study was submitted to the social partners, the general population and the academic and scientific communities; following this, the issue was debated in Parliament. Only then was the Contract finalised and published.

One of the Contract's objectives is to increase, from 2004 onwards, the population's active participation in training by 50%. This would mean that, on average, 7.5% of the adult population would be involved in training at any one time. In 2003, the Walloon region drew up an agreement on LLL with all its social partners to involve the whole of the public and private sectors in the drive towards training. Following this, seven sector-based agreements were made by the various social partners, the Walloon regional government, FOREM (*Formation à l'Emploi*) and IFAPME (*Institut de Formation en Alternance pour les Petites et Moyennes Entreprises*). These agreements are intended to make the partnership-based policy a reality. The region's budget specifically for training has risen by 60% since 1999.

The right to be trained can only be put into effect on a voluntary basis and the personal motives of trainees are essential to the success of this policy. The principle of compulsory education, which applies up to the age of 18 in Belgium, cannot be used in the case of adults. It is therefore important to stimulate enthusiasm for training amongst the adult population. This can be done by:

- Training unqualified people in new technologies. This will mean training 100,000 job-seekers in three years;
- Recognising their skills and qualifications; and
- Finding more attractive training methods, for example by alternating practical and theoretical training.

Increasing accessibility to training requires initiatives at many levels. Particularly relevant is the fact that detailed information and advice on training is available throughout the region in its ten Training Information Centres (*Carrefours de Formation*) or via Formabanque, an interactive and well-maintained database for adult education, which has been available since March 2002.

The staff providing the training necessarily work flexible hours and the course programmes provided are determined by the needs of the local economy, building upon the educational and skills profiles of the workers involved. The Regional Employment Service is required to base its programme on a survey of the training needs of the market: there is a permanent survey going on at the FOREM and also at the *Observatoire Wallon de l'Emploi.* If the region is unable to provide appropriate training of its own, the service can, with the agreement of the Education Department of the Francophone Community (*Ministère de la Communauté Française*), allocate funds to vocational and technical schools equipped to provide the training needed. The region is also able to provide financial support for training providers and individual Walloon companies wishing to develop their own tailor-made training programmes.

One provider, the Institute for Long-Term Training for Small and Medium-sized Enterprises and the Middle Classes (*Institut de Formation Permanente pour les Classes Moyennes et Petites et Moyennes Entreprises*) is charged with the development of training for future company managers and self-employed workers. The need for training is not yet fully recognised by the Walloon people, however. To help overcome this problem, the region is supporting the creation of start-up companies and soft loan pilot schemes, as well as placing a team of human resources advisers in the Regional Employment Service. The aim of this team is to encourage a more entrepreneurial spirit by giving advice on the creation of new enterprises, identifying the logistical support needed in such enterprises and organising a suitable training programme for future leaders of small- and medium-sized enterprises (SMEs). The University of Liège set up, in 1998, in partnership with Meusinvest, a public regional partner, a company called 'Spinventure' aiming to foster enterprise projects and to bring them to maturity for investors.

The various social partners acknowledge the growing importance of investment by businesses in the training of their employees. In the inter-professional accord of the *Conseil Central de l'Economie*, 2003/04 it was agreed that, by the end of 2004, 1.9% of the total salary bill of companies in Wallonia should be spent on training. The use of sector-based funds should provide the most appropriate courses for people to enable them to develop the new skills that are needed.

Amongst the most recent training courses that have been set up, priority has been given to the training of handicapped people and to women and the course subjects have been directed particularly at the professions stemming from technological change. Other priorities are courses related to careers in farming and agribusiness. Here, particular emphasis is placed on youth training. It was also decided in the early 1980s that paid training leave (which allows workers to follow training courses while continuing to receive their salaries) should be extended at the federal level to employees in business. The universities in Wallonia are one of the providers of this training through *Interface Université-Entreprises*.

Funding arrangements

The Walloon Government has put in place two different financial incentive schemes relating to worker training: '*Chèque-Formation*' and '*Crédit-Adaptation*'. Chèques-formation was introduced to give financial support to companies employing up to 250 people. For each training hour, the Walloon Region offers 15 euros. Here the trainers must be accredited by an official accrediting centre. Since the establishment of the Chèque-Formation scheme in 1998, 1,275,000 cheques have been reimbursed. The scheme covers part of the costs involved in qualifying worker training in the form of 'guidance' (*tutorat*): young workers are trained by more experienced people employed by the same company. In this case, twenty percent of the salaries of the trainers are reimbursed by the Walloon Region.

In addition, the Employment Service offers, free of charge, high-quality training to both employed and unemployed workers, which takes into account the particular skills requirements of SMEs. Moreover, all job seekers in receipt of training from any provider approved by the region have equal rights to claim training grants. Crèche and day nursery expenses are also reimbursed in this case.

The Walloon Skills Centres

These training centres have been formed by a public-private partnership between the region, its Employment and Training Office, the social partners, the research centres, and the universities. All the universities are involved through their continuing education centres or through specific initiatives, for example, by providing training for the trainers. Furthermore, the universities offer some courses to meet the demands of the market. These form an integral part of the local economy. Provided with up-to-date equipment, these centres are creating a new technological culture for workers, job seekers, students, academic staff, company managers and executives.

At the time of writing, there are 11 centres in existence and it is intended that this number will rise to 24 by the end of 2005. These centres will cover a wide range of sectors including metallurgy, ICT, logistics, timber, graphics, transport, the environment, construction, the automobile industry, and agribusiness. Training modules provided by e-learning are increasingly being used.

Information and Communication Technology Mobilisation Plan

Already established in the region, this equal opportunities plan is directed particularly towards those members of the workforce whose jobs are far removed from the new technologies and who have limited access to retraining for such technologies. Women have been especially targeted because of their limited access to such training in the past.

Language Proficiency Plan

The region is particularly keen to develop the language skills of both employed and unemployed young people and workers generally. Specific action plans have been developed to tackle this need including the provision of scholarships, work placements, and exchange visits between workers, students and trainers from the region to the Flemish and German Communities.

Skills and qualification recognition: accreditation of prior experiential learning (APEL)

Everyone, including job seekers, can have their skills, wherever they have acquired them, accredited in order to gain access to training and, above all, to employment. To achieve this, the Walloon-Brussels community's government has put in place a procedure to give credits for skills associated with the various training programmes established by the region. This will facilitate APEL and make certificates more transparent. The universities are carrying out research in this area but are not involved in this directly. The people involved, working at the European level, are from the Communauté Française de Belgique, FOREM (Wallonia), Bruxelles-Formation (Brussels Region), IFAPME and Promotion Sociale. They are working on the implementation of Skills Validation Centres and these should be working by the end of 2004.

This APEL programme will follow the European standards, emphasising transparency, harmonisation and consultation. This is in line with Europass (1999). Within this, the two interrelated core concepts of the scheme, 'European pathway for training' and 'Europass Training', promote the idea of European pathways for work-related training. There is an urgent need for the Walloon-Brussels community and the Walloon region to develop a system of equivalence between work-related educational diplomas and certificates and professional training.

One of the structural changes needed to facilitate access to all types of education and training is the introduction of a modular approach to social advancement. This should become widespread throughout the various professional training programmes, regardless of the body that has organised it. The involvement of businesses in this programme will allow the wider recognition of accreditation carried out in this way.

University adult education

Compared with the other providers, university adult education is distinguished by the following characteristics: the process of analysis (it tackles the question of 'why' as well as 'how'); it maintains a balance between theory and practice (unlike training which concentrates mainly on vocational skills); and it is also able to draw upon research. University adult education programmes are frequently multidisciplinary, cutting across traditional academic subject divisions.

The amount of education provided for adult students by universities has grown considerably in recent years, particularly in the area of distance learning, which has developed with funding from the Walloon Government. This is intended for people in work as well as those seeking work; they cannot be awarded an academic diploma or a post-graduate degree, however. Further information on the education for adults organised by the nine French-speaking university centres is given by Dehousse (2003).

E-learning at the University of Liège

At the University of Liège, LabSet, (the *Laboratoire de Soutien à l'Enseignement Télématique*, i.e. support laboratory for e-learning) helps in devising and implementing e-courses intended for companies and organisations related to the Ministry of Employment, which are dedicated to professional training. Two among its many projects deserve a special mention: the ICT plan (*Plan TIC*) and the FORMADIS project. Some thirty employees work for LabSet on these and similar projects in partnership with CTE (the *Centre de Technologies au service de l'Enseignement* of the Free University, Brussels). This receives financial support from the European Social Fund, the Walloon Region and the government of Belgium's French Community.

Commissioned by the Walloon Region, *Plan TIC* is part of the Contract for the Future mentioned earlier and it sets out to help citizens face professional and technological changes by introducing them to information technologies. The contribution of the University of Liège to *Plan TIC* consists of three course modules, containing 48 hours of instruction, dedicated to the use of the Internet and office software. It also shares experience among the instructors.

The FORMADIS Project helps selected bodies to convert the training they already offer into the e-training format. A technological template, training courses and ad hoc support are provided to stimulate the development of both initial and continuing training programmes. FORMADIS also organises an annual conference to highlight the advantages of e-learning.

Conclusion

In Flanders, lifelong learning is incorporated into day-to-day life. Adult education is the responsibility not only of the government but, in the first instance, is also a priority for teachers and, most importantly, for the learners themselves. Adult education in the universities is largely carried out by the Open University, which attracts thousands of students every year.

In the French speaking part of Belgium, universities are far from being the main providers in adult education. They focus more on training the trainers and theoretical issues of education such as the validation of skills. The universities offer many courses for adults but these are generally intended for graduates. In recent years, e-learning has grown considerably, especially in the University of Liège.

References

Dehousse, N., 2003. University continuing education in the French-speaking part of Belgium. In: M. Osborne and E. Thomas, eds. *Lifelong Learning in a Changing Continent: continuing education in the universities of Europe*. Leicester: National Institute of Adult Continuing Education.

Europass, 1999. The 'European pathway for training' and 'Europass Training'. Official Journal of the European Communities, L17, 22.1.1999.

Gehre, G., 2003. University continuing education in the Dutch-speaking part of Belgium. In: M. Osborne and E. Thomas, *ibid.*

Useful Websites

Flanders

Education in the Flemish Community: http://www.ond.vlaanderen.be/english/

Information on LLL in Flanders (in Dutch): http://www.ivo.be

Learners' Week: http://www.groteleerweek.be/

Lifelong learning debate in the Flemish Community: http://europa.eu.int/comm/education/policies/lll/life/report/belgium_flemish_be.pdf

Open Universiteit: www.ou.nl

University of Ghent Open University: http://www.ou.nl/info-alg-english-introduction/profile_OUNL_2003.pdf

Wallonie

Conseil Central de l'Economie: http://www.ccecrb.fgov.be/cce/text/f.HTM

Courses offered by the universities in Wallonie: http://www.cfwb.be

Information on adult education (Formabanque): http://www.formabanque.be/ (in French)
Interface Université-Entreprises: http://www.interface.ulg.ac.be/
Plan TIC: http://www.pmtic.net
LabSet and the FORMADIS Project: http://www.labset.net/modules/tinycontent/index.php?id=2
Université Libre de Bruxelles: http://www.ulb.ac.be/docs/formationpermanente/fc.2;html
Université de Liège: http://www.ulg.ac.be/aacad/fcont/

ROSSICA BETCHEVA

3: Adults in Bulgarian Higher Education

Introduction

This chapter examines the involvement of adults in universities in Bulgaria. Particular attention is given to those adults who did not enter a university immediately after completing their secondary schooling and who subsequently experienced barriers to returning to education (Ministry of Education, 2004). University continuing education in Bulgaria more widely has recently been described by Betcheva and Velev (2003).

In Bulgaria, there are two routes by which adults can enter higher education (HE). The first of these assumes that the person concerned will have successfully completed secondary schooling. According to the Bulgarian Higher Education Act (1995, amended in 1999), adults must graduate from a secondary school before enrolling on a higher education (HE) degree programme. The other possibility is for adults to undertake short vocational training courses in a university. In this case a certificate is awarded. These courses are at the level of a first degree and, although there are no strict entry requirements, those entering are normally expected to have completed at least their secondary education.

Some specific characteristics of these types of HE for adults, within the framework of the Bulgarian educational legislation and the existing economic and social conditions, will be reported here.

The Bulgarian system of higher education

The HE system in Bulgaria is based on the Higher Education Act adopted in 1995. This Act introduced important conditions regarding the status, structure and organization of studies in universities leading both to degrees and to accreditation. These changes arose from the major social and economic transformation that began in Bulgaria in 1989 and related mainly to the restructuring of the national economy. Higher education in Bulgaria is now provided by universities, specialist higher schools (offering university-type degrees) and colleges (which offer non-university-type degrees).

The university degrees that are currently on offer in Bulgaria are the following:

- First degree – Bachelor – with a curriculum lasting at least four years;
- Second degree – Master – lasting at least five years in total (i.e. one year after the bachelors degree); and
- Third degree – Doctor – at least three-years after the masters degree (or four years after the bachelors degree).

A non-university degree (known as the 'Expert in…') is also provided by the colleges. Students on these courses can continue their education, following the successful completion of their secondary school qualifications, for a period of three more years. Universities decide whether or not to allow the graduates from these courses to transfer to the normal university degree programmes. Usually this is seen as a privilege given only to the best students (perhaps the top 5% of the course). Only a limited number of subjects are recognised for this purpose and marks are later transferred directly to the university degree records.

Admission is based on passing an entrance examination set by each university individually. The government approves a State register of qualifying degrees by profession or specialty. Approval is also given annually for the number of places to be supported financially at each university for each subject. Bachelors degrees can only be taken if the students have state-approved places (for which they have to compete). Masters studies are more flexible. If universities have the teaching capacity, they can admit masters students for so called 'paid studies'. This offers a good opportunity for adults to update their knowledge or to obtain a new qualification.

Access for adults to degree programmes in higher education

According to the Bulgarian Higher Education Act, there should be no obstacles for anyone possessing a secondary school diploma to apply for university study. On the other hand, there is no specific mention of the particular need to involve adults in universities or to encourage their participation.

Between 1960 and 1990, special provisions were made for certain groups of adults (for example, redundant army officers and other professional groups) to enter without sitting the university entrance examinations. Each professional group had its own method of selection and these were highly competitive. This approach was part of the Communist Party's policy for widening access to HE and it was also dependent on the applicants' political involvement in the Party. This was seen as one way of distributing well-educated and reliable people across a wide range of occupations. This aim was also achieved by the *Rabfak* (Workers' Faculty) found in the major Bulgarian industrial towns. There selected workers received an education that was seen as the equivalent of secondary schooling. Successful completion of *Rabfak* therefore guaranteed adults a university place. This favouritism towards those who engaged in particular forms of politics is now seen as undemocratic, however, and it has been stopped.

The criteria for university admission of adults are now the same for everyone; that is, they must hold a secondary school diploma and also be successful in the university entrance examination.

Adult access to non-degree university courses does not require the adult to pass an entrance examination or to possess a secondary school diploma. The award of a certificate following these courses does though require each student to demonstrate that they have reached a prescribed level. According to the Bulgarian Higher Education Act, however, these courses cannot lead to a degree. For this reason, adults are not motivated to participate in the non-degree courses offered by universities. In some universities, these courses are organised by the Ministry of Labour and Social Care for unemployed people when the universities themselves cannot organize them.

The organisation of adult learning in universities

According to the Higher Education Act, there are several ways in which adults can choose to study in Bulgarian universities for degree or non-degree programmes; it is possible for adults to enrol on full-time courses, part-time courses (generally in the evenings) or by distance education. The most popular form for adults is the part-time format. Participation in other modes is restricted by the lifestyle of many adults who generally have limited time available for study due to home or work commitments or who lack appropriate facilities for working at home, e.g. for distance learning.

The organisation of part-time learning in the universities usually extends over two semesters. Students generally have contact hours of 2–3 weeks per semester and to attend lectures, seminars and laboratory practice with a duration of approximately one-third of the full-time classes. Part-time students are examined and assessed in the same way as full-time students. The number of places available for learning is determined by the State and part-time students pay 50% of the tuition fees set for full-time students.

Motivation and barriers for adults in higher education

The preferences for adults to study are largely influenced by the labour market in Bulgaria or the prospect of getting a better job abroad.

Before 1989, the economic situation in Bulgaria was relatively good. The chemical industry and metallurgy, mining and machine tool industries, the textile and food industries, agriculture and tourism were all functioning normally. Imports of raw materials, including oil and gas, were readily available from the Soviet Union to service the industrial sector and there was a huge unsaturated and non-competitive market to absorb all the goods produced. At this time, employment for well-educated people was guaranteed and, as a result, every kind of study was sought, particularly related to the technical sciences. These courses were also in demand from adults.

Since 1989 the political changes, followed by the economic reforms, have led to a restructuring of the labour market. Unemployment, almost unknown before 1989, has since grown regularly. Many highly qualified people working in industry have had (and still have) to change their professions. Very often these changes have led to jobs that require fewer, or no, qualifications: engineers, for example, have become construction workers or taxi drivers.

This situation still exists at the time of writing and has reduced the motivation for adults, particularly in the technical sciences. On the other hand, medical doctors and lawyers are in high demand and competition for places for these courses is high. In Bulgaria, adults have access to employment in the legal profession since part-time legal courses are available. The number of medical places, however, is very limited and entry is therefore extremely competitive. What is more, only full-time courses are available and the result is that there are essentially no adults on courses for doctors. In medical colleges, access to nursing and medical laboratory courses is also competitive but these still remain accessible to adults. Those who have made several unsuccessful attempts to enter a university medical school often turn to these medical-related courses.

Other professional courses which are proving popular are those connected with computing and economics (i.e. management, micro- and macro-economics, banking and insurance). These courses all offer good opportunities for professionals in the labour market.

Approximately 80% of Bulgaria's universities offer undergraduate and postgraduate courses in the field of economics. These courses are popular both with adults and with younger students as they enable individuals to establish and manage private businesses. On the other hand, it is sometime difficult for adults to gain access to computer science courses which are very competitive. These require a high level of mathematical knowledge and this can also sometimes act as a barrier for mature learners returning to study.

Conclusion

In conclusion, the motivation for adult access to universities in Bulgaria is generally strongly influenced by the improved job opportunities that will result and the subsequent improvements in their salary prospects. The barriers to access are twofold. First, there are those barriers linked to competition for places from a number of relatively highly qualified people. The number of places available on the popular courses is limited and many adults are unable to find a suitable place. On the other hand, in those cases where places are available, the courses are often not attractive because the salaries of their graduates are likely to be lower.

The future Bulgarian entry to the European Union will bring Bulgarian universities into the common European higher educational area where they will have to compete for students. Inevitably this will result in a more flexible policy towards providing study options for adults not only with more appropriate course content but also adopting a more flexible framework within the HE policy. Steps like the development and implementation of a National Strategy for Life Long Learning or the formalization of practices such as the accreditation of prior learning and the European credit accumulation and transfer system (ECATS), will contribute considerably to the widening of adult participation in Bulgarian universities. Scholarships are very low, however, and it is not possible to support a family on one. Many adults therefore have to give up their aspirations to go to university as a result. In addition, in Bulgaria many adults who currently wish to study do not have sufficient knowledge to pass the university entrance examinations or the skills needed to succeed if they do manage to get there.

References

Betcheva, R. and Velev, K., 2003. University continuing education in Bulgaria. In: M. Osborne and E. Thomas, eds., *Lifelong Learning in a Changing Continent: Continuing education in the universities of Europe*. Leicester: National Institute of Adult Continuing Education.

Bulgarian Higher Education Act, 1995. State Gazette, No. 112.

Ministry of Education, 2004. Available at: http://www.minedu.government.bg

MILOSLAVA CHOVANCOVÁ AND ANDRAS CHERNEL

4: Adults in Czech Higher Education

The development of adult education in the higher education sector

In the Czech Republic, the important role that adult education can play in the economic development of the country is increasingly being recognised. This view of adult education has been incorporated into the concept of lifelong learning. Links are now developing between schools and higher education (*terciální vzdělávání*) to provide an ongoing and accessible education system for Czech citizens throughout their lives. (The direct translation of *terciální vzdělávání* is 'tertiary education'. The term used for this stage of education in the rest of the book is 'higher education' and this will be used here except in the translation of the titles of Czech government documents.)

The education of adults in HE institutions (HEIs) has undergone significant changes in recent years. The higher education (HE) sector is taken to be all types of education recognised by the State that follow general upper secondary education or upper secondary technical education which end with the State-recognised final examination (*Maturita*).

Over the past decade, the HE sector as a whole has grown from taking 14% of the school leaving population in 1989 to 40% in 2000, and this is likely to rise to 50% by 2005 (National Report on Adult Education in the Czech Republic, 2003). In 2002, a total of 0.3% of the overall population in the Czech Republic was enrolled in university adult education programmes of one type or another.

It is possible to differentiate three main sectors in adult education in the Czech Republic:

- *Adult education leading to formal higher education.* In the main, this involves adults studying in all types of state and non-state secondary education, further education and university-type schools as a so-called 'second chance' opportunity for those who, for whatever reason, did not obtain such an education earlier;
- *Further professional education.* This covers all compulsory (i.e. normative) and non-compulsory education leading to the qualification and requalification of employees or of applicants for employment; and
- *Other sectors of adult education.* For instance, interest-related education, citizenship-related education and the education of Senior Citizens.

In the year 2000, about 2,000 educational institutions offered adult education, of which 15–20% was made up by schools, 10% by company education centres, and 2.5% from foreign educational companies. Approximately 38,000 educational courses were offered with a total of approximately 650,000 participants, approximately one-seventh of all employed persons (National Report on Adult Education in the Czech Republic, 2003).

The wide diversity of students now entering HE has required a significant broadening of the range of courses offered. In spite of the wide diversity of forms, the HE sector has several common features that distinguish it from other sectors and enable it to be treated as a whole. It provides education for adults, who have full legal responsibility, are autonomous in their decision-making, and have clear motivation combined with a responsible attitude to their education.

The legal basis of adult education in the higher education sector in the Czech Republic

Higher education in the Czech Republic is based upon the following laws:

- Act No. 29/1984 § Coll., 'On the System of Primary, Secondary, and Higher Educational Establishments and Schools'. This stipulates the operational conditions, entry and completion requirements, organisational and technical matters such as compulsory attendance, planning of the school year and teaching materials. Moreover, it contains regulations related to the teaching staff;
- Act No. 111/1998 § Coll., 'On Universities; On Higher Education'. This reorganises the concept of the university and non-university forms of HE and provides for the establishment of private HEIs. Article 60, legislates for lifelong education: HEIs may provide lifelong education programmes, either free of charge, or subject to payment, within the framework of their other educational activities and beyond the scope of their study programmes. Lifelong education can either be vocation-oriented or interest-oriented; and
- The National Programme for the Development of Education in the Czech Republic (White Paper, 2001). This builds in part on the outcomes of the PHARE Reform Programme funded by the European Union (EU). It is based on the principles of lifelong learning and determines the preconditions supporting concepts at the policy level. The document was approved by the Czech government in February 2001. The objective process was to 'make education an issue for society as a whole', and to pave the way for considerations about future developments beyond the boundaries of the education sector.

Apart from the overall objectives for the further development of education, the White Paper contains a number of quantifiable targets (programmes aimed at gaining a certain educational level, further professional education, and adult education courses), which are in line with the EU's Lisbon Convention (the agreement on mutual recognition of qualifications, i.e. degrees, diplomas and certificates, for HE in Europe, adopted in Lisbon in April 1997).

A problem is that the development of adult education in the Czech Republic is slower than elsewhere. Key problems include uncertainty about the areas of competence, lack of motivation, and the absence of a systematic approach to adult education. Some specific problems are typical of the adult education sphere, e.g. HEIs call for large numbers of adult students, demand easier access to adult studies (i.e. through the official recognition of shorter programmes), and require wider implementation of distance learning programmes, higher financial allowances per adult student, and reimbursement for study leave of absence from their jobs (National Report on Adult Education in the Czech Republic, 2003). Furthermore, the White Paper suggests increasing the numbers of participants in requalification courses; the launching of new requalification programmes for specialist applicants; stronger motivation of the unemployed to requalify themselves; and the updating of related information and counselling services. The authors of the White Paper even propose that the expenses incurred by individual adults on education should be tax-deductible for hobby courses and civic education.

The structure of higher education

Educational programmes in HE will focus on the future work of graduates in society and the rapidly changing composition of the labour market. This differing learning context has led to a different relationship between teachers and students and, as a result, new modes of teaching have emerged e.g. the increasing use of case studies in the classroom and various forms of distance learning. The structures of HE programmes can be viewed at the following levels:

- *Extension Technical Studies* (Post-Maturita Studies). One or two year modular courses, completed with a Certificate. Students can apply and exploit knowledge gained from these modules in their further higher-level studies and thereby attain higher levels of qualifications;
- *Post-secondary Technical Education* (Higher Professional Education). These exist in a three-year form. Upon graduation the student is awarded the title DiS … (Diploma Specialist in the field of …) It is essential that greater permeability between these programmes and normal bachelors degrees study programmes should be created;
- *Bachelors degree study programmes*. In accordance with the principles of the Bologna Declaration (June 1999), these represent a group of courses that not only enable graduates to find appropriate employment on the labour market but also to continue with their studies at the masters degree level;
- *Masters degree study programmes*. These are focused on acquiring theoretical and practical knowledge based on scientific research and other creative activities. In accordance with the development of bachelors degrees, they can be seen as following on from these. As in the other cases above, their structure is modular to maximise the possibility of mobility throughout the HE sector;
- *Doctoral studies study programmes*. As the highest level of HE, these are predominantly focussed on individual research and are thus independent 'creative scientific activities'; and
- *Studies within the framework of lifelong learning.* Studies provided by state or non-state institutions, which are recognised by the State, and are focussed on participants' professional needs or interests.

Higher education is intended to build on the knowledge gained in the course of studies at the secondary school level. However, access to the course of one's choice is not necessarily dependent on the curriculum studied at a secondary school. The candidates each come, depending on the nature of their schools, with (sometimes widely) differing levels of knowledge and skills. *Gymnasia* are the most prestigious type of secondary school in the Czech Republic and they provide a general education. They offer a broad background of general knowledge primarily aimed at preparing students for university studies (entry rate: 18.5% in 2000/01, compared to 15% in 1996) (Vojtech, 2001). The curricula of *Secondary Technical Schools* (entry rate: 36.4% in 2000/01), contain a relatively high proportion of general education (about 40%), and are mainly developed to enable the students who have completed their courses to enter the labour market with mid-level qualifications. The limited transparency of programme contents and outcomes, linked to non-uniform examination standards in different schools throughout the country, have been a matter of concern for some time, especially with the Maturita, which entitles graduates to apply for admission to higher level education. This has led to extensive discussion on a new model of the Maturita (which should be standardised and uniform throughout the country). Pilot versions have been in the testing stage since the late 1990s and this concept has been included in the White Paper on Education (2001).

The institutional structure of higher education

The existing organisational structure of public HEIs of a university type, including the foundation of new HE establishments of a non-university type (private as well as public), will eventually provide sufficient numbers of HE places.

There are currently five types of HEIs in the Czech Republic:

- Universities (*univerzita*). These offer all types of HE study programmes and various types of study in lifelong education programmes. These can be bachelors degree programmes (lasting three or four years) which lead on to masters degree programmes (of one, two, or three years' duration); or in specific instances, masters degrees study programmes (of four, five, or six years' duration) in cases where it is inappropriate to create a precursor bachelors degree study programme at the lower level of such studies (e.g. in medicine or veterinary sciences). It is also possible to study in doctoral degree programmes.
  A totally new element in this system is the private university. These were established under Act No. 111/1998. One new public university has recently been founded, the Tomas Bata University in Zlín in 2001. Universities provide adult education programmes, especially in economics-, finance- and psychology-related subjects, technology, science, humanities and in medicine. A complete list of the universities in the Czech Republic, together with their Web addresses, can be found at the end of this chapter;
- Non-university higher education institutions (*neuniverzitní vysoké školy*). These mainly provide bachelors degree type study programmes (of three or four years' duration) and follow-on education courses. They should be established with a vision of larger multidisciplinary educational institutions, offering courses that will satisfy the educational needs of a region. A wider spectrum of subjects is on offer, with greater possibilities for combinations, wider options and variability, and also a sufficient number of students are necessary to achieve quality and the effective use of funds. Part of these institutions' activities are based on joint projects undertaken with firms, in consulting and training activities, applied research projects, and in international cooperation ventures.
  Some twenty-one private HEIs of a non-university type have been founded since the change in regime (November

1989) by the amendment of Act No. 138/1995 § Coll., 'On Schools', which legalised HEIs;

- Post-secondary Technical Schools (*vyšší odborné školy*). These offer post-secondary technical (two-, three- and five-year) programmes and extension technical studies. They can also offer bachelor degree programmes but only in co-operation with a university. A post-secondary technical school can apply for a change in its status and become a non-university HEI if its study programmes are accredited as bachelor degree courses. In some regions, the main role of post-secondary technical schools may lie in the provision of further education.
  By 1999, study programmes at the post-secondary technical school level were on offer in some 170 post-secondary technical schools, of which only 13 had more than 400 students, and in 90 of them fewer than 150 students study. The majority coexist in some form of combination with secondary technical schools (126 are post-secondary technical schools and secondary technical schools). Only 44 post-secondary technical schools are completely independent.
  The majority of the programme contents provided by post-secondary technical schools is from the economics/finance disciplines (about 40%). This is followed by health care services with about 20%; technology with about 17%; humanities (about 15%); agricultural and forestry, ecology and environmental protection (about 5%); and arts-related subjects (about 3%) (Development Strategy of Tertiary Education, 2001); and
- Institutions Providing Extension Technical Studies. These are planned primarily as upper secondary technical schools which have extended their work into the higher sector, most often in the same discipline that they offer at the upper secondary level.

Other higher sector educational institutions also offer types of study recognised by the State. As a rule, these are personal interest or requalification courses of several months' duration which should, under certain conditions and in the spirit of the Bologna Declaration, enable movement between the various types of formal education.

Barriers to adult lifelong learning

The major barriers in the Czech Republic are:

- Traditionalism – The traditional concept of a university in the Czech Republic is that it is an academic institution whose mission is to provide a unified university education and to conduct the research and development activities associated with such activities. This largely excludes life-long learning; and
- The ability to cope with the content of accredited study programmes.

Lifelong learning should offer individual subjects, courses, and unified modules that enable adults, especially those who are employed, to upgrade their qualifications or to educate themselves in the areas of their interests. It should provide easy access to educational opportunities as and when needed and without regard to age, social standing or personal creed.

Problems with adult education that need to be resolved

The main problems concerning adult education that need to be addressed are:

- Satisfaction of the demand for HE, especially in the humanities, law and arts disciplines. The study opportunities currently on offer still do not correspond to the interest or abilities of those interested in studying;
- There are very high failure levels in these study programmes, especially in the first year, both at universities and in the higher professional schools; and
- It is difficult to move between the different sectors of the HE sector, particularly between the higher professional school and university sectors.

Student numbers in the higher education institutions

In 2002, a total of 266,516 students were studying in all types of HE, i.e. 2.7% of the population of the Czech Republic. Of these, 11.2 % of the students (29,838) were adults. Table 1 shows a detailed breakdown of student numbers in the bachelors, masters and doctoral degrees and other studies programmes. Some 251,195 students were enrolled at the 24 public universities, which represents 94.3% of the total number of university students. Of these, 10.6% were adults. A total of 8,863 students were enrolled in the 21 private universities. The percentage of adults at the private universities was 18%. The so-called 'State Universities' are in fact Military and Police Academies. In 2002, some 6,306 students were enrolled in these establishments. These institutions are undergoing radical restructuring at the time of writing.

Some 24.3% of all students were enrolled in bachelor degrees studies programmes offered by institutions in the HE sector. It is expected that these numbers will rise in the future (Annual Report on Tertiary Education, 2002). One of the main goals of the Czech Government's educational policy is to enable half of all 19-year-olds in any given year to enter some type of HE by 2005.

The future size of the HE sector also has to take into account the growing interest of middle-aged and older people with an interest in studying. These may want to study for formal qualifications or they may be interested in courses as a part of their own lifelong education. Only a small fraction of these groups would be interested in applying for full-time studies and the rest therefore need to be offered new forms of education. New forms of study may include distance education, exploiting the use of information and communication technologies, thereby enabling students to shape their own educational paths and study loads according to their personal abilities. This will make a significant contribution to the vision of an HE system that facilitates entrance to education throughout one's life (National Programme for the Development of Education in the Czech Republic, 2001).

The provision of distance learning courses by technical universities in a country with a relatively dense network of universities could be the problem. However, it is an advantage to apply these methods in subjects with a scientific basis or those in the social sciences and economics/finance-related studies. On the other hand, there are branches of technical universities where the application and exploitation of such methods is practically impossible (Kopecny and Polák, 1999).

Special attention is paid to the training of teachers in the application of different teaching methods as well as to the training of the authors of the study-support materials for distance learning programmes. Academic staff from a number of universities, including the Tomas Bata University in Zlín, have attended a series of short courses provided by the National Centre for Distance Education, based in Olomouc.

Table 2 shows the growing interest of adults in education. In the 2000/01 academic year, some 17,099 adult students were enrolled in courses. For 2002/03, this rose to 29,838 students in the same group, i.e. an increase of 74% in two years. In 2000, the numbers of adults studying in HE programmes was 0.17% of the overall population of the Czech Republic; by 2003 this figure had grown to 0.3 %.

Adult education programmes

In 2002, HEIs in the Czech Republic were offering a total of 944 courses in accredited adult educational programmes (see Table 3). The largest number of adult education programmes (i.e. 265, or 28.1%) is found in the teaching and social care disciplines. The reason for this high number is that teacher education is oriented towards changing the goals and contents of education (i.e. curriculum reform) and the related development of new teaching forms and methods while social care assists the overall change in approach taken by Czech society to social issues.

The greatest share of paid courses, i.e. 53.4% (31 out of 58 actually ran), was for economics/finance-oriented courses. This was in response to the reaction of the population to the current economic changes and the transformation of Czech society as a whole. It also reflects an intense interest in going into business for oneself. A significant component of these courses is the acquisition of new knowledge and skills, especially in the areas of sales and marketing (Chovancová, 2001).

In the technical and theoretical disciplines, adults most frequently wish to increase their computer and foreign language skills.

Fifteen public universities organised activities in the area of the University of the Third Age. Their programmes not only include sociological and psychological issues but also history, politics, philosophy, management, economics and the natural and technical sciences. Interest expressed by senior citizens in these courses continues to grow. The effectiveness of these forms of study has yet to be evaluated.

Meeting the needs of disabled students

Support frameworks in the area of adult education for individuals with special educational needs are created either at the state level or through non-government organisations such as civic organisations and private companies. The conditions for disabled students studying in universities and other HEIs in the Czech Republic have improved greatly since 2002. The need to integrate students with special needs into the university-level educational system is now fully accepted. The support available includes personal assistance, translation services, the adaptation of study materials, copying services and advisory services. As a result, the number of disabled students has grown considerably.

The number of places on offer in the 1999/2000 academic year increased by 216%, and in 2000/01 by 196%. However, the HE sector is still not fully able to meet the demand for disabled student places. Accommodating the requirements of these students, unlocking their potential and ensuring that sufficient high quality education is available, will only be possible if their numbers are expanded further (Annual Report on Tertiary Education, 2002). The requirements of the disabled students need to be resolved on an individual basis.

The accessibility of higher education programmes

The concept of equality of access to higher institutions is supported by the fact that, by law, everyone in the Czech Republic who has completed their secondary education has the right to apply to any HE institution and to take the entrance examination without fear of discrimination. Unfortunately, the existing conditions for education leading to a recognised qualification offer only limited opportunities for adults since they are mostly based on study programmes that last several years. This is difficult for some learners, and their employers, to accept and reduces the take-up of adult education opportunities. For this reason, adults still make up only a small fraction of the total number of the learners in universities. (National Programme for the Development of Education in the Czech Republic, 2001).

So-called 'equalisation' (*vyrovnávací*) courses are organised by university centres for those students who have an interest in studying at university. In 90% of cases, these are 'top up' courses designed to increase the participants' knowledge in mathematics and foreign languages.

Examples of good practice

Examples of good practice in the adult education sector can be found in the work of the Faculty of Management and Economics at Tomas Bata University in Zlín. This Faculty provides bachelors and masters degrees and doctoral studies programmes in, for instance, the fields of economics and management, economic policy, public sector administration and regional development, marketing, company finance and industrial engineering. Courses in all of these disciplines are also offered in a distance learning format. At the time of writing, distance learning courses are also being prepared in economics and management at the bachelors and masters degree levels.

Other courses provided for adults include:

- University entrance examinations preparatory courses: (language and mathematics); and
- University of the Third Age courses.

Courses specifically designed for the general public include:

- Entrepreneurial Activities in Small and Medium-Sized Enterprises; and
- New Approaches to Doing Business, focussing on entrepreneurial activities.

All these courses are specifically designed to meet the particular needs of the University's local region. Special courses with an educational or training orientation are also organised in conjunction with the Zlín region's branch of the Unemployment Bureau in collaborative ventures with other private educational institutions.

Conclusion

Building the structures and institutional framework for adult education is currently at an initial stage in the Czech Republic. Since 1989, adult education has been allowed to develop independently and has thus been exposed to the full effect of market mechanisms. A fundamental document in the education field is the National Programme for the Development of Education in the Czech Republic (the 'White Paper').

The educational systems in place for adult education in the Czech Republic are evolving very slowly, with the core problem being the tradition of copying existing HE programmes (which were created to meet the needs of full-time students). Despite this, virtually all Czech universities are gradually developing programmes specifically designed to meet the needs of adult students in the lifelong education system. Emphasis is being placed on:

- All forms of distance education;
- The transferability of the various course modules between educational institutions operating in the HE sector; and
- The creation of short-term requalification courses.

The quality of such forms of studies is being assured by training university specialists in the education of adults.

References

Act No. 29/1984 § Coll. 'On the System of Primary, Secondary, and Higher Educational Establishments and Schools'.

Act No. 111/1998 § Parliamentary Proceedings. 'On Universities; On Higher Education'.

Act No. 138/1995 § Parliamentary Proceedings. 'Educational Law'.

Annual Report on Tertiary Education, 2002 (*Výroční zprava o stavu vysokého školství za rok* 2002). Ministry of Education, Youth and Sport, IX, 2003.

Chovancová, M., 2001. *Schopnosti a dovednosti marketingového managera.* (The Skills and Abilities of Marketing Managers). In: *Manažment 2001. Enterprises Competitive Ability in Slovakia.* International Scientific Seminar. Bratislava: Economics University in Bratislava, Slovakia.

Development Strategy for Tertiary Education, 2001. (*Strategie rozvoje terciálního vzdělávání*). Ministry of Education, Youth and Sport, X.

Kopecny, J. and Polak, J., 1999. *Is There any Future for Distance Education at Technical Universities in the Czech Republic?* Technical University, Ostrava. Available at: http://www.fs.vsb.cz/akce/1999

National Report on Adult Education, Czech Republic, IX, 2003. Available at: http://www.unesco.org./education/uie/pdf/country/CzechRep.pdf

Vojtech, J., 2001. *The Distribution and Numbers of Students in the System of Educational Routes in Secondary and Higher Professional Education and their Situation in the Labour Market.* National Institute for Vocational Education (*Ustav pro informace a vzdělávání*).

White Paper, 2001. National Programme for the Development of Education in the Czech Republic. (*Národní program rozvoje vzdělávání v České republice. Bila kniha*). Institute for Information and Education (*Ustav pro informace a vzdělávání*).

Appendix

Table 1: Number of Universities, Faculties and Students by Town/City in the Czech Republic (as at: 31.10.2002)

Town or City[1]	Numbers		Students in the Czech Republic in all forms of studies							Foreign
	Unis.	Facs.	Study Programmes: Bachelors Degree	Study Programmes: Masters Degree[2]	Study Programmes: Doctoral Studies	Students Overall	Newly Registered[3]	Graduates[4]	Further/ Other Education	Foreign Students Overall[5]
Universities	49	122	64,745	152,373	19, 560	236,678	44,760	31,671	29,838	12,078
Prague	23	36	18,740	62,584	9,459	90,783	14,193	11,453	11,904	6,654
Brno	8	28	14,356	29,890	5,023	49,269	9,433	6,553	4,880	2,373
Ostrava	3	11	6,461	14,686	1,375	22,522	5,425	3,180	2,900	478
Plzeň	2	7	3,372	9,374	622	13,368	2,842	1,818	634	389
Hradec Králové	2	4	2,290	5,011	454	7,755	1,400	1,261	1,131	328
Olomouc	1	7	2,592	10,277	1,170	14,039	2,273	1,704	1,740	824
Liberec	1	6	1,555	4,751	332	6,638	1,200	791	812	405
České Budějovice	1	5	1,823	4,903	345	7,071	1,486	1,099	651	57
Ústí nad Labem	1	4	2,804	3,819	23	6,646	1,605	874	978	41
Pardubice	1	4	2,697	2,290	374	5,361	1,411	776	756	47
Zlín	1	3	3,065	917	170	4,152	1,103	594	223	152
Vyškov	1	2	634	299	99	1,032	295	229	895	1
Opava	1	1	866	835	38	1,739	419	340	179	60
Kunovice	1	–	535	0	0	535	209	175	229	52
Karlovy Vary	1	–	462	0	0	462	196	0	0	2
Mladá Boleslav	1	–	209	0	0	209	82	0	0	3
Cheb	–	1	898	560	0	1,458	448	248	1,441	15
Lednice na Moravě	–	1	539	218	76	833	179	136	0	63
Jindřichův Hradec	–	1	538	482	0	1,020	233	204	67	35
Karviná	–	1	309	1,477	0	1,786	328	236	418	99
Public Universities	24	117	54,862	150,330	19,245	224,437	40,588	30,224	26,758	11,437
Prague	8	36	12,500	61,922	9,459	83,881	11,787	10,724	10,538	6,171
Brno	5	25	13,451	28,942	4,874	47,267	8,934	6,307	4,442	2,356
Ostrava	2	11	5,683	14,686	1,375	21,744	5,082	3,137	2,900	396
Plzeň	1	7	3,263	9,374	622	13,259	2,733	1,818	634	388
Olomouc	1	7	2,592	10,277	1,170	14,039	2,273	1,704	1,740	824
Liberec	1	6	1,555	4,751	332	6,638	1,200	791	812	405

Town or City[1]	Numbers		Students in the Czech Republic in all forms of studies							Foreign
	Unis.	Facs.	Study Programmes: Bachelors Degree	Study Programmes: Masters Degree[2]	Study Programmes: Doctoral Studies	Students Overall	Newly Registered[3]	Graduates[4]	Further/ Other Education	Foreign Students Overall[5]
České Budějovice	1	5	1,823	4,903	345	7,071	1,486	1,099	651	57
Ústí nad Labem	1	4	2,804	3,819	23	6,646	1,605	874	826	41
Pardubice	1	4	2,697	2,290	374	5,361	1,411	776	756	47
Hradec Králové	1	4	2,279	4,877	387	7,543	1,367	1,236	1,131	328
Zlín	1	3	3,065	917	170	4, 152	1,103	594	223	152
Opava	1	1	866	835	38	1,739	419	340	179	60
Cheb	0	1	898	560	0	1,458	448	248	1, 441	15
Lednice na Moravě	0	1	539	218	76	833	179	136	0	63
Jindřichův Hradec	0	1	538	482	0	1,020	233	204	67	35
Karviná	0	1	309	1,477	0	1,786	328	236	418	99
Private	21	0	6,981	287	0	7,268	3,161	399	1,595	623
Prague	14	0	4,351	287	0	4,638	1,962	181	1,366	476
Brno	2	0	537	0	0	537	260	0	0	7
Ostrava	1	0	778	0	0	778	343	43	0	82
Kunovice	1	0	535	0	0	535	209	175	229	52
Karlovy Vary	1	0	462	0	0	462	196	0	0	2
Mladá Boleslav	1	0	209	0	0	209	82	0	0	3
Plzeň	1	0	109	0	0	109	109	0	0	1
State Universities	4	5	2,902	1,756	315	4,973	1,011	1,048	1,333	18
Prague	1	0	1,889	375	0	2,264	444	548	0	7
Brno	1	3	368	948	149	1,465	239	246	438	10
Hradec Králové	1	0	11	134	67	212	33	25	0	0
Vyškov	1	2	634	299	99	1,032	295	229	895	1

1 All towns or cities in which there is at least one faculty are indicated here (without regard to the actual seat of their university). They are organised in descending order according to the number of Universities, Faculties, and number of students in Full-time, Distance, and Combined Studies programmes.

2 Including follow-on Masters Degree studies programmes.
3 The overall numbers newly registered in the 1st Year do not include those accepted into follow-on Masters Degree and Doctoral Studies programmes.
4 For calendar year 2002.
5 The figures shown for 'Foreign Students Overall' include student numbers in the Bachelors, Masters and Doctoral Studies programmes, and in Full-time, Distance, and Combined Studies programmes.
6 Data for the Private Universities: Shows studying and newly registered students only for those institutions included in the SIMS system. Graduate numbers are complete, and were discovered in other ways. For the figures for the overall numbers of Universities, the data has been adjusted according to the actual numbers in accredited universities.

(Source: Annual Report on Tertiary Education – 2002)

Table 2: Other Forms of Higher Studies by Individual Education Level

	2000/2001		2001/2002		2002/2003	
Education Level	Student Numbers	% at this level	Student Numbers	% at this level	Student Numbers	% at this level
Higher Profess. Schools	3,914	14.7	4,121	15.5	4,726	17.1
Universities						
B.A., M.A.	27,631	14.5	30,793	15.3	37,054	16.3
Postgraduate	9,672	58.4	10,572	58.8	12,092	57.3
Adult Education	17,099	–	27,865	–	29,837	–
(of this, Distance Education)	3,397	–	8,956	–	7,596	–

(Source: Czech Statistics Office (National Report on Adult Education, Czech Republic, 2003))

Table 3: Adult Education Programmes Offered by Higher Education Institutions in the Czech Republic

Disciplines	Accredited Adult Education Programmes		Other	Total
	Courses (without fees)	Courses (with fees)		
Natural Sciences and Theoretical Disciplines	9	15	61	85
Technical Sciences and Theoretical Disciplines	2	9	122	133
Agricultural, Forestry, Veterinary Sciences and Theoretical Disciplines	0	0	22	22
Health Care, Medical and Pharmaceutical Sciences and Theoretical Disciplines	1	7	90	98
Social Sciences and Theoretical Disciplines and Services	0	58	144	202
Economics	0	31	27	58
Law, Legal and Public Sector Administration Activities	0	2	37	39
Pedagogy, Teaching and Social Care	14	47	204	265
Psychology and Psychiatry	0	4	15	19
Cultural and Fine Arts Sciences and Theoretical Disciplines	0	6	17	23
Total:	26	179	739	944

(Source: Annual Report on Tertiary Education, 2002)

University Web Addresses

Public Universities

The Academy of Arts, Architecture and Design, Prague: http://www.vsup.cz/
Brno University of Technology: http://www.vutbr.cz/
Charles University, Prague: http://www.cuni.cz/
The Czech Technical University, Prague: http://www.cvut.cz/
The Czech University of Agriculture, Prague: http://www.czu.cz/

The Institute of Chemical Technology, Prague: http://www.vscht.cz/
Jan Evangelista Purkyne University in Ústi nad Labem: http://www.ujep.cz/
Masaryk University, Brno: http://www.muni.cz/
Mendel University of Agriculture and Forestry, Brno: http://www.mendelu.cz/
The Silesian University in Opava: http://www.slu.cz/
The Technical University of Liberec: http://www.vslib.cz/
The Technical University of Ostrava: http://www.vsb.cz/
Tomas Bata University, Zlin: http://www.utb.cz/
Universitas Palackiana Olomucensis: http://www.upol.cz/
The University of Economics, Prague: http://www.vse.cz/
The University of Hradec Kralove: http://www.uhk.cz/
The University of Ostrava: http://www.osu.cz/
The University of Pardubice: http://www.upce.cz/
The University of South Bohemia in Ceské Budejovice: http://www.jcu.cz/
The University of Veterinary and Pharmaceutical Sciences, Brno: http://www.vfu.cz/
The University of West Bohemia in Pilsen: http://www.zcu.cz/
The Academy of Fine Arts in Prague: http://www.avu.cz/
The Academy of Music and Performing Arts in Prague: http://www.amu.cz/
The Janacek Academy of Music and Performing Arts in Brno: http://www.jamu.cz/

State Universities

The Military Academy in Brno: http://www.vabo.cz/
The Military University of the Ground Forces in Vyskov: http://www.vvs-pv.cz/
The Purkyne Military Medical Academy in Hradec Kralove: http://www.pmfhk.cz/

Private Universities

The Finance and Policy College in Prague: http://www.vsfs.cz/
The Writers Academy, Prague: http://www.lit-akad.cz/
The College of Banking, Prague: http://www.bivs.cz/
The J. A. Komenský College of Higher Education in Prague: http://www.vsjak.cz/
The European Polytechnic Institute in Kunovice: http://www.vos.cz/
The Academy Sting, Brno: http://www.sting.cz/
The College of International Affairs and Public Relations, Prague: http://www.vip-vs.cz/
The International Baptist Theological Seminary: http://www.ibts.cz/

AUNE VALK

5: Adults in Estonian Higher Education

The context of university adult education in Estonia

The history of university adult education in Estonia can be traced back to the beginning of the nineteenth century when the University of Tartu was the centre of one of the six 'learning districts' in Czarist Russia (Seene and Valk, 2000). The establishment of Estonia as an independent republic in 1918 brought an urgent need for teachers' training courses and the University of Tartu launched these even before its official reopening as an Estonian university on 1 December 1919. During the Soviet Occupation (1945–1991), universities were considered to be the main providers of adult education (Märja, 2000). Besides specialist continuing education (CE) and retraining courses and extramural degree programmes, courses in psychology and leadership that started in the 1970s were considered to be of the utmost importance for the development of the country. Although adult education operated quite well during that time, its contents were rarely free from Marxist-Leninist influences, however. Estonian universities started to change and rebuild their adult education systems early in the 1990s following the restoration of independence in the country.

During the 1990s, the number of students in Estonian universities increased very rapidly: in 1993 there were about 25,000 students (*Riiklike hariduspoliitikate ülevaated. Eesti*, 2001); in 2003, the number of students in higher education (HE) reached almost 61,000. This rapid increase has been achieved in large part due to the increasing number of adult students. Currently every year universities enrol more students than there are secondary school graduates. This rapid increase can also be seen in the case of university continuing education (UCE) and retraining programmes. There are several reasons for the vastly increasing interest in HE among adults. The reasons can be split into two groups. First, the great need for new skills associated with the enormous changes in the job market and in society; many people cannot manage in the 'new society' with an 'old education' obtained in the 1980s or earlier. This group is related also to the gradual formalisation of the job market where more and more professions have set up entry requirements. There is also a need for language retraining (from Russian to English), for IT skills and entrepreneurial attitudes and skills. The second group of reasons why more adults have come to the universities is most probably related to the greater opportunities: the increasing openness of the HE system and the curricula. In addition to the six public universities in Estonia, six private universities have now been established, together with a number of applied HE institutions. The public universities have adopted a third mission, providing services to society (in addition to teaching full-time students and research). They have considerably diversified their forms of tuition, opened numerous new (mainly masters level) courses to adult students and made major efforts to assist regional development by opening colleges in regions far away from the two big cities, Tallinn and Tartu.

In parallel with the developments in society more broadly, all the education laws have either been newly adopted or have been considerably changed since the restoration of independence in 1991. Taking into account the context, it is noteworthy that the Adult Education Law was adopted as early as 1993 (*Täiskasvanute koolituse seadus*, 1993; latest amendments, 2003). This is the main document besides the University Law (*Ülikooliseadus*, 1995; latest amendments 2003) and the Law of Applied Higher Education Institutions (*Rakenduskõrgkooliseadus*, 1998; latest amendments, 2003) that regulate adult participation in HE. According to this Law, adult education includes basic, secondary and higher education in forms suitable for adult learners, professional continuing education (including retraining) and liberal adult education. Retraining is referred to as continuing education (CE) later. Higher education is considered as adult education if it is delivered in either the part-time or distance learning modes. Alternatively, students can take their examinations as 'external students'.[1] In addition to defining the forms of adult education, the Law deals with a number of issues such as the responsibility of the different actors in adult education, the providers of adult education, the general principles of adult education management, financing, and the rights of adult learners. Depending on the aims and level of the activities, adult education is provided mainly by special adult-oriented secondary schools, vocational schools, applied higher education institutions, universities,[2] folk universities and other similar kinds of liberal adult education institutions, and private training companies.

The Adult Education Law lists the main actors responsible for guaranteeing adult education and states their responsibilities. The Government is responsible for defining state priorities and strategy, for finding finance for adult education and the related research and for forming the Adult Education Council (*Täiskasvanuhariduse Nõukogu*). This Council, led by the Minister of Education, is responsible for advising the Government on issues of adult education. Local governments are responsible for guaranteeing that adults have the opportunity to obtain basic and secondary education, to support the training of unemployed people, people with disabilities and people with low incomes. Public service employers are obliged to give in-service leave to staff of a minimum of seven days per year to participate in liberal adult education courses (though without salary), 14 days for participating in professional CE courses (with salary), 30 days for participating in degree education and an additional 42 to 49 days to defend bachelors, masters or doctoral degrees (maintaining the basic salary for the first 10 days and with a reduced salary thereafter). In January 2002, the Ministry of Education introduced the first version of its Strategy for Lifelong Learning. This provides a strategic vision, mainly of adult education development,[3] which gives an overview of

1 External students take pass examinations without participating in the teaching activities. However, only a small part of a course can be passed in this way.

2 While universities provide research-based, more generally oriented, education at three levels (bachelor, master and doctor), applied higher education institutions provide more vocationally-oriented higher education, as a rule at the first level.

3 For more information see the Ministry of Education Website: www.hm.ee

the state of the art in this field; the political, economic, legal and informational principles for developing lifelong learning environments, issues of motivation, financing, barriers to learning and the priorities for action for 2002/04. At the end of 2003, however, the strategy had still not been approved.

Management and delivery of adult education in Estonian universities

All Estonian universities offer learning opportunities for adults by providing both CE courses and part-time degree education as evening courses or distance learning programmes. Distance education usually includes short learning sessions at weekends once or twice a month, learning with Internet-based courses and independent work with study materials. About 25% of the total student body (of altogether more than 60,000 students) can be defined as adult students as they study either in the evenings or part-time in the distance education mode (see Figure 1). The number of adult students is highest in the public universities.

Figure 1: Full-time students and part-time (adult) students in Estonian higher education, 2002. (Statistics from the Ministry of Education and Research)

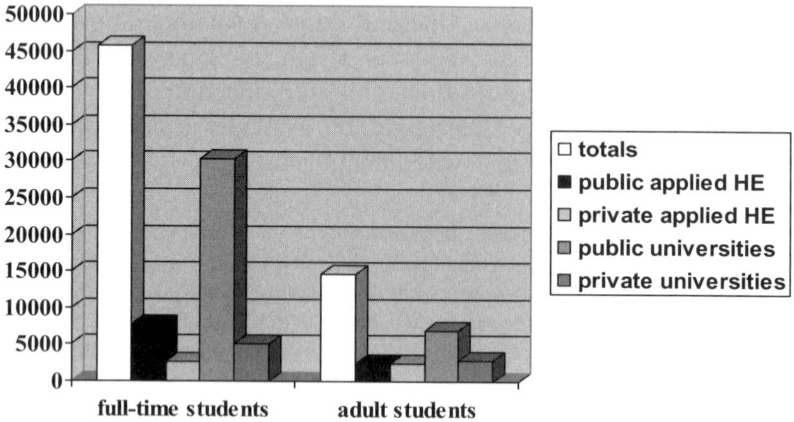

Although the management of adult education differs from one university to another, all the Estonian public universities[4] have established Open Universities for the purpose of providing services for the community and offering opportunities for lifelong learning. A similar system operates in some private universities. The Open University is a defined function within each university. It is the symbol of flexible university-level lifelong learning opportunities, including UCE, part-time degree education and degree education given in the form of distance learning. In most cases, the same lecturers who are responsible for the full-time teaching provide adult education in the faculties and colleges. Only a few universities have special staff responsible for delivering UCE.

Adult education courses and curricula generally include a wide range of different topics and approaches. Universities are, however, mainly engaged in professional and scientific degree education, the retraining of graduates and providing UCE programmes for professionals such as teachers, doctors, engineers and civil servants. Subjects of wider interest are considered within Summer Schools and at public lectures. At the same time, Folk Universities, Adult Education Centres and other training institutions provide more general courses directed to adults' personal and social interests.

According to the sociological research (*Elukestva õppe vajaduste analüüs*, 2002)[5] on Estonians' interests in learning, it is possible to conclude that adults prefer shorter courses. The most popular length of a course for adult learners is 40 hours. Compared to the interest in short courses (about 15%), only 1.7% of the respondents wanted to acquire basic or secondary education and 7.9% were interested in undertaking higher education or obtaining an academic degree.

4 These are: the University of Tartu, Tallinn Technical University, Tallinn Pedagogical University, the Estonian Agricultural University, the Estonian Academy of Music, and the Estonian Academy of Arts.

5 The study was organised by the Adult Education Association, Andras, and conducted by the social and market research company Saar Poll in November 2001. The sample of the study included 1,008 people, aged 15–74 years. The study investigated adults' participation in degree education and continuing education oriented for professional development; the questions also included liberal adult education.

Summing up, altogether 13% of Estonian adults participated in 2001 in some kind of course (not taking into account liberal adult education). The proportion was highest (22%) among the 20 to 29-year-old cohort. This does not, however, exactly represent the number of people participating in university education since the question did not specify the provider of education. The main motive for participating in adult education was self-development, followed by enhancing one's professional qualification. The first of these was clearly the most important for women (64% considered it as their main motive); the second was the most important motive for men (45%).

Adult participation in education leading to degrees

To illustrate better the reasons why adult students choose to participate in university education, some data from research carried out in 1998, 1999 and 2001 are presented (Dsiss, 2000; *Avatud ülikooli esimesed lõpetajad,* 2003). Altogether about 620 Open University students and graduates (median age 30 years, 70% female) from the University of Tartu answered the question why they had chosen the Open University as the particular medium for their studies. The results are summarised in Figure 2. It can be seen that three factors prevail among the reasons: first, the suitability of this form of studies for adults in full-time employment; second the high quality of the teaching; and third the prestige of the University. Amongst the graduates, 32% also mentioned finishing previously interrupted studies as one of the reasons for choosing the Open University.

Figure 2: Motives for selecting the Open University (%)

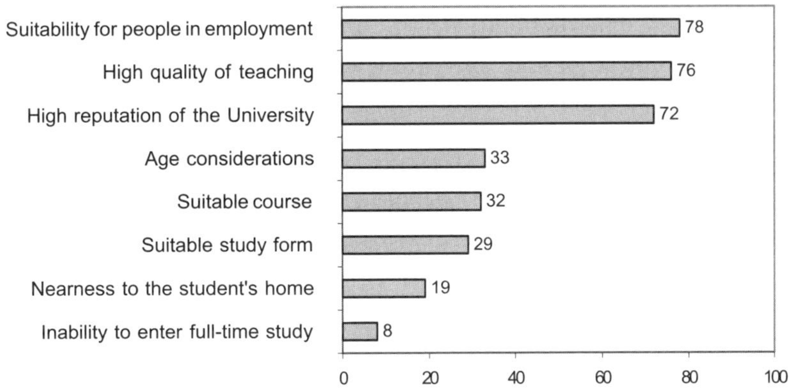

Longitudinal surveys have shown that decisions regarding the continuation of studies at the university level and the choice of a course to be taken are generally made at different times and may often be fairly independent of one another. The decision to continue studying at the university level is generally made long before the choice of a particular course, except in a few subject areas such as music or medicine where the two decisions need to coincide; the subject area may even be selected before the university. A number of students have known for a long time that they want to continue their education but decide on a particular university programme only at the time of registration. What matters most for these students is the intention to acquire a university degree; the subjects they study are of less importance. In these cases, particular factors may come to influence the selection of a programme, e.g. the number of applicants (students prefer programmes with less competition for entrance), lower fees and the wish not to leave one's home, home town or friends. Figure 3 reveals that three-quarters of the respondents mentioned the wish to get a university degree as the dominating motive for beginning a course.

Using factor analysis, four characteristic groups can be distinguished from these data: the first group includes people whose choice of course has been determined by its social prestige, profitability and career prospects. Interestingly, students belonging to this group have often been advised to begin studies with the Open University by their families. The second group could be called the professional development sector. This includes people who are studying in order to cope better with their jobs, to gain knowledge and skills applicable in their everyday work and to achieve future success. In most cases, these people have been advised to undertake their studies by their employers. The incentive to begin studies for this group can also be the prospect of getting a new occupation. The third group contains people whose aims are general self-development and the acquisition of a university diploma or degree for its own sake. The fourth, the least numerous group, is made up of people induced to study by job-related risks and fears; for example, the risk of losing their job or the fear that their level of education or qualifications might be considered unsuitable for their present occupations. For them, the size of the fee plays a very important role.

The motives that graduates of the Open University mention differ considerably from those who are still studying. While students consider university degree and work-related motives as very important (Figure 3), graduates stress more general self-development (see Figure 4). This may reflect their experiences during their studies. 'Opportunity for self-development' was the main answer to the question of what they got from their studies in the Open University. 'Obtaining a university degree' was only the fourth most important benefit, coming after 'better and higher salary' and 'programme corresponds to my abilities'.

Figure 3: Reasons determining the selection of the programme among the Open University students of the University of Tartu (%), (Dsiss, 2001)

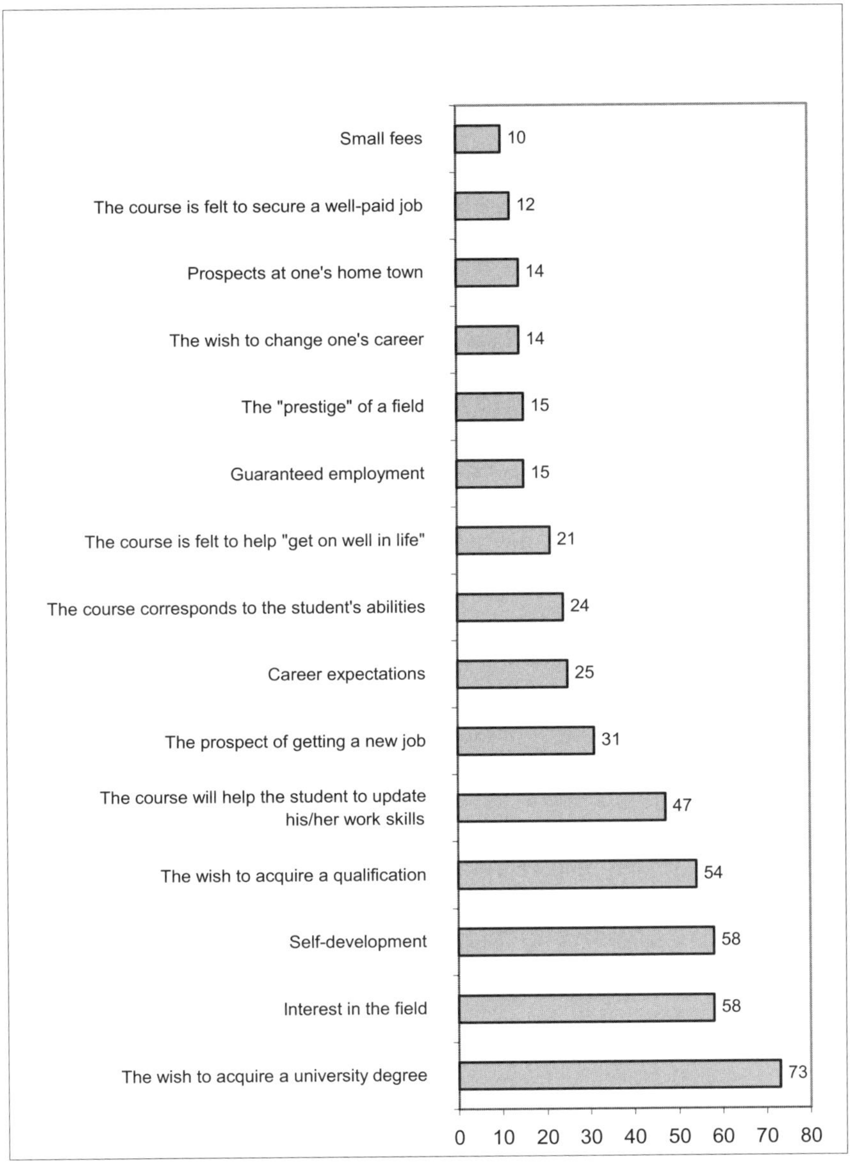

*Figure 4: Reasons determining the selection of the programme among graduates of the Open University of the University of Tartu (*Avatud Ülikooli esimesed lõpetajad, *2003)*

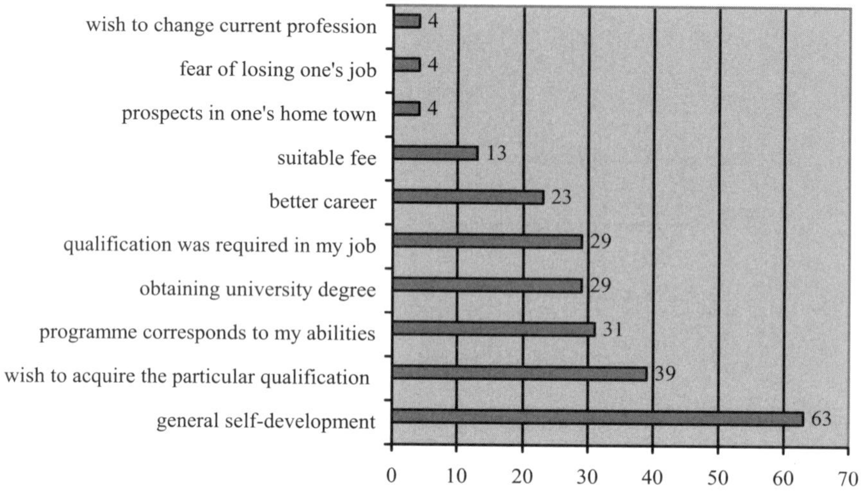

The prevalence of work-related motives amongst Open University students is also evident when looking at the relation between studies and work. For approximately half of the students, irrespective of their sex, studying is directly related to their full-time employment and only about one in five of the students are studying subjects not related to their present employment. A comparison with the information concerning status at work shows that most of the students who are working classified themselves as being freelance or self-employed. Three-quarters of the senior executives and nearly two-thirds of the non-executive employees study subjects that are directly related to their occupations.

Adult participation in university continuing education

The popularity of CE depends to a certain extent on the regulations set for particular occupations. For example, medical doctors and schoolteachers have to complete specified hours of training to maintain or enhance their qualifications. In the case of schoolteachers, this is also supported by the requirement that 3% of their total salary bill should be spent on continuing professional education. These kinds of regulations create demand for UCE.

The scope and content of the UCE provision of each university depends on its size and specific orientation. A wide range of UCE opportunities is offered by Tallinn Pedagogical University (mainly oriented towards teachers' education and training) and the University of Tartu (the only classical university in Estonia and the only one providing medical CE). The University of Tartu delivers CE courses for both teachers and doctors, amongst others, while Tallinn Pedagogical University focuses on teachers' professional development. Engineers' professional continuing education takes place entirely at Tallinn Technical University.

We can see from Figure 1 that, in most universities, the number of CE students is clearly small compared to the number of students in traditional undergraduate programmes. The biggest UCE provider is Tallinn Pedagogical University, where the number of CE learners in 2003 (about 11,500) and distance students (about 1,800) exceeds the number of full-time university students (nearly 6,000). The University of Tartu's 9,000 UCE learners and 4,500 Open University students equal the number of full-time students (13,500). In addition to teachers and doctors, local and national government officials are active participants in CE courses. To a lesser extent, members of other professions also engage in updating their skills and knowledge.

University continuing education courses include requalification programmes, which have become popular following the recent profound political and economic changes in Estonian society. Due to these changes, several professions (mainly in agriculture, but also in Russian language teaching, for example) became less useful and different skills were required. Requalification programmes are meant for people who already have one university degree and who wish to get an additional qualification for job-related reasons. Current courses are aimed mainly at practising teachers. Programmes last for two or three years and lead to a new teaching qualification. In recent years, there have been requalification programmes in English, German, History and Estonian language and literature.

Community outreach and learning based on information and communication technology

In addition to organising courses in the evenings and during weekends and using traditional methods of distance education (with printed study material), universities try to make the courses more adult-oriented with community outreach and information and communication technology (ICT). The three largest Estonian public universities have regional colleges where students can study for a degree without leaving their home regions. Open University studies are very popular in some of these colleges. In addition, colleges serve as support centres for organising UCE courses and delivering public lectures in the counties. Regular *Studia Generale*[6] are held in the counties and increasing numbers of lectures are also made publicly available via the Internet.[7] These provide alternative ways for the universities to offer adults the opportunity to participate in university education without requiring their long-term commitment and not for work-related reasons.

There is a growing tendency to deliver individual lectures, seminars, UCE courses and also longer programmes via the Internet. Technology is also increasingly being used in traditional classroom teaching, leading to the emergence of joint methods where traditional lecturing and seminars are combined with Web-based study materials using forums and e-mail for communication. Although technology offers new opportunities and enables the inclusion of new target

6 *Studia generale* are public lectures delivered by university teachers that are open to everyone free of charge.

7 Some of these lectures can be seen, both in English and Estonian, at http://video.ut.ee

groups to university education, it also creates problems, especially for adult learners. In the year 2000, 200 Open University students of the University of Tartu were asked about their experiences and wishes with reference to ICT-based learning (Valk and Pilt, 2001). Most (88%) of the students were eager to participate in ICT-based courses. Approximately two-thirds of them had good Internet skills and access to the Internet. Only 12% had experience in ICT-based learning, however. Besides lack of skills and lack of access, some students were worried about the costs of using telephone lines for Internet access. One of the main problems is also the fear of loosing face-to-face contact with teachers and fellow students. In addition, some people enjoy lectures and consider that taking notes helps them to remember. In summary, most of the students were eager to participate in Internet-based courses as an addition to their current learning. They were not keen, however, to substitute it for their face-to-face learning.

Problems of adult participation in universities

According to the sociological research referred to earlier (*Elukestva õppe vajaduste analüüs*, 2002), the major obstacles to adults' participation in training are either attitudinal (they feel that they are too old or do not need any training) or situational (they view lack of finance and time as overwhelming problems). Respondents did not mention the distance from a training institution as a problem. They were also satisfied with the opportunities to choose between courses.

One of the major problems for adults in obtaining education is lack of money. Currently only about 53% of all the students studying in Estonia's universities and other higher education institutions are state financed. Other students pay their own tuition fees or these are paid for them by their employers. As a rule, the State finances only full-time studies and these are not usually taught at times that are suitable for adult students. Until now the only exception has been for teachers who are working in schools but who do not yet have a university qualification or who are qualified in the wrong speciality. The fees for their part-time bachelors or masters studies or re-qualification programmes taken by distance learning are paid by the State.

Figure 5. Sources of finance for studies among Open University student

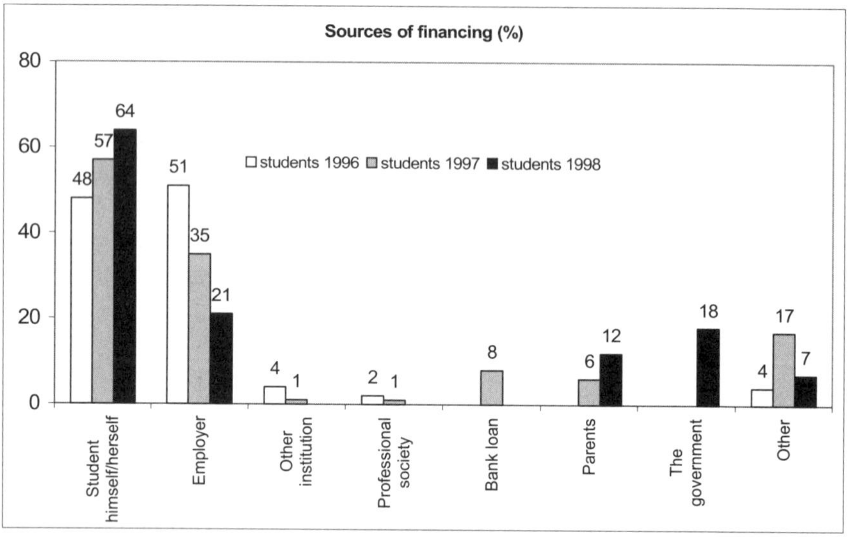

Figure 5 presents statistics about the sources of financing Open University studies at the University of Tartu in the recent past (Dsiss, 2000; *Avatud ülikooli esimesed lõpetajad*, 2003). The role of employers in financing education and training has decreased for several reasons. One of these is that the Estonian tax law considers payment for degree education (bachelors, masters and doctoral studies) as a special favour to employees and it is therefore taxed at a special rate. This is a major legal problem which, added to the lack of state participation in financing adult education, hinders further development of adult participation in degree education.

Almost 85% of the Open University students are currently self-financing; the remaining 15% are practising teachers whose studies are mandatory and who are therefore financed by the State. Approximately half of the self-financing students pay their tuition fees from their own income, one-third of students have their fees paid by their employer, one in ten students were assisted by their parents or spouses, and about 5% use a bank loan. In comparison with the students who began their studies in 1996, the percentage of self-financing students has increased by almost 20%, and the percentage of those funded by their employers has diminished.

Research among Estonian adults (*Elukestva õppe vajaduste analüüs*, 2002) and other research on Tartu University graduates (carried out on graduates and their employers) (*Tartu Ülikooli lõpetanute uuring*, 2003) shows, however, that employers generally have a positive attitude towards employee training. 90% support their employees' university studies, e.g. by giving free time for regular participation in study sessions and they consider that investments in the education of their employees are useful to the company. More than 80% of employers also find that education obtained while their employees continue working (part-time university studies) is more practical and better related to the company's activities than full-time studies. In the case of CE, people can usually select for themselves the courses they wish to take and they continue to be paid while they study. Taking into account participation in degree education and CE in both universities and other training institutions, 45% of adults' participation in education is entirely paid by employers and 30% is self-financed. The rest of the courses were paid partly by the employers and partly by the learners jointly, some by official bodies (e.g. the Employment Office or local governments), and some were free of charge for the learner (paid for by project-based initiatives financed by different Estonian or EU foundations).

One of the problems that adults can face when they enter a university is the orientation of some lecturers towards traditional students and their inability to take account of adults' needs. As a rule, university teachers have no training in teaching and learning (and particularly none in teaching adults). It was only in the late 1990s that the Estonian Institute of Humanities, the University of Tartu and Tallinn Pedagogical University started to organise teaching development courses for university teachers. Since 1997 Tallinn Pedagogical University has also offered bachelors, masters and doctoral studies in andragogy. For students in other specialities, 'adult training' or the 'management of adult training' are sometimes offered as a subsidiary subject.

Another of the obstacles for adult participation referred to in the above research (*Elukestva õppe vajaduste analüüs*, 2002) is the attitude found in some learners; in addition to thinking that they do not need training or that they are too old to learn, they also lack learning skills (Dsiss, 2000). On average, Open University students have not engaged in any systematic study for eight years. This means that they may have difficulties both in starting their studies and in obtaining the skills and habits required for independent learning.

One of the specific problems concerning adult participation in university education in Estonia is the language of the study materials. The small number of Estonian speaking people (approximately one million of the 1.4 million inhabitants of Estonia) does not warrant the publication of up-to-date university textbooks in Estonian. This forces students to use other languages for learning. Nowadays it is mainly English, and in some specialities German, that is used. For younger students this does not cause a problem since they have learnt these languages at school. However, older people speak Russian as their first, and often only, foreign language (since the previous political regime imposed the use of Russian and inhibited contacts with the rest of the world). The fact that most of the current subjects on offer are based on textbooks and research articles in English causes problems for many adult students.

Examples of good practice from Estonia

Organisation of adult education in universities

As already mentioned, the management of adult education differs from one university to another in Estonia. One of the models that has proved most efficient is to centralise the management of all non-traditional teaching opportunities in one place. In the case of the

University of Tartu this is the Open University, which is responsible for the coordination of degree education for adults, UCE, ICT-based teaching, and the regional activities of the university. This close co-operation enables effective planning of the lifelong learning strategy and allows the university to use its intellectual and material resources more effectively. It also enables students to move more easily from degree courses to CE and vice versa. One way of doing this is by offering single courses or modules of courses from degree curricula (especially at the masters level) for people who do not wish to take the whole curriculum. It also makes it possible to count credit points from CE courses towards a university degree.

Community outreach

Flexibility and openness are important principles but they are difficult to achieve in providing education for adults. There are different ways of being open and flexible, one of which is to provide community outreach. Estonian universities have the provision of services to society as part of their mission statements. This they do by providing additional learning opportunities for local people via their colleges in the counties. Universities have representatives in the counties and contracts are signed between the universities and counties to provide co-operation in information exchange, training and retraining, research and consultancy services, and cultural activities.

Another way of increasing the flexibility for working people is to offer Internet-based learning opportunities. In a number of universities and subject areas, in recent years there has been a rapid growth in this field. An example from the University of Tartu is shown in Figure 6. At the beginning of 2003, six Estonian higher education institutions, together with the Ministry of Education and Research and the Estonian Information Technology Foundation, initiated the Estonian E-University to facilitate cooperation, use the available resources effectively and enhance the quality of e-learning. The initiative includes both universities and applied HE institutions, as well as public and private institutions. One of the main aims of this initiative is to facilitate access to university education for adult learners and other 'non-traditional' target groups.

Figure 6: Internet-based courses at the University of Tartu

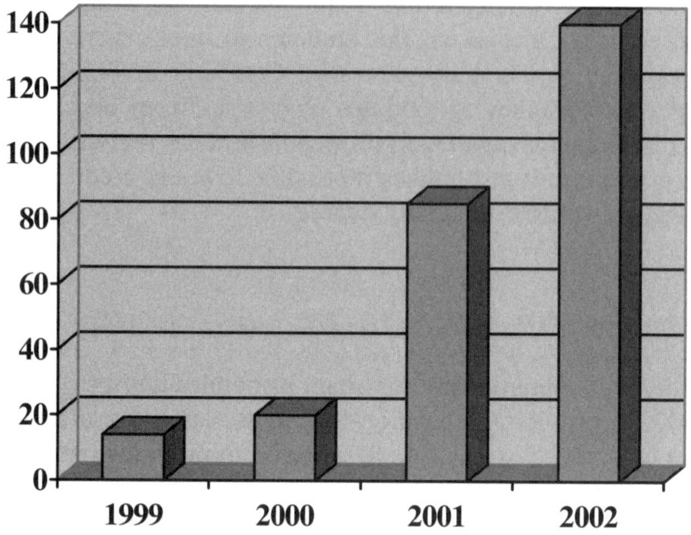

Although there are a number of issues in the Estonian political system that hinder adult participation in education, it is worth mentioning two points that support the development of adult education in the universities: the Adult Education Law allows people who work in the public services, as already mentioned, to have up to 79 days of part-paid leave for learning. This is clearly helpful and encourages their staff to participate, especially in longer courses and degree education. The other positive example is that the tax law permits the refund of income tax (up to 26% of total salary) paid by individuals for their own education.

Conclusion

Estonian society is accustomed to change. One of the usually traditional areas, university education, has had to change considerably during the 1990s, opening itself to society and to the rest of the world. Two higher education reforms,[8] the rapid increase in student numbers, the establishment of private universities, the change of the first foreign language (including the language of text-books) from Russian to English, quick adoption of ICT-opportunities for teaching and learning and the setting up of new adult education systems are some examples of the changes that universities have had to undertake to answer the needs of a changing society and job market. At the time of writing, the universities have established their Open Universities, which include a variety of activities directed towards adult students, and these are functioning well. In 2002 the Estonian universities adopted new curricula in line with the Bologna proposals. In the near future, we should see the response towards the ideas of lifelong learning (LLL) in the universities: an increase in their adult education provision; the Accreditation of Prior Learning (APL);[9] adult-oriented masters curricula, and so on. In addition to relating university LLL to the Bologna process, new trends for university adult education should include the following activities: setting up Accreditation of Prior Experiential

8 Until 1992, higher education studies in Estonia lasted for five years, followed by studies for Candidate of Sciences. The highest degree, the Doctor of Sciences, was normally obtained only after decades of research. At the beginning of the 1990s a new system was introduced: four years for a bachelors degree, two years for a masters, and four years for a PhD. The previous higher education diploma obtained in five years was made equal to the new Bachelor of Education. Candidates of Sciences as well as Doctors of Sciences were given the same rights as new PhDs. In 2001, a second reform of higher education started following the principles of the Bologna Agreement. Since 2002 students have been admitted to the new 3+2 curricula. These reforms have created a need for APL.

9 The recently changed University Law allows students to take into account APL and APEL up to 50% of the curriculum.

Learning (APEL) systems; enhancing cooperation in e-learning; and developing and supporting teachers.

References

Avatud Ülikooli esimesed lõpetajad, 2003. *Tartu: TÜ avatud ülikool.* (First graduates of the Open University, 2003). Tartu: Tartu University Open University.

Dsiss, H., 2000. *Three Years of the Open University. A sociological study*. Tartu: Tartu University Multimedia Centre.

Elukestva õppe vajaduste analüüs, 2002. ETKA, Andras. (*Analysis of lifelong learning needs, 2002. Estonian Adult Education Association, Andras*).

Märja, T., 2000. Jäljed. Meenutusi täiskasvanuhariduse lähiajaloost Eestis. Tallinn: SE&JS. (*Tracks. Memories from recent history of adult education in Estonia*).

Riiklike hariduspoliitikate ülevaated. Eesti, 2001. OECD. (*Reviews of National Policies for Education. Estonia*).

Rakenduskõrgkooli seadus (RT I 1998, 61, 980; 2001, 65, 375), 10.06.1998.

Seene, T. and Valk, A., 2000. Continuing Education in the University of Tartu, Estonia. In: V. Mitchell, ed. *European University Continuing Education. The Managers Handbook*. EUCEN: Liège.

Tartu Ülikooli lõpetanute uuringute, 2003. Career Centre of the University of Tartu. Available at: http://www.ut.ee/career/Tooandjatekysitlus2003.pdf

Täiskasvanute koolituse seadus (RT I 1993, 74, 1054; 1999, 10, 150; 60, 617), 10.11.1993. (*Adult Education Law*).

Valk, A. and Pilt, L., 2001. Virtuaalõppe väljakutsed õppijale ja õppejõule. (Challenges of virtual learning for students and teachers). In: L. Pilt, ed., *Elukestev Õpe Eestis*. Tartu: Tartu Ülikooli Kirjastus.

Ülikooliseadus (RT I 1995, 12, 119; 2001, 16, 71; 2003, 20, 116), 12.01 1995. (*University Law*).

Useful Websites

Estonian Adult Education Association, Andras: http://www.andras.ee
Estonian E-University: http://www.e-uni.ee
Estonian Network for University Continuing Education: http://www.ut.ee/av/koostoo/EATK_eng.php
Ministry of Education and Research: http://www.hm.ee
Open University of the University of Tartu: http://www.ut.ee/AV
Open University of the Tallinn Pedagogical University: http://www.tpu.ee/avatud_ylikool.html
Open University of the Tallinn Technical University: http://www.ttu.ee/
Public videolectures from the University of Tartu: http://video.ut.ee/

JYRI MANNINEN AND TINA ENGBLOM

6: Adults in Finnish Higher Education

The Higher Education System in Finland

Finland is one of the Nordic welfare states and has approximately five million inhabitants. They mainly live in the far south and the rest of the country is rather sparsely populated. However, for regional development purposes some universities are located in the midlands and the north. The population of Finland is characterised by its high educational level and it is usually considered to be in the forefront of the information society. The education system is bilingual: the official languages are Finnish and Swedish. The Swedish speaking minority, 5.6% of the population (Statistics Finland, 2004) has separate educational facilities. These are organised either through bilingual university faculties or Swedish higher education institutions (for example, Åbo Akademi University or the Swedish School of Economics).

The Finnish higher education system[1] is divided into universities and polytechnics. These complement one another in their own areas of strength and each has its own well-defined profile. Scientific research and related teaching are the major characteristics of the universities. There are 20 universities and 29 polytechnics in Finland and the supply of higher education is extensive. In 2002, the student intake was 68.4% (polytechnics 37%; universities 31.4%) as a percentage of all the school leavers.

1 The main source for this country report has been Heinonen, V. (2001).

Universities

Of the 20 universities in Finland, ten are multidisciplinary institutions, six are specialist and four are arts academies. They all offer adult education (AE) (*aikuiskoulutus/vuxenutbildning*). (Here the Finnish word is given first and the Swedish second.) The universities are autonomous and they make independent decisions on their teaching and research activities. Approximately 70% of the finance for Finnish universities comes directly from the State. However, the share of the State's contribution to the total funding varies a good deal from one to another.

Polytechnics

A dual system of institutions of higher education was introduced in Finland in the early 1990s. As an experiment, a network of polytechnics was established to complement the universities. At first the polytechnics were provisional institutions but more recently they have all been established permanently. Most of them are multidisciplinary institutions and their basic and professional studies are generally funded partly by their municipalities and partly by the State. Polytechnic courses leading to degrees are mainly vocational and aim to give the students the necessary knowledge and skills to succeed in their working lives.

Fairly soon after their establishment, the polytechnics adopted AE as one of their basic tasks. Today approximately one fifth of their courses leading to degrees are targeted at adult students. In addition, the polytechnics organise 20 to 40 credit professional studies courses targeted at adults and Open Polytechnic studies (no entry qualifications, studies are open to all). Polytechnics are fairly large organisers of additional vocational training and they also organise short-term continuing education (CE) (*täydennyskoulutus/fortbildning*).

Unlike universities, polytechnics provide education and training leading to basic degrees (at the bachelor level) specifically targeted at adults. There are also many adults (aged 25 years or older) studying on basic education programmes aimed at young people (57% of all polytechnic students are aged 25 or over). Correspondingly, 11% of those studying in programmes designed for adults are under 25.

University adult education in Finland

Strictly speaking, only continuing education and the Open University (OU) (*Avoin yliopisto/Öppna universitetet*) (that is, university programmes open to all age groups, carrying no entrance requirements) are regarded as AE provided by the universities. This definition is mainly for administrative use, however, since the OU is also very popular with younger people. For example, approximately one third of the OU students in Finland in 2000 were 25 years old or younger. (Kess *et al.*, 2002)

On the other hand, in the university degree programmes, the majority (51%) of the degree students are adults (aged 25 years or older) and 18% of the students beginning their studies belong to this group (Statistics Finland, 1999, p.29).

The basic degrees of universities are the same for adults and for younger people and students complete the same studies irrespective of their age. Therefore the whole university is an AE institution in practice. There are several reasons for this. In Finland the university entrance age is significantly higher (19–25, and even higher in some cases) than in most other European countries and students usually complete masters degrees. This in theory takes 4–5 years but in practice 6–8 years is more usual. The reasons for this are structural: the students are free to select their own combinations of subjects to study (there are no predetermined programmes except in medicine and similar professionally oriented areas); and financial (many students work during their studies, often entering the labour market when they reach the bachelor level). They therefore take several years more to complete their masters degrees.

It is clear that there is a growing number of mature students in the higher education system. What is happening is an 'adultification' of higher education (Parjanen and Tuomi, 2003). This trend is clearly visible, for example in Åbo Akademi University, where in 1997 36.5% of the undergraduates were over 25 years of age and in 2001 there were already more than 40%.

The forms of university AE in Finland can be summarised as follows:

- Open university: open to all age groups, no entrance requirements;
- University of the Third Age (*Ikäihmisten yliopisto/ Senioruniversitetet*): for retired people, part of the OU system;
- Continuing education: short courses and long programmes, open learning centres, including labour market training for unemployed university graduates and professionals.

In practice, regional, national and international development projects and programmes provided for public and private organisations are also considered as AE and are usually organised by CE centres within the universities.

Some of the main activities are described in the following.

Open university

All Finnish universities organise OU teaching. This has become a well-established and extensive activity with 85,100 enrolments in 2002. University of the Third Age teaching is also connected with the OUs and these had almost 9,500 registered students in 2002 (KOTA database[2] 2002).

Universities and polytechnics both offer open teaching leading to basic degrees. The universities have offered OU courses for some years and these have reflected their traditional courses. The polytechnics, however, began to offer open teaching only at the end of the 1990s. In the OU, teaching is open to all irrespective of age and initial

2 Kota database: See http://www.csc.fi/kota/kota.html

education and the students can complete modules and gain credits. Objectives relating to liberal education are set individually by each student. When they have collected the required number of study credits in the OU, students can apply to transfer to a traditional university, becoming regular students and working for higher education degrees. In 2002, a total of 696 students were accepted for degree programmes at universities on the basis of studies taken through the OU (the so-called 'Open University channel'). This was around 70% of the target set for the year by the Ministry of Education. (Ministry of Education, 2002)

In 2002, 76% of the OU students were women. Statistics from the year 2000 show that the OU provides a good opportunity for less well educated adults to access university level education; 27.5% of the entrants had lower secondary vocational training and 29.2% an upper secondary qualification. Only 2.3% had a university degree while studying at the OU. The same statistics show that 57.8% were fully employed and 8.9% unemployed (Rinne *et al.*, 2003).

In 2002, the OUs organised 64% of the teaching themselves and the rest was arranged in cooperation with other AE organisations such as workers' institutes, summer universities and folk high schools.

In 1996, regular weekly broadcasts of OU courses began on television. From the point of view of educational policy, the decision to do this was closely linked to the significant increase in the amount of OU teaching.

Continuing education centres

The 1980s saw the creation of a significant number of initiatives, both to facilitate adults' participation in training and to create a clearer administrative system for AE. One of the most important reforms was the establishment of the CE centres in universities.[3] In the early 1990s, the operations of the university CE centres expanded considerably. Funding was mainly directed at the training, or retraining, of unem-

3 A more detailed analysis and description of the Finnish system can be found in Osborne and Thomas (2003, p.125–52).

ployed university graduates, those under threat of unemployment and people coming from outside the labour market, through the so-called 'Relander' programme. (The extra funding programme was named after Secretary of State, Mr. Timo Relander, who chaired the employment and industrial policy programme.) This increased funding expanded the operations of the CE centres considerably and their activities remain at a high level today even though the level of funding, which was targeted during a period of high unemployment, has gradually decreased during the subsequent economic recovery. The Relander programme has also contributed to the increase in the activities of the OU. (See Heinonen, 2001 for details).

At the moment all the Finnish universities have at least one CE centre providing specialised education for graduates. In 2002, 88,600 people participated in university CE courses. Nearly 4,100 courses were held and approximately 330 of these were specialised programmes offering more than 20 credits (Ministry of Education, 2002).

Direct State funding is no longer directed to CE centres. Instead, they are expected to finance their own operations, mainly by selling education services. However, in 2003 it became possible for them to apply for funding (3 million euros, in total) from the Ministry of Education to develop specialised programmes.

Education institutions are major purchasers of additional vocational training and the Ministry of Labour buys a considerable amount of labour market training. Continuing education centres also sell in-service education to companies and public corporations.

The university CE centres offer graduates a non-certificated opportunity to update and broaden their professional competence and skills. Moreover, these centres also offer courses on professional topics which complement the university degree system and promote professional development. The professional courses offer a minimum of 20 credits each and can be taken by university graduates or others who meet the set criteria.

Some trends can be seen in the following table. The dramatic reduction in the number of UCE students since 2000 reflects the changes in the funding principles and the changes in the labour market: employment opportunities improved between 2000 and 2002.

Table 1: Total numbers of degree students, UCE students and OU students, 1996–2002.

Year	1996	1998	2000	2002
Degree students	138,200	147,300	157,200	170,000
UCE students	108,900	133,600	121,200	88,600
OU students	74,900	77,500	80,000	85,100
Totals	322,000	358,400	358,400	343,700

(Source: Ministry of Education, KOTA database, 2002)

Adults may also take professional courses in polytechnics. These are arranged as long CE programmes which promote vocational and professional development. Courses are arranged for graduates, those with vocational post-secondary or vocational tertiary education qualifications and others with adequate study skills.

Current Trends and Innovations

Provision for adults

The principles of lifelong learning (*elinikäinen oppiminen/livslångt lärande*) have been successfully implemented in Finland for around 100 years. There is a loose network of AE institutes (folk high schools, workers' institutes and summer universities) and a well-established OU system. As described above, adults also increasingly participate in the traditional undergraduate programmes. The courses and contents of the university provision are the same for universities and for the OUs but the format of the studies and the methods of delivery vary according to the adult learners' needs. Even in some undergraduate programmes, mature students are taken into consideration so that some seminars and lectures are organised during the afternoons and evenings. These enable students to study and work at the same time.

Innovative methods of course delivery especially for adults have been developed within the OUs. As early as the beginning of the 1980s, a system called 'multiform studies' (*monimuoto-opiskelu/ monimuoto-opetus*) was developed using a variety of teaching methods. This involved a combination of local study groups (usually organised by local workers' educational institutes or AE centres) with a tutor, distance study materials (books and audio- and videotapes) and lectures at a distance (using telephones, videoconferencing and computer mediated communication). This system enabled adults in all parts of the country to participate in OU studies and it also guaranteed flexible study programmes for adult learners.

In 1997, the Virtual Open University[4] (*Suomen avoin virtuaali-yliopisto*) was established as a national umbrella organisation and most individual OUs established their own virtual services. For example, the Virtual Open University at the University of Helsinki[5] is one of the forerunners in this area. Almost all Finnish universities now have some virtual courses and, in the year 2000, over 3,000 OU students participated in these. Even though this is only 4% of the total number of OU students, it is expected that both the need and provision for Web-based courses will rise dramatically in the near future. Web-based courses are especially popular amongst middle-aged adults and those who are working in white-collar positions (Mannisenmäki and Manninen, 2004). At the moment most OU students (64%) participate in face-to-face courses but a substantial number also take part in mixed-mode courses or courses at a distance.

In CE course programmes, similar forms of delivery are used. Depending on the type of training (labour market training, self-initiated training, professional development or CE), the courses are long full-time studies, short one- or two-day expert seminars or mixed

4 Virtual Open University: See Website www.avoinyliopisto.fi
5 University of Helsinki see Website: www.avoin.helsinki.fi

format programmes with face-to-face meetings and distance learning periods. Web-based services are also in common use here.[6]

Policy issues

The current policy changes in Finland are directed mainly towards two aims. The first is to increase the number of young students in initial university level studies. This is related to the Bologna process, especially on the harmonisation of the Finnish higher education system with the European universities. The purpose is to shorten the length of the courses and facilitate access for school leavers into universities. (This will, incidentally, lower the graduation age which, as mentioned earlier, is currently much higher in Finland than in most other European countries.) Second, the role of traditional adult learning organisations within the higher education system is becoming stronger. The State budget guarantees basic funding for the OUs, and it is intended to make the Open University Channel a significant route for entry to university. A forthcoming University Law also requires universities, in addition to their two traditional missions of teaching full-time students and research, to provide a service to their surrounding regions. This latter includes responding to the educational needs of the adult population in their region and also developing innovative activities for regional development. This additional task will further strengthen the roles of CE centres within their universities.

Access and equal opportunities

In principle, the higher education system is open to all and the social security system, together with a free education system, have made it possible for all social classes to enter higher education, in practice as well as in theory. Even though there is a much higher proportion of students from white collar families in the universities and the OU, the numbers of students with blue collar and working class backgrounds

6 See for example: www.studium.helsinki.fi

are not far different from their share in the population (Rinne *et al.*, 2003, p.73).

However, OU studies carry a fee (of around 20 to 100 euros per course), which may limit participation. University CE is usually targeted at university graduates and is therefore not open to all adults. In practice the structures of participation follow the general adult participation trend: the more basic education people have, the more often they are likely to participate in OU studies. The majority of OU students are female, reflecting the content of the course provision (which is biased towards behavioural and educational sciences).

To overcome the regional barriers, the best innovations have been mixed format distance education, and more recently Web-based, courses. The OU's regional networks have also been effective in facilitating access.

Conclusion

University adult education in Finland is a well-established and institutionalized activity with an extensive network of continuing education centres and the OU. The development of these activities was especially rapid in the 1990s and, even though the number of students has been lower during the past few years, the range of activities is still tending to grow. One reason for this is that the forthcoming University Law will add a 'third task' to the universities' traditional activities of research and teaching full-time students. The new requirements include interaction and cooperation with society and the local community; both of these are traditional tasks of the continuing education centres.

There is also a tendency to reduce both the length of undergraduate studies and the number of degrees a student can take. In the longer term, this will increase the pressure to organize more CE and university level learning opportunities for mature students.

As a leader in the use of modern communications technology, the Finnish university system will make increasing use of virtual learning methods and, in this area, the OU and continuing education centres are the key developers. There is evidence (Mannisenmäki and Manninen, 2004) that Web-based OU courses provide new learning opportunities for those adults who have no access to traditional courses due to work or family responsibilities. Both the need for, and provision of, new flexible study possibilities are expanding and this will reshape Finland's university level adult education of the future.

References

Heinonen, S., 2001. Policy perspective on programme evaluation. Case of a labour market oriented training programme in Finland. In: S. Kontiainen and K. Nurmi, eds. *Effectiveness of Adult Education. Historical and Evaluative Studies in Finland.* Helsinki: University of Helsinki, Department of Education.

Heinonen, V., ed., 2001. *A review of Finnish adult education – background report for OECD country survey on adult education policies.* Helsinki: Ministry of Education.

Kess, P., Hulkko, K., Jussila, M., Kallio, U., Larsen S., Pohjolainen, T. and Seppälä, K., 2002. *Suomen avoin yliopisto. Avoimen yliopisto-opetuksen arviointiraportti.* (The Finninsh Open University). Helsinki: Edita.

Mannisenmäki, E. and Manninen, J., 2004. *Avoimen yliopiston verkko-opiskelijan muotokuva.* (The portrait of Open University Web-students). Helsinki: Palmenia-kustannus.

Ministry of Education, 2002. Finnish Universities. Available at: http://www.minedu.fi/julkaisut/YOvsk2003/YliopEnglVSK2002.pdf

Osborne, M. and Thomas, E., eds., 2003. *Lifelong learning in a changing continent: Continuing education in the universities of Europe.* Leicester: National Institute of Adult Continuing Education.

Parjanen, M. and Tuomi, O., 2003. Access to Higher Education – persistent or changing inequality? A case study from Finland. *European Journal of Education*, 38(1).
Rinne, R., Jauhiainen, A., Tuomisto, H., Alho-Malmelin, M., Halttunen, N. and Lehtonen, K., 2003. *Avoimen yliopiston opiskelija.* (The Open University student). Kasvatustieteiden tiedekunta, julkaisusarja A: 200. Turku: Turun yliopisto.
Statistics Finland, 1999. Annual. *Statistics of educational institutions.* Helsinki: Tilastokeskus.
Statistics Finland, 2004. Available at: http://www.tilastokeskus.fi/tk/tp/tasku/taskus_vaesto.html

Useful Websites

Kota database: http://www.csc.fi/kota/kota.html
Ministry of Education: http://www.minedu.fi/minedu/education/index.html
University of Helsinki, Open university: http://www.avoin.helsinki.fi
University of Helsinki, Continuing education: http://www.studium.helsinki.fi
Virtual Open University: http://www.avoinyliopisto.fi
Åbo Akademi University: http://www.abo.fi/aa/engelska/

GUY ARQUEMBOURG AND ARNAUD HAERINGER

7: Adults in French Higher Education

Introduction

French universities have provided education for adults for a very long time, opening their doors to unregistered students (*auditeurs libres*), who could attend courses and take examinations.[1] The idea that people of all ages should be allowed education as a continuing activity was advocated, for the first time in French history by the philosopher and mathematician Condorcet in 1792 (Terrot, 1997). This egalitarian approach was linked to the ideal of social justice which found its origin in the French Revolution. Since then, a number of laws designed to support the up-grading of workers' skills have repeated this principle of equality-based lifelong education. This system was developed on the principle of social promotion (*promotion sociale*) (Dif, 2000; Jallade, 2000a) and worker's promotion (*promotion ouvrière*) to enable workers to upgrade their skills. The CNAM (*Conservatoire National des Arts et Métiers*), which was created in 1794, became the cornerstone of 'second chance' education. This higher education (HE) institution had been created initially to enable engineers and technicians to improve their professional skills by taking evening and weekend courses. This was the start of the tradition of professional development for adults in France. Since then, CNAM has developed into one of the largest providers of adult continuing education (*formation permanente*) in France, with a wide range of courses provided in 55 regional centres and 33 institutes (Jallade, 2000b).

1 See Terrot (1997) and Jallade (2000a) for comprehensive accounts of the historical development of lifelong learning in French universities.

A law, passed in 1939, enabled engineers without professional or higher qualifications, but with more than five year's experience, to present a dissertation based on their work experience in order to gain the official title of 'engineer' (Feutrie, 2000). This measure foreshadowed the present process of accreditation.

French universities began to play a significant role in the education of adults in 1951 when they started to set up institutes specialising in continuing education (CE), initially through evening classes. These are the IPST (*Instituts de Promotion Sociale du Travail*) which have since been integrated within the universities' structures, while retaining some degree of autonomy (Feutrie, 1998).

In 1957, a specific examination was created to give access to university for people who had left school without the secondary education qualification (*baccalauréat*). This was another important landmark which predated the creation in 1969 of the *Examen Spécial d'Entrée à l'Université* (ESEU). Although it only became an official national diploma in 1994, this first step to what is now termed the *Diplôme d'Accès aux Etudes Universitaires* (DAEU) is very important in the history of university education for adults in France. Together with the procedure enabling the Accreditation of Prior Experiential Learning, APEL (*Validation des Acquis Professionnels*, VAP), and the preparation of specific professional diplomas (*diplômes d'université*, DU), its administration is the responsibility of the university continuing education (UCE) departments and is one of their major functions.

Following the events of May 1968, it was acknowledged that universities had an obligation to help everyone, whatever their age, social background or profession, to increase and refresh their knowledge so that their advancement was based only on their capabilities. The status of UCE in French universities was officially defined in 1968 by the Act of Guidance on Higher Education (*Loi d'orientation sur l'enseignement supérieur*). A second Act of Guidance in 1984 established CE as one of the three fundamental missions of universities, together with initial[2] higher education (HE) teaching and research. This led to the official creation, in 1985, of a specific 'service' in every university (*service commun de formation continue*) usually with a department of continuing education (*département d'éducation permanente,* DEP).

This development was closely linked to a growing concern in France about vocational training. Since 1971, companies had been compelled by law to contribute to the cost of training their employees. This led university continuing education departments to design and provide courses for employers and their employees. These courses were organised through a contractual arrangement in which the Ministry of Higher Education gave the universities and other institutions delivering HE an initial financial resource to set up their continuing education services. A new concern for professional development arose in the 1970s due to the rising level of unemployment. This resulted in a noticeable shift in emphasis from the concept of lifelong learning (*éducation permanente*) to professional continuing education (*formation continue professionnelle*) focussed on continuing professional development (CPD) rather than CE (Jallade, 2000a).

The creation of CE centres (*centres de formation continue*) with a widened range of responsibilities marked the beginning of a further increase in the responsibility of universities for the education of adults. It was the task of these centres to provide short-term training for professional development (though not leading to certification) financed by companies. Gradually they were also required to organise evening courses preparing students for diploma examinations which, until then, had been available only to initial HE students. This training was cofinanced by the State and by the regions. The CE centres were also required to extend their training to prepare adult students for the DAEU.

The next important step was the creation in 1979 of new training programmes for young job-seekers (16- to 25-year-olds). These were designed for young adults who had left the education system with few

2 In the French university context, university initial education, UIE (*formation initiale*) refers to undergraduate studies and is for students who have just left secondary education and enrolled at university.

or no qualifications. They were financed by the State and the trainees received a salary.[3] They also marked a considerable step forward in the evolution of adult training since, for the first time, these training programmes led to specific university diplomas (*diplômes d'université*, DU). These were created to meet the specific needs of the local employment market.

The effect of these changes on universities was considerable: they had to take on new responsibilities and fulfil new tasks. In order to achieve these, however, universities had to fight to obtain recognition from the three key players: the Ministry of Employment, the employment agencies (*agence nationale pour l'emploi*, ANPE), and the Chambers of Commerce (*Chambres de Commerce*). Here the universities had to account for their use of the money, the quality and efficiency of the training and the results of the trainees.[4]

This policy also had the effect on the UCE departments of giving them a well-defined status:

- The specific courses that developed required a different approach to teaching; and
- They were required to meet local professional needs-generated innovative programmes for DUs alongside traditional HE national diplomas. Thousands of different DUs have since been created by the various continuing education services.

Since the 1990s, however, there has been a gradual decrease in the development of DUs, giving way gradually to State professional diplomas: professional bachelors degrees (*licences professionnelles*) and masters degrees (*Diplôme d'Etudes Supérieures Specialisées*, DESS).

3 The '*Plan Barre*', named after the Economy Minister, Raymond Barre, agreed to pay the trainees an allowance equivalent to the minimum wage (*salaire minimum d'insertion*, SMIC).

4 Official surveys have been carried out on the later professional achievements of the trainees.

Current situation

In the past decade, the training of young adults has become a major concern for two reasons. The growing number of young people who leave school without qualifications (recently estimated at 60,000 per year)[5] and the rate of youth unemployment, which is one of the highest in the European Community. These have led both the State and the regions to undertake large programmes such as the Youth Training and Employment (*Formation Emplois Jeunes*), day or block release (*formation en alternance*), training contracts with employers (*contrats d'insertion*) and apprenticeships (*apprentissage*) to help young people integrate actively into society.

These training programmes for young adults, which provide information, careers advice and assistance as well as specific training activities, added further to the traditional CE activities. As a consequence, an increasing number of adults are enrolling in French universities at many different levels. The provision of training has always varied from one university to another and the differences have been increased by this trend.

Adult participation in initial training programmes

Increasing numbers of adults who have at least the baccalauréat or the DAEU and who wish to take up specific studies again after an interruption are enrolling in universities for courses which are provided by the various academic university departments (Unités de Formation et de Recherche, UFR) and institutes. There, the adults attend the same courses as the initial HE students.

Integration into programmes leading to national diplomas can also be achieved either through tailor-made programmes (block- or day-release, evening classes, modularised curricula), or through the

5 The objective set by the Ministry that 80% of each age cohort should achieve the *baccalauréat* has not yet been met. In fact, the situation has been unchanged since 1995.

reorganisation of existing programmes to suit the needs of the adult client groups. It can also be done simply by integrating adult students into existing programmes without any rearrangement of the timetables or curricula (Feutrie, 1998). These programmes offer progression from the *baccalauréat* or DAEU to higher post-graduate diplomas, equivalent to a masters degree. Most of the changes made to the mainstream curricula have concentrated on courses with vocational strands since these are more suited to the needs of applicants. The figures for 2001 reveal that 300,300 adult students enrolled on the wide range of continuing education programmes organised in universities.

These courses can be free of charge for job seekers or adults benefiting from CPD leave (*Congé Individuel de Formation*). Here adults are able to follow a full-time curriculum (unless they are on leave). In this latter case special arrangements are made to allow them to follow part-time curricula and they are given more time to prepare for their examinations. Some UFRs and institutes appoint an instructor specifically to deal with the problems which these students may have.

Medium- or short-term courses organised for adults

Traditionally, the UCE services have always offered a range of programmes, not necessarily leading to diplomas. In this case, the adults who attend do so for personal or professional reasons and they may enrol individually, in which case they pay their own fees, or at the wish of their employers, who then pay for the training. (See Tables 1 and 2.) The types of courses which universities initially offered to adults were essentially aimed to meet local needs, or the national or international needs in case of specific subjects closely related to research. However, the programmes categorised as short-course provision are often designed for, and negotiated with, companies or public administrative services, usually in response to calls for tenders on the open market. They do not offer diplomas but give only certificates of attendance for participants (Jallade, 2000a, p.307). In 2001, the average number of hours per student in higher education institutions was 124 hours (compared with 70 hours in 1996).

These courses are usually based on the competencies of the existing university teachers and researchers and cover a very wide range of topics. This accounts for the considerable variations between the provisions of the different universities. For vocational reasons, languages and computer science attract growing numbers of adults and these constitute the major part of the activities of a number of UCE departments. In many universities, however, they are outnumbered by the courses preparing adults for the specific university diplomas.

The following examples are given here to illustrate the kinds of courses offered. They are taken from three universities which have had very different, but equally active, UCE departments: the University of Lille 1 (USTL)[6] (*the Centre Université-Economie d'Education Permanente*, CUEEP); the University of Lille 3 (*Service Universitaire de Formation Continue – Education Permanente*, SUFCEP); and the University of Haute Alsace in Mulhouse, (the *Service d'Enseignement et de Recherche en Formation d'Adultes*, SERFA).[7] All these universities provide some or all of the courses that follow.

Language courses

Language courses have a long tradition in adult education and constitute an important part of training provisions. Although a growing number of adults enrol on language courses for vocational purposes, adults attend for many different reasons. It is, therefore, not compulsory to take examinations but these courses may constitute an appropriate preparation for a number of diplomas such as: the Diploma in Language Competencies (English, German, Italian, Spanish),[8] the Test

6 USTL: Université des Sciences et Technologies de Lille.

7 The UCE structures vary considerably from one university to another according to the university authorities' awareness and willingness to promote UCE. In this respect, in spite of its important role in the history of French UCE, the CUEEP (Lille 1) has lost much of its dynamism. If, similarly, the University of Lille 3 seems to show a lack of interest in its UCE service, SERFA in Mulhouse represents the growing dynamism that is seen in a number of UCE services in France.

8 The DLC aims to test practical abilities as well as knowledge of the language and breaks with the traditional evaluation processes. Candidates are involved in

of English for International Communication; the Test of English as a Foreign Language – American diploma; the Cambridge Certificates (First and Advanced) – British diplomas; the *Diplôme d'Etudes en Langue Française* – French Diploma; the Zertifikat Deutsch (ZD); the Zentrale Mittelstufenprüfung (ZMP); the Zertifikat Deutsch; and Deutsch für den Beruf (ZDfB).[9]

Some universities also prepare adult students for local specific language diplomas. Thus, the Universities of Lille 1 and Lille 3 offer the DIUL (*Diplôme Inter-Universitaire de Langues*).[10] Like other university diplomas, this has a local value and is recognised by the Regional Councils (*Conseils régionaux*).

Computer sciences courses

Understandably, an important and growing number of courses are offered by most university CE services to meet adults' needs for computing and the use of the Internet (cf. Hofstetter and Haeringer, 2000). These courses may lead to specific university diplomas[11] but adults can, in the case of languages, choose to follow courses which do not lead to certification on topics such as the use of specific programmes, databases, the Internet and multimedia tools. As an example, the Université de Haute Alsace in Mulhouse offers six diplomas dealing with the Internet and computing.[12]

the simulation of professional activities which requires them to practise the four skills (speaking, listening, reading and writing) in role-play situations. It accredits 'operational' competencies in foreign languages for people who have been working for at least two years in relevant areas. It is organised both by secondary and HE authorities and is recognised nationally.

9 In agreement with the Goethe Institute.

10 This concerns languages such as Chinese, Dutch, English, German, Italian, Spanish, and Russian.

11 Such as the *Diplôme Universitaire de Capacité en Informatique* (DUCI) at Lille 3.

12 *DU Applications bureautiques*; *DU Conception et Maintenance de sites Web d'entreprise*; *DU Responsable Internet dans l'entreprise*; *DU Projet Intranet*; *DU Administration de réseaux*; and the *Licence professionnelle 'Réseaux et télécommunications, option conception et administration des services des réseaux d'entreprise'*.

Specific courses

The main activity of UCE departments in adult education and training is the preparation of adults for specific university diplomas. These diplomas, which respond to the need for employment-oriented training, especially to integrate young adults into the workforce, will be presented in the next section. They are offered in a very wide range of fields including human resources, communication techniques, accounting, management, communication, psychology, law and fields related to industry (for example, chemistry, mechanics or electronics).

Universities also prepare adults for competitive examinations (*concours*) for entry into the French civil service (*administration*). For example, SUFCEP and SERFA provide courses for several civil service competitions (*concours administratifs*) including the entry examinations to nursing colleges and the institute for nursing and health management, as well as national diplomas which have been especially designed for adults (for example the DESS prepared by SERFA in information technology and various management topics). They may also prepare adults for the national vocational bachelor degree (*licence professionnelle*) in areas such as social service management (*management de l'action sociale*).

The diversity of the adults who attend such courses requires that funding for them comes from a variety of sources. For example, a group of students following a language course may contain adults sent by their employers who are financing their training (*formation*), job-seekers whose courses are financed by the ANPE and individuals who are self-funding, often with some support from regional authority grants.

'University of All Ages' courses and lectures

Although a number of older adults attend the courses mentioned above for what is called 'continuing education with a cultural or general purpose' (Feutrie, 2001), older adults are also offered a range of educational and cultural activities by what is widely called the University of the Third Age (*Université du Troisième Age*, U3A). Although it is mainly attended by older adults, because it does not prepare them for any diploma, this designation is unsatisfactory since it includes at least two different main providers and is open to all kinds of individuals, whatever their ages, who have free-time and who are willing to enrich their cultural knowledge. (These include retired workers, job-seekers, salaried workers with free-time and non-active individuals). The main providers are:

- The People's University (*Université populaire*) claims to belong to a tradition which dates back to the end of the nineteenth century when philosophers, writers, professors and many others offered free lectures to the working-class. Its updated aim is to provide free knowledge for the great majority. It offers lectures by media personalities (about ten per year, usually on Sundays) followed by a debate; and
- The University for All Ages (*Université pour Tous Ages*, UTA), also called the University of Free Time (*Inter-Ages* or *Université du Temps Libre*, UTL) are more in keeping with the university principle of lifelong learning and provide far more lectures (about 160 per year) by university lecturers. 44 regional UTAs, linked to 200 centres throughout France, are regrouped in the French Association of Universities of All Ages (*Union Française des Universités Tous Ages*, UFUTA). The UFUTA is a non-profit-making association (*Association Loi de 1901*) which was created in 1980 and is itself linked to the International Association of the Universities of Third Age (*Association Internationale des Universités du Troisième Age*, AIUTA). The UFUTA now has more than 70,000 students (compared with 61,000 in 1996).

These structures are more or less integrated into the university services of CE but they are financially independent: enrolment fees represent about 50% of the income of UTA. Subsidies from the local authorities, sponsorship and the good will of volunteers provide the remainder.

Courses for young adults and job-seekers

As far as general adult education is concerned, three goals have been identified regarding professional development (*formation professionnelle*) (Feutrie, 1998):

- To reduce the social exclusion of particularly disadvantaged sections of the population (such as prisoners, immigrants and those with literacy problems);
- To update the competencies of salaried workers to improve business competitiveness; and
- To facilitate social mobility to guarantee the opportunity for all active members of society to improve their situations in society.

Under the pressure of unemployment, the UCE services are now increasingly urged to offer education and training services which aim to reintegrate young adults into HE by offering diploma courses which are directly linked to the labour market. These courses focus on preparation for the DAEU and other specific university diplomas such as the DU and DESS (Table 1).

Diplôme d'Accès aux Etudes Universitaires *(DAEU)*

The origin of this 'second chance diploma' dates back to the creation, in 1969, by the Ministry of Education, of two specific diplomas.[13] These allowed access to universities for candidates who had failed, or simply not taken, the *baccalauréat* but who had at least two years of work experience. Because of the low rate of success from these examinations, the University of Lille 1 began, in 1971, to organise a specific programme at different levels adapted to the needs of adults who

13 The ESEU A (*Examen Spécial d'Entrée à l'Université*) gave access to humanities, economics and legal studies in universities; the ESEU B gave access to scientific and medical studies. A similar distinction exists between the DAEU A and B.

wished to enter a university. In 1976, other universities proposed a two or three year programme, (in some ways similar to British access courses, at least in their intent) taking into account each individual's starting point and the amount of time that they could make available for study.

As mentioned earlier, this diploma was recognised as a national diploma in 1994, the *Diplôme d'Accès aux Etudes Universitaires* (DAEU), and has since become an important tool for social advancement. The UCE departments, which are entirely responsible for these programmes, have developed an efficient pedagogical system including the creation of specific teaching materials, teacher training, distance learning and specific tutoring arrangements.

The organisation of the programmes varies considerably from one university to another reflecting the wide range of situations in which the candidates find themselves. This flexibility, together with the experience which has been developed by the UCE departments in this area, accounts for the impact of the DAEU in promoting access to HE for adults who have previously been failed by the education system. The DAEU is no longer an end in itself for the majority of candidates. It has been observed, over the years, that candidates' self-confidence has also gradually increased and that, contrary to what happened initially, students now commonly propose ambitious projects, with some 70–80% of them moving on to HE once they have obtained the DAEU.

Diplômes d'université *(DU)*

Although national diplomas are awarded by the French Ministry of Education, universities are also entitled to offer their own diplomas. The development of vocational training linked to the specific needs of the labour market and the demands of local or national companies, led UCE departments to create specific university diplomas which cover a range of very diverse subjects.[14] These usually represent innovative

14 For example, the University of Lille 3 offers such different courses as Knowledge of Religions (*Connaissance des religions*) to help understand

responses to the demand for different qualifications from very diverse client groups, such as private and public employees, job-seekers, and people seeking to have their experience recognised and accredited (Feutrie, 1998). Thousands of different diplomas have been created during the past twenty years and the preparation of adults to take these diplomas constitutes a major part of the current activities of UCE departments.

These courses are usually open to students who have completed their secondary studies, or who have passed the DAEU, as well as to adults whose experience has been accredited.[15] The personal and professional experience of young job-seekers can also be taken into account, either through the procedure of the Accreditation of their Prior Learning (APL), or of their prior experiential learning (APEL). The length of the training may vary from one diploma to another: some diploma courses last for two years, some for one year or less. The number of hours varies from one diploma to another[16] and from one university to another. According to the availability of the students, the courses may be organised full-time or part-time through evening sessions or one- or half-day meetings each week. They may in some cases give access to second level HE studies (level 2: *Baccalaureat +3* or *+4*).[17] In order to cope with their wide range of situations, special arrangements and different periods of training can be undertaken by different students.[18]

behaviours in health, education, social care departments, or Psychological Approach to Judicial Problems (*Approche psychologique des problèmes judiciaire*) as well as DUs linked to tourism, the management of companies, trade and so on. The University of Mulhouse, Haute Alsace has created 23 different courses leading either to national or local diplomas.

15 In some cases, a prior DU may be required to give access to further training. For example, in Lille 3, preparation for a DU TTA (DU *des Techniques du Tourisme d'Affaire*) is offered to students with a DU STAAF (DU *des Sciences du Tourisme d'Agence et d'Affaires*).

16 DU STAAF: 707 hours over two years; DU TTA: 301 hours in one year.

17 E.g. a student with the DU STAFF or the DU TTA may follow an HE degree course in University Professional Institute (*Institut Universitaire Professionnel*, IUP) or a *Métiers des Arts et de la Culture (section Tourisme).*

18 E.g. in Lille 3, students may choose to start the preparation of a DU on four different dates in the year: September, November, February or March.

Students may benefit from help and advice in the choice of their personal development planning (*parcours personnalisé de formation*) as well as from special grants, and sometimes a salary, to pay for their programme. Although attendance at these courses does not commit students to taking the examination, their work on the course gives them the opportunity to take the examination later if they wish. Trainees can also receive financial support from their employers (from the company's staff development budget) if they are in employment or from the appropriate professional or social agency if they are not.

Jallade (2000a) noted that more adult students sought university diplomas (37%) than national diplomas (17%). This highlights the role of a UCE department in offering innovative programmes. In 2001, 22% of the CE students were registered for national diplomas and 15% for university diplomas. State professional diplomas (*licence professionnelle*) and the DESS have tended to take over from the DU in the past five years. This will require the UCE departments to develop new strategies.

Additional support for adults in higher education

The focussed subjects of adult education courses and the need to help the various publics to define their individual career plans and move on to HE following appropriate training, has led UCE departments to provide accompanying measures and structures with the aim of informing students, advising them and assuring quality.

Centres of information and careers advice

In order to help adults with work experience to cope with the difficulties they may encounter when shifting back and forth between their professional activities and professional development, several universities have created centres which can provide assistance and advice at various levels. Their remit is to provide:

- Information on career opportunities, professional development and CE programmes;
- Tools for self-evaluation. Candidates can either evaluate themselves with the help of specific software tools or they can be assessed by a university subject specialist; and
- Contacts with careers advisers who can help them design a development programme relevant to their professional plans.

Candidates may benefit from assistance from advisers and teaching staff throughout their programmes until they start or resume work (Feutrie, 1998). This facilitates the connection between their work-based experiences, their social lives and the professional development opportunities offered by the university. It also constitutes a useful device to aid the identification of competencies when this is needed for the purpose of accreditation.

Self-directed learning

In 1987, the continuing education department within the Ministry of Education created the University Network of Self-directed Learning Centres (*Réseau Universitaire des Centres d'autoformation*)[19] in order to help update and promote the use of ICT for teaching and learning in UCE.

A number of UCE departments have developed e-learning facilities and offer specific distance education preparation for university diplomas.[20] Some are equipped with specific ICT environments (multimedia classrooms and networks, units for the development of multimedia products, and so on) which give access to

19 Centres were opened in Bordeaux, Lille, Grenoble, Nancy and Paris.
20 E.g. CUEEP in Lille I offers several training programmes based on e-learning.

vocationally-oriented courses based on the use of vocational software as well as experimental initiatives such as the 'virtual company'.

To provide this service, the UCE department of Lille 3 has been equipped with a multimedia classroom since 1998. Various experimental pedagogical products have been developed since then for the teaching and learning of languages (English and French as foreign languages). Specific ICT environments are also available for the preparation of several DUs (for example, on tourism, trade and management).

In 1992 SERFA, in the Université de Haute Alsace, created CLAM (*Centre de Langues en Autoformation Multimédia*) in order to provide equipment, tools, tutoring and guidance for both adult and full-time students, mainly for language learning. Here both types of students can benefit from advice and access to tools in order to evaluate their level. They can also define their needs in relation to a professional or training project which the teachers within CLAM can then help them design. Course attendance is also planned by the students in consultation with the organisers and their progress is evaluated periodically by the teachers in face-to-face meetings.

The Digital Campus

The concept of the Digital Campus (*Campus numériques*) was developed in 2000 by the Ministry of Education within a vast programme aiming to develop the use of information and communication technology (ICT) in secondary education and higher studies[21] and has had a considerable impact on the development of new practices in the education of adults. Digital Campuses are partly funded by the gov-

21 This programme specified that by the year 2002, all secondary school children should have used ICT and that all students should become familiar with ICT. It includes networking, production and use of multimedia resources, training of teachers, creation of firms and development at the European and international levels. It provides financial support for equipment and networking. Several governmental Websites provide information about the policy and plans. (See the Useful Websites below.)

ernment and each one usually covers a small network of French universities that is developing the use of ICT in adult education.

As an example, the creation of a Digital Campus of the University of Lille 3 marks a new step in the development of self-directed learning centres available to both adult and full-time students. In addition, to help students to use a methodology adapted to their needs, these centres have also been involved in pedagogical and methodological research as well as in the production and diffusion of specific learning tools[22] adapted for use by a variety of student groups.[23]

Within a partnership of six universities, SERFA has developed a full on-line course devoted to preparation for the DAEU.[24]

The Quality Assurance National Plan

The considerable move towards increasing access to higher studies, and their subsequent integration into professional activities through appropriate CPD programmes, has stimulated a concern for quality which, in turn, has led to the application of industrial quality assurance norms such as ISO 9000 to UCE. The creation, in 1981, by the University of Franche-Comté, of a Quality Management course for Managers (*Diplôme de Responsable de gestion de la qualité*) led the Ministry for Education to set up a working group to develop a National Plan on Quality for UCE (*Plan National d'Action Qualité*). This plan aimed to introduce the concepts of quality to UCE in France and to encourage the creation and dissemination of projects on quality management. It also included an advisory service, diagnoses and

22 E.g. multimedia modules for learning French as a foreign language developed by the CUEEP, Lille 1 (*'Pour tout dire'* 1 and 2 for beginners) and by Lille 3 (*'Je vous ai compris'* 1, 2, 3 and 4 to support students preparing for the DELF and DALF).

23 E.g. the Self-Directed Learning Centre of the University of Nancy 1 and 2.

24 This preparation consists in 24 courses of 20 lessons each in diverse topics. They have been made available on the Website http://www.campus-pegasus.org

audits carried out by quality specialists and the transfer of methods and techniques through the development of guidelines for heads of UCE departments, trainers, quality consultants and members of the teaching staff.[25]

Examples of students in UCE programmes

The following examples provide useful information on the types of students who attend CE courses as well as on the distribution and proportions of the training on offer.

Table 1: Outline of the student body and the programme offered in 2000/01: SUFCEP, University of Lille 3

A. CATEGORIES OF STUDENTS		
	Number of students	Student-hours
Salaried	855	71,819
Job-seekers	466	97,450
Individuals	393	41,329
Others	26	1,404
TOTAL	1,740	212,012

B. LEVELS OF THE TRAINING			
		Number of students	Student-hours
I & II	Baccalauréat + 3 or more	125	16,681
III	Baccalauréat + 2	237	89,755
IV	Baccalauréat + 1	227	38,040
IX	Others	1,151	67,536
TOTAL		1,740	212,012

25 These objectives have been defined in six stages (Feutrie, 1998).

C. TYPES OF COURSES		
	Number of students	Student-hours
General training courses	127	27,108
DAEU	284	44,574
DUs		
psychology	12	1,452
adult training	45	10,060
trade and management	46	16,325
human resource management	36	7,685
tourism	45	15,996
Computer sciences	113	9,861
Foreign languages	663	39,909
Human resources	208	4,056
Expression techniques	110	7,176
DUT		
transport	16	9,330
social careers	35	18,480
TOTAL	1,740	212,012

Table 2: Outline of the student body and the programmes offered in 2002: SERFA, University of Mulhouse, Haute Alsace

A. CATEGORIES OF STUDENTS		
	Number of students	Student-hours
Salaried	971	89,039
Job-seekers	133	50,293
Individuals	627	68,515
Others	52	6,507
TOTAL	1,783	214,354

B. LEVEL OF THE TRAINING			
		Number of students	Student-hours
I & II	Baccalauréat + 3 or more	471	72,015
III	Baccalauréat + 2	243	76,400
IV	Baccalauréat	532	54,621
IX	Others	534	11,318
TOTAL		1,783	214,354

C. TYPES OF COURSES		
	Number of students	Student-hours
Multidisciplinary specialities: trade and management	240	47,561
Multidisciplinary specialities: human sciences and law	367	36,423
Business and sales	76	32,387
Computer science and networks	167	23,121
Security of property and people	104	13,679
Multiscience specialities	87	10,911
Secretarial work, office automation	251	8,946
Health	74	6,553
Education, training	85	5,481
Social work	76	5,454
Industrial control technology	9	4,759
Foreign languages	68	2,892
Electrical, electronic	24	2,891
Literature specialities	31	1,804
Behavioural and human relations skills development	71	826
Other	53	10,666
TOTAL	1,783	214,354

In his study of four universities, Jallade (2000b) reviewed the role played by the University of Lille 1[26] in the development of courses for adults made redundant following the decline of the traditional industries in northern France. Its *Centre Université-Economie d'Education Permanente* (CUEEP) and *Service Universitaire de Développement Economique et Social* (SUDES) (created out of CUEEP), have helped the University to interact actively with its outside clients and partners and to foster, coordinate and manage its programmes for adult students across the University's departments.[27] This process has been efficiently complemented by the practice of VAE; with a team of 15 counsellors and an information and resource centre open to students and prospective students, SUDES handles 5,000 applications a year, of which around 1,000 are successful.

The CNAM's provision, also reviewed by Jallade (2000b, 2001), equally reflects its curriculum strength, namely in engineering, business management and related fields. Its programmes range from short courses for unemployed adults (for example the Certificate of Competence in Marketing and Trade) to distance education courses in foreign languages and the use of the Internet. These courses, which are also on, for example, commercial law, accounting, finance and banking, do not lead to a formal qualification level (for example, Bac+2 or Bac+4).[28]

26 The University of Lille 1 has developed the largest department in France. Its activity represents 'about ten per cent of the total in all the 80 French universities'. (Jallade, 2000b, p.20).

27 For more details on UST's CE provision, see Jallade's report (2000b).

28 For a diagram of the French HE qualifications structure, see Davies (1995). Here, Bac+2 is roughly equivalent to a two-year university diploma, Bac+3 to an ordinary degree, Bac+4 to an honours degree, Bac+5 masters, Bac+6/7/8 doctorate. Here the numbers indicate the level of the qualification. This is defined by the number of years of full-time study needed to gain the qualification following the *baccalauréat*.

Accreditation of personal and professional experience

France started the process of accreditation through a decree (*Décret*) in 1985. Agreed by the Ministry of Education and the heads of UCE departments, the process gave the right of access to adult students to HE establishments on the grounds that personal and professional experience could be recognised as the equivalent of the diplomas required to follow HE courses. The decisions were taken by a pedagogical commission.

A second *Décret,* in 1993, extended this to diplomas coming from other ministries: the Ministry of Education; Ministry of Agriculture; and, since 1999, the Ministry of Youth and Sports (Amat, 2002). Here, a jury decides whether the candidate's experience or knowledge corresponds to the chosen course level, in order to grant credit up to the level of the full diploma less one unit. This decision is then conveyed to the Board of Examiners of the diploma.

In order to apply for the APL process, candidates have to demonstrate five years of relevant professional experience, whether salaried or not. Two procedures are available: the audit of competences (*bilan de compétence*); and the accreditation of prior experiential learning, APEL (*validation des acquis professionnels*, VAP).

All French nationals have the right 'to an analysis of their personal and professional skills and competencies and of their aptitudes and motivations, with a view to defining an individual career plan (*un projet professionnel*) and, if appropriate, to identify training needs and possibilities' (Davies, 1999). Higher education institutions are even allowed to accredit prior learning in order to admit students to courses leading to national diplomas or to competitive entry examinations prepared in the same university (Feutrie, 1997; Feutrie, 2000).

The French APEL process has had a significant impact on UCE: in 1996/97, nearly 8,000 of the 10,000 applications made under the APL scheme were successful (Davies, 1999). The process can be applied in different ways, according to the subject area:

- The USTL model, which gives an essential role to UCE departments, follows the candidates until their integration into training programmes or university courses;
- The second mode corresponds to a long tradition in French universities: exemptions are granted by lecturers or departments of studies. Here the criteria for accreditation vary considerably from one department to another. No particular assistance is provided to the candidate in this case; or
- Accreditation can be delegated to a specific administrative service within the university which assembles the files and passes them on to the admission panels within the appropriate departments or to the accreditation commission.

Table 3: Number of APL applications examined in 2002 in the universities of the Nord-Pas de Calais Region

	Total number of candidates	Job-seekers
Université d'Artois	43	9
Université de Lille 1	1,619	825
Université de Lille 2	40	5
Université de Lille 3	976	124
Université du Littoral	200	74
Université de Valenciennes	100	44
TOTAL	2,978	1,081

The new trends in adult education provision: the Law on Social Modernisation and the Accreditation of Prior Experiential Learning

As a result of the social context and the involvement of the social partners in recent years, the provision of adult education has evolved considerably. An important reform has recently been put in place to restructure UCE. Based on a report by experts commissioned by the Ministry of Labour, a new Law on Social Modernisation (*Loi de Modernisation Sociale*) was approved in 2002 which aimed to meet a number of these challenges:

- To cope with the rapid technological and economic transformations;
- To ensure better preparation of young people for the labour market;
- To deal with the issues of social and professional integration; and
- To update individuals' competences.

The Law on Social Modernisation represents a most important landmark in the history of adult education and vocational training for two main reasons. First, it established a National Framework of Qualifications (*Répertoire national des certifications professionnelles*) which, by including all the national diplomas and professional qualifications, clarified this complex system. Some Ministries,[29] as well as private training organisations, have also produced their own diplomas and titles while professional training bodies also offered a variety of professional certificates (*certificats de qualification professionnelle*, CQP).[30] Contrary to the CQPs, which have to be added to the

29 Ministries of Education, Social Affairs, Agriculture and Youth and Sports.

30 The CQPs were introduced through the Act of 6 July 1971 (Blachère, 2002). They reflect employers' and social partners' determination to have an alternative training and qualifications system. This is delivered not by the State but by a joint National Commission on Employment (*commission nationale*

approved list (*Répertoire*), the diplomas and titles delivered by the Ministries or the State, appear on the list automatically (Blachère, 2002). The *Répertoire* is designed as a classification of all the diplomas, titles and certificates offered by the State, the professional bodies and private organisations.

The 2002 legislation also introduced a new process of accreditation, the Accreditation of Prior Experiential Learning, which is based on the recognition of experience to obtain the qualifications registered in the *Répertoire* (Amat, 2002):

> Any person engaged in active life (whether employed or not) has a right to have his/her experience accredited towards the award of a diploma, a professional title or a certificate of professional qualification, which appears on a list established by a joint national commission on employment registered in the *Répertoire*. (*Code du travail, livre IX*, quoted by Grandin 2002, p.1)

The only condition required to apply is to have practised an activity for at least three years that is linked to the outcome of the diploma aimed at by the candidate.

Table 4: Number of APEL applications processed by the jury on 31/7/2003 in the universities of the Nord-Pas de Calais Region

	Total number of candidates	Job-seekers
Université d'Artois	20	5
Université de Lille 1	229	16
Université de Lille 2	123	2
Université de Lille 3	24	9
Université du Littoral	50	15
Université de Valenciennes	55	13
TOTAL	501	60

paritaire de l'emploi) of the appropriate professional training body (Perker *et al.*, 1998) which is made up of the social partners and employers.

Table 5: Number of applications examined by the CE service for the whole university of Lille 3 in 2003

	APL		APEL	
Number of applications	Male applicants	Female applicants	Male applicants	Female applicants
Under 30	115	273	1	0
30 to 45	116	322	10	7
Over 45	26	41	3	4
Total	307	636	14	11

Table 6: Distribution of the participants in the various training programmes and diplomas

	APL		APEL		APEL applicants who were accredited with the entire diploma	
	M	F	M	F	M	F
DEUG	47	88		1		1
DUT – DEUST – DNST	1	3	4	3		
Licence	175	426	1	2		
Licence professionnelle	8	4	1			
Licence IUP	1	1				
Maîtrise	22	26	2	2	1	
DESS – DEA	17	10	5	3		1
Other diplomas			1			
TOTAL NUMBER	271	558	14	11	1	2

Table 7: Distribution of the beneficiaries according to status and sex

	APL		APEL		APEL applicants who were accredited with the entire diploma	
	M	F	M	F	M	F
Working salaried	198	423	13	8	1	1
Job-seekers	68	96	1	3		1
Non-working	5	39				
TOTAL NUMBER	271	558	14	11		

The importance of the new legislation for UCE rests in the fact that all the qualifications, in their entirety, registered in the *Répertoire* can be obtained through APEL linked to activities, whether paid employment or voluntary work, or other non-certificated competencies gained through experience. These can all be accredited using the APEL process and the credits put towards an appropriate qualification. As Blachère (2002, p.101) points out, this marks a shift from the principle of giving dispensations for units and specific qualifications to that of evaluating competencies. 'Before the new law, the candidate's professional profile was compared to the content of the examination questions. The new approach enables it to be compared to the professional profile required by the holder of that specific qualification.'

Conclusion

The development of adult education in French universities has been firmly supported by legislation which favours the rights of workers to social security (*promotion sociale*). The increasing importance of the notion of 'second chance' education and the trend towards providing professional training both indicate the determination of the Government to cope with the changing socio-economic environment. The emphasis for a number of years was on the DAEU and the specific diplomas to respond to the demands of the labour market. More recently these have been complemented by the provision of APL and, more recently still, by APEL.

In spite of the changing environment however, there is still a gap in French universities between the teaching of full-time students and research on the one hand and adult education on the other due to a tradition of academic prestige which largely prevails in human sciences universities. SERFA in the University of Haute Alsace in Mulhouse is a good example of the attitude of a progressive university following the new political trend. Many universities, however, still give greater importance to the traditional academic curricula and are slow to respond to the changing educational needs or to attach sufficient value to the programmes of their CE services. Far from acknowledging the increasing importance of lifelong learning and of promoting adult education to a central position, most universities still worry to a large extent about the cost of CE and tend either to decrease their CE services or to dilute their activities by moving them into other organisations.

This university-held view of adult education conflicts with the views put forward by the government and the measures that it has been taking. It is still not clear how universities will deal in future years with the integration of their teaching for young adults and the preparation of adults for vocationally oriented qualifications. In this respect, the increasing concern for accreditation, and particularly the recent introduction of APEL, present a major challenge for universities. These are likely to appear in the near future, raising again the issue of the role of adult education in French universities.

Acknowledgement

This account builds partly upon information contained in a chapter written by Guy Arquembourg and Mireille Pouget (2003). We therefore wish to thank Mireille Pouget for her former contribution and the editors of that book for their helpful comments and guidance.

References

Amat, F., 2002. La Validation des Acquis de l'Expérience: La Nouvelle Législation. *Actualités de la formation permanente.* 177 (mars–avril). Paris: Centre INFFO.

Arquembourg, G. and Pouget, M., 2003. University Continuing Education in France. In M. Osborne and E. Thomas, eds. *Lifelong Learning in a Changing Continent: continuing education in the universities of Europe.* Leicester: National Institute of Adult Continuing Education.

Blachère, M., 2002. La VAE entre dans le code du travail. *Actualités de la formation permanente*, 177 (mars–avril). Paris: Centre INFFO.

Cloonan, M., Haeringer, A., Matarazzo, B., Murphy, M. and Osborne, M., (1999). The use of cost-benefit analysis in funding continuing education: steering the fifth wheel? *International Journal of Lifelong Education*, 18(6), 492–504.

Davies, P., ed., 1995. *Adults in Higher Education. International Perspectives*. London: Jessica Kingsley.

Davies, P., 1999. Rights and Rites of Passages: Crossing Boundaries in France. *International Journal of Lifelong Education*, 19(3), 215–24.

Dif, M., 2000. On the Development of the Lifelong Learning Concept in the French Context. *Lifelong Learning in Europe*, 1, 23–30.

Feutrie, M., 1997. *Identification, Validation et Accréditation de l'apprentissage antérieur et informel, France.* Thessaloniki: CEDEFOP.

Feutrie, M., 1998. University Continuing Education in France. Available at: http://www.fe.up.pt/nuce/FRA.html

Feutrie, M., 2000. Accreditation of Experiential Learning in Higher Education in France. In: N. Evans, ed. *Experiential Learning Around the World: Employability and the Global Economy.* London: Jessica Kinsley.

Feutrie, M., 2001. La formation continue universitaire en France. Situation et Perspectives. Unpublished paper.

Grandin, P., 2002. *Historique et apports du dispositif.* Supplément à Info Flash, 588–9 (15 avril au 15 mai). Paris: Centre INFFO.

Hofstetter, C. and Haeringer, A., 2000. The Role of the Internet Manager in a Corporate Environment – An emerging job; a custom-tailored training programme. *Scottish Journal of Adult and Continuing Education*, 6(2), 129–36.

Jallade, J.-P., 2000a. Lifelong Learning in French Universities: the State of the Art. *European Journal of Education*, 35(3), 301–15.

Jallade, J.-P., 2000b. *From Continuing Education to Lifelong Learning: A Survey of Current Practice in Four French Universities.* Paris: IEEPS (Institut Européen d'Education et de Politique Sociale), Université de Paris-Dauphine.

Jallade, J.-P., 2001. From Continuing Education to Lifelong Learning in French Universities. *European Journal of Education*, 36(3), 291–304.

Perker, H., Martel, D. and Guilloux, P., 1998. *Les certificats de qualification professionnelle.* Paris: Centre INFFO.

Terrot, N., 1997. *Histoire de l'éducation des adultes en France.* Paris: L'Harmattan.

Useful Websites

Ministère de l'Education Nationale, de la Recherche et de la Technologie

http://www.education.gouv.fr
http://www.educnet.education.gouv.fr
http://www.educasource.education.gouv.fr
(Adult education and the European dimension): http://www.cr2i.com

Ministère du travail

http://www.travail.gouv.fr/dossiers/vae

Accreditation of personal and professional experience. Information centres

http://www.eduscol.education.fr/D0077/carteacad.htm
http://www.dep.u-picardie.fr/confdir/vae/visitannu/annuairevisit.htm
http://www.univ-lille3/suvac/

e-learning. On-line courses programmes

Fédération Interuniversitaire de l'Enseignement à Distance: http://telesup.univ-mrs.fr
Audiosup.net (Internet audio courses): http://handel.u-paris10.fr
University of Lille 3. Distance Education programmes: http://cteu.univ-lille3.fr
CUEEP (Lille1): http://cueep.univ-lille1.fr/e-learning
SERFA seminars: http://www.ellproft.org
On-line preparation for the DAEU: http://www.campus-pegasus.org

Universities of All Ages

Union Française des Universités Tous Ages: http://www.unicaen.fr/unicaen/uia/UFUTA.htm
Association Internationale des Universités du Troisième Age: http://www.aiuta.asso.fr
Université populaire: http://perso.wanadoo.fr/michel.onfrav/

MARTIN BEYERSDORF

8: Adults in German Higher Education

Introduction

In Germany, the meaning of 'adult education' (AE) (*Erwachsenenbildung*) varies from one State (*Land*), and one university, to another and is often replaced by the term 'continuing education' (CE). In the context of the universities, the term 'continuing education' (*Weiterbildung*) or university continuing education (*wissenschaftliche Weiterbildung*) are more common. The following paraphrases an extract from the Continuing Education policy (*Weiterbildungsstrategie*) (2003) of the University of Hanover:

> Continuing education describes university outputs aimed at a resumption of organised learning (*Organisiertes Lernen*) leading to the updating, extension or deepening of knowledge and competences acquired earlier.

This seeks to outline the main characteristics of CE in the majority of German universities.

According to the Higher Education Act (*Hochschulrahmengesetz, § 12*), CE is all education which begins once the first compulsory education period has been completed. It is conducted after a period of employment (usually professional in the case of higher education), normally part-time, and with a flexible schedule to suit the needs of those in work. It involves the acquisition of specialised knowledge using teaching methods suitable for the adults concerned.

'Adult education' is a term with a political history in Germany and is associated with the idea of active citizenship. It has a long tradition reaching back to the Weimar Republic in the 1920s and its beginnings can be traced back even further to the workers' movements of the second half of the eighteenth century and the educational associations of workers (*Arbeiterbildungsvereine*) of that period. After the national socialist regime, this tradition was resumed in post-war Germany. During this revival, numerous offices were established in German universities jointly between the trade unions and the universities. The rationale for these grew out of a common view of social responsibility in the academic sphere and in the world of employment. This led to regional development which supported AE through conferences and the provision of advice. This form has remained a marginal area in the wider provision of university continuing education (UCE) and of the learning culture which was shaped decisively by UCE. The reason might be that the political tradition, which is more closely associated with the term adult education, has been repressed by the currently dominant form of CE for academic and vocational training in a more restricted and pragmatic sense.

Adult education provision

Extra-mural courses

Extra-mural courses (*Erwachsenenbildung*), courses provided outside the universities, used to be the key activity in university AE. The seminar courses (*Seminarkurse*) developed in Lower Saxony and spread throughout Germany. The intention in this case was to pose questions and to present the results of academic and scientific research to interested adults, regardless of their previous educational levels.

Willy Strzelewiczs, Fritz Borinski and Hans-Dietrich Raapke were the first to be named amongst those who disseminated this educational-democratic idea and who put it into practice. This form of AE was adapted from a similar idea in English universities (Seifert, 1975, p.187; Schneider, 1999, p.16). As early as the mid-1950s, a centre for seminar courses was established at the University of Göttingen. University teachers travelled through the surrounding region and gave lectures and seminars on topical subjects. These seminars outside the university walls are still a constitutuent element of the provision of AE in Germany. The courses provide an important channel in making the knowledge in universities widely available (see Prokop, 1981a, p.89). Prokop (1981b) noted that this form of provision was criticised on the grounds that a mutual fertilization of the university (theory) and of AE (educational practice) was unlikely to take place if there was no academic model on which the activity could be based. It was also claimed that no research was being undertaken to support its development.

This form of extramural AE reached its peak in Germany between the 1960s and early 1980s. Since then, AE has been regarded as an additional conventional task for university teachers in addition to their research and full-time student teaching. Lecturers receive only a relatively small amount of additional financial compensation for this work but this does not seem to present a problem: most regard the small payments as minor compensation for something that is, in any case, a proper activity for an enlightened and committed member of the academic staff.

In German universities, the courses are organised by CE offices (*Zentrale Einrichtungen für Weiterbildung*, ZEW) located centrally and cooperating with other CE institutions, for example regional institutions providing CE programmes within their States. In Lower Saxony, described as the 'model state', the courses are subsidised by the State as specified by the Adult Education Act (*Niedersächsisches Erwachsenenbildungsgesetz*). The seminar courses are considered to be orientated towards public welfare and are therefore eligible for public subsidies. The commitment to running joint seminar courses in Lower Saxony was proposed by the Association of University Adult Education (*Arbeitskreis Universitäre Erwachsenenbildung*, AUE, http://www.aue-net.de) and was closely linked to the central office in Hanover where it was founded. The office is now situated at the University of Hamburg. The AUE is a nationwide association presenting a nationwide policy and further information about it is given by Dikau *et al.* (1996). In September 2003 the AUE was renamed the German Association for University Continuing Education and Distance Learning (*Deutsche Gesellschaft für wissenschaftliche Weiterbildung und Fernstudium*). Greater emphasis on vocational training is implicit in the new title.

In the 1970s and 1980s courses related to nuclear energy, ecology, the consequences of new technology and the women's movement were in high demand. The response to these issues has greatly diminished, however, and only 5% of the programmes now offered deal explicitly with social topics. These seminar courses began to decline in many parts of Germany in the 1990s. New ways of learning, a shift in academic discourse towards a career-centred understanding of self-directed learning, the development of the mass media, the creation of additional centres for learning and the changes in subsidy and sponsorship regulations all contributed to this decline. In spite of this, however, many CE offices continue to uphold their educationally democratic ideals. The University of Hanover's seminar programme, for example, continues to reach 3,500 participants annually.

Higher education staff training

In the 1980s another area of responsibility, normally financed by state funds, was added to the CE profile. This was the training of university staff, in those cases where this task had not already been assigned directly to the university administration. On the basis of a contract between the CE office and staff representatives, the central CE offices were given the task of developing the professional skills of the administrative and academic staff. This new area has grown and may grow further if universities increase their autonomy and the competition between them requires enhanced skills for their staffs.

These programmes centre around functional qualifications and are intended to help staff to adapt, for example before new computer programmes are installed, when commercial bookkeeping methods are introduced or when international contacts are developed. In this latter case, language skills and intercultural competence are particularly supported.

Since the mid-1990s, new subjects linked to staff development have shown a strong increase. Courses support the cooperation between the administrations, staff representatives, lecturers and CE. Working methods in which different interest groups work closely in project teams seem to be much more successful than methods relating to the traditional single-subject areas within the university. This initiative has added a new task, organisational development (*Organisationsentwicklung*), to the work of the central CE offices. This requires CE that is related to the needs of different groups within the context of the organisation.

Tailor-made courses

In the late 1960s new courses of study were established to meet the developing needs of adults and the universities started to offer tailor-made courses for special target groups in the region. The German Association of University Rectors (*Hochschulrektorenkonferenz, HRK*) proposed a wide variety of courses and a number of these were developed to meet the needs of new student groups. They included training courses for teachers, including adult educators, and for managers. These courses, together with those for the general public, are now usually required to be financially self-supporting.

Courses for senior citizens

A fourth working area for university CE is courses for senior citizens or 'guest students' who attend part-time. The intention here is to open existing or slightly modified lectures to further target groups. Some universities provide this service free of charge, demonstrating their commitment to providing a general education. Most universities, however, charge fees sufficient to cover their costs.

By 2001, 50 universities had established a Third Age University with 25,000 students older than 55 years (Faulstich *et al.,* 2004). The idea of the Third Age University is to acquire general knowledge, rather than to qualify for a profession, deepening experiences, skills and knowledge and supporting intergenerational learning. At the University of Hanover a 'Third Age University syllabus' is produced each semester. In addition to the regular university lectures and seminars, special courses are also offered to the guest students, e.g. library guidance tours, computer courses and an introduction to research methods. The development of their academic skills encourages adult students to register for longer study programmes. Each student can seek advice before registering and the courses themselves lead to certificates. With senior citizens, it is particularly important to respond to their personal rather than their vocational needs within each subject.

Three study programmes have been established at the University of Hanover in recent years:

- In cooperation with several faculties, the ZEW offers a *Cultural Studies* programme for guest students. Participants can be awarded a certificate after four terms. This programme was attended by 70 people during the Winter Term 2003. Only 33 of these had a qualification for entry to higher education;
- For a certificate in the *Aesthetic Education* programme, the students attend courses in literature, social studies, architecture and educational studies for two terms. In 2003, 42 people chose this programme, 34 women and 8 men; and
- In the Summer Term 2001, the ZEW began a new practice-orientated programme for active citizenship called *Profile.* Here 34 students registered (28 women and 6 men) to gain skills for voluntary work. Regular university seminars and lectures are recommended for the participants of this programme. The subjects are art, culture and media, intercultural life, health and environment. In addition participants are offered special courses in, amongst other things, project management, fund raising, public relations, mediation and new media.

Interdisciplinary courses

Whereas theory and research over the decades have developed almost exclusively within the academic disciplines, AE has raised issues which cross these boundaries. From the start, AE in Germany has been regarded as a university responsibility, not only to make university education accessible but also to provide impartial advice for the general public. These tasks are frequently difficult for individual university academic departments to fulfil because of the multidisciplinary interests of many adults. To cope with this, two approaches have been proposed:

- Central CE offices, functioning as operational units and working with regional groups, have been set up to meet specific task-oriented educational needs. In doing this, they discuss and advise on the courses needed. They then create and run these courses; and
- 'Theory and practice streams' have been set up to enable the direct involvement of practitioners in the development, running and evaluation of courses.

In recent years adult learners have increasingly indicated their wish to learn across the traditional academic boundaries and new courses have emerged which contain mixtures of traditional subjects, e.g. economics and engineering, and economics and computer science.

Meeting the needs of the market

In the 1980s, the need to producc CE courses that could be successfully marketed increased greatly. Those CE institutions that were particularly successful in continuing to recruit students for their courses hardly dared to celebrate this openly, however, as the reputations of the centres at this time normally depended on their degree of involvement in 'politically correct' projects.

In the 1990s the role of AE in Germany underwent another transformation. Diminishing public funding, followed by cutbacks in CE staff recruitment, meant that new and profitable sectors had to be found. Tippelt (1996), amongst others, took the view that easily marketable CE was essential and could only be developed by separating the interests of individual CE staff from the needs of the CE market. The provision of courses in marketable academic areas became essential to the central CE offices during this period.

One of the results of the cutbacks in central funding for CE was that the courses became more orientated towards business and management topics rather than research issues or general regional needs. This led to a movement away from interdisciplinary courses providing a social critique and towards courses with a vocational emphasis which focussed on the needs of employers. These latter courses attracted participants and companies who could afford economic fees. The CE offices' new mission was based on the needs of employers and also of the unemployed. Courses for this latter group were generally funded by external projects, including those of the European Union (EU), like Key Skills for Managers, Marketing for Women, Listening Skills for Men, E-learning for Volunteers or Transnational Quality Management.

These new approaches to AE also led to new international partnerships. The results of these included the development by a Japanese university of an academic 'feng shui' certificate run in Germany and an open university course in Buddhism at the University of Hamburg.

Continuing changes in the EU funding rules are likely to mean that less funding will be available in the future and the CE offices will once again have to look for new funding models. For example, some courses will have to look for mixed funding with courses receiving support from central university funds, project funding and from student fees. Most of the future courses are likely to be run for target groups that are eligible for public funding or that have other sources of financial support. In particular, the open university for women and the third age university, are likely to require top-up fees. A possible way to keep the fees for students low would be to find private sponsorship. One possibility here could be to liase with health insurance companies as strategic partners for the third age universities.

A nationwide discussion and research on funding policies for education have been encouraged by the government. The Research Institute for Educational and Social Economy in Cologne (*Forschungsinstitut für Bildungs- und Sozialökonomie*, FIBS) provides a pool of information on the current debate on the Internet (http://www.fibs-koeln.de). However the frequently stated idea of cross subsidizing appears difficult to put into practice when few CE courses can be run that are both appropriate and profitable.

Another consequence of the new funding policies is that the workload for academic and administrative staff in CE has become higher, as more courses have to be organised in order to work cost-effectively.

The increasing availability of the Internet is also having a major impact on the way that CE in German universities can be made available to a wider audience. The Internet offers opportunities for new methods of learning in what can be regarded as a 'global learning village'. Critics of this idea, however, have pointed out that communication between teachers and learners will be considerably restricted if the computer is the only teaching medium used. The numerous advantages of distance learning are well-known: the possibility of the asynchronous exchange of information from many different teaching and learning sites; the differentiation of learning levels, learning periods and paces; and the possibility of developing learning profiles for individual students by monitoring the way in which they navigate complex learning programmes. The Learning Lab in Lower Saxony has conducted several surveys whose results are presented on their Website (http://www.learninglab.de).

Good learning programmes are normally expensive to develop. The cost of producing a multi-media learning programme, for example, is currently around 50,000 euros per hour, according to the German publishing firm Schlütersche. A great many users are needed to justify this level of expenditure on a programme. Furthermore, regional relevance can be difficult to provide. It has also been questioned whether central CE offices have the expertise that is needed to develop virtual learning environments.

Central CE offices have to ask themselves if they can be successful on a global scale or whether they should aim to satisfy only local markets. Clearly Web-based learning sequences can be inserted into existing programmes with less expense and, in this way, the virtual classroom might be used cost-effectively as a supportive medium rather than as the only one.

This context suggests another field of activity for CE in universities. The use of new technologies is normally dependent upon the learner having sufficient computer skills in order to benefit from the learning programmes. The technical skills might eventually become more important than the contents of the courses. What are needed are multi-media learning programmes that enable potential students to develop learning programmes for themselves.

The department of educational studies at the University of Hanover has started a programme that helps students to develop their own learning software. Students can work on a simple form of user interface which takes only a half a day to learn. The users can add recorded sequences of seminars, exercises, texts and results to their interface and thus create learning software for themselves, for a learning group or for external users. The students acquire technical skills together with knowledge of their particular subject area. The completed programme can then be transferred to the Website of the department (http://www.hanub.de).

Life-accompanying learning (*Lebensbegleitend*). A new way forward?

In the new millennium, lifelong learning (*Lebenslanges Lernen*) has become 'life-accompanying learning' (*Lebensbegleitendes Lernen*), i.e. learning that accompanies life in the same way that the institutions that support learning should. This new German model, which is part of the national programme 'Learning Regions' (*Lernende Regionen*), was formulated by the Ministry of Education, (http://www.bmbf.de/563_1492.html). It emphasises the need to develop local and institutional learning concepts for well-defined target groups. This should lead to courses being offered on appropriate subjects and using appropriate learning media.

Learning groups having members with a wide range of ages have been formed to discuss specific subjects and also to consider the learning biographies of the individual group members and the learning projects that they might undertake. In many places in Germany, participants have put the knowledge acquired by these groups into practice in order to promote their regions. Senior citizens also participate in 'Agenda 21' groups which offer consultancy on environmental issues, such as energy saving, or they are committed to cultural topics or to social self-help issues. Volunteer Centres exist in the big cities and these function as agencies for honorary work or civil commitment.

Conclusion

The characteristic achievements of AE in German society could be described as 'to open up meaningful perspectives, to demand responsibility and to guarantee humaneness' (Prokop, 2000, p.97). These can be seen as aims for academic AE. Is the strong emphasis on the achievement of these a defensive reaction on the part of the universities? If the market approach is driven entirely by the economy, these benefits would disappear from society. The attempt to open up meaningful perspectives based on financial criteria and cost covering fees makes education a fleeting commodity. The one-sided application of marketing concepts could lead to the separation of the central CE offices from their universities to enable them to operate in a more business-like way: the university would think and steer; the central CE office would maintain the necessary links to society and to businesses. This unbalanced approach is likely to lead first to the outsourcing of AE and then to the abandonment of the educational-democratic ideals that presently underlie much of this work.

Schäfer (2000, p.22) has summarised the key tasks for university AE as to:

- Integrate the essential AE tasks into the broad university planning;
- Define the value of AE within the university profile;

- Clarify the relationship between training and AE within the framework of the university reform;
- Make AE an instrument of regional structural development;
- Consider the needs of AE when broad policy goals are defined, for example, for the recruitment of staff and for funding; and
- Improve the general conditions for AE in line with the higher education policy recommendations.

Finally, universities must decide how they can, in practice, continue to engage with an ever-widening range of adult groups.

This chapter was translated from the German by Susanne Hermeling.

References

Beyersdorf, M., ed., 1999. *Zur Zukunft der – wissenschaftlichen – Weiterbildung*. Hanover: Schriftenreihe der ZEW.

Brown, S., 2000. *Feng Shui Berufs-Praxis. Vom Restaurant bis zum Therapie-Zentrum, von der Schule bis zum Büro des Selbständigen*. Neuhausen: Urania.

Dikau, J., Nerlich, B.P. and Schäfer, E., eds., 1996. *Der AUE an der Schnittstelle zwischen tertiärem und quartären Bildungsbereich – Bilanz und Perspektive*. Bielefeld: Selbstverlag AUE.

Faulstich, P., Graeßner G. and Tippelt, R., 2004. Wissenschaftliche Weiterbildung als bildungswissenschaftliche Aufgabe. In: R. Tippelt, T. Rauschenbach and H. Werßhaubt, eds., 2004, *ibid.*

Hochschulrektorenkonferenz, 2000. *Weiterführende Studienangebote an den Hochschulen in der Bundesrepublik Deutschland.* Bonn: HRK.

Pöggeler, F., ed., 1975. *Geschichte der Erwachsenenbildung.* Stuttgart: Kohlhammer.

Pöggeler, F., ed., 1981. *Neue Theorien der Erwachsenenbildung.* Stuttgart: Kohlhammer.

Prokop, E., 1973. *Erziehungswissenschaft und Erwachsenenbildung.* Brunswick: Westermann.

Prokop, E., 1981a. Widersprüche zwischen Wissenschaft und Praxis – Ansatzpunkte einer Theorie der Weiterbildung. In: F. Pöggeler, ed., 1981, *ibid.*

Prokop, E., 1981b. *Universität und Erwachsenenbildung.* Munich: Minerva Verlag.

Prokop, E., 2000. Bilanz und Perspektiven wissenschaftlicher Weiterbildung – AUE. In: *Beiträge zur Hochschulforschung* 1/2-2000, pp.85ff.

Schäfer, E., 2000. Strukturen wissenschaftlicher Weiterbildung. *AUE-Informationen Hochschule und Weiterbildung*, H. 2/2000, p.14ff.

Schneider, W., 1999. Der Anfang. In: M. Beyersdorf, ed., 1999, *ibid.*

Seifert, E., 1975. Geschichte der universitären Erwachsenenbildung. In: F. Pöggeler, ed., 1975, *ibid.*

Siebert, H., 1999a. *Pädagogischer Konstruktivismus. Eine Bilanz der Konstruktivismusdebatte für die Bildungspraxis.* Neuwied, Kriftel: Luchterhand.

Siebert, H., 1999b. Wissenschaftliche Weiterbildung in der Wissensgesellschaft. In: M. Beyersdorf, ed., 1999, *ibid.*

Siebert, H., 2001. *Selbstgesteuertes Lernen und Lernberatung. Neue Lernkulturen in Zeiten der Postmoderne.* Neuwied, Kriftel: Luchterhand.

Tippelt, R., Eckert, Th. and Barz, H., 1996. *Markt und integrative Weiterbildung. Zur Differenzierung von Weiterbildungsanbietern und Weiterbildungsinteressen.* Bad Heilbrunn/Obb: Klinkhardt.

Tippelt, R., Rauschenbach, T. and Weißhaupt, H., 2004. *Datenreport der Erziehungswissenschaft 2004.* Wiesbaden: Leske and Budrich.

Useful Websites

Hochschulkompass der Hochschulrektorenkonferenz: http://www.hochschulkompass.hrk.de

Hochschulrahmengesetz (HRG) vom 16.02.2002: http://www.bmbf.de/pub/hrg_2002.pdf

Niedersächsisches Erwachsenenbildungsgesetz vom 17.12.1999: http://www.nbeb.de/nbeb/NBEB.htm

Weiterbildungsstrategie der Universität Hannover. Senatsbeschluss vom 25.06.2003 http://www.uni-hannover.de/gremien/zswk/intern/unterlagen_archiv/weiterbildungsstrategie_120603.pdf

ATHINA SIPITANOU

9: Adults in Greek Higher Education

Introduction

Globalisation, socio-economic changes and technological developments taking place worldwide have led to a dramatic increase both in the amount of knowledge available and in the number of ways in which it can be transmitted. In Greece, education for adults in higher education institutions has emerged as one response to these changes and it is now an expanding field of practice. Since 1990, an increasingly wide range of course programmes for adults has been established in Greek universities. So far, however, the nature of these programmes has been under-researched and it is difficult at the moment to write authoritatively about the developments (Kokosalakis, 2000).

This chapter examines adult education at the undergraduate and postgraduate levels, particularly continuing education (CE) for teachers in primary education and the role of the Institutes of Lifelong Learning attached to Greek universities. Given the fact that there is a serious shortage of research data, with all too few studies based on primary evidence, this chapter will draw on data taken from relatively recent surveys undertaken by the research team of the Department for Educational and Social Policy of the University of Macedonia

The Greek universities have implemented numerous programmes in-service training of primary and secondary teachers. Some are also organising special re-education programmes for the CE of primary school teachers who qualified in other countries. In addition, the University of Macedonia has introduced special skills programmes, 'Programmes of Specialization' (*Programmata Exeidikeusis*), for graduates of universities and technical educational institutes (*technologika ekpedeutika idrimata*), who are either unemployed or who wish to attend for other vocational reasons.

Many of the traditional universities are now also developing CE opportunities for distance learning and the Greek Open University (*Elliniko Anoikto Panepistimio*), which provides only distance learning programmes, is also offering a range of flexible and up-to-date courses.

The development of continuing education in Greek universities

A recent study of the provision of CE since 1985 (Sipitanou and Papakonstantinou, 2004) revealed that all of the 18 Greek universities are offering courses for adult students, mainly in the Faculties of Philosophy and Pedagogy, Human and Social Sciences, Educational Sciences and Humanities.

The stimulus for the development of CE came from several sources. First, from the mid-1980s the European Union began to show a keen interest in CE. This reached its present level during the 1990s and the publication of the White Paper (1995), the establishment of the European Year of Lifelong Learning in 1996 and the publication of the Commission's Memorandum on Lifelong Learning (2000) all illustrate this interest (Sipitanou, 2002). As a result, CE began to emerge as a priority for both academic staff and higher education policy makers.

This period was also one of considerable change in Greek universities. In 1982, legislation had been passed (Law No.1268/1982) upgrading the pedagogical academies that, until then, had been responsible for the training of primary school teachers. These became primary education pedagogical departments in universities. In the same way, the schools for training kindergarten teachers were up-graded to university kindergarten pedagogical departments These reforms led to changes in university curricula which led in turn to the development of CE courses.

During this period, a large number of new university CE departments were set up offering courses linked to the needs of the labour market. From the late 1980s, courses began to emerge seeking to respond to the new social and educational needs. The findings from the ten Greek universities that were examined in detail, show that eight of these offer undergraduate CE courses and three offer postgraduate courses. The first university to enter the field was the Aristotle University of Thessaloniki in 1988. This was soon followed by two relatively new universities: the Panteion University of Social and Political Sciences in Athens and the University of Macedonia in Thessaloniki. Both of these responded to meet the social and educational needs of their regions. The University of Macedonia also established a Department for Educational and Social Policy in 1996 containing a designated Continuing Education section. This provides not only courses in CE as a subject but also carries out research in the field.

A number of other issues merit attention in relation to the courses in the universities studied. First, they offer a total of 89 CE courses, 59 of which are undergraduate and 30 are postgraduate. These courses are also open to the departments' full-time students: in particular, 31 of the undergraduate courses are offered to these students free of charge. In the case of the undergraduate courses, students from other departments normally have the right to take them too. Of the postgraduate courses, 18 are elective and 12 are compulsory. The classification of a postgraduate course as an 'elective', however, usually indicates that the department can choose whether or not to offer it each term, depending on the resources available, rather than on the students' right to choose.

The courses fall within the following broad categories:

- Adult Education: Pedagogy, Methodology, Learning Theories;
- Lifelong Learning: Evolution, European Policies;
- Continuing Education: Design, Development, Evaluation, National and European Institutions in the field;

- Training of Teachers of Primary and Secondary Education; and
- Distance Learning and the New Technologies.

In these courses, 62 members of the academic staffs were involved either directly or indirectly. The high numbers of CE courses on offer and of staff who are active in the field have considerable implications since they increase the provision of qualified adult educators and they also raise awareness of the essential role of CE (Sipitanou and Papakonstantinou, 2004).

Continuing education for primary school teachers

Since 1982, the law in Greece (Law No. 1268/1982) has required university education departments to provide courses to enable teachers to raise their qualifications. This grew out of the need for some practicing teachers, particularly those who had previously graduated from the two-year courses of the pedagogical academies, to raise their skills and knowledge to the current standards. In this way they would become equivalent to graduates from the new university pedagogical departments (Presidential Decree 130/1990). Particular emphasis was placed on the need to modernise Greek primary education making it more responsive to the changing economic, social and cultural relations (Programme Prospectus, 1998). In the period from 1997 to 2001, a total of 18,214 teachers (15,111 primary school teachers and 3,103 kindergarten teachers) attended these courses (Sipitanou and Samara, 2004).

All the students who passed the final examination were awarded a university diploma. Perhaps the most important aspect of these CE programmes, however, was the opportunity that they gave teachers to continue their studies, sometimes at the postgraduate level, at a university. It was recognised that the previous qualifications from the two-year pedagogical academies were not sufficient to do this. Another significant benefit of these programmes was that they made school teachers more aware of the need to update their own education to stay abreast of the new challenges of the age and more able to meet the changing requirements of children at school (Antoniou, 2002, p.409–10).

Secondary school teachers already have university level diplomas but they can still benefit from CE. Since 1995 many CE programmes have been run to improve teachers' knowledge and skills and to enable them to be more effective in their educational roles. These programmes have covered topics such as the New Technologies in Education, Environmental Education, Migrants and Foreign Children's Education, and Muslim and Gipsy Children's Education. Within these programmes, about 25,000 secondary school teachers have received additional training (Samara, 2003).

The Institutes of Lifelong Learning

Institutes of Lifelong Learning (ILL) (*Institouta Dia Biou Ekpaideusis*) (Law No. 2525/1997) are to be established in higher education to replace the programmes of elective studies (Platsidou *et al.*, 2003) currently on offer in universities and technical education institutes.

Lifelong education (*dia biou ekpedeusi*) will be the term applied to all forms of educational programmes in Greece, whatever their duration, which are designed for adults over the age of 25 who have completed the standard secondary school (*lykeion*) programme or who hold a certificate from a technical vocational education secondary school (*technologika epagelmatika ekpedeutiria*). The ILLs will broaden the educational and vocational options available to adult students and will enable them to update their knowledge and skills and, if they wish, embark on an academic higher education qualification.

The educational objectives of the ILLs will be achieved through lifelong learning programmes organised in parallel with programmes offered by other institutions. Their courses will be based on a flexible timetable to meet the needs of the students and distance learning methods will be available, with each course consisting of 40–50 hours of teaching. Each ILL will be an autonomous administrative organisation but will be attached to an existing institution of higher education. They will be administered by a President, an Academic Director and a Council to be appointed either by the Rector's Council or the Senate, if linked to a university, or by the Council or Assembly if linked to a technical education institute. All the administrative bodies and administrators serve three-year terms in both cases. The ILLs will have their own teaching and support staffs and their courses will lead to one of two qualifications:

- Further training programmes will lead to the award of a Further Training Certificate; and
- Educational courses, lasting for about 100 teaching hours, will lead to the award of a Continuing Education Certificate. Courses with more than 250 teaching hours will lead to a Certificate of Complementary Education.

These courses will be open to both university and technical education institute graduates.

The ILLs will also engage in research on general issues connected with lifelong learning. They will also be involved in innovative activities to support the ongoing development and qualitative improvement of lifelong learning. These activities are likely to include the development of educational materials and tools, and the effective use of modern technologies and teaching methods for different kinds of lifelong learning. The institutes will also engage in research on the general development of lifelong learning systems.

Lifelong learning courses will be subject to regular evaluation by the Council of the Institute of Lifelong Learning. Evaluation criteria may include the level of student demand for individual courses, the levels and backgrounds of the students, the opinions of students and teachers on course contents and other issues, and the opinions of graduates on the relevance of their courses to updating and enriching their knowledge. Employers' views on the usefulness of the courses and of the research they carry out will also be taken into account.

The attached universities will provide the funding for these institutes with money allocated for this purpose by the Ministry of National Education and Religious Affairs.

It is anticipated that these institutes will soon be making a major contribution to the provision of education for adults in Greek institutions of higher education.

Conclusion

This study has gone some way to covering the research gap in respect of the education of adults in Greek universities. This form of education is assuming increasing importance in view of the relative inadequacy of initial formal education and training in the past and also because of the dramatic developments that are currently taking place in many areas of science and technology. It also highlights the important role of the universities in the broader field of continuing education.

References

Antoniou, C., 2002. *Η Εκπαίδευση των Ελλήνων Δασκάλων (1828–2000)*. (The Education of Greek Teachers). Athens: Ellinika Grammata Press.

European Commission, 1995. *White Paper on Teaching and Learning: Towards the Learning Society*. Brussels: Commission of the European Community.

European Commission, 2000. *Memorandum on Lifelong Learning*. Brussels: Commission of the European Communities. Available at: http://www.bologna-berlin2003.de/pdf/MemorandumEng.pdf

European Commission, 2001. *Making a European Area of Lifelong Learning a Reality*. COM (2001) 678. Brussels: Commission of the European Community.

European Commission, 2001b. *The European Union programmes for 2000–06*. Directorate-General for Education and Culture. Luxembourg: Office for Official Publications of the EU.

Kokosalakis, N., 2000. Lifelong learning at the Universities in Greece: the state of the art. *European Journal of Education*, 35(3), 229–343.

Law 1268/1982. On the structure and operation of universities.

Law 2525/1997. Unified secondary schools. Student access to higher education. Evaluation of teaching and other provisions.

Platsidou M., Valassiadou, M. and Varvati D., 2003. University Continuing Education in Greece. In M. Osborne and E. Thomas, eds., *Lifelong Learning in a Changing Continent: Continuing education in the universities of Europe*. Leicester: National Institute of Adult Continuing Education.

Presidential Decree 130/1990. Conditions and procedures for the equivalency of Pedagogical Academy and Kindergarten Teacher Training College graduates with graduates of University Pedagogical Departments.

Programme Prospectus, 1998. *Academic and Vocational Upgrading for Primary School Teachers*. Athens: National and Capodistrian University of Athens, Pedagogical Department of Primary Education.

Sipitanou, A., 2002. *The European Union's agenda concerning policies and actions for Lifelong Learning during the period 1994–2002*. In handouts for the module 'The Role and the Mission of International Institutions in Continuing Education'. Thessaloniki: University of Macedonia.

Sipitanou, A. and Papakonstantinou, M., 2004. Μαθήματα Συνεχιζόμενης Εκπαίδευσης στα Προπτυχιακά και Μεταπτυχιακά Προγράμματα Σπουδών των Ελληνικών Πανεπιστημίων. (Continuing Education Courses at Undergraduate and Postgraduate Level in Greek Universities). Επιστήμες Αγωγής, 'Δια Βίου και Εξ Αποστάσεως Εκπαίδευση στην Κοινωνία της Πληροφορίας' (Journal of Education Science, Special Edition 'Lifelong and Distance Education in the Information Society'). Rethymno: University of Crete.

Sipitanou, A. and Samara, E., 2004. Τα Ελληνικά Πανεπιστήμια ως φορείς Επιμόρφωσης των Εκπαιδευτικών Πρωτοβάθμιας Εκπαίδευσης (1990–2001). (Greek universities as agencies of further training for teachers in primary education). Μακεδνόν. Florina: Aristotle University of Thessaloniki.

Samara E., 2003. Τα Προγράμματα Συνεχιζόμενης Εκπαίδευσης στα Ελληνικά Πανεπιστήμια (1985–2003). (The Programmes of Continuing Education in Greek Universities). Πτυχιακή εργασία, Θεσσαλονίκη. Dissertation, Thessaloniki: University of Macedonia.

Useful Websites

Agricultural University of Athens: http://www.aua.gr
Aristotle University of Thessaloniki: http://www.auth.gr
Athens University of Economics and Business: http://www.aueb.gr
Democritus University of Thrace: http://www.duth.gr
Greek Open University: http://www.eap.gr
Greek University Network: http://www.gunet.gr In Greek.
Harokopeio University: http://www.hua.gr
Ionian University: http://www.uion.edu.gr
Macedonia University of Economic and Political Science: http://www.uom.gr
National and Capodistrian University of Athens: http://www.uoa.gr
National Technical University of Athens: http://www.ntua.gr
Panteion University of Social and Political Sciences: http://www.panteion.gr
Polytechnic of Crete: http://www.tuc.gr

School of Fine Arts: http://www.asfa.gr
University of the Aegean: http://www.aegean.gr
University of Crete: http://www.uoc.gr
University of Ioannina: http://www.uoi.gr
University of Patras: http://www.upatras.gr
University of Piraeus: http://www.unipi.gr
University of Thessaly: http://www.uth.gr

Anikó Kálmán

10: Adults in Hungarian Higher Education

Introduction: the political and economic background

The year 1989 was a turning point in the history of Hungary although, even now, it is difficult to appreciate fully how fundamental the resulting changes have been. Discussions of these changes often identify the whole of the 1945–1989 period with the 1948–1953 Stalinist era and the Soviet regime. In fact, there was a period of rapid development in Hungary between 1945 and 1948, with a multi-party political system, community participation and free elections (with 93% of the electorate voting). During 1953–1957, the dictatorship weakened and power became more openly devolved. This revived the Hungarian tradition of fighting for freedom and, in 1956, without external intervention, it led to the uprising and its subsequent repression by the Soviets. Between 1957 and 1989, during periods of alternate loosening and tightening of the political hold, the communists tried to use a system of 'market socialism' to coordinate the activities of the State and the market. (Balázs, 1996; Halmos, 1999; Kálmán, 1997).

The one-party political system, although always predominant, lost its meaning towards the end of the communist era, when the main aims of the Hungarian people generally became acquisition and consumption. Even in educational programmes, the 'entrepreneurial spirit' was encouraged. Discussion of international relations and privatisation still remained taboo but there were parliamentary and local elections and local matters were considered in the national parliament. (This contrasts with the present parliamentary position in Hungary which seems to be more concerned with party political in-fighting.) It was characteristic of earlier times that local matters could only be resolved if they reached the level of central government, when a member of parliament (possibly a minister or the prime minister himself) intervened, or if a television personality or a film producer took the matter up.

This situation was brought about by the revival of two traditional antagonisms. One was the division between the capital city and the rest of the country. This is now even more acute: the gross domestic product per capita of the most remote region in Hungary is only one-third of that of Budapest (Benedek, 1999; Zachár, 2003; Kálmán 1998). This tension within the public administration reflects a thousand years of dissension between the power of the central State and that of the regions. A second major factor influencing the present situation is the ancient conflict between those holding liberal views and those with traditional values. The community values of brotherhood, communal solidarity and liberal values, centred on liberty, currently have the greatest support. Socialist values, centred on equality, have relatively few followers and social inequality in Hungary remains acute.

It is apparent that gypsies have been the main losers in the change of regime; most of the gypsy population in Hungary today is unemployed. This compares with the previous situation where the gypsy unemployment rate was no worse than the national average. Local authorities are responsible for finding a solution to this difficult problem.

Human Capital Development

The World Bank (2000, 2002) has launched a number of initiatives (in partnership with the European Commission, the Organisation for Economic Cooperation and Development, the European Bank for Reconstruction and Development, and the European Investment Bank) designed to assess the progress made by the Central European accession countries that entered the European Union (EU) in 2004. In the case of Hungary, they have clearly identified important key opportunities and priority areas for action, in particular the increasing importance of its knowledge economy (Fretwell and Colombano, 2000).

The major lesson learned from this process is that lifelong learning operates as a social, as well as an economic, benefit. There are overlapping policy issues concerning the way in which lifelong learning should be funded, both from public and from private sources. The new practice of lifelong learning in Hungary is focussed on meeting learners' needs. This approach encourages the opening of new pathways both within and between the different sections of the education system (for example, between the various educational levels of the formal system and between the formal and informal systems).

The World Bank (2002) has shown that Hungary's adult literacy and unemployment rates, expressed as a percentage of the labour force, come close to those for Western Europe while the numbers of mobile phones and television sets per 1,000 people in Hungary is nearly as high as in Western Europe. The numbers of computers and of people with Internet access, however, are very much lower.

The Hungarian economy and human resource development in the 1990s

Unemployment

One of the most important current objectives for Hungary is to raise its employment level. It has a functioning market economy and, between 1995 and 2000, its productivity increased faster than the average growth rate of the EU's member states, albeit starting from a much lower base. Compared to the other central European candidate countries, in 2001 the overall Hungarian unemployment rate was one of the lowest: 5.7%, compared to the EU average of 7.3%. Unemployment statistics, however, continue to demonstrate the vulnerability of poorly qualified groups in the population.

At the beginning of the transition period, the Human Resource Development Plan (*Nemzeti Fejlesztési Terv: Humán erőforrás fejlesztés*) was launched with the objectives of:

- Helping unemployed people to find jobs;
- Helping employers to find properly trained staff;
- Developing employment services and job creation programmes;
- Promoting adults' continuing professional development (CPD);
- Helping higher education to meet the demands of the market economy concerning both new technology and management;
- Reducing the technological gap between Hungary and the developed countries;
- Ensuring good educational standards for young people in secondary vocational education and providing vocational training better suited to the changing labour market;
- Improving scientific research; and
- Promoting the teaching and learning of foreign languages.

For further details of the Plan, see: http://www.medinfo.hu/kgy/fazekasm/

Between 1990 and 1999 the percentage of employed people who had at least a secondary education rose from 60% to 82.4%, while the percentage of those with only elementary education fell from 28% to 15.4%. At the same time, a public employment service network was established to help the unemployed find work and training programmes have been set up to meet the needs of the current labour market.

The New Vocational Training Model

The introduction of the New Vocational Training Model (*Új magyar szakképzési model*), (Zachár, 2003) marked the start of an exciting period in Hungarian human resource development. Between 1992 and

1998 almost 310 secondary and vocational schools, including those providing adult education, were supported by the Hungarian government (Nemzeti Szakképzési Intézet (Hungary), 1997).

In addition, the successful application by Hungary in 1992 for EU Phare funding allowed an increasing number of schools to use the new curricula (EAEA, 2001) and introduced new CPD programmes for teachers, including mentoring programmes (Kálmán *et al.*, 1995).

The Phare programme (http://europa.eu.int/comm/enlargement/pas/phare/) was one of the three pre-accession instruments financed by the European Community to assist the applicant countries of central Europe in their preparations for joining the EU, helping them through a period of massive economic restructuring and political change.

Following the 1993 Copenhagen Council's invitation to central European countries to apply for EU membership, the Scheme's support was reoriented, including a marked expansion of support for infrastructure investment. In 1997, in response to the Luxembourg Council's launch of the present enlargement process, Phare funds were focussed entirely on the pre-accession priorities highlighted in each country's Accession Partnership. Civil servants from member states were seconded to assist their counterparts in preparing for accession. Lastly, Phare's management was integrated into the government structures of the applicant countries through the creation of the National Fund and a number of implementing agencies.

In 2000–06, Phare is providing some 11 billion euros of co-financing for institution building support and technical assistance and for investment support to help applicant countries in their efforts:

- To strengthen their public administrations and institutions to function effectively inside the Union;
- To promote convergence with the European Community's extensive legislation and reduce the need for transition periods; and
- To promote economic and social cohesion.

Regional Training Centres

A national network of regional workforce development and training centres has been developed in Hungary with the primary aim of helping the unemployed. It was clear when the system was set up, however, that the most up-to-date centres of adult training were, because of budgetary limitations, being created in a restricted number of regions of the country. This initiative does not concern universities.

Policies and programmes: Second phase (1997–2001)

A programme called the Vocational Training of Young People (*Fiatalok szakképzése*) (Benedek, 1999) launched in 1991, made the first significant investment in vocational training in Hungary and provided the basis for long-term development. The number of daytime students in vocational secondary schools increased from 168,000 to 260,000 between 1990 and 2000.

Repeated efforts have been made to adapt the structure and content of higher education and training to the needs generated by the political transformation process, aided by the establishment of new cooperative projects with EU countries, through the Tempus and Phare programmes. Tempus (http://www.etf.eu.int/tempus.nsf) is one of a number of European Community programmes designed to help the process of social and economic reform in the partner countries. It focuses on the development of the higher education systems in these countries through cooperation with institutions from the member states of the European Community. The programme is based on the concept that higher education institutions are of particular importance for the social and economic transition processes as well as cultural development; they are also pools of expertise and of human resources and provide for the training of the new generation of leaders.

Tangible changes took place in the nationwide administration of education and training, with a move towards deregulation and overall decentralisation of the system. In addition, an EU-compatible National Training Register (*Országos Képzési Jegyzék*) was established in 1993 (Zachár, 2003) and this is constantly being adjusted to the current requirements of the economy and the labour market. The Register is a major outcome of the transition period and has influenced the whole Hungarian education and training system.

Equally, the Hungarian Youth Training Project (1997–2001) extended and updated the new vocational training model, moving towards the European standards and providing qualifications relevant to the labour market. This project was extended beyond 2001 in specific fields (e.g. career guidance, methods of applying for employment, competency based modular training) and does involve also universities (Ministry of Education, 2002).

Resources for lifelong learning and training

Central resources for education and training development in 2002/03 were provided from four main sources. A significant part of the resources for mainstream education came from the central State budget and the budgets of local governments. Overall issues of training and education were also financed from the vocational training contributions (i.e. the funds for professional training coming from the employers' training levy) and some 19 billion HUF (about 74 million euros) from the Labour Market Fund. Before Hungary's accession to the EU, some European resources were also available (for example from the Phare and Tempus programmes, as already mentioned). Since accession, these have been supplemented by considerably greater funding from the EU's Structural Funds. This funding has been further supplemented by contributions from the business sector and non-governmental organisations. The development and training fund segment of the Labour Market Fund (which has been allocated from the government's central budget to finance its employment policy) generated by vocational training contributions, constitutes the most significant part of the total resources for the training system. This plays an important role in adult training and is the main domestic resource following Hungary's accession.

The Hungarian Adult Education Act, 2001: tax benefits and lifelong learning

The Adult Education Act (2001), (Kálmán, 2000) has created new opportunities in the field of adult education. Its stated aims are:

> [...] to enable the exercise of the constitutional right to learning throughout the whole life of citizens, to enhance the possibilities of accessing adult education and training for all members of society, to enable citizens to meet the challenges imposed by economic, cultural and technological developments and to participate successfully in the labour market and continue to be successful through their lives, and to ensure the improvement of the quality of life through adult education and training.

The Act regards training for a second qualification as an 'adult education' activity in terms of funding. Additional degree and diploma courses are normally funded by employers, or by the employees or both, rather than by the State. To help with this, however, since January 2002 a 30% annual tax benefit has been made available to learners participating in accredited lifelong learning programmes. This covers the cost of the training costs paid (including examination fees) up to a total of 60,000 HUF (about 240 euros) in any tax year after deducting the tax benefits available on the purchase of information technology equipment.

The introduction of a system of continuing professional education in the framework of the Act is one of the most important higher education innovations for adult students. Hungarian higher education offers several hundred programmes that have been accredited by this system from which graduates can choose throughout their lives. These generally last for one to two years and they include specialised, practice-oriented and competence-based courses. The courses are developed for adults allowing them to take part without difficulty and they can carry on working while they are studying. Employers will need to play an increasing role in their design and they are the main funding providers for these programmes.

In 2002, 7,807 adult education courses in total were organised for adult learners; of these, 6,273 were recognized by the State. The numbers of students in the different categories of courses were:

Vocational basic training	5,058
Training for vocational qualifications recognised by the State	125,296
Training for vocational qualifications not recognised by the State	6,089
Vocational training	2,249
Rehabilitation training for adults increasing their work skills	391
Training to help adults get jobs	974
Other training	9,416

These figures come from the 'Felnőttképzés/Statisztika' folder in the government's Website: http://www.fmm.gov.hu This training is provided by a number of different organisations, not only by universities.

The aims of the Hungarian Government

The National Development Plan (*Nemzeti Fejlesztési Terv*) (see http://www.nfh.hu) drawn up by the Ministry of Employment and Labour in the period leading to accession to the EU, put forward specific objectives for the improvement of the overall quality of life. A section of the Human Resource Development Plan, which is an integral part of this, seeks to raise Hungarian's qualification and knowledge levels, improve the employability and adaptability of the workforce, reduce inequalities, facilitate the integration of people with disadvantages into society and the labour market, and to improve the education and training infrastructure. The Hungarian National Development Plan has already been approved by the European Commission and, since 2004, individual Operative Programmes within the Plan have been in place to achieve its aims.

Hungary's transition to a market economy has involved a learning process requiring traditional educational institutions to embrace change and to work with new frameworks for individual learning. The economic and institutional transformations which have taken place in the past decade have been of historic importance. The Hungarian government considers the following issues to be strategic priorities:

- Establishing a comprehensive lifelong learning framework within which adults can move according to their needs. As economic restructuring continues across the various sectors of the economy, the development of an effective lifelong learning system represents an important tool to combat job losses and to respond to the changing labour market requirements;
- Raising the literacy and numeracy skills of young people. The government intends to strengthen the basic education provision, for example by helping them to learn how to learn; and
- Focussing on 'catch-up' training to address the problem of school dropouts. Programmes are currently being developed by mainstream education providers, including universities, and additional funding will be made available to extend this to the vocational and professional education sectors.

The comprehensive framework for lifelong learning currently being developed by the government integrates all the measures already taken into one system. This framework is taking shape with the following requirements:

- Transparency: better publicity and easily accessible services are needed to enable adults to enrol on training programmes more simply. This objective is supported in the case of

vocational training by the Training Providers' Register, a list of adult training organisations first compiled in 1997, and by the accreditation process for training programmes launched in 2003. Similarly, statistics are now being collected to enable more accurate analyses of adult participation levels to be made;
- Guaranteed funding: the Adult Training Act, introduced from the beginning of 2003, has set up specific funding arrangements via bodies such as the National Adult Training Council, the Adult Training Accreditation Council and the National Institute for Adult Training. This provides a framework for the training available for unskilled adults with disabilities, encourages organisations to train their own staffs and provides a system of training tax benefits; and
- Quality assurance: this is provided through appropriate statistical and accreditation mechanisms.

Participation rates in education

The Hungarian education system, which is based on a long-standing tradition, is well developed in the European context since the enrolment rates in higher education are relatively high. Public expenditure on education and training, expressed as a percentage of the gross domestic product, remains somewhat below the Organisation for Economic Cooperation and Development average, however. In spite of this, the education system's output has greatly improved over the past decade. Both the absolute level and the ratio of participation in higher education compare well with those in other countries.

Higher education in the market place

Over the last decade, higher education in Hungary has begun to operate in a market place in which the State acts as an intermediary between the institutions and the students in order to create a modern and competitive workforce. The government has also introduced new legislation to create private higher education institutions, including requirements for quality assurance and high educational standards. As a part of this process, Hungary has also adopted the proposals of the Bologna Declaration (2003).

The development of higher education accelerated during the second half of the 1990s. In 1990, 101,000 people applied for places in higher education institutions; in 2001, 149,000 people applied (of whom 125,000 were 18 years old); in 2002, the figure increased to 165,000.

A cooperative project with international organisations (OECD, World Bank, EU) launched an intensive innovation programme, which included the establishment of a quality assurance system linked to European practice. The newly established Hungarian Accrediting Committee accredits the higher education institutions and their programmes every four years. The project is also:

- Introducing a student loan system. From 2001, a full-time student has been able to receive a student loan for ten months of each academic year at a favourable interest rate, financed by the State;
- Introducing of a system of grants to higher education institutions through an institutional development plan based on transparent criteria. Higher education institutions are financed through a five-channel system in Hungary: per head formula funding; maintenance of the institution; its development; textbook formula funding; and programme financing on an application base. This affects the full-time students; and

- Allowing the higher education institutions that were formed following the Higher Education Act, 2000 to carry out targeted multi-cycle education.

An example of good practice in university adult education

The creation of the Lifelong Learning Centre at the University of Debrecen in 2000 marked a significant step in providing adult education for all at the university level. Its unique position as the only university centre of adult education in the Hungarian Eastern Great Plain Region enables it to take the scholarship of the University to the adults in the region. (Kálmán *et al.*, 2002).

Taking into account the University's resources, the following characterise the Centre's function and priorities:

- To carry out research and development of learning and improvement throughout life together with institutional support;
- To implement a high performance computer service, to provide realistic simulations for teaching and to run a complex administrative system;
- To emphasize the measurement and improvement of their competencies for all who support the education of others with lectures, teaching material, assessment and advisory activities, and for everyone who needs human resource development;
- To evaluate the education and training needs and expect-ations, providing continuous monitoring using market research methods;
- To study the present financial, physical, organisational, legal, informatics, methodological, technical and human resource needs evaluation and continuous updating of the human resource maps;

- To provide communications, marketing, public relations, the formation of partnerships, peer- and team-activities (including tutoring and assessment), and neighbourhood networking to redefine and increase the social funds of learning, social capital and transformation; and
- To evaluate accreditation and quality assurance in higher educational vocational training systems.

More information is available at http://www.lifelong.hu

Special departments for adult education have also been set up in many of the faculties of the University of Debrecen. In 2002, 69 courses were started in the field of adult education. The Lifelong Learning Centre records these different courses and also runs its own courses (e.g. on adult education as a subject and also providing training for EU project officers).

The University of Debrecen was one of the first to be accredited by the central government for Adult Education. The institutional accreditation procedure was arranged by the Centre and it now also manages the different programme accreditation procedures.

The 'Training for the World of Work' project

The Lifelong Learning Centre has coordinated a number of successful projects including 'Training for the World of Work'. This programme ran from July 2002 to April 2004 and had six partner organisations (including other departments of the University of Debrecen). Six courses were implemented within the project's framework, the most successful of these being led by the Agricultural Centre of the Department of Managerial Sciences. The rationale for this educational and training development was the region's need for effective and well-qualified managers set against the tradition of a centralised Hungarian government in Budapest and with many training organisations still reluctant to accept the need for change. In this context, the University of Debrecen has played a considerable role in the training of agricultural experts for the Eastern Great Plain Region of Hungary, thus contributing to the implementation of the economic priorities of the region.

Target groups

The aim was to establish a training programme to support young agricultural graduates in the process of becoming managers and practising agricultural managers who need to develop their skills.

Project activity and methodology

A competency-based training method was chosen for this project with a range of modules designed to suit the participants' specialisation, develop their communication skills and prepare them for a successful career in professional management. Management theory and management psychology modules provided information and developed their entrepreneurial attitudes.

Results

Once they have left the university, young agricultural graduates in Hungary face many difficulties for which they are not prepared by their degree programmes. The 'Training for the World of Work' programme contained the following education modules: Management Theory; Management Psychology; Training; and a case study. The participants learned how to manage staff conflicts and changes, how to solve the management problems that may arise and, following the course, they could apply for attractive management positions. For the young agricultural graduates, this programme also gave them practical knowledge and helped them to choose posts which best matched their personalities. During the programme the young agricultural engineers were given realistic tasks that they had to solve as managers and, after each of these, the participants had to present their solutions as case studies.

When designing the training programme, syllabuses were developed which were suitable both in standard and content for accredited postgraduate training. Programmes were set up within a standard national syllabus which was taught using agreed training methods. This has enabled the programme to remain viable once the external funding for the programme ended.

Conclusion

This paper has focussed on adult education for the newly established Hungarian knowledge economy and the inherent challenges related to management and supervision, including the role of public and private stakeholders. The accession countries' experience gained from the transition process is that adult education operates as a social as well as an economic framework. There are overlapping policy issues concerning the way in which a proper financing of adult education should be formulated, including the role of public and private sources. The new practice of adult education is seen from the learner's perspective, opening new pathways between the different sections of both the formal and informal education systems.

References

Adult Education Act, 2001. Adult Education Act No CI, 2001. Available at: www.mkogy.hu (See the *törvények* folder for the modified version: Adult Education Act No CVI, 2003).

Balázs, I., 1996. Közigazgatás a '90-es években: tendenciák és újítások. (Civil service in the 90s: tendencies and innovations). *Magyar Közigazgatás*, 7, 441–2.

Benedek, A., 1999. *Piacgazdaság és szakképzés – A XXI. sz. kihívásai Magyarországon.* (Market Economy and Professional Training – The twenty-first century's challenges in Hungary). Szakképzés – Finanszírozás. Budapest: Oktatási Minisztérium.

Bologna Declaration, 2003. Hungarian Report on the implementation of the Objectives of the Bologna Declaration, July 2003. Available at: http://www.bolognaberlin2003.de/en/national_reports/index.htm

CEDEFOP, 2002. *Making Learning Visible, Identification, Assessment and Recognition of Non-formal Learning in Europe.* Thessaloniki: CEDEFOP.

EAEA, 2000. European Studies on Lifelong Learning: Learning space in non-governmental organisations. Central/Eastern European Link Office of EAEA. Available at: www.eaeabudapest.hu

EAEA, 2001. Focus on Lifelong Learning, Making Lifelong Learning a reality. Available at: http://www.eaea.org/doc/focus-en.pdf

ETF, 2001. *Cross Country Report: The Consultation on the Memorandum of Lifelong Learning in the Candidate Countries.* Turin: European Training Foundation.

ETF, 2002. *Synthesis of the monographs exercise. Interim report, October 2002*. Turin: European Training Foundation.

ETF, 2000. *Country Monograph of Hungary. Working Document, June 2002*. Turin: European Training Foundation.

EU, 2001. *Making a European Area of Lifelong Learning a Reality.* Brussels: European Commission.

EU, 2002. *Human capital in a global and knowledge-based economy. Employment and social affairs*. Brussels: European Commission.

EURYDICE, 2000. *Lifelong learning – the contribution of education systems in the member states of the European Union*. Brussels: Eurydice.

Fretwell, D. and Colombano, J., 2000. *Adult Continuing Education: An Integral Part of Lifelong Learning – Emerging Policies and Programs for the 21st Century in Upper and Middle Income Countries*. Washington: World Bank.

Halmos, C., 1999. *Rendszerváltás a munkaügyben.* (Change of regime in employment). Pécs: Pécsi Tudományegyetem

Higher Education Act No CVII, 2000. Available at: http://www.mkogy.hu – under the *törvények* folder.

Kálmán, A., Ferencné, B., Tamásné, K. and Jenő, S., 1995. *Képzési és oktatási technikák (Oktatói kézikönyv), Phare program a Magyar Közszolgálat fejlesztésére és oktatásra – sorozat.* (Training and teaching methods (A Teaching Handbook)). Budapest: Phare Programme series for the development and the Hungarian public service, pp.12–26.

Kálmán, A., Ferencné, B., Tamásné, K. and Jenő, S., 1995. *Képzési és oktatási technikák (Elvek és eljárások kézikönyve), Phare program a Magyar Közszolgálat fejlesztésére és oktatásra – sorozat.* (Training and teaching methods (Principles and Procedures Handbook)). Budapest: Phare Programme series for the development and of the Hungarian public service, pp.48–65.

Kálmán, A., Ferencné, B., Tamásné, K. and Szigeti Jenő, 1995. *Képzési és oktatási technikák (Melléklet gyűjteménye). Phare program a Magyar Közszolgálat fejlesztésére és oktatásra – sorozat.* (Training and teaching methods (Supplements)). Budapest: Phare Programme series for the development of the Hungarian public service, pp.12–21.

Kálmán, A., 1995. *Tanítási technikák (Oktatói kézikönyv) Phare program a Magyar Közszolgálat fejlesztésére és oktatásra – sorozat.* (Teaching methods (A Teaching Handbook)). Budapest: Phare Programme series for the development of the Hungarian public service, pp.26–41.

Kálmán, A., 1997. Strategies of Adult Education and Methods in Change Management. In: *The Training of the Administrative Staff in the Light of an Educational System.* Cambridge: Proceedings of Crisis in the Human Services Seminar, pp.7–9.

Kálmán, A., 1998. Experience of an OECD Country Report. Lifelong Learning, International Seminar, The Role and Organisation of Adult Education in the Period of Transition. Available at: www.andras.ee/papers/kalman.html

Kálmán, A., 2000. *Felnőttképzési törvény: alapelvek, javaslatok.* In: *A fejlettek sarkában lenni.* (The Adult Education Law: principles and proposals. In: On the heels of the developed). Budapest: Oktatási Minisztérium, Nemzeti Szakképzési Intézet. A felnőttképzési törvény előkészületeinek keretében szervezett nemzetközi szakértői szeminárium dokumentumai, pp.25–9.

Kálmán A. and Gábor, E., 2002. *A Lifelong Learning Központ empirikus távoktatási felmérése az Észak-Alföldi Régióban, valamint a távoktatás regionális helyzete.* (The empirical distance education survey in the North-Plain Region by the Lifelong Learning Centre and the situation of regional distance education). Debrecen: Debreceni Egyetemi Lifelong Learning Központ. (University of Debrecen Lifelong Learning Centre). Debrecen: Lifelong Learning Booklets, Nr. 2, pp.5–28.

Kálmán, A., 2002. *Teaching and Learning Methodologies: Changing Attitudes in University Continuing Education at the University of Debrecen.* THENUCE Socrates-Erasmus Thematic Network in University Continuing Education, Thematic Group 9: Adult Teaching and Learning. Available at: http://www.thenuce.net

Kálmán, A., 2002. The Condition of Distance Learning in the North-Alföld Region of Hungary. In: V. Mitchell, ed. *The Managers' Handbook Online, Case Study 49.* THENUCE European Socrates-Erasmus Thematic Network in University Continuing Education. Available at: http://distance.ktu.lt/thenuce/ebook

Kálmán, A., 2002. *Az életen át tartó tanulás koncepciójának és a Debreceni Egyetem Lifelong Learning Központ működésének bemutatása.* (Presentation of the concept of Lifelong Learning and the activity of the Debrecen University Lifelong Learning Centre. Partnership for Lifelong Learning Series. The European process of modernisation in Hungarian Higher Education). Felnõttoktatás, továbbképzés és élethosszig tartó tanulás. (Adult Education, Further Training and Lifelong Learning), 27, 43–57.

Kálmán, A. and Janko M., 2002. *Felsőoktatás és folyamatos tanulás. Lifelong Learning a Debreceni Egyetemen, Művelődés – Népfőiskola – Társadalom.* (Higher Education and Continuing Education. Lifelong Learning at the University of Debrecen.) Available at: www.nepfoiskola.hu/mntlap/archiv/2002_1/debrecen.htm

Kálmán A., 2003. *Vállalkozási készségek fejlesztése a felsőoktatásban. 3 kötetes tanulmány: 'Vállalkozási ismeretek a Debreceni Egyetem képzési rendszerében'.* (The development of entrepreneurial skills in Higher Education. A three volume study: Entrepreneurial skills in the educational system of the University of Debrecen). Phare project HU-0105-03-ESZA: Debrecen: A kutatás címe: 'A vállalkozási készségek fejlesztése a középfokú és felsőoktatásban'. To be published.

Ministry of Education, 2002. *Career Guidance and Counselling: Theory and Practice for the 21st Century*. Budapest: Regional Conference.

Nemzeti Szakképzési Intézet (Hungary), 1997. *Training Centres 1994–96*. Budapest: Nemzeti Szakképzési Intézet (Hungary).

Putnam R.D., Feldstein L.M. and Cohen D., 2003. *Better Together: Restoring the American Community*. New York: Simon and Schuster.

UNESCO, 2001. *National Consultation Process in Hungary with a European Outlook*. Report for the UNESCO Institute for Education. Available at: www.nepfoiskola.hu/eng/news.htm

World Bank/ETF, 2000. *Knowledge and skills for development: The role of secondary education and training in the Middle East and North Africa*. A Policy Makers' Conference, 7–10 May 2000. Jointly organised be the World Bank and the European Training Foundation, Turin.

World Bank, 2000. *Hidden Challenges to Education Systems in Transition Economies*. The World Bank European and Central Asia Region Human Development Sector.

World Bank, 2002. *Lifelong Learning in the Global Knowledge Economy: Challenges for Developing Countries, October 2002*. A World Bank Report.

Zachár, L., 2003. *Felnőttképzés, munkaerőpiaci képzés tervezése*. (Adult education, the planning of training for the labour market). Pécs: Pécsi Tudományegyetem.

PATRICIA-ANNE MOORE

11: Adults in Irish Higher Education

Introduction

The recent past has been one of unprecedented activity in Ireland in terms of policy papers and discussion concerning adult education and lifelong learning. This began with the White Paper 'Charting our Education Future' (1995) and was soon complemented by the OECD Literacy Report 'Literacy Skills for the Knowledge Society' (1997). They were followed by the Universities Act (1997) which required universities to provide adult education as part of lifelong learning. Then came the publication of the Green Paper 'Adult Education in an Era of Lifelong Learning' (1998), followed by the White Paper 'Learning for Life' (2000) and the Report of the Task Force on Lifelong Learning (2002). Clearly the period since 1995 has been very busy for those involved in adult education in Ireland.

The debate that that took place during this period highlighted the need for change. It has taken place against a background of unparalleled economic growth in Ireland, falling unemployment and increasing engagement by women in the labour market. Not everyone has been able to take advantage of the employment opportunities on offer, however, and the downside of these changes is that the gap between the rich and the poor in our society has grown (Allen, 2000). In order to redress the balance, the Government put in place the National Anti-Poverty Strategy (1997), a key component of which is enhanced educational opportunity. The aspiration of adult education and lifelong learning policy in Ireland, therefore, is in line with the twin pillars advocated by the European Union (EU): looking to education to provide economic growth and productivity; and as a means of bringing about social cohesion.

Ireland has a low rate of adult participation in higher education as acknowledged in the White Paper (2000, p.138):

> According to the OECD Education Policy Analysis (1997) just over 19% of new entrants to degree level programmes in all OECD countries in 1995 were aged 26 or over, compared to an Irish figure of 2%. With regard to Certificate and Diploma level programmes the OECD figure was almost 37% compared to an Irish figure of just over 1%.

In order to address these points, specific targets for raising the level of mature student entry were set by the government:

> Colleges will aim to provide that, by 2005, 15% of the intake each year will be comprised of students aged 23 or over [...] Increasing the mature student intake over the next five years will involve increasing part-time provision and other flexible options such as distance learning opportunities. (White Paper, 2000, p.148).

With these proposed changes in mind, this chapter will examine:

- How increasing 'commercialisation' (treating education as a consumer choice like any other 'product' in the market), competition and demand can create opportunities for learners and, arguably, threats for institutions;
- The importance of information, advice and timing in adult learners' decision-making;
- The significance of the National Qualifications Authority in Ireland (NQAI) and its sister institutions, the Higher Education and Training Awards Council (HETAC) and the Further Education and Training Awards Council (FETAC) in mapping out pathways of learning and providing accreditation; and
- The role that lifelong learning can play in all these processes.

Student identity – a changing profile?

Irish universities have begun to react to the challenges posed by societal, and specifically demographic, changes. Only a few years ago, the average student was a young person aged 18 or a little over, probably either living at home full-time during his or her studies or commuting with a bag of laundry home to a country town at weekends. This began to change in 2004 as the demographic drop in the number of 'traditional' students began to affect higher education institutions.

The need for change has been particularly apparent at the higher education level where our traditional definition of a 'student' began to change faster than anticipated, partly because many school leavers are now working part-time to support themselves. This latter change in the student profile calls into question the distinction between full-time and part-time students. Unfortunately, however, institutional funding is still determined on the basis of full-time equivalent students, thus creating a bias towards full-time course provision. Irish university undergraduate courses have been free to all Irish citizens, EU nationals and to those who meet certain residency requirements, since January 1996.

To counteract the drop in the number of 18-year-olds, major efforts are now being made to attract adult learners into full-time undergraduate courses as 'mature students'. However, this focus on mature students has not yet resulted in more flexibly delivered part-time courses. These would require major institutional change. Indeed it is possible to speculate that the concentration on the recruitment of mature students actually preserves the status quo and is delaying the kind of radical reappraisal of adult education in universities that is required.

The adult students' pathway that is currently on offer appears to be more concerned with the wish of institutions to fill their places rather than to meet the needs of the adult students who are taking them. As recently as February, it was reported that:

> The numbers applying for third level places have dropped significantly for the first time [...] from 62,500 to 60,000 [...]. By some estimates, the numbers taking the leaving certificate will decline from a peak of over 60,000 five years ago to only 46,000 by 2007. One report for the Higher Education Authority has predicted a 35% drop in leaving certificate numbers up to 2012 [...] The new [...] figures would appear to show that the government's efforts to widen access – for both mature students and disadvantaged groups – have still to make a significant difference. (*Irish Times* February 12, 2004)

Some incentives work better than others. For example, the fact that adult learners studying part-time are able to claim back the tax on the fees they have paid for their courses, if certain requirements are met, is a step in the right direction. The fact remains, however, that adult learners (who in most cases are tax payers whose contributions already go, in part, to support free full-time undergraduate education) still have to pay fees for part-time and distance learning courses. This is an inequitable situation and creates a major barrier to adult learners' potential participation in university education. As Clancy argued (1999, p.33):

> One policy option which should now be re-examined is the introduction of a level playing pitch with respect to the funding of full-time and part-time courses. For many adults the part-time route is more suitable than the full-time route. Yet the present arrangements discriminate against those who choose to pursue higher education as part-time students [...] it is difficult to justify a policy which gives preference to full-time students both in respect of fees and maintenance.

What is the market for Irish Higher Education?

The impact of the demographic decline has led higher education managers in Ireland to look for other potential target groups for the courses they have on offer. Marketing plans often begin with a SWOT (Strengths, Weaknesses, Opportunities and Threats) analysis. Here the key questions are: who are the potential customers; and what do they want? Arguably, education has become a market-led product. In putting together their strategic plans, it can be presumed that Irish universities are looking at all the stakeholders in society, especially those concerned with making policies allied to funding and to determining the market for their product (which is a university accredited learning experience).

There is one area in which universities have already sought to increase their market share: the marketing trend of increasing the 'internationalisation' of universities has emerged strongly. Recruiting non-EU students at high fee rates introduces cultural diversity to most Irish campuses which, until recently, have had mainly young and largely Irish student populations. As a small example of the effect of taking overseas students, the fee for a student from the EU for a part-time evening degree in law leading to the award of an LL.B degree was 2,873 euros in the academic year 2003/04; the non-EU fee was 8,505 euros. While the rich learning opportunities that this change brings are to be welcomed, the new needs that the change has created must be carefully handled.

There is likely to be a tension between the different requirements of the various student groups who are now being enrolled by our institutions. On the one hand, the adult learners who are now entering our institutions may well need financial support; on the other, the international non-EU students are likely to need support with their use of English and with issues of adapting to the Irish culture, particularly at the beginning. In financial terms, the fees of the international students may offset the additional teaching costs of the more diversified student body. However, they in turn have cultural needs, which the present system may not be able to meet. These have first to be understood, and then met, by meaningful changes of attitude and culture within the universities themselves. This includes providing appropriate training for staff and appropriate physical facilities for the students where necessary.

The Irish Universities Act, 1997 (Part III, Chapter I) states that the objects and functions of a university should include 'facilitating lifelong learning through the provision of adult and continuing education'. Further, Skilbeck (2001 p.139) points out in his report, *The University Challenged – A review of international trends and issues with particular reference to Ireland* commissioned by the Irish Higher

Education Authority (HEA) and the Conference of Heads of Irish Universities (CHIU):

> Ireland's relatively low ranking among OECD countries in respect of mature age participation in higher education has been identified as a significant weakness on both economic and equity grounds. There is now a more pressing concern with shortages in the labour market of highly trained personnel and the need for continual upgrading of knowledge and expertise. Targets have been set which include substantial enrolment increases and a variety of support measures including finance. There is a need for greater openness, flexibility and innovativeness if suitable conditions are to be established to attract mature age, part-time students and suitable programmes of study provided. Marketing strategies will be required related to university strengths and to national needs. There are clear definite challenges here for partnerships involving all tertiary level institutions as well as for government, the HEA, employers, the adult education agencies and indeed the wider community to recognise and support moves towards continued studies for adults.

The report of the Task Force on Lifelong Learning (DETE, 2002, p.33) noted that:

> Current delivery systems are not optimally adapted to lifelong learning. With the exception of community education, the predominant delivery model remains that of full-time attendance during office hours [...] there has been little subsidisation of lifelong learning, and adult learning in particular. Fees for full-time undergraduate courses were abolished from the academic year 1996/97 and as a result there is now a significant discrepancy between the costs of learning for full-time and part-time students, with the latter paying full fees.

In many of our universities, adult and continuing education is still the Cinderella provision, required to be self-funding and to obtain its revenue on the basis of full-time equivalent student calculations. This is so even though, for many adults, it is the point where the pathway into the university system begins. Former extra-mural courses in, for example, the National University of Ireland (which has university colleges in major centres of population, including Dublin, Cork, Maynooth and Galway) can now lead to credits which can be offset or banked against entry to undergraduate degree programmes within their system.

Whether through a funded course aimed at a particular constituency or through the need to acquire further or higher qualifications for employment, the adult learning route is an important pathway for older learners, whether they are vocational students, leisure learners, 'second chance' students or individuals who have 'unfinished business' with education. Adult education provides a pathway or even a 'taster' experience prior to the return to learning, possibly beginning with a non-accredited evening course and moving on through accredited modules perhaps to the award of a full degree.

The underlying philosophies now are access, transfer and progression, the approach which underpins the National Qualifications Authority of Ireland. Flexible delivery, a critical feature of the adult learning experience, may embrace distance or e-learning, or a mixture of the two, and it may (and indeed should) offer a range of student support services in addition to the teaching. Issues for these students such as the reconciliation of the demands of work, study and family life are delicately balanced and are a matter of constantly shifting priorities. It is time that the needs of adult students moved closer to the core of university values with funding provided to meet these different requirements.

The importance of signposts, maps and pathways

Clancy (1999) made the point that social justice considerations require the universities to seek to tackle generational inequalities and that access to higher education is no longer the sole prerogative of school leavers. Later in the same paper, Clancy (p.33) refers to:

> the increasingly close links between education and employment opportunity. The transformation of the occupational structure, which has seen very rapid growth in those occupations requiring technical and professional qualifications and the demise of employment opportunities for those who lack educational credentials has increasingly led to a view of education as a form of cultural

> capital, which is analogous to economic capital. The opportunity to acquire this capital is a human right and should not be an accident of birth or of generation.

The White Paper (2000), which was published after extensive debates, discussions and submissions from interested parties, also reported that almost all the submissions stressed the urgency of developing streamlined nationally available mechanisms for the accreditation of prior learning and work-based learning.

The National Qualifications Authority of Ireland (NQAI), which was set up under the Qualifications (Education and Training) Act 1999, has access, transfer and progression as its key underpinning principles. In the NQAI (2002, p.19) discussion document, the centrality of the learner within formal, non-formal and informal learning experiences has been identified as a key characteristic of the national framework of qualifications which the Authority seeks to establish 'for the development, recognition and award of qualifications based on standards of knowledge, skill or competence to be acquired by learners'. The Act also provided for the establishment of two other bodies: FETAC (the Further Education and Training Awards Council) and HETAC (the Higher Education and Training Awards Council). This sets out interdependent roles for these Councils, the Higher Education Awards Council, and a range of other stakeholders, including the universities who are represented through the Committee of Heads of Irish Universities.

The relationship between the universities and the NQAI is not defined in the sense that universities retain their autonomy in regard to the content of the courses they offer and in the level of awards that they make. It is likely however that, as the work of the NQAI and of HETAC and FETAC develops, the universities will have to take the standards and levels that they set into account because of the demands of the education market. In particular, the need for work-based learning to be accredited will be driven by competition both from corporate training organizations and from the private sector, especially those providers who use information and communication technology to provide flexible course delivery. Similarly, the demand from adult learners for the accreditation of programmes, which they themselves negotiate, will eventually be met by other providers of accreditation if the university sector does not respond to the demand. At present, university adult education departments act as brokers between the student groups and the institutions. These are the kinds of issues that, from a practitioner's point of view, will drive the development of new learning pathways based on the accreditation of prior learning.

What are the implications for universities?

First, there needs to be a change in terminology. The term 'mature student' has been defined in Ireland on the Higher Education Authority Website as 'a candidate who is at least 23 years of age in the year of entry or re-entry to an approved course [...]'. This does not embrace the full range of adults participating in higher education in Ireland, however, as other institutions, such as the private colleges and institutes of technology, may have different approaches. Most universities have now appointed Mature Student Officers whose remit is to assist these adult learners in full-time undergraduate programmes with their entry into the university by, for example, providing access and study skills courses, return to learning courses and the acquisition of transferable skills. They also provide support with issues such as financial assistance, time management and personal development.

Increased attention needs to be paid to the role of information, advice and guidance to help adult learners make choices regarding an appropriate learning experience. If this is to be objective, it may not be suitable for pre-entry advice and guidance to be given by a provider. Especially for those adult learners whose motives for choosing to engage in learning are complex, it is essential that advice and guidance should be person-centred and also ideally that it should be given by a professionally trained guidance counsellor. In Ireland a major initiative, the Adult Education Guidance Project, has taken on the provision of adult guidance centres which are available to adults free of charge in a number of areas of the country. Funded as projects aimed at providing 'a quality adult educational guidance service to adults' it is envisaged that a comprehensive countrywide service will be in place by 2006. In addition universities have careers services available to all students. In the University of Limerick for example a career development module, which can be taken as part of a student's accredited learning experience, is available and much use has been made of developing software to provide an enhanced service. (Details of this module can be seen at www.ul.ie/careers).

The importance of pre-entry guidance, backed up by events such as open evenings, is that it gives the adult learner an impression of what the institution is actually like. During a course of study, guidance may also be offered at critical times such as during the application period or towards the end of a course when an adult learner may require career management advice or information about further study. The Task Force on Lifelong Learning Report (DETE, 2002, p.40) recommends that 'education institutions develop formal plans to move towards flexible opening hours and put in place the necessary arrangements to achieve this'. Additionally it recommends that 'the funding for providers of education and training should be assessed to ensure that there is a coherent structure for the funding of post-secondary level education, i.e. further and higher education courses'.

A major initiative on e-learning is long overdue in Ireland. This would offer at least some students another pathway into higher education, helping them to learn at a convenient time and place, not constrained by having to be physically present in an institution. This is an area where global competition is already beginning to develop and where ground lost now may be impossible to make up later. As Skilbeck (2001, p.85) states:

> The technological challenge to universities posed by commercial educational networks capable of offering a wide range of global products and the number and variety of providers of part-time professional education growing in number and scale to meet expanding demand, cannot be disregarded. While some institutions have mobilised themselves to treat the challenge of competition as an opportunity, others have not.

The development of partnerships with other providers to increase market penetration, as well as to enhance the provisions for learners, will provide another challenge for the universities which have long been accustomed to autonomy and to their unchallenged position as providers of accredited higher education. These partnerships with community groups, accrediting bodies and professional bodies for continuing professional development, are essential in the creation of pathways for adult learners, as advocated by Skilbeck (2001, p.85).

> Increasingly as professional associations, large employers and governments introduce requirements or strong incentives for continuing professional development, conventional universities will have the opportunity to become major providers. They will not enjoy a monopoly, however, and those active in this field are already finding themselves in competition with private training firms, the training arms of the professional associations – and the virtual universities.

Where do we go from here?

From the adult learner's perspective, it looks as though the range of learning provision on offer to future adult students can only increase. The need for a diagram of learning pathways, underpinned by appropriate information, guidance and advice, is acknowledged and is being addressed by the NQAI and its related agencies, FETAC and HETAC. The consultative approach of the National Qualifications Authority and the guidelines which is has now produced in terms of describing levels of learning are already very helpful in marking out routes to qualifications for learners. Nationally agreed and transparent procedures for the recognition of prior learning will also help many people to gain access to university education and make learning an integral part of their lives.

The White Paper (2000) proposed that a National Adult Guidance and Counselling Service should be set up and that 35 million euros should be provided for staff development and programme support initiatives over the period of the National Development Plan, 2000–2006 (p.161).

The Government has made substantial funds available to Irish universities under the Targeted Higher Education Mature Student Fund to develop initiatives to support greater flexibility and college-based outreach and support programmes for students from disadvantaged backgrounds, second chance mature students, students with disabilities, and those at the lowest income levels. Industry has been asked to consider giving paid leave to employees for learning which is considered relevant to the employee's current career development. (DETE, 2002, p.45.). It must be the case, however, that major moves to encourage adult learners to participate in Irish universities are also required from the universities themselves without sacrificing their standards or risking their academic integrity.

Conclusion

This chapter has briefly examined the possible future role of adult and lifelong learning might be in assisting learners. From the viewpoint of many adult learners, this engagement is essential to enable them to participate in a knowledge-based society and to be able to compete in a labour market which is very conscious of qualifications. Many of the issues considered in the White Paper (2000) remain unresolved in institutions which are being constrained to focus increasingly on research outputs. Where initiatives have been funded, however, there have been benefits for students throughout the institutions. Study skills and other academic support, for example a Maths Learning Centre and a Science Learning Centre, have been set up in the University of Limerick. Better facilities have been provided to students with disabilities.

Universities themselves are beginning to realise the benefit of having a new market for their existing product but they are still slow to respond to the fact that new products with new distinguishing features (part-time courses, work-based learning initiatives, blended learning delivery) are required to service new market segments. The government also has an important role in providing incentives to others stakeholders, especially employers, to do likewise. For their part, the universities have to evaluate the quality of their own performance according to the requirements of the 1997 Act and follow the recommendations of Skilbeck (2001). Finally, lifelong learners themselves have to mobilise and make their voices heard so that their needs can be met in a realistic way.

The how, why, and when, of the acquisition of knowledge relevant to the development of a knowledge-based economy are the main challenges of the future. If the universities do not accommodate society's demands for change, their role in the process of accreditation and validation will diminish to their detriment. The university 'brand' is the unique selling point which it has in the marketplace of educational provision. It is the learners and those who work with them who must drive and accelerate the pace of change on the issues of realistic provision, access, transfer and progression. We are still in the process of becoming a learning society.

References

Allen, K., 2000. *The Celtic Tiger and the Myth of Social Partnership in Ireland*. Manchester: Manchester University Press.

Clancy, P., 1999. Participation of Mature Students in Higher Education in Ireland. In: *Report of the Commission on the Points System*. Dublin: Stationery Office.

DETE, 2002. *Report of the Task Force on Lifelong Learning*. Department of Enterprise Trade and Employment. Dublin: Stationery Office.

Green Paper, 1998. *Adult Education: Adult Education in an Era of Lifelong Learning. Green Paper*. Dublin: Stationery Office.

National Development Plan, 2000–2006. Dublin: Stationery Office.

NQAI, 2001. *Towards a National Framework of Qualifications – A discussion document*. Dublin: National Qualifications Authority of Ireland.

National Anti-Poverty Strategy, 1997. Dublin: Government of Ireland Stationery Office.

OECD, 1997. Literacy Skills for the Knowledge Society. In: *International Adult Literacy Survey*. Paris: Organization for Economic Cooperation and Development.

Qualifications (Education and Training) Act, 1999. Dublin: Stationery Office.

Skilbeck, M., 2001. *The Universities Challenged – A review of international trends and issues with particular reference to Ireland*. Dublin: Higher Education Authority.

Universities Act, 1997. Dublin: Stationery Office.

White Paper, 1995. *Charting our Education Future: White Paper on Education*. Dublin: Stationery Office.

White Paper, 2000. *Learning for Life: White Paper on Adult Education*. Dublin: Government of Ireland Stationery Office.

Useful Websites

AONTAS (Adult Education Lobbying body): http://www.aontas.ie

Committee of Heads of Irish Universities (CHIU): http://www.chiu.ie This provides a gateway to the Websites of all the Irish universities.

Further Education and Training Awards Council (FETAC): http://www.fetac.ie

Higher Education Authority (HEA): http://www.hea.ie

Higher Education and Training Awards Council (HETAC): http://www.hetac.ie

National Centre for Guidance in Education: http://www.ngce.ie

National Qualifications Authority of Ireland (NQAI): http://www.nqai.ie

MARGRIT WETTER

12: Adults in Italian Higher Education

Introduction

Recent reports indicate that the number of people enrolled in adult education is increasing rapidly in Italy: it has increased from 150,000 in 1999 to 310,000 in 2001 (Dell'Aringa, 2001). The number of adults involved in education has more than doubled in two years and this is a clear indication that Italians wish to increase their knowledge and skills.

Another interesting finding in Italy is that the number of students in work has recently risen above the number of full-time students (Fondazione Rui, 2002). This high number of working students, most of whom are presumably studying part-time, is interesting because the needs of working students clearly differ from those of full-time students. Working students, for example, have many more problems in finishing their studies than do full-time students.

According to the Evaluation Committee of the University System (*Comitato di Valutazione del Sistema Universitario*) which, amongst other things, examines the student enrolment figures, a clear trend is emerging of an increasing number of older adults in the university student population. The data show that in Autumn 2001 about 20% of all new students enrolling were over 22 years of age and that they had already worked for between one and three years. In the same period, the total number of new enrolments rose from 310,924 in Autumn 2000 to 331,368 in Autumn 2001 and the provisional enrolment figure for Autumn 2002 is 347,160 (*Ufficio di Statistica*, MIUR URST at http://www.miur.it/ustat). This increase has taken place despite an overall demographic decrease in Italy.

This chapter starts with a short discussion of the meaning of the term 'adult education'. In recent years, Italian universities have been undergoing changes which favour adult education and the old and the new positions are then compared, showing how the system, with its increased flexibility, has moved to meet the needs of adult students. A number of courses are finally described as examples of good practice to illustrate the efforts made in the last few years to help students complete their studies.

The meaning of Adult Education

In Italy the concept of 'adult education' (*educazione degli adulti*) has not been defined specifically. The term 'adult' has a number of different meanings: it is used, for example, to refer to 'a person who has attained maturity' and also to 'a person who has attained the age of legal majority', (18 years of age in Italy). This is also the age when young people, after having obtained their school leaving certificates (*esami di stato*), roughly equivalent to the International Baccalaureate, can move on to higher education (HE).

However, the term 'adult education' is not used in the sense of persons who follow university courses between the ages of 18 and 24 or so but commonly refers to education for older people who participate in educational programmes at all levels to achieve better living and professional conditions or to increase their personal cultural development. Referring to people who attend university classes, the Italian Education Ministry (*Ministero dell'Istruzione, dell'Università e della Ricerca,* MIUR)[1] uses the term students (*studenti*) or young people (*giovani*).

The term 'adult higher education' is used in practice to designate HE for people who, for any reason, could not move on to HE immediately after they had obtained their secondary school leaving certificate. Often the term 'adult education' is used to mean the same

1 In 2001 the Ministry of the Public Instruction (*Ministero della Pubblica Istruzione*, MPI) and the Ministry of the University and Research (*Ministero dell'Università e della Ricerca Scientifica*, MURST) were unified.

as 'continuing' or 'permanent education'. The English term 'lifelong learning' has also been adopted by Italians.

In Italy, a distinction can also be drawn between 'education' and 'learning': education is 'the act or process of imparting knowledge' (from the Latin *ducere* 'to lead'); learning is 'the act of gaining knowledge (by study)'. The perspectives of education and learning are therefore different. When offering education, the initiative comes from an institution or an educator (teacher, parents, or whoever else wishes to improve the knowledge of the learners); the act of learning is centred on those who acquire knowledge.

National policies on adult education

While there were some initiatives to develop adult education in Italian universities before 1995,[2] recent developments have been greatly influenced by the European Union's 'White Book on Growth, Competitiveness and Development' (Delors, 1993). This book, whose main goal was to reduce unemployment, was a cornerstone for the agreement signed in 1996 between the Italian Government and its social partners. Chapter 7 stressed the catalytic role of education in a changing society and it has played an important part in convincing the Italian authorities to increase the provision of adult education at all levels.

In 1997, a Ministerial Decree called for the establishment of centres of adult education (Ordinanza MPI No. 455/1997; Corradi, 2000, pp.317–29) and, in 1998, the Italian Government and the trades unions signed a Social Agreement for Development and Employment (*Patto sociale per lo sviluppo e l'occupazione*). This agreement contains an appendix in which the government agreed to provide adequate finance and organisational support to develop continuing education for employees and managers, with special consideration for disadvantaged

2 For instance, the Consortium for a Distance University (CUD), founded in 1984, and the NETTUNO project (see later).

adults. In this agreement, the central and regional governments guaranteed that education and professional training would be provided at a range of levels (schools, professional schools and universities). It is also intended that professional experience can be taken into account when credits are given for learning (Corradi, 2000, p.99). One result of Ministerial Decree 455/1997 and the Social Agreement has been the setting up of permanent outreach centres (*Centri Territoriali Permanenti, CTP*) where adults can catch up on functional and cultural literacy, learn languages, get professional qualifications and prepare for re-entry to education (including to the universities).

In 1999, following an earlier Social Agreement, the Italian government established a high-level committee with the following tasks:

- To examine the suitability of current employment training schemes;
- To ensure that disadvantaged people would benefit from training in schools and universities;
- To reorganize the educational system, with more autonomy for schools and universities and the introduction of a credit system; and
- To introduce new forms of assessment and a credit system suited to the needs of adult learners.

The so-called 'Master Plan' emphasized the need to pay particular attention to southern Italy and other disadvantaged regions and to the development of distance education (Corradi, 2000, p.102). As a result of the decisions taken in 1997 and 1998, the government allocated the sum of 26,970 million Italian lire (corresponding to about 13.5 million euros) which offered the educational system, and in particular adult education, the opportunity to develop.

In 2000, a national conference, attended by representatives of the State, regional and local institutions, developed a strategy for increasing the development of lifelong learning (Corradi, 2000, pp.345–69). It also increased the number of CTPs, which began to appear in the academic year 2000/01, to nearly 550 and it increased their importance.

The Law 'Legge 8 marzo, No. 53/2000' (Article 5), states that workers employed in the public and private sectors with at least five years' service (*anzianità di servizio*) with the same employer, can apply for educational leave for a maximum period of eleven months, continuously or over the whole of their working lives, to participate in educational activities. These activities do not have to be related to their particular work and this leave does not have to be financed by the employer. Article 6 of the Law approves leave for continuing training throughout a person's working life to increase their professional knowledge and competence. This training may be chosen by the employee or by the employer but needs to be by agreement (Corradi, 2000, p.21). Employers are not obliged to finance further training of their employees. If they refuse, however, employees can ask to receive some of their pension early or to extend their working lives beyond the normal retirement age.

The steps described above are concerned particularly with formal and vocational adult education. In addition, non-formal adult education is offered by many cultural associations. It is also worth mentioning in this context the many cultural associations, mostly with the help of local administrations, set out to help the integration of immigrant workers. They offer Italian language courses, often combined with the teaching of everyday Italian customs, and they also provide some legal and administrative information about Italy. Knowledge of the Italian language is a milestone for integration and facilitates participation in further education programmes, for instance enrolling in a CTP.

Non-formal education also takes place in open universities which nowadays are present throughout the country, not only in big cities but also in the towns. In the province of Rome, for instance, 20 branches of the UPTER (*Università Popolare e della Terza Età di Roma*) are located. In addition, the city itself has 38 centres. Altogether, during the academic year 2000/01, nearly 20,000 people enrolled in UPTER in the Rome region. Throughout the whole of Italy during the same period, more than 42,000 people took part in educational activities organised by the Italian open universities (*Federazione Italiana per l'Educazione Continua*, FIPEC).

The structure of higher education

Higher education in Italy is organised either in one of the 62 State universities or in the 13 State-recognised institutions. (These latter are independent institutions which have been approved by, and are partially funded by, the State.)

Between 1996 and 1999 the introduction of a number of legislative and administrative measures signalled a major change in Italy's university education. One of the main aims of these reforms was to implement the universities' autonomy (statutory, regulatory, financial and budgetary) and the new system has been followed since the academic year 2000/01. These reforms, which have allowed greater flexibility, will support the development of HE for adults.

One of the reasons for the reform was that the old system of degree courses[3] (most with a statutory length of four years) was very rigid.[4] One consequence of the old system was that a large number of students did not complete their courses within the scheduled period during which the course was taught, becoming so called long-term students (*studenti fuori corso*). Under the old system, only 15% of students managed to graduate within the statutory period and 41% became long-term students taking, on average, two to three years more than the statutory length of their courses to complete them.

3 There was little diversification: the academic degree course was for a long time the only type of university course available. University diplomas were abolished in the reform and the possibility of studying for masters and doctoral degrees was added.

4 Students registered under the old system until the academic year 1999/2000. For this reason, Italian universities will have to carry on with the old system until at least 2005.

Figure 1: The percentages of long-term students, by subject, during the academic year 1999/2000 (De Bernardi et al., 2001, p.12). This refers to only one specific academic year but the figures for other years are similar.

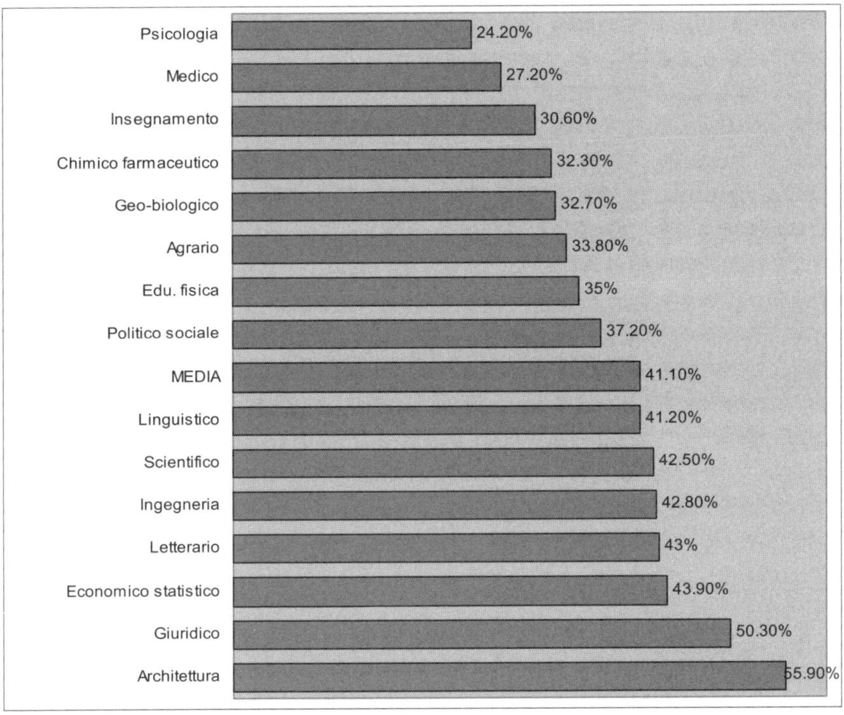

With the old system the dropout rate was very high; approximately 60% of all the students who matriculated did not complete their first degrees. Of these, about half had left by the end of their first year.

Figure 2: The percentages of students who did not renew their enrolments in the academic year 1996/97 (De Bernardi et al., 2001, p.12). Once again, the figure refers only to one specific academic year but the numbers in other years are similar.

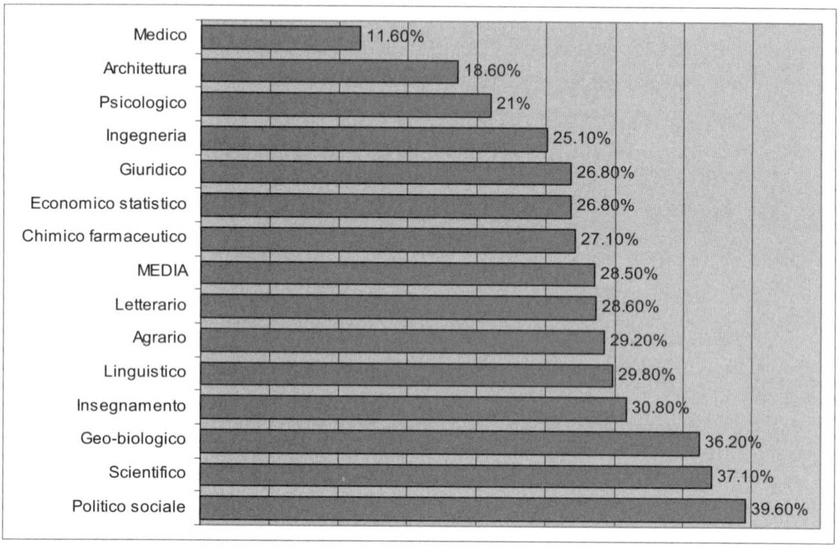

Other problems with the old system included a number of mismatches:

- Between the social and cultural demands for a higher and more widespread level of education and the small number of young people who acquired a university qualification. (Graduates only accounted for 14% of their age cohort.);
- Between the available university education and the demands of the production and social systems. This is clear from the high rate of unemployed graduates (currently 23% of all graduates) and from the average age on graduation (26 years); and
- Between the Italian HE system and other European systems (De Bernardi *et al.*, 2001, pp.13, 14).

The objectives of the reform are to:

- Give the universities autonomy on decisions concerning the curriculum;
- Extend and diversify the range of HE courses and introduce greater flexibility;
- Enhance the curricula and syllabuses and improve teaching, by introducing competition between universities and creating an efficient national system for assessing and fostering higher standards of excellence in teaching;
- Reduce the time needed to obtain a qualification by ensuring that the actual time taken corresponds to the statutory length of the courses;
- Relate the objectives of the courses to the structure of knowledge, skills and professionalism required by the socio-cultural and labour market demands and opportunities;
- Define criteria, rules and procedures which will enable the universities to ensure that the courses keep pace with social change and the changes in the labour market; and
- Bring the structure of Italian HE into line with the other universities of the European HE area by 2010 (De Bernardi *et al.*, 2001, pp.15–18).

The most important actions and measures adopted were the:

- Organisation of study around two cycles: the first taking three years and leading to the award of a first degree; and the second taking two years and leading to a specialised degree;[5]
- Special one-year courses after the first and second degrees to be organized for the acquisition of specialised scientific education as well as higher continuing education and training. These can lead to masters degrees;
- The introduction of educational credits as a means of recording students' progress and facilitating their mobility;
- The introduction of training courses, lasting for up to twelve months; and

5 With the old system there was only one degree.

- The requirement for meetings and discussions with students, as well as with representatives of the social and production systems, the professions and representatives of the local authorities, in order to determine syllabuses and curricula (De Bernardi *et al.*, 2001, p.18).

These reforms will clearly contribute a great deal towards the development of adult education and the concept of lifelong learning within the university system.

Adult involvement in higher education

The introduction of the special, masters and doctoral degrees offers adults who have left the university following their first degree the opportunity to return to further study. Furthermore their work experience can be accredited within the new credit system which is geared to meet their needs.

The new regulations also make it possible for part-time students to be charged reduced fees (so that they no longer have to pay the same amount each term as the full-time students). Instead of having to complete the first degree in three years they may take up to six years to complete and distribute the payment of the fee over the period of the course.

Another important regulation in favour of adult students has been valid since 2002: before the reform, results awarded in examinations lost their validity after eight years if the degree had not been awarded by that time; now, with the statutory autonomy that they have been given, individual universities are free to decide for themselves on the length of time that their examinations are valid.

Before the current reforms, students who had previously given up their studies and returned later had to pay the fees for the intervening period when they were not studying (together with an additional penalty for late payment). This was so expensive that, in most cases, they were prevented from returning. Now each university is free to set the fee to be paid if a break in a student's studies occurs. This has resulted in many universities making special arrangements to encourage students who have not completed their degrees to return. In some cases this is now a token sum. For example, the University of Venice Ca'Foscari charges around 10 euros per year. This may encourage adults who interrupted their studies some years ago to come back.

The reforms have made it possible for individuals to obtain a degree in three years rather than four. At the same time many adults can now return to study and convert their previous uncompleted study into credits towards a new degree. This, along with the conversion of credits for work experience, brings many candidates appreciably nearer their desired degrees.

The autonomy recently given to universities also allows them to offer new courses to meet a wider range of educational demands. Another trend which is emerging is the development of specialised vocational courses and courses to improve professional and cultural skills. These are shorter and can lead to the award of a certificate. A broad range of such courses is on offer and programmes differ from one university to another according to local needs.

The new-found autonomy of the universities is clearly very important for the expansion of higher education for adults.

Degree programmes

Adult learners who wish to take a university degree enroll in the same way as other students. There is no age limit for obtaining a degree. The daytime programme can be taken by adults who are free to attend and can be particularly attractive to those who are required to pass only a few more units before completion.

Some universities have encouraged adults already in work and who are interested in taking a degree, or those who had to leave part way through their degree programmes, to return. For example, since 2001/02, the Faculty of Economics of the University of Rome 'La Sapienza' has run classes in the evenings with the teaching taking place from 6 to 10 pm and on Saturday mornings. This allows working and other part-time students (and also full-time students who for one reason or another cannot attend classes during the day) to take their degrees in a more flexible way. Although, at the time of writing, it is only in its second year, the number attending this evening programme is already over 10% of the total student number. Recently other universities, who until now have offered only short courses, have also begun to promote evening degree programmes. For example, the Faculty of Economics in Bologna University provides an evening degree course in Business Administration while the Faculty of Political Science of the University of Milan offers a degree programme on the Organisation of Human Resources that is taught only in the evenings.

Information technology is revolutionizing the way in which adult students can find out about the learning opportunities that are available to them. Information, for example about the course content, time tables, examinations and the availability of teaching staff, are now all made available through university Websites.

Students who are unable to attend classes can get information through the course Website and keep in contact with teaching staff from home. The quality of the information varies greatly from university to university and from lecturer to lecturer. E-mail exchanges between students and teaching staff, together with Web-based forums organised by lecturers, are particularly helpful for working students and for those who live at a distance from the university. Until now, contacts have depended upon individual initiatives.

While learning support using information and communication technology has become quite common, university teaching using e-learning methods is still quite rare in Italy. Some universities promoting e-learning, organize courses for teaching staff to encourage them to organize not only e-learning support but also courses on e-learning itself. The Polytechnic of Milan, for example, is a pioneer in this area and has just graduated its first cohort of students who completed their degrees in computer engineering entirely on-line. It will be some time, however, before e-learning goes beyond downloading information from the Web to the provision of regular interactive lessons.

Distance learning is becoming closely connected with e-learning. One of the best known distance teaching projects in Italy is provided by NETTUNO (the *Network per l'Università Ovunque*, the Network for the University Everywhere). This is a consortium of 38 Italian universities which is offering an alternative to traditional classroom courses. Courses are disseminated via two satellite TV channels (Rai Nettuno Sat 1 and Rai Nettuno Sat 2) and the Internet (Eutelsat Open-Sky). In addition to using e-learning materials, students on these courses can keep in contact with their tutors not only by e-mail but also by audio and video chat, and using a forum. Already 20,000 hours of video lessons and 20,000 exercises on the Internet are available. Initially the consortium offered only diplomas and short courses but, since 2003, it has also offered 25 complete degree courses in the areas of architecture, cultural assets, economics, engineering, psychology, sociology and communication sciences. About 500 students graduated via NETTUNO in the year 2003, more than half of them in economics from Bologna University.

Specialised degree courses and masters courses

A number of specialized courses are also available for adults. For example, the masters course in lifelong learning organised by the University of Roma Tre is a distance course in which adults learn by video- and audiocassettes and by reading selected texts (Corradi, 2000, pp.105–31). Books and cassettes can be borrowed from the University and the participants meet each month on Saturday afternoons for instruction and discussion. These meetings are recorded and are available on videocassettes for students who cannot attend. Tutors guide participants and encourage them to follow cultural, social and scientific events. Every year this course produces new and highly qualified adult educators to add to the number of specialists in the field. This in turn assists with the expansion of adult education in the universities.

Single courses

Most Italian universities, at present, still see their main roles to be the preparation of full-time students for bachelors and higher degrees and to carry out research. Single courses in the field of lifelong learning are therefore underdeveloped, especially when compared to other providers of training courses and professional continuing education. There are, however, some exceptions. One of these is the University 'Gabriele D'Annunzio' in Chieti which, in the year 2000, established a Continuing Education Centre situated in the nearby town of Torrevecchia. The Centre runs classes in professional development which seek to meet the needs of public and private organisations and companies, especially in the fields of economics, management, medical sciences and new technologies. These courses are highly professional and contain 380 hours of classes and 220 hours of practical training. Credits from the courses can be put towards a specialized degree or masters programme.

The University of Rome, 'Tor Vergata' also offers over twenty courses at different levels and in different subjects by distance education online. The course credits awarded to successful students on these courses have the same value as traditional university credits.

Conclusion

It is clear that the Italian system of HE is changing to meet the needs of lifelong learners and a number of examples have been given of new opportunities that are being provided for adults who wish to participate. These indicate how HE can best be organised for adults.

Much still has to be done to increase adult numbers in HE and to enable them to obtain qualifications if they wish. Particularly since 2000, many new initiatives have been taken and the universities have become increasingly aware of the growing importance of HE for adults. Italian universities are also becoming more aware of the need to take account of the growing numbers of students who do not fit the traditional learning model. The opportunities presented by the new technologies to enable adults to gain access to HE are also being realised and, by increasing its flexibility in time and space, will undoubtedly increase the participation of adults in HE.

References

Corradi, S., 2000. *Lezioni di Educazione degli Adulti. Europa, Occupazione, 'Lifelong Learning'*. Roma: Aracne.

De Bernardi, G., Lanzoni, F. and Winters, M., 2001. *3 + 2. La nuova università*. Milano: Alpha Test.

Dell'Aringa, C., 2001. *Rapporto ISFOL 2001*. Milano: Franco Angeli.

Delors, J., 1993. *White Book on Growth, Competitiveness and Development*. European Commission. (An extract can be found in Italian in Corradi, S., 2000, pp.135–239).

Fondazione Rui, 2002. *Università, Uno studente su due lavora. Boom dei 'nuovi' lavori*. Available at: www.fondazionerui.it/escomunicato.html

Useful Websites

Circular about the institution of permanent regional centres for adult education (1997). Available at: www.set-mi.net/ofi/aree/eda/eda-norm/om455.htm

Direttiva Ministeriale No. 22/2002. Available at: www.fnada.it/Norme/2001/dir22-2001.htm

FIPEC (numbers of participants on open university courses). Available at: www.fipec.it/Dati/2000-2001.htm

Information about the Masters course in Lifelong Learning. Available at: www.encanta.it/unversità_learning.html

Law '*Legge 8 marzo 2000*'. Available at: www.parlamento.it/parlam/leggi/00053l.htm

Protocollo d'Intesa Ministero Pubblica Istruzione. ISFOL, 15.12.1998. Available at: www.istruzione.it/argomenti/qualità/testi/documenti1b.htm

Social agreement for Development and Employment (*Patto sociale per lo sviluppo e l'occupazione*). Available at: www.fnada.it/Norme/patto.htm

Ufficio di Statistica, MIUR – URST. Available at: www.miur.it/ustat

Web addresses of the cited institutions

Continuing Education Centre CEC, Università 'G. d'Annunzio', Chieti. Available at: http://www.unich.it/cec/

CTP (*Centri Territoriali Permanenti*) operating in the academic year 2000/01. Available at: www.fipec.it/documenti/ctp.html

EDA (*Educazione permanenti degli Adulti*). Available at: www.europalavoro.it/eda.asp

Federazione Italiana per l'Educazione Continua, FIPEC. Available at: www.fipec.it

MIUR (*Ministero dell'Istruzione, dell'Università e della Ricerca*). Available at: www.miur.it.

Nettuno (*Network per l'Università Ovunque*). Available at http://www.nettuno.it/

University of Bologna: distance learning (*teledidattica*). Avalilable at: http://www.economia.unibo.it/Economia+Bologna/Didattica/Teledidattica/default.htm

University of Bologna: evening courses. Avaliable at: www.economia.unibo.it/Economia+Bologna/Didattica/Corsi+serali

University of Milan: evening courses. Available at: www.cosp.unimi.it/Corsi%20serali%20SP%2003-04.pdf

University of Rome: evening courses at the Faculty of Economics. Available at: www. eco.uniroma1.it/serale.

UPTER (*Università Popolare e della Terza Età*). Available at: www.upter.it

INETA KRISTOVSKA

13: Adults in Latvian Higher Education

Introduction

The University of Latvia is the largest university in the country and has approximately 33,000 students. There are two views of its mission amongst the University's academic staff: the first is that it should concentrate on its traditional academic functions, be conservative in its attitude towards innovation and inflexible in its activities; the second view is that, in addition to its earlier academic functions, the University should offer wider learning opportunities for the citizens of Latvia, helping them both to become better educated and to gain the professional skills that are necessary to compete in the labour market, not just in Latvia but throughout the European Union.

Higher education in Latvia

Brief history

The University of Latvia, the first university in the country, (initially called the Latvia Higher School) was founded in 1919. This new university was based on Riga Polytechnic which had been founded in 1862. The facade of the former Polytechnic building still serves as the symbol of the University. In 1923 the Higher School received its present name, the University of Latvia (*Universitas Latviensis*).

During the period between 1919 and 1940, the University of Latvia was the major centre of higher education in the country; in 1940 it was occupied by the Soviet Army. In the pre-war years it was possible to obtain higher education only at the University, at the Conservatoire of Latvia and the Academy of Arts.

More recently, higher education establishments such as the Latvian University of Agriculture, the Latvian Academy of Medicine and Riga Technical University have gained independence from the University of Latvia and have become well-known centres of education and research in their own right. At the present time there are five universities and 22 other institutions of higher education in the country. (For more information, see: http://www.izm.lv). Following independence in 1991, one of the first acts of the new Republic was to confirm the Constitution of the University. This took place on September 18, 1991 when it was described as 'a state establishment of academic education, science and culture which serves the needs of Latvia and its people'. (Further information is available on the University's Website at: http://www.lu.lv).

General characteristics of the University of Latvia

There are 13 faculties in the University and the numbers of full-time and part-time students in 2001 and their academic levels, taken from the University's Website, are shown in Figures 1 and 2 below.

Figure 1: Number of full-time and part-time students, 2001.

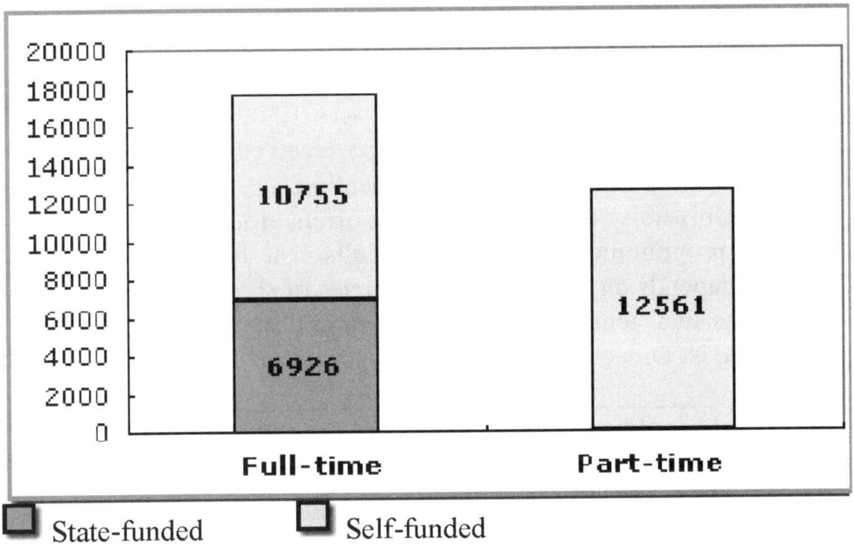

Figure 2: Number of students at different academic levels, 2001.

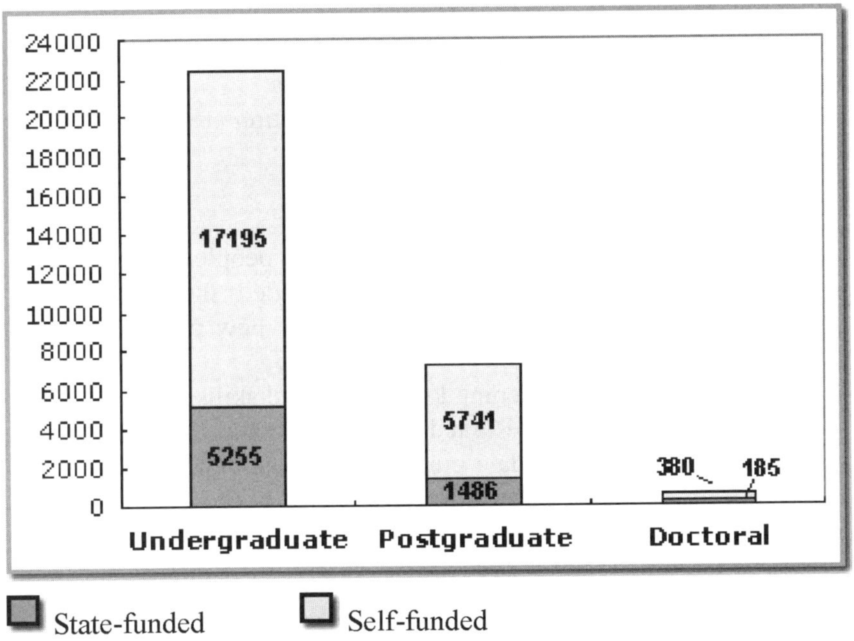

There is considerable demand for continuing education courses from adults wanting to increase their knowledge and skills, particularly following their first degrees. They can choose courses offered by fifteen centres within the University. The total number of students who took these courses during 2001/02 was 1,302: of these, 427 had only basic initial education; 77 had also received vocational education; and 821 had undertaken higher education.

The University of Latvia currently offers around 145 continuing education programmes each year for adults. The length of these programmes depends on the content. (Examples of short programmes are: Innovations in Chemistry, Modern Literature; an example of a long programme is: Didactics.) The current distribution of lengths is:

Hours	Number of programmes
<13	27
13–36	13
37–72	2
>72	4

These courses are provided by staff who are specially trained to teach adults: of these, 38 are full-time, 63 are part-time.

The following possibilities for adult education are offered by the University:

- Re-qualification
  These courses are intended for people whose former qualifications are no longer needed: the new political and economic situation requires new professions and new skills;
- Updating and widening knowledge and skills
  These are designed for people who studied courses with out-of-date curricula or those where regular updating of knowledge is required because of the socio-economic changes or technological advances;

- Courses to enable people to achieve their personal goals
  These help people to develop foreign language or computer skills, for example, as well as to increase their general knowledge. These skills, in turn, help people to adjust more easily to the new society, for example by being more willing to take risks and make decisions;
- Courses for government and municipal officials
  The Local Government and Project Management State Training Centre within the University is responsible for this area of work. Since the establishment of the Centre, several thousand local government officials and civil servants have been helped to solve the problems that they face. The Centre currently employs a permanent staff of lecturers who in 2001 offered about 60 programmes. It also offers project management programmes that are attended by specialists from local government offices, businesses and institutions. Together with partners from Germany, the Centre has developed a considerable body of training material for these groups and this has been translated into Latvian;
- Professional development courses for university staff
  With the introduction of information and communication technology (ICT), there is a great need to design courses based on the principles of adult learning, using the new methods; and
- Courses within international and local projects.

Analysis of the programmes of a range of departments shows that the most popular subject areas are practically based Computer Sciences courses; Management; Languages; Law; and Project Design and Management. Special attention is paid to target groups such as schoolteachers and educational managers to help them obtain computer skills, to update their knowledge in specific subjects and to develop the skills needed in student-centred teaching.

Courses for adult students are publicised using the Internet and the mass media as well as through direct contact with schools, municipal governments and companies. Courses are organised close to students' homes whenever possible. Most adult students use the same facilities as the full-time students. In some centres, however, adult learners have separate facilities and use more advanced equipment. For example, the computer laboratories and classrooms of the Continuing Education Centre for Librarians are located in the National Library of Latvia and there the students use the Library's information systems.

Some University departments organise face-to-face teaching sessions at weekends and in the evenings in order not to disturb the working day. Tutorials and examinations are also organised close to students' homes. To facilitate the development of the courses, questionnaires are issued to the students at the end of each course. The views of students provide effective evaluations of the content, course formats and teaching methods.

The accessibility of different programmes and study modes provides an opportunity for people to broaden their knowledge, especially those who are not able to do so through traditional programmes. The University of Latvia therefore fulfils the mission of providing lifelong learning for all people in Latvia. This mission poses a challenge to the traditional understanding of the higher education learning and teaching processes. The E-university of the University of Latvia is an example of good practice. Since 2003, the E-university has offered more than 100 different e-courses for full-time and part-time students. This is a challenge to everyone, especially to some older members of the academic staff. Many teaching staff feel hesitant in this new situation and fear that their work will not be needed by students in the future. It is important to understand, however, that students should experience innovations: they should come into contact not only with new theories but also with the new forms of education.

The process of adult education in the University of Latvia

Adult education in the University of Latvia is governed by the following laws of the Republic and regulations of the University: the Law of Education of the Republic of Latvia, the Law for Higher Educational Establishments, the Law of Vocational Education, the Law of Adult Education, the Concept of Adult Education of the Republic of Latvia, the Constitution of the University of Latvia, the Mission of the University of Latvia and the Concept of the Academic Development of the University of Latvia. The regulations of the European Commission (European Commission, 1998; European Union, 2000) are also very important, especially to predict how the interaction between the labour market and continuing education is likely to develop.

Problems facing the development of education for adults

The following issues concerning adult and continuing education in the University have emerged during the writing of this chapter:

- There is no unified understanding of the questions concerning adult education and lifelong learning within the University;
- Many members of the teaching staff are not yet sufficiently motivated to participate in the development of adult education;
- The University has no unified system for the development of adult education: for example, there are no University-wide systems for publicity, course registration, quality assurance and accreditation. This is true not only within the University of Latvia but for the whole country;
- The content of the existing courses does not always reflect the changes that are currently taking place in the labour market or the changing needs of society more broadly;

- The status of the documents that confirm the award of credit points for adult education courses has not yet been defined; and
- A funding model to encourage faculties and departments to offer adult education courses has not yet been developed.

The University has a number of options from which to choose in becoming more open to Latvian society. These include:

- Enabling adult students to take the full-time academic courses, providing them with personal development planning and allowing them to take the examinations and obtain academic credit;
- Allowing them to take professional and other vocational courses as part of continuing education programmes (with or without certification); and
- Offering general interest courses (for example on foreign languages and psychology).

Some solutions

The University's aims should include not only the provision of opportunities to acquire academic qualifications but also to offer a wide range of educational opportunities for adults, including general interest courses. The University of Latvia should offer modern and flexible study programmes, using ICT and mixed learning models (including, for example, video- and audio-conferencing).

At the present stage of development, the following suggestions are put forward:

- To develop mutual understanding and cooperation in the process of providing and designing programmes using ICT, by organising seminars and workshops for course developers and managers, and producing a database of courses for adults in cooperation with other regional adult education centres, non-profit-making organisations and municipalities;

- To encourage the work of the faculties and departments in order to offer effective, open and flexible continuing education courses, possibly obtaining new ideas from participation in international projects;
- To develop self-funding course structures for these activities, possibly in collaboration with non-profit making organisations;
- To analyse the labour market in order to respond more effectively to its needs and to involve potential students in future decision making; and
- To improve the content, design and implementation of courses. This can be done, in particular, by:
  - Using ICT and mixed learning environments;
  - Cooperating with the best specialists and practitioners from elsewhere in order to produce programmes that meet the needs both of the target groups and of the labour market;
  - Increasing the distance learning provision as the most effective open and flexible study mode;
  - Creating a favourable study environment and an effective support system for students and teaching staff; and
  - Establishing a quality assurance system for the evaluation of courses. This needs to provide the stimulus to ensure consistent quality throughout the life of each programme and to ensure an effective learning experience for all students.

Examples of good practice using distance learning in Latvia

Distance learning using ICT can be considered as a development of the correspondence education that was widely available, and well liked, in Latvia in the 1960s and 1970s. Unfortunately there is no information on how many people used this system but it was certainly very popular amongst the adults who needed to combine their studies with their jobs. Practically all academic programmes were available using correspondence education. For various reasons its prestige was low, however, since people thought that high quality education required face-to-face communication, mainly through boring lectures. Nevertheless, for many people it offered the only opportunity to continue their education, combining study with their working and family lives.

The worldwide development of ICT offers Latvia the possibility of participating in this new era. Why does Latvia, which is a small country, need distance learning? The reason is that many people are not able to undertake full-time studies because of their personal circumstances. The main groups who should be targeted to undertake distance education are:

- Adults who are very busy because of their job activities;
- Unemployed people;
- Young people without previous experience; and
- Disabled and other disadvantaged people.

The successful application of distance education depends on the level of computerisation of the country and the level of skills that people have to work with what is, for many of them, a new system.

Latvia has recently experienced remarkable growth in the IT service sector. The software industry in Latvia in 2001 had an annual turnover of 28 million euros, with an annual growth rate of 150%. Generally the country's IT service sector is well supported by related business services which include front and back office operations, customer care centres, billing, Web-design, testing and localisation services. Globalisation has created exciting new opportunities in the field of information technology, opening new markets, clearing the way for new investment possibilities and providing worldwide access to skilled IT professionals.

Latvia has the highest percentage of IT students in central Europe and an extremely high computer literacy rate. (See Figure 3. This shows actual figures for 1999 and 2000 and forecast figures thereafter.) More than 90% of all people aged 15–30 are computer literate.

Figure 3: Number of IT university students in Latvia.

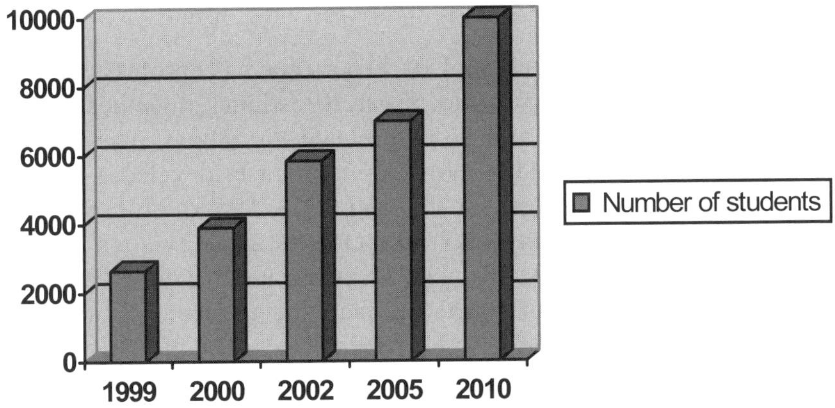

The Latvian government is actively encouraging foreign investment in the IT sector in order to make it a powerful exporter of software services and to promote it as a favoured location for high-technology industries. The country offers a wide range of opportunities to the IT investor, particularly in:

- Software development outsourcing;
- High-technology manufacturing and assembly;
- Development and hosting of e-commerce and Internet-based solutions; and
- Call centres and telemarketing.

It provides substantial competitive advantages to the IT investor, based on the following factors:

- Availability of skilled IT professionals;
- Relatively low cost of these professionals;
- High educational standards;
- Advanced systems and software engineering traditions;
- Well-developed communications and logistics infrastructure;
- Strategic geographic location and a Western-style culture; and
- Foreign language skills.

There is a significant pool of experienced IT professionals in Latvia today, particularly in the research institutes, together with a large number of graduates in IT and related disciplines. The Latvian government has made a long-term commitment to develop a pool of IT specialists. In the budget for the year 2000, for example, the government increased funding for IT education by 20%. This is expected to translate into a significant increase in the number of IT students from the current level of 5,500. In fact, the number of first year university students enrolled in IT programmes has grown by 33% from 1999 to 2000 and the number of graduating IT students is expected to triple over the next three years.

Higher education in computer-related fields is provided by:

- The University of Latvia;
- Riga Technical University;
- Regional Universities in Daugavpils, Rezekne, Liepaja, Ventspils, Valmiera;
- Riga International College of Business Administration, which is now offering professional training for future e-commerce managers; and
- The Stockholm School of Economics in Riga, which offers business administration courses in English, taught by Western-educated professors.

Software companies such as Lotus, Oracle, Novell, and Microsoft also offer IT training programmes and IBM has sponsored a computer course at the University of Latvia.

A high level of foreign language skills is another outstanding feature of Latvia's educational system. Although the country's official language is Latvian, about 25% of the population speak at least three languages. This is particularly relevant for IT functions such as call centres and telemarketing. There is clearly a good basis for using modern technologies at all stages of education in Latvia.

The main problem is to define the most effective kind of IT for adult education. Taking into account the country's present circumstances (including the economic situation in Latvia and the psychological preparedness of the students and teaching staff), the most effective tools could be the following:

- Telephones;
- Audio and video materials;
- Computer-based learning programmes;
- CD-ROMs;
- Internet-based resources;
- Internet-based communication tools (including e-mails and chat lines); and
- Web-based interactive learning materials and learning platforms.

The role of virtual training organisations in adult education is currently a matter of debate. The author's view is that, at the moment, most Latvians are not yet ready for virtual courses and virtual student management services and tools. The additional face-to-face communication is still very important for them. This view comes from a theoretical review of the situation. There are also practical indications that the use of IT tools in adult education in Latvia can lead to difficulties.

Premises and equipment are two of the most important factors in the process of using distance learning in Latvia, especially in the countryside. There are well-equipped study centres only in the largest cities; people in small towns are not able to use modern technology in their studies. In the academic year 2002/03, correspondence education students in the University of Latvia were surveyed by questionnaire. The responses showed that only one of 60 students had a personal computer at home and only two students were able to use e-mail when studying in the country. The experience in other universities may, however, be different.

The University of Latvia has some experience of distance learning for adults. The first courses, on Baltic Studies, were mounted in 2002/03 in collaboration with colleagues from the Universities of Tartu (Estonia), Vilnius (Lithuania) and Turku (Finland). To support these courses, a Website and written material were produced and audio-conferencing and face-to-face tutorials were established. All the teaching materials in this case were created specifically for these courses and had not been used on full-time courses previously.

At the end of the courses a number of common advantages and disadvantages of the use of ICT were identified:

Advantages	Disadvantages
The courses gave the opportunity to:	*However:*
Study specially created courses that were not part of the traditional university programmes;	These courses were not acceptable to all students and lecturers. Not all students were sufficiently motivated to study effectively using these methods;
Learn independently at times that were suitable for the students;	Some students and tutors were weak in the use of the foreign languages needed;
Use the English language in real situations;	Some students lacked the skills required to use ICT effectively;
Learn the culture of communication in the different countries (cross-cultural education);	Some students were not used to working either independently or in teams. They lacked the necessary learning skills;

Advantages	Disadvantages
The courses gave the opportunity to:	*However:*
Work in teams (and develop social skills while doing so);	Some academic staff were prejudiced against the use of ICT (sometimes because they lacked the necessary skills to use it);
Use new non-traditional methods;	Some academic staff were also not sufficiently experienced as tutors or in the preparation of study materials;
Enable academic staff to develop skills in the use of ICT. From the point of view of the tutors, they gained experience of a new university role.	There was insufficient student support, especially a lack of learning materials and of highly motivated tutors.

In cooperation with the Distance Learning Centre of Latvia, a ‘Handbook of Distance Learning’ and a ‘Handbook for Tutors’ were prepared (Ivanova *et al.*, 1999; Kristovska, 2000). These have been issued to help teaching staff who are creating new learning materials and learning environments.

Because of their likely future importance, it is considered necessary to train future schoolteachers to use distance learning techniques. The course ‘Distance learning and its future development in Latvia’ is therefore offered to all students as an optional unit in the University of Latvia’s Faculty of Education and Psychology.

Conclusion

Universities, other higher education establishments and adult education institutions must share the responsibility with the Ministry of Education, the Ministry of Welfare and the municipalities to work together in the field of adult education. The existing legislation will be implemented more effectively if the existing financial sources are used more rationally.

Higher education institutions (HEIs) have many opportunities to carry out research in the field of adult education but these possibilities are currently not fully exploited. For example, students working on bachelors, masters and doctoral theses on the problems of adult education could be of great help for the development of adult education.

The social non-governmental organisations such as adult education associations, the Association of Virtual Education and the Association of Teachers and University Staff could also play a valuable part in the organisation of adult education. Furthermore, HEIs have to become more active in taking part in international projects to gain experience and to raise the funds to help the citizens to help reduce course fees for adult students.

It is necessary to point out that Latvia's HEIs already have sufficient resources to educate the specialists needed to create the infrastructure for adult education throughout the country. It is, however, necessary to improve the flow of information on adult education, especially to those living outside the main towns and to the municipalities and adult education centres.

All these proposals support the development of adult education in Latvia. It will be possible to achieve them, however, only with the combined efforts of HEIs, the government, non-governmental organisations and business enterprises. The deeper involvement of HEIs will benefit the people of Latvia; in turn, their personal development will enable them to compete even more successfully in the labour market of Europe.

References

European Commission, 1998. Teaching and Learning: Towards the Learning Society. (*Eiropas komisijas 'Baltā grāmata par izglītību un apmācību: Mācīšana un mācīšanās-ceļi uz izglītotu sabiedrību'*). Riga: APA.

European Union, 2000. *Memorandum on Lifelong Learning*. Commission Staff Working Papers. SEC (2000) 1832. Brussels: Commission of the European Communities.

Ivanova, I., Kristovska, I. and Slaidiņš, I., 1999. Handbook for Tutors. (*Tālmācības konsultanta rokasgrāmata*). Riga: Mācību apgāds.

Kristovska I., 2000. Handbook of Distance Learning. (*Tālmācības konsultanta rokasgrāmata*). Riga: Mācību apgāds.

Useful Websites

Ministry of Education and Science, Republic of Latvia: http://www.izm.lv

University of Latvia: http://www.lu.lv

DAIVA DUMČIUVIENĖ, MARIUS MIKULĖNAS AND
DANGUOLĖ RUTKAUSKIENĖ

14: Adults in Lithuanian Higher Education

Introduction

Lithuania has a population of approximately 3.8 million people, made up of Lithuanians (80%), Russians (9%), Poles (7%), and other nationalities (4%). The capital city is Vilnius, which has approximately 600,000 inhabitants. There are four other large urban conurbations: Kaunas (430,000), Klaipeda (208,000), Siauliai (150,000), and Panevezys (130,0000). Approximately 69% of the population live in urban areas and 31% in rural areas. The official language is Lithuanian. Students at the primary and secondary schools and at the gymnasiums may choose to learn English, German, French or Russian as a foreign language.

The present-day educational system in Lithuania has several branches: pre-school education, school education, junior college training, higher education (HE) and adult education. In this chapter we examine higher and adult education in Lithuania taking into account the recent reform of the education system.

Higher Education

Lithuania's HE institutions consist of two types; universities and colleges. To be educated to the bachelors degree level currently requires the completion of four or five years of undergraduate studies in an HE institution. After completing a bachelors programme, it is possible to proceed to a specialized professional or to a masters programme in a university lasting one-and-a-half to two years. Doctoral studies are completed over four years, with one-and-a-half to two years devoted to preparing for doctoral examinations. To be awarded a doctoral degree, candidates must prepare and publicly defend a doctoral thesis.

Adult Education

Adult education in Lithuania is characterised by the need for accessibility, openness in time and place and in the learning and teaching methodologies used. Adult education is influenced by overriding principles which are defined in the education policy. These are (Beresnevičienė, 1997):

- Equality in education: learning opportunities should be accessible to adults at all levels;
- Permanent lifetime learning: flexible and available both at work and in the individual's free time;
- Openness to society; and
- Oriented towards the needs of the individual: the goals and content of education are determined by the need for self-improvement which will enable the individual to adapt to a new social order in a changing world.

Reform of the Education System in Lithuania

Educational reform in Lithuania started in 1988, when the establishment of national schools was announced. Attention was focused on three areas: general education, higher education and vocational education and training. The following laws have since been passed in the Parliament (*Seimas*):

- The Law on Science, February 1991;
- The Law on Education, June 1991; and
- The Law on Vocational Education and Training, October 1997.

The Lithuanian Law on Education sets the following main goals for the educational system:

- To develop people's spiritual and physical powers, to lay a firm foundation for morality and a healthy way of life, to educate the intellect, and to create the necessary conditions for developing individuality;
- To provide general and vocational training which complies with the present level of science and culture for the young;
- To provide adult education for every Lithuanian;
- To instil a sense of citizenship, individual rights and duties to family, nation, society, and the Lithuanian State and to encourage participation in the cultural, public, economic, and political life of Lithuania; and
- To ensure the same rights and conditions for members of religious communities as for everyone else, including the right to educate their children at educational institutions according to their beliefs.

In the first stage the different types of school were developed and institutions that administer education (i.e. the Ministry of Education and the education departments of municipalities) were reorganized. Later the reform of vocational schools and colleges began and the university system was reorganized.

Non-formal adult education

The Law of Non-formal Adult Education of the Lithuanian Republic was issued in 1998. This regulates the system of non-formal adult education and lays down the basic principles of the structure, operation, and management of the system. The aim of the Law is to (*Lietuvos Respublikos*, 1998):

- Provide guarantees to the participants and providers of non-formal adult education and the social partners;

- Assist individuals in exercising their inherent right to life-long development;
- Ensure that individuals have the opportunity to acquire the knowledge and skills needed to be both a citizen of a democratic society and a qualified specialist; and
- Facilitate creative and meaningful recreation.

Non-formal adult education is defined as the learning, development or studies appropriate for personal and/or social development. Certificates awarded following this form of education are not recognized by the State. Accreditation in the non-formal adult education sector is recognized however by employers, employers' organisations and the unions.

The principal tasks of non-formal adult education formulated in this Law are to:

- Help individuals develop their cultural interests;
- Raise their creative powers and abilities;
- Help them to become active citizens of a democratic society; and
- Enable them to gain the theoretical knowledge and practical skills necessary for vocational work.

The Law introduced new rights for the participants of non-formal adult education:

- It is obligatory to sign a contract between the non-formal education provider and the customer if a fee is charged; and
- The customers of non-formal education have a right to paid leave of absence from work to meet their educational needs when this is agreed between them and their employers.

Non-formal vocational adult education is becoming widespread in modern-day Lithuania. The need to adapt continually to changes at work and the possibility of having to change one's profession during a lifetime is recognized more than ever before. One of the reasons for this is a rapidly changing job market in the country. Economic and social changes mean that there is continual change in the labour force. The relatively recent change to a market economy brought with it additional demands on the workforce and, for the Government, the problem of educating the unemployed who resulted.

A unified permanent system of Lithuanian education, which includes both formal and informal education and state and private educational institutions, has now emerged. Reform is characterised by change in all the elements of the educational system. These include policy goals, structures, curricula, teaching methods, processes, management structures, teacher training and qualifications.

In Lithuania the education system defines adult education as a major part of the permanent education system, for people who are over the age of 18 and not engaged in the initial education system (i.e. in schools). It is also characterised by its voluntary nature and by specific training methodologies (Beresnevičienė, 1994).

The political, economic, and social changes in Lithuania which began in 1990, have had a major impact in the field of adult education. Between 1992 and 1993 the foundations for the development of adult education were laid with the establishment of adult education units within various bodies such as the Ministry of Education and Science, the Ministry for Social Protection and Labour, the Institute of Pedagogy, and the Lithuanian In-service Teacher Training Institute.

This view of Lithuanian adult education is characteristic of a modern adult education system currently under construction. The existing adult education system is being transformed to take account of worldwide cultural and educational developments while retaining the national traditions.

The Ministry of Education and Science in Lithuania described the priorities of the second phase of Educational Reform in Lithuania in 1999 as:

- The need to modernise and develop the quality of education and study programmes;
- The need to improve the social and educational foundation for learning and studying; and
- The need for harmonisation of the educational system.

The priorities for this harmonisation of the whole of the education system, including adult education, are to:

- Develop a continuous system of education;
- Organise educational institutions:
- Develop democratic management models; and
- Develop information systems appropriate to self-governing bodies within educational institutions.

As stated earlier, the education of adults embraces both the formal and non-formal provision. The non-formal sector includes both cultural education and the development and improvement of the knowledge and skills necessary for work. This sector is also called 'popular adult education' (*populiarusis suaugusiųjų švietimas*) and promotes personal development, including the development of creativity, initiative and social responsibility (Beresnevičienė, 1994).

Formal education includes general education, vocational, college and (parts of) university education which are regulated and managed by the State or other authorised institutions. Vocational education and training is concentrated in vocational schools, colleges and training centres. While there are no special departments in vocational schools for adults, colleges have separate adult education departments, usually providing distance education.

The universities have also developed a new in-service training infrastructure which is organised through university faculties, adult education centres and business training centres.

In Lithuania, HE is provided by twenty-six higher education institutions, fifteen state universities, four private universities, four non-university state institutions and three non-university private institutions. The cities of Vilnius and Kaunas are the principal HE centres. Although the Government subsidises the universities, the universities also charge fees. Scholarships and bursaries are also available for individual students.

Government financing of adult education

The Government currently provides all the financial support for non-formal adult education (including special projects, development programmes and research into adult education). Adult education generally is financed by the State, by municipalities, employers, sponsors, and by the trainees themselves. The training of trainers for adult education is a high priority, as well as is the development of centres where non-formal adult education activities can take place.

State funding ensures that general education is accessible to all. State support for adult education is provided by the following means:

- Direct funding of educational bodies;
- Financing state, municipal, individual and group educational projects and programmes;
- Granting favourable leases on state-owned premises;
- Supporting education through the tax system;
- Giving full or partial coverage of education-linked expenses incurred by socially vulnerable people;
- Supporting participants in adult education through grants;
- Granting free access to information and publications in state-funded libraries; and
- Funding research on adult education needs.

Adult education can also be financed from municipal budgets in the manner prescribed by the Government or its authorised institutions. Up to 3% of the salary budgets of state and municipally financed institutions can be used to finance the in-service training or re-qualification of state and municipal officials. Non-formal adult education programmes and special projects commissioned by the municipalities are also funded from municipality budgets. Non-formal education of individuals and groups eligible for social support are financed by the State.

The Ministry of Education and Science has licensed 90 institutions to offer non-formal studies. About 700 institutions are listed in the Register of the Ministry of Economics for adults and others. These include 63 state-owned companies, 288 joint-stock companies, 271 individual companies and 46 foreign investment companies. In addition, special departments for adult training have been set up in the universities. The courses offered here include training and retraining, particularly in the fields of pedagogy, psychology, and special education (*Kultūra, spauda, sportas*, 1998).

The changes in the educational system and the need of employers to sustain the competency of their workers provides ever-increasing opportunities for the development of adult education in Lithuania.

The development of adult education is also linked to Lithuania's membership of the European Union (EU). The main goals and objectives of adult education in the EU countries are formulated in joint projects such as the EU Phare, Leonardo da Vinci and Socrates programmes. Lithuania has become an active participant in these projects. This means that it will have the same strategy for the development of adult education as other EU countries.

Further possibilities for taking university courses were created using distance education. This widens the participation of adults in different age groups who have different aims: to get a diploma, or to be retrained or to develop a professional qualification.

Case Study 1. Adult Education in Small- and Medium-sized Enterprises

Provided by the Association of Adult Education of Lithuania

More than 100 managers and 400 employees were interviewed for this study which was carried out in 1998. This was not a representative sample but the results nevertheless give some useful indications. Adult education was defined to the respondents as 'qualification improvement' and included provision made by the institutions of higher education.

The results indicate that 55.4% of the respondent employees had improved their qualifications during the previous two years, 51% of heads of enterprises had information about learning in similar enterprises and 89.9% of these heads knew where their workers could retrain. The view in Lithuania is that enterprises still do not have sufficient access to adult training and qualification improvement. However, 46.9% of the company heads evaluated the training possibilities of their enterprises positively; of the employees who had improved their qualifications, 66.8% indicated that their employer was the main source of funding for their courses.

The responses of the managers to the question on the participation in programmes to improve qualification are given in the following Table:

	%
1. Practically all the employees in the company	16.3
2. Approximately half of them	30.6
3. Minority	43.9
4. It is hard to say	2.0
5. Nobody has had this opportunity yet	4.1
6. Other responses	3.1

Source: Kvalifikacijos tobulinimo situacija smulkaus ir vidutinio verslo įmonėse, 1998.

Responses of employees to the question 'Have you improved your qualification during the previous two years?' were: Yes, 55.4%; No, 44.6%.

The managers were asked whether they had the necessary information concerning adult education. The majority of them (89.8%) knew which teaching institutions provided this. The problem was clearly not one of the quantity of information available but rather of its transmission from the source of the information to the employees (Osauskas, 1999).

When asked how much they knew about qualification improvement in their companies, the responses of the employees were:

	%
1. A good deal	24.4
2. Some, but not too much	30.6
3. Very little	19.7
4. Hard to say	13.0
5. Have heard nothing yet	11.3
6. Other responses	1.0

It is seen that a good many employees here (44%, if one sums responses 3, 4 and 5) have very little, if any, information about the possibilities for improving their qualifications.

Financing adult education

In the sample, 46.9% of the managers reported that their companies would provide financial support for adult education. Problems were found, however, in the provision of this support. The responses showed that qualification improvement is not yet an integral part of most company policies. Only a minority of company managers (20.6%) reported that they had a qualification improvement plan.

Learning applicability is very important in Lithuania since the practical application of the knowledge acquired strongly influences employees' proficiency. Only 33.3% of the employees who participated in qualification improvement courses were completely satisfied by the applicability of the knowledge they had acquired, 60.6% were partially satisfied, 0.5% were dissatisfied and 5.1% found the question difficult to answer (*Pranešimas apie profesinio*, 1998).

Problems for adult education can also be predicted for the future. This is how employees saw their future prospects for improving their qualifications:

	%
1. I am planning to improve my qualification this year	13.6
2. I expect some possibilities in 2–3 years	22.9
3. It would be fine but I am not planning it at the moment	38.3
4. It is hard to say	20.1
5. Other responses	5.1

The sum of the last three responses in this Table indicates that the majority of employees (63.5%) have no definite plans to take part in adult education.

In interpreting the above figures, certain peculiarities of the Lithuanian socio-cultural context should be considered, including the State policy, the law regulating adult education in companies, tax policy, the attention paid by government institutions to adult education generally, and the law on non-formal adult education. Managers who are interested in quick profits pay little attention to the long-term vocational needs of their employees.

The data also show that there are no serious initiatives by the trades unions to support adult education. In addition, it is important to consider the mentality of the Lithuanian population. Many of them expect direct help from the State; they are not self-confident and they do not have a clear understanding of the need to learn.

The responses to the questioning in this investigation showed an increase in the number of people who understood the new requirements of their workplaces. This was especially so for young people (up to the age of 30). Attitudes change slowly, however, and it is not surprising that the survey does not predict a rapid expansion in the demand for adult education.

Case Study 2. Adult Education Provision at Kaunas University of Technology

Marius Mikulėnas

Since the move from the former education model to the European model, as required both by the Law on Research and Higher Education, 1991 and the application of the total quality system ISO 9001 to research at Kaunas University of Technology (KTU), the attention of the KTU leaders has focussed on the improvement of its adult education and particularly on the model that is used.

Prior to 1991 a single faculty within the university, the Specialist Training Faculty (*Specialistų tobulinimosi fakultetas*) focused on the professional development of a range of occupations. As this range grew, however, it became increasingly difficult for this faculty to provide the appropriate level of specialization in all the required fields. For this reason, the university decided to create a new Professional Development Centre (*Profesinio tobulinimosi centras*).

An even greater impact on the University, however, arose from a second management decision: to remove the administrative barriers to the establishment of new training units, focussed either on teaching methods (including technology-based methods, for example for distance education) or on a customer target group (for example the Municipal Training Centre which provides training for administrators in public institutions). These all provide training for people who are already working.

After 1991, a new model began to evolve and since then a large programme of adult education courses has been established in the University. Most of these are now delivered regularly. It was also common for many KTU professors to work on a contract basis for private training institutions. This tradition continues today since KTU professors are seen as top-level professional lecturers in the Lithuanian market. For example, more than half the lecturers of the International School of Management[1] came from KTU. Even the School itself is a spin-off from the former KTU Business Training Centre following a decision in Norway in 1999 to invest heavily in Lithuania.

In KTU there are 14 faculties with a number of faculty-level adult education units (centres, departments, institutes and laboratories), 11 university-level institutes and 27 university-level research and training centers. (For more information, see http://www.ktu.lt). The adult education units provide training in many areas: for example in business management, public administration, information and communication technologies, environmental protection, management and chemical engineering. There are a number of active adult education providers in each faculty of the university. The great majority of these focus on the local market in Lithuania. Some also provide courses in English; for example, the Distance Education Centre co-operates with the Environmental Engineering Institute to deliver training in English in Zimbabwe.

There are now more than 200 courses, modules and programmes for adults available at KTU. Some examples of popular course for adults include short courses and seminars of a few days' duration on managerial and technological subjects. A two-year Executive MBA Programme for top and mid-level managers is also offered.

In April 2002, a new phase of improvement of adult education began with the formation of a liaison unit with the mission of expanding and developing partnerships with external organisations and the alumni. This unit started by listing and evaluating the current courses, modules and programmes which compete in the open Lithuanian market. It now helps all the providers in the University to acquire contracts.

Today there is also an Adult Education group within the Corporate Relations Office. This has four functions:

- To prepare and upgrade the catalogue of adult education courses, modules and programmes;

1 The International School of Management is a branch of the Business Institute which has its headquarters in Norway. It is the first private HE non-university institution in Lithuania.

- To disseminate information about KTU to external organizations;
- To collect requests for, and assist providers of, adult education at KTU; and
- To organize the annual *Contacts for Adult Education* event. This aims to build further links between KTU and its community.

Another part of the university which participates in organizing adult education is the Office of Academic Affairs. The functions of this institution include the assurance of study quality, the preparation and granting of certificates and the preparation of an adult education catalogue.

At the time of writing, KTU's management is preparing a further stage of adult education improvement with the aim of moving into e-learning for adults, so realising more of KTU's potential in this field. The University is also expecting to develop further adult education projects in the fields of technology, management, sociology, education and science.

Case Study 3. The development of open and distance learning in Lithuania

Provided by Danguolė Rutkauskienė

The 'Development of Distance Education' project has made a significant contribution to the development of open and distance learning (ODL) in Lithuania. A total of thirteen universities and colleges from eight Lithuanian cities were involved in its implementation. The project ran from 1998 to 2003 and during this time it created an infrastructure for the development of distance learning. The student target groups of the project included:

- Full-time students;
- Part-time students;
- Teachers improving their pedagogical and vocational qualifications;
- Local government staff gaining vocational skills in administration;
- Specialists from other fields improving their professional skills or seeking to re-qualify; and
- Unemployed adults seeking to improve their qualifications.

In the future, the project will be expanded to include other target groups such as school children and the staffs of state and private enterprises.

A total of twenty-one remote classrooms were established, supported by three teaching video studios located at the Distance Education Centres at Kaunas University of Technology, Vilnius University and Vilnius Gediminas Technical University. The Kaunas Videoconference Studio is connected to the World Bank Global Development Learning Network.

Much of the teaching and learning is based around videoconferencing and other teaching material such as videotapes and output from document cameras can also be included. Multimedia projection systems allow students to see shared application windows and video windows in remote classrooms that switch automatically to voice-activated remote sites.

Open and distance learning and higher education

Universities are increasingly being asked to provide knowledge-based services for their regions and for society as a whole. In Lithuania, this challenge has been taken up. By using ODL, the universities have provided new opportunities for more flexible study and this enables students to use their time more effectively.

Kaunas University of Technology (KTU), located in the second city of Lithuania, provides a good example of how a university can use advanced computing and other technology to promote access to university courses for adult students using ODL. The project has shown that, in order to establish an ODL system, a number of steps must first be taken. These include:

- Establishing a system of professional development for organisers and teachers of ODL programmes;
- Encouraging the development of ODL programmes and independant modules;
- Devising procedures for the evaluation and quality assurance of ODL;
- Developing support systems for the participants;
- Developing a computer network and other means of telecommunication adjusted to distance education;
- Establishing a legal framework for ODL; and
- Developing effective funding mechanisms.

Open and distance learning at Kaunas Technical University

Since the late 1990s, KTU has worked closely with other educational institutions and with representatives from Chambers of Commerce, Industry and Crafts, and the Municipality of Kaunas in the development of ODL. The main aims of these partnerships are not only to train local government and other officials but also to raise the interest of the partners more generally in ODL. It is important that they should understand the benefits that individualised continuing training using information and communication technology (ICT) can bring.

Kaunas Technical University is developing a step-by-step approach using current ODL courses and is seeking ways to develop other courses using national and international funding. Open and distance learning has been developed both for single modules and for diplomas. In doing this, KTU has accumulated a great deal of experience in providing Web-based and videoconferencing courses. One of its major tasks has been to create the infrastructure for the delivery of courses and involving teachers in ODL course development and delivery. The University has encouraged its staff to transfer their traditional course modules to an ODL format.

At the same time, the University is developing a strategy for becoming an e-university with an E-studies Council working to establish a policy for organizing and implementing e-learning. This strategy will allow ODL to develop in two directions: through traditional university studies; and through continuing professional training (CPT). At the time of writing, there are two ODL programmes (a masters course and a CPT programme) delivered via videoconferencing and a number of other courses are being planned. The KTU strategy is to develop full ODL study programmes as well as to modernise full-time studies using e-learning. The most important objectives for the development of ODL currently at KTU are the following:

- To determine the priorities for e-studies at the University;
- To identify and prioritise the potential consumer groups;
- To create a database of technical and other information on ODL as a subject;
- To create an approval and certification system for e-study;
- To ensure the quality of the e-study educational material together with overall quality assurance;
- To ensure that there is career progression for the programmers;
- To establish mechanisms to enable the work of e-study organizers and teachers to be recognised;
- To develop a system to encourage teachers to contribute to the development of e-learning courses; and
- To carry out research into ODL as a subject.

E-university development

The main guidelines for e-studies at KTU were developed from European Union funded research which foresees four priority areas for e-learning development. These are:

- Infrastructure and equipment;
- E-learning and support;

- Quality of service; and
- Opportunities for European cooperation.

The University has used a step-by-step approach to achieve these objectives:

- To use information and communication technologies more effectively as *tools* for teaching and learning;
- To promote the application of ODL *elements* in the delivery of traditional study to support individuals, to develop the necessary ICT skills among teachers, and to prepare them to create and deliver ODL modules;
- To promote the development of new *modules* using ODL, as well as the adaptation of existing modules for distance study;
- To promote the creation of ODL *study programmes* to develop university staff;
- To accredit ODL modules with the professional bodies leading to improved *professional qualifications*;
- To *apply ODL* in continuing education; and
- To promote the creation of *independent ODL courses* as well as modules for programmes leading to qualifications.

In future it will be necessary to stimulate scientific research to support the development of new training modules. Issues which need to be examined include the influence of ICT on learning skills, student-oriented educational tools and the social impact of ICT. Interdisciplinary research will also be needed to underpin a vision for the e-university.

The Board of E-studies has highlighted the following key issues for the development of an e-university:

- Procedures for e-studies at university;
- Target groups for e-studies;
- The technical and information base for e-studies;
- Developing and approving e-studies programmes;
- E-studies material development and publication;

- Delivering e-studies programmes;
- E-studies quality assurance;
- Procedures for handing e-studies graduation;
- Salary and payment for e-studies coordinators and teachers;
- Research into e-studies as a subject; and
- Teacher motivation.

Key tasks for the development of university open and distance learning

The KTU Rector, the Senate and the whole academic community have agreed the following conditions for the development of e-learning:

- The establishment of a Board to oversee the implementation of an e-university;
- The preparation of a programme for university ODL development;
- The dissemination of information about ODL to students, teachers and others by:
  - Increasing the number of channels for the dissemination of information about ODL; and
  - Encouraging the exchange of good practice concerning ODL throughout the University;
- The raising of the professional ODL skills of university teachers and managers by:
  - Organising seminars, conferences, and synchronous and asynchronous discussions;
  - Encouraging university teachers to participate in research programmes on e-learning;
  - Developing modules on 'Basics of ODL' and 'Introduction to Distance Education' to improve teachers' qualifications through CPT; and
  - Developing a support system for university teacher training in ODL course development and delivery;
- The creation of a system for teacher motivation to participate in ODL development by:
  - Funding teachers to develop ODL courses;

  - Developing an ODL course in curriculum preparation;
  - Evaluating the ODL elements used in traditional study modules;
  - Legitimizing ODL study as an alternative form of university study; and
  - Introducing a system for ODL course accreditation by:
    - Forming a group of ODL programme experts; and
    - Approving only courses which have ODL expert approval;
- The establishment of a technical base for software and ICT and the improvement of access to this information using the Internet;
- The integration of university ODL into the global education market and the development of an international orientation; and
- The development of a legal basis for ODL.

Kaunas University of Technology staff training

The KTU Distance Education Centre (DEC) is undertaking some of the teacher training required and is also responsible for raising its staff's competence in ODL. This has been done by developing training modules. Teachers are charged only a low fee to attend and the courses have recently also been delivered for teachers from other higher education institutions. Both face-to-face training and Web-based and videoconferencing methods are used.[2] Teachers who complete these modules successfully are competent to start preparing ODL courses and ongoing professional support is also made available to them.

WebCT is used as the platform for the Web-based courses and Macromedia and Tool Book software are used for the creation of CD-based courses. Printed materials, videotapes and audiocassettes can also

2 More details about the network are available at: http://www.liedm.lt[.] A list of courses open to teachers can also be found on this Website and potential students can register there.

be used to support courses when required. A course development kit is currently being developed, aimed at improving the development process, particularly for teachers whose computer skills are weak. The KTU DEC staff coordinate the registration of students on these courses.

To encourage teachers to participate in ODL course development, the University has organized competitions. The winners here receive additional financial and technical support and they also benefit from help with ODL methodology and IT consultations. The evaluation of these competitions is carried out following set criteria. These include the assessment of how well the proposed course addresses the needs of part-time students and the likely number of students who will use the proposed ODL course. Funding for ODL development is a priority within the University.

Kaunas University of Technology sees a huge potential in the use of the new medium of ODL. Lithuanian students have a positive attitude towards technology-enhanced learning and there are increasing opportunities to use ICT in continuing education studies. Such is the size of the problem, however, that it will only be possible to meet these needs through ongoing collaboration with other universities, government institutions and business enterprises in the creative process of ODL.

References

Beresnevičienė, D., 1994. Adult education in former Eastern Europe: Lithuania. *Life and Education in Finland (LEIF*), 3, 61–3.

Beresnevičienė D., 1997. Adult Education in Lithuania: The Context of Central and Eastern Europe. *Adult Education Research Exchange*, Bulletin for Central and Eastern European and the Baltic Countries, 2, 11–12.

Kultūra, spauda, sportas, 1998 (Culture, the press, sport). Vilnius: Statistikos Departamentas.

Kvalifikacijos tobulinimo situacija smulkaus ir vidutinio verslo įmonėse. (Qualification development in small- and medium-sized enterprises), 1998. Ataskaita.

Lietuvos Respublikos neformaliojo suaugusiųjų švietimo įstatymas. (Lithuanian Republic Informal Adult Education Law), 1998. Valstybės žinios Nr. 66–1909.

Osauskas R., 1999. *Jonavos rajono profesinių mokyklų absolventų įsidarbinimo galimybių darbo rinkoje tyrimas.* (Employment opportunities for graduates of professional schools in the Jonava region). Vytautas Magnus University (magistro tezės).

Pranešimas apie profesinio rengimo sistemą Lietuvoje socialiniame-ekonominiame kontekste. (The social and economic context of the professional development system), 1998. Vilnius: Profesinio mokymo informacinė tarnyba. (Professional development information agency).

Useful Websites

Adult Education in Lithuania: http://www.vsy.fi/evk/material/baltlit.html

Association of Adult Education in Lithuania: http://www.andras.ee/issue/zemaitaityte.htm

Association of Adult Education in Lithuania: Publications: http://www.andras.ee/papers/tadas.html

Distance Education in Lithuania: http://www.liedm.lt

Graduate Programmes: http://www.euroeducation.net/prof/lithuaco.htm

Kaunas Regional Distance Education Centre: http://distance.ktu.lt

Kaunas University of Technology: http://www.ktu.lt

Learning in Lithuania: http://cwr.utoronto.ca/Cultural/english/lithuania/learning.html

Ministry of Education and Science: http://www.smm.lt/en/
National Distance Education Association: http://www.ndma.lt
Non-formal Adult Education in Lithuania: http://www.andras.ee/issue/zemaitaityte.htm

DIMTCHO TOURDANOV

15: Adults in Polish Higher Education

Introduction

The recent development of adult education (*kształcenie dorosłych*) in Polish universities has been closely linked to the transition from a socialist to a market-orientated economy which began in the early 1990s. Resulting from the political changes that took place in Poland during this period, every part of society, including the education system, has been reformed. These changes led to the emergence of new attitudes towards education and these, in turn, raised the demand for adult education.

At the same time that the economic changes were taking place, laws were also introduced to guide the educational transition. One of the effects of these was to break the monopoly that the state universities had previously held on higher education; private universities were now also able to provide higher education. Several Government Acts[1] passed by the Parliament during the 1990s laid the foundation

1 The following are the most important Acts setting up the new education system in Poland:
Act on the Education System, 7 September 1991. (*Ustawa z dnia 7.9.1991 o systemie oświaty*);
Act on the School of Higher Education, 12 September 1990. (*Ustawa z dnia 12.9.1990 o szkolnictwie wyższym*);
Act on the Academic Title and Academic Degrees, 12 September 1990. (*Ustawa o stopniach i tytułach naukowych*);
Teachers' Charter Act (with later amendments), 26 January 1982. (*Ustawa z dnia 26.1.1982. Karta Nauczyciela*);
Act on Vocational Higher Education Institutions, 26 June 1997. (*Ustawa z dnia 26.6.1997 o wyższych Szkołach zawodowych*);
Act on Loans and Credits for Students, 17 July 1998. (*Ustawa z dnia 17.8.1998 o pożyczkach i kredytach studenckich*); and

for the development of a flexible, open and market-oriented higher education system suited to the needs of a market economy. The rise of the private universities created new challenges in meeting the demand for higher education, not only from young people seeking degrees but also for continuing education from adults seeking to update their qualifications.

The transition to a market orientated economy in Poland brought with it fundamental changes in the labour market and in professional needs. At the same time the attitudes of adults towards the development of their knowledge, qualifications and skills began to change. New knowledge and modern qualifications became important prerequisites for personal advancement in society and, in particular, in the labour market. As a result, the education of adults has now become an important part of the Polish higher education system. Since 1990, the immense growth of private universities has created a modern basis for providing adult education on a large scale.

This chapter considers the expansion of higher education, particularly for adults, that took place in Poland in the 1990s. The part played by the private universities in this change, and the government control that was established to assure the quality of the teaching, can be seen as examples of large-scale good practice. More recently, the Government has published a strategy to increase adult access to higher education even further and this is considered. Major challenges still remain, however, and these are briefly mentioned at the end. Issues of university continuing education in Poland more broadly have been considered recently by Wiercińska *et al.* (2003).

The Act on the Education System (1991). This defines education as a common good for the whole of society. The Constitution of Poland ensures the right of each citizen to be educated.

The expansion of adult higher education in Poland

A number of factors have led to the rapid development of adult education in Poland. The establishment of a democratic society, together with the shift from a socialist to a market-orientated economy, led to the demand for new knowledge and skills at all levels and in every age group. While the transition to a market economy required workers with different skills and knowledge, the replacement of workers was not an option. A considerable amount of retraining was therefore necessary, not just for those holding key positions but for workers at all levels. Intensive education for working adults of all ages and social backgrounds, especially to update their knowledge and qualifications, had become essential.

The dynamic and radical restructuring of some parts of the economy and of society has meant that many adults have been faced with the choice either of updating their skills or of leaving work. This has been seen, for example, in the teaching profession where the development of new school curricula has brought about major change. A further problem has been the low level of the qualifications of many Polish adults. On the other hand, qualifications, particularly at the diploma level and above,[2] clearly increase the chances of employment and provide career enhancement.

2 Students can generally be divided into two categories according to their aims and the qualifications that they are seeking: the first group contains those who seek new skills and who are working for diplomas; the second group has those studying for certificates. The first group generally contains adults who are updating their qualifications to enable them to continue working in their professions. Part-time and weekend students, who generally have fewer previous qualifications, belong mainly to the second group.

The development of new structures to encourage involvement

In Poland, adult education is now provided both by public and private higher education institutions. The private institutions differ from the public universities in that they are more flexible and open, providing programmes near to adult learners' homes. These establishments meet effectively the needs both of adults who are thinking of starting university study and of those who want to update their skills and qualifications. Private higher education institutions focus mainly on the provision of adult education for those aged 25 years or over. The majority of their courses are part-time and they are generally held in the evenings or at weekends. Some students, usually those under 25 years of age, also attend full-time.

The 1990 Education Act gave wider autonomy to the existing higher education institutions, reducing the State's power to supervise and define their policies. It also made it possible for new private higher education institutions to be established. At the time of writing, more then 200 private universities exist in Poland providing higher education accredited by the Ministry of Education and Sports (*Ministerstwo Edukacji Narodowej i Sportu*). Degrees and diplomas obtained in these establishments have the same value as the qualifications obtained in the public universities.

Figure 1: The growth in the number of universities in Poland (1990–2002). Source: Higher Education Institutions in Poland and their Finances. Central Statistical Office of Poland, 2002.

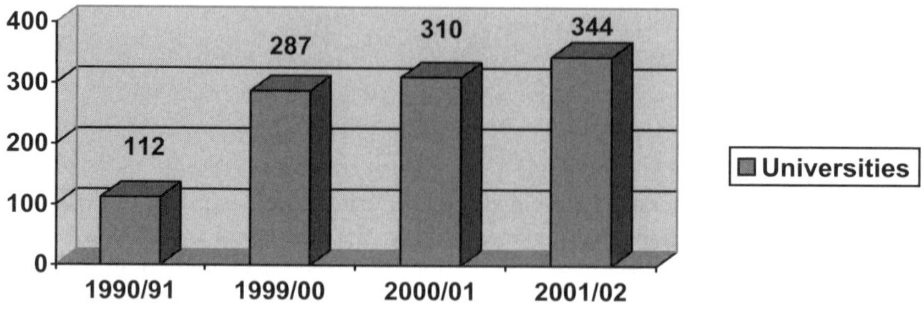

Figure 2: The number of private universities in Poland, 1990–2002. Source: Higher Education Institutions in Poland and their Finances. Central Statistical Office of Poland, 2002.

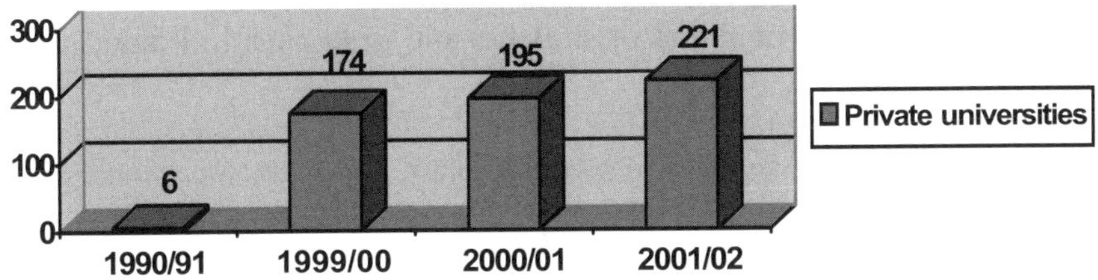

Figure 1 shows the rapid rise in the number of universities following the publication of the Act. It can be seen from Figure 2 that almost all of this growth has taken place in the private sector. Today the private universities provide an opportunity for many more people to pursue higher education. It is seen that, in 2002, 221 (64%) of the 344 universities in the country were private.

The changes that have occurred since the introduction of the new educational system have greatly improved access to education for many adults. A market for higher education courses has been created which reacts to supply and demand and this now regulates the courses offered by the institutions. Most of the private universities offer courses both at the first degree and diploma levels, mainly in management, marketing, finance, banking and accountancy. However, only 23% (51 out of 221) of the private universities are currently able to offer accredited courses at the postgraduate level.

This transformation in the higher education system has also led to an increase in the number of vocational higher education institutions. The first of these was opened in 1998. Their courses last for six terms and, on completion, their students obtain a vocational title, e.g. a licence as an engineer. Students can also be awarded a masters degree after attending supplementary courses for another two or three years. In 2002 some 100,000 students enrolled in vocational higher education institutions in Poland, nearly 6% of the total student number.

The growth of student numbers in Poland since 1990

Figure 3 shows the numbers of students and graduates in Poland from 1990/91 to 2001/02.

Figure 3. Student and graduate numbers in Poland, 1990–2002 (in thousands). Source: Higher Schools and their Finances. Central Statistical Office of Poland, 2002.

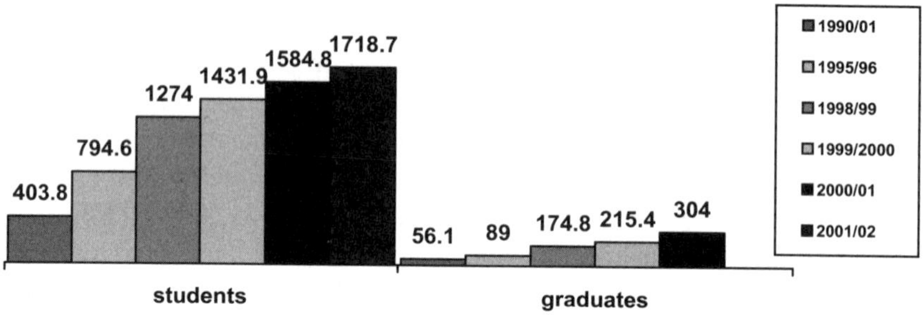

It is seen that the number of students in Polish universities increased by over 400% during the period. It is also clear that the number is still increasing. The figure provides a statistically based picture of the development of the Polish higher education system in the years following 1990. The rapid growth in the total number of students is due mainly to the growth in the number of adult students. The social and economic transition in the country during the last decade has created a quite different situation on the labour market. Requirements and qualification standards have also risen and, in doing so, have increased the pressure on adults. Many adults are affected by this trend and are under pressure to update their knowledge and qualifications in order to improve their position in the labour market. It is this labour market pressure that has produced the enormous growth in the number of adults among Polish students.

Table 1: Total number of university students in Poland 2001.
Source: Higher Schools and their Finances.
Central Statistical Office of Poland, 2002.

Students	Total numbers	Percentage	Doctoral students	Percentages
Part-time	939,458	54.7	6,817	24.1
Full-time	765,273	44.5	21,455	75.9
Distance education	14,016	0.8	–	–
Total	1,718,747	100.0	28,272	100.0

The rise in the number of students is also caused by the increasing number of weekend and part-time students, mainly in the private universities mentioned earlier.

Table 2: Numbers of evening and weekend students in Poland, 2001.
Source: Higher Schools and their Finances.
Central Statistical Office of Poland, 2002.

	Student Numbers			
	Evening students	%	Weekend students	%
Aged 18 and below	236	0.3	937	0.1
Aged 19–20	20,585	24.9	130,342	15.2
Aged 21–22	24,132	29.2	198,290	23.2
Aged 23–24	17,207	20.8	174,905	20.4
Aged 25 and above	20,495	24.8	351,452	41.1
Total	82,655	100.0	855,932	100.0

Organisation of adult education and meeting adult learners' needs

The organisation of Polish private universities is specifically directed to meeting the needs of adult learners, particularly through the flexible mode of delivery that they offer. Many of these universities have been established in smaller cities where there is no public university. The private universities have clearly filled a gap in the market for adult education at a regional level that had not previously been met by the public universities. Even though they must pay fees,[3] many students prefer to study in the private universities in their own regions since this saves the travelling and subsistence costs which they would otherwise have to bear. In this way, private universities play an important social role, establishing an educational infrastructure within the smaller towns and their surrounding regions; these often lag behind the rest of the country in other ways (for example, in their social and economic development).

To assure the quality of their service, the private universities are required to have a licence. An Accreditation Commission (*Państwowa Komisja Akredytacyjna*), set up by the Ministry of Education and Sports, monitors their provision. This body has common rules and standards for both public and private higher education and each private university is reviewed every year. The universities are required to modify their programmes and organisation following these reviews. More recently, there has been a move towards introducing common features in the curricula that are offered across the provision. Private universities can have their licences for accreditation withdrawn; in 2003, three universities lost their accreditation in this way. The work of the Accreditation Commission has led to rising standards in universities across the country. Universities in Poland are often rated by the media using the detailed data on quality published by the Commission. This monitoring increases the value of the qualifications

3 Full-time students in public universities do not pay fees. Their part-time students do, however, have to pay and these fees are often comparable to those paid by all students in the private universities.

that are awarded and universities frequently quote it when they are marketing their courses.

Most private universities in Poland provide adult education at the undergraduate, and to a lesser extent the postgraduate, level. Students over the age of 25 are generally seeking to update their knowledge and qualifications in order to use this in their subsequent employment. As seen in Table 1, adult learners rarely decide to extend their qualifications by, for example, working for a doctorate. One important factor determining the attitudes and motives of adult students is that most of them have family responsibilities. It is extremely difficult to combine family duties with these longer-term studies.

One major problem for private universities is to provide the range of subjects required to meet the diverse needs of adult students. Many overcome this problem by specialising in narrow subject areas. Since the late 1990s, however, there has been a diversification of courses and this has increased the competition in attracting students. This diversification occurs mainly in the private universities which provide mainly one or two core subjects. Because of the pressure of the competition between them, they have now started to offer subjects which often do not fit their initial purposes: for example, a University for Law and Commerce has recently started political science and European integration courses; a Pedagogical University is now offering a wide range of political science subjects; and a Management School is offering law courses for managers.

Government policy and increasing adult access to higher education

A recent paper produced by the Polish Government (*Strategia*..., 2003) has provided a strategy for the development of the education of adults until the year 2010. This was adopted in July 2003 and provides a new direction for adult education in Poland, setting it firmly within the context of lifelong learning and the development of a knowledge-based society. This strategy seeks to involve all Polish citizens in their personal development, both through increasing their access to continuing education and in improving their access to the labour market.

The Government strategy has defined six key tasks for the development of adult and continuing education. The first of these is to increase the access to all forms of adult and continuing education for all Polish citizens regardless of their age, gender, family situation, social and physical disadvantage, location, social status, level of education or ethnic origin. The provision is intended to be open, flexible, transparent and comparable to other European educational systems, offering a variety of educational services and allowing the mutual recognition of qualifications. To bring about the first of these objectives, the Polish Government has undertaken to:

- Improve access to information on adult and continuing education;
- Ensure that a wide range of adult and continuing education programmes is offered;
- Break down social and psychological barriers towards adult education;
- Implement information and communication technology (ICT) in the educational process; and
- Improve the professional qualifications of those who are already in employment.

The remaining five tasks in the strategy are to:

- Improve the quality of adult education;
- Strengthen cooperation between institutions providing adult and continuing education;
- Increase human investment;
- Provide information and guidance services; and
- Promote the role of adult and continuing education generally.

Financing adult education in Poland

The demand for adult education, especially at the higher education level, has grown considerably since 1990. Funding this increase, however, is a major problem. The rise in the student numbers has not been matched by increased funding to the universities. Without additional funding, it is questionable whether the education system can be developed much further to meet the needs of modern Polish society while, at the same time, maintaining a quality comparable to that of other European countries.

In 2001 Poland spent 4.6% of its gross domestic product on education. This is comparable to the average spent by other European countries. There is a significant gap, however, between Poland and the other European countries when the amount spent on any one learner is taken into account. While Poland spends 1,900 US dollars (1,580 euros) per learner in its primary schools, Hungary spends 2,200 US dollars (1,830 euros) and the Czech Republic 3,400 US dollars (2,830 euros). This compares to a European Union (EU) average of 4,200 US dollars (3,500 euros). In higher education, the EU countries spend, on average, 8,500 US dollars (7,090 euros) per student; the equivalent figure in Poland is only 3,900 US dollars (3,250 euros) per student.[4]

The Polish Ministry of Education and Sports has also noted the poor level of provision of equipment, especially in ICT, in Polish universities. This is inhibiting the development of the educational system. In Poland one computer is available for every 44 students in primary schools (the average across the fifteen members of the EU is for every 13.2) and for 22.6 pupils in secondary schools (compared to an EU average of 8.6.) Considering access to the Worldwide Web, in Polish primary schools there is one computer with an Internet connection for every 79 students (compared to 32 in the EU) and one to 26.1 pupils in secondary schools (compared to 14.9 in the EU).[5]

4 All these data come from the statistical report of the Polish Ministry for Education and Sports. (*Strategia…*, 2003).

5 Statistics of the Polish Ministry of Education and Sports for the year 2002. (*Strategia…*, 2003).

The greatest obstacle to developing adult and continuing education in Poland is the very low level of funding available. In 2002, the Polish government spent only 0.6% of its education budget (41 million euros) on developing adult education. This is clearly not enough to develop a modern adult education system in a European country with a population of almost 40 million people. This government underspending was not compensated by the employers. They spent only 0.8% of their total labour costs on adult education and vocational training in 2002. Some 1.2–1.5 million, i.e. 8–10% of those employed in the Polish economy, continued their education during the year. This compares to around 20% of the workforce in the EU as a whole. What is more, in Poland adults spend approximately two hours each year continuing their education; this compares with an average of 50–70 hours per year[6] for the EU as a whole.

How can the Polish government finance the new policy for adult education that it has introduced? The government's view is that Poland will not be able to implement the strategy from its own resources and it hopes to cover the additional cost, at least in part, with support from the European Social Fund. The total funding needed for the development of adult and continuing education in Poland in the years 2004–2006 is estimated to be about 395 million euros.

Reaching new target groups

Adult education in Poland is orientated largely towards the labour market and mainly attracts people between 25 and 50 years of age. Adult higher education is largely targeted at those wanting to update their qualifications and knowledge or to advance in their profession rather than towards socially excluded groups such as older learners. Decisions in Poland to invest money and time in higher education are almost always linked to the needs of the labour market, either current or in the near future. Examples of disadvantaged adults, people with disabilities, ex-offenders, prisoners, people living in rural isolated communities or even ethnic minority groups enrolling on university

6 Estimated by the Polish Ministry of Education and Sports. (*Strategia*…, 2003).

courses are rare. When they do occur, they are the result of personal decisions and personal investment rather than government policy or state finance.

The Government's policy does provide support for those who have had to leave their jobs, for example in the mining industry, the agricultural sector or the textile industry. This enables them to retrain for another area of work. At the time of writing, however, there is no adequately resourced government strategy for wider economic development.

The public universities are very limited in their ability to offer access to adults since they depend upon the financial support of the State. This is certainly not sufficient to provide high-quality courses for everyone wishing to update their skills and knowledge. Public universities have to charge part-time students for the courses they attend and these charges are almost the same as those of the private universities.

This gives the private higher education institutions an advantage on fees in rural areas, where more than 35% of Polish people live, since they provide courses near to many adult learners' homes. The charges for their courses are high, however: the usual cost per semester is more than double the average monthly Polish salary. These charges are a major barrier for those adults who wish to learn.

Family commitments often prevent adults from attending classes. Because of these, their only option is often to enrol on part-time classes taking place in the evenings or at weekends. The universities have responded to this situation by allowing students with particular family problems to make special arrangements, for example by sitting examinations at times that are convenient to them.

Conclusion

While the Polish government's policy clearly favours the expansion of adult education, the steps needed to bring this about are far from being realised at the time of writing.

Improving quality is one of the major issues facing Poland today. Monitoring the provision against national standards is one way in which the Polish Ministry of Education and Sports is assessing the suitability of individual institutions. Where this is not satisfactory, the university's licence to offer accredited qualifications is withdrawn.

To develop well-organized and efficient adult education, in line with current EU thinking, it is not sufficient just to meet the demands of the labour market or the expectations of the adult learners. Considerable investment will be needed if participation in adult education is to be significantly increased and the current plans for investment are unlikely to meet the anticipated demand.[7] The rapid economic and social development of Poland means that adult education has become an absolute necessity requiring considerable investment from public funds. The arguments in favour of expansion are both economic and social and are based on the right of every adult to have access to education, just as younger people have. Failure to meet this challenge will not only lower the rate of Poland's economic growth but it will also raise tensions between the excluded groups and the rest of the population.

7 In the *Strategia…*, (2003), the Polish government has stated that it will invest 527.4 million euros to achieve its education strategy in the period 2004–2006.

References

Strategia rozwoju kształcenia ustawicznego do roku 2010, 2003. Warsaw: Ministerstwo Edukacji Narodowej I Sportu. (Strategy for developing continuing education until 2010. Ministry of Education and Sports).

Szkoły wyższe i ich finanse, 2002. Warsaw: GUS. (Higher education institutions and their finances. Central Statistical Office of Poland).

Wiercińska, A., Auleytner, J. and Piotrowski, M., 2003. University continuing education in Poland. In: M. Osborne and E. Thomas, eds. *Lifelong learning in a changing continent: Continuing education in the universities of Europe.* Leicester: National Institute of Adult Continuing Education, 2003, pp.351–65.

NILZA COSTA, PEDRO MANTAS AND LUÍS MARQUES

16: Adults in Portuguese Higher Education

Introduction

This chapter focusses initially on the University of Aveiro's (UA) developing approach to adult education (AE). To meet the requirements both of the national educational system in Portugal and the social context of the country, two organisations with different aims have been created within the University with responsibility for AE. These are the Integrated Centre for Teacher Training (CIFOP) and the Association for Research and Professional Development of the University of Aveiro (UNAVE), an association located outside the institution and concerned mainly with continuing professional development (CPD).

The next two sections report the historical issues that determined the present activities and the structures of these two units and they describe the work that is currently being done. The trends in the development of education for students at UA who have previously had no opportunity to follow higher education are then described. Moving on from this detailed description, the final section presents an overview of AE in Portugal as a whole.

Training of teachers (CIFOP)

The national education system in Portugal consists of twelve years of schooling before university, divided into two levels: the Basic Education level, with nine years of compulsory education, and the Secondary Education level, not compulsory, for the last three years.

The Basic Education is itself divided into three cycles: four years for the first cycle, two for the second and three for the third. In 1974, the teachers of the second and third cycles of the Basic Education level were required to have a university *license* (with a few exceptions, for example Music, Physical Education, Athletics and Handicrafts). Universities could only prepare teachers for the second and third cycles of the Basic Education and for the Secondary Education level. Consequently UA offered degrees for teaching in different curriculum areas: in science (including Mathematics, Physics-Chemistry and Biology-Geology) and in languages (Portuguese-French, Portuguese-English, English-German, etc.). Since different curriculum areas were required to merge with educational topics in order to confer a final 'teaching degree' (for example, a teacher of Physics and Chemistry needs to know about physics, chemistry, pedagogy and the science of education), in 1986 UA created a centre where the curriculum is integrated. This is the function of the Integrated Centre for the Training of Teachers (*Centro Integrado de Formação de Professores*, CIFOP).

CIFOP currently has a range of activities, all of them concerned with teacher training. Today, teachers at all levels need to follow short courses in order to get credits within the national In-service Teachers Training Programme (*Programa de Formação Contínua de Professores*, FOCO) to progress within their careers or to follow a masters degree at a university. At UA, the FOCO Programme is located in CIFOP. Another activity is the undergraduate CPD programme for teachers who do not yet have a teaching qualification, a programme called *Formação em serviço*. CIFOP also includes a local unit of the Open University, again only for teachers.

The FOCO Programme is directly concerned with continuing education, since participants take courses (on new perspectives, new trends or refresher courses) that follow on from their initial area of expertise. The other programmes, CPD and the Open University, do not necessarily relate to the students' initial training and are therefore better viewed as 'permanent education'.

The experience so far acquired in CIFOP is sufficient to characterise the strengths and weaknesses of this model. Teachers follow the CIFOP teacher training programmes because they are required to do so: these teachers are either obliged to have a *license* (obtained through CPD or the Open University) or they need to earn a fixed number of credits per year from FOCO. All these programmes are supported financially by the Ministry of Education and, in return, the attendees must follow the courses in their own time. These characteristics have the following strengths and weaknesses:

Strengths

- Expectations: It is possible to choose the course one wants to follow, since there is a wide choice;
- Time schedule: Courses normally take place outside working hours;
- Distance: UA draws attendees from a distance of roughly fifty kilometres which, at the most, corresponds to forty-five minutes travel; and
- Financial support: The State supports this type of training.

Weaknesses

- Compulsory element: This often militates against teachers' goodwill to participate;
- Time schedule and/or distance: The total time needed to follow a course is not always compatible with the demands of family life and the need for leisure time; and
- Financial support from the State: Attendees do not normally feel this is a benefit for their own education.

These strengths and weaknesses together provide a picture of the present situation of teacher training through the AE route in the Aveiro region. More widely, other factors need to be taken into consideration; for example, not all schools are directly involved in this CPD process. In the case of the FOCO Programme, schools can set up an association among themselves to form a centre to provide CPD courses. This overcomes some of the above weaknesses, for example the timetabling and the travel issues. The appearance of these centres is closely related to the type of training the schools need to develop in their annual planning. Again, this carries strengths and weaknesses:

perhaps the greatest weakness is the conflict between the schools' needs and the teachers' motivation. As will be discussed later, the same tension between institutional and personal requirements appears in other branches of AE (Soares, 1998; Neves, 1998).

Professional development and training (UNAVE)

In 1998, UA restructured its system linking the University and society in general. In this new structure, UNAVE was committed to professional development provision. It is not a centre within UA but is a private non-profit-making association. This situation brings an advantage in those cases when there are no tutors in UA for a specific CPD activity since UNAVE is able to contract them from outside. However, a disadvantage, discussed later, is that UNAVE cannot confer academic credit. Because it is private, all the CPD programmes offered by UNAVE must be paid for by the attendees or their employers.

Currently, UNAVE's main activity is concerned with professional development and training (*acções de formação*). This activity is divided into two sectors with different approaches: traditional professional development; and distance learning (DL). In the traditional case, access to CPD activities can be open, either by being included in an annual plan promoted by UNAVE to the general public or within a programme delivered specifically for institutions or private sector companies. These specific programmes involve an analysis of the institution's or company's needs, the proposal of a training plan, its execution and the final evaluation.

It also offers DL based exclusively on the Internet. This consists of courses put together by selecting a number of independent modules. In this case, there is no restriction on the background of the participants so, in theory at least, some of them may be below 18 years of age (although this has not yet happened).

As in the case of CIFOP, the experience acquired in its first three years by UNAVE is enough to reveal some of the strengths and weaknesses of this model:

Traditional continuing professional development

Strengths:

- Expectations: It is possible to choose the course one wants to follow; it is possible to have a plan for the whole organisation;
- Timetabling: Courses normally take place after working hours; courses can incorporate *in situ* training during working time;
- Distance: UA draws attendees from a distance of roughly fifty kilometres which, at most, corresponds to a forty-five minutes journey; and
- Financial support: The institution or employer supports this training.

Weaknesses:

- Motivation: A compulsory element often hinders the willingness of potential trainees to follow a particular course;
- Time of provision and distance: The total time needed to follow any course and its timing are not always compatible with the demands of family life and the need for leisure time; and
- Financial support from the institution or company: Attendees do not necessarily feel this is a benefit for their own education.

Distance learning

Strengths:

- Expectations: It is possible to take the course of one's choice (or only one module, if necessary);
- Timetable: Distance learning is asynchronous; and
- Distance: There is no limit.

Weaknesses:

- Personal Internet skills: Up-to-date DL is confined to people who are already able to use the Internet;
- Development of modules: Relatively few tutors feel comfortable with this type of learning at the moment; and
- Advertising the courses: More than 90% of the attendees found out about this type of learning through the Internet. (Traditional advertising channels such as newspapers, magazines and radio fail to capture the attention of significant numbers of potential adult students.)

The strengths and weaknesses are different in these two cases. In the traditional case, the CPD programmes face similar problems to those of CIFOP. In practice, when training is directed at institutional or private-sector clients, there is always likely to be some incompatibility between the client's requirements and those of the individual participants. This incompatibility is much less evident, however, in professional development than it is for CIFOP. This needs further analysis but it seems clear that two major factors contribute to the greater satisfaction with professional development: the attendees are more aware of the financial support from their employers (which changes their attitude to their own education); and, according to their type of work and working environment, the willingness of attendees to engage in new professional development activities is much more pronounced.

It is important to focus on the types of requirement that different clients have. Large organisations normally have their own training departments while small- and medium-sized enterprises generally do not. The existence of training departments is beneficial for organizations since they can regularly survey the training needs of their personnel. In these cases training is seen as an investment, rather than a cost, and their approach is substantially different: these institutions and companies look at all the stages of a training programme, from the training needs analysis to the final evaluation of the programme. These departments are also generally able to look for external funds, either from the State or from EU programmes. Small and medium enterprises, on the other hand, having no training departments, generally consider professional training and development as a cost. They also lack information about the availability of external funds and how to get them. In addition, they generally do not know where problems are located (since they do not carry out needs analyses) and the training activities that they do provide are likely to be dependant on individual decisions and to be chosen because they are offered at the lowest costs. Effective training is less likely to flourish in these cases.

When using a DL method, the achievements of the participants are obvious. A good indication of its success is that most students following DL courses return to undertake a second module. It seems clear that the following factors contribute to DL's success: its non-compulsory nature, its choice and flexibility; its asynchronous nature; and the self-financing element. If the trainees pay for it themselves, they want to complete it successfully. The weaknesses mentioned above hinder the wider acceptance of this form of education, however, despite the fact that we are all now part of an 'information society'. After about 18 months, roughly, 200 people were engaged on UNAVE's DL courses. All of them were successful. In the same period, about 1,000 people were engaged on non-DL courses, with 80% success. Steps that would support the wider acceptance of this type of training include the upgrading of the hardware available, the wider availability of Internet navigation skills amongst potential students, and increased confidence on the part of tutors in the process.

Lifelong education: formal education and *disciplinas avulsas*

The descriptions of CIFOP and UNAVE outline the current situation for AE short courses at UA. In addition, in some cases adults who had interrupted their formal education earlier look for further formal education while those who already have a first degree may look for postgraduate studies. For the latter group, UA offers postgraduate courses in a relatively wide range of areas.

These courses are generally masters degrees but it was realised that they did not necessarily fulfil people's needs. Adults often look for advanced knowledge without a research component and with recognition by the university of their prior learning. These requirements are easily provided within the framework of a credit system. In particular, this allows the taught part of the masters degree to be separated easily from the research component. This procedure enables postgraduate courses to be offered with a wide interdisciplinary content which, in turn, offers new educational possibilities (Costa *et al.*, 2001). These courses are not always substantially different from the existing CPD courses, however, and the boundary between the two is unclear.

Since 2002, UA has also made it possible for the general public to take courses from its traditional teaching programmes, both at the undergraduate and postgraduate levels. Previously these courses had only been available to full-time students. In these cases, candidates are said to follow 'detached disciplines' (*disciplinas avulsas*) and the units do not carry academic recognition. (This process is commonly referred to as 'auditing'.) In spite of this, however, and despite the fact that the teaching follows the existing full-time student timetable, twenty individuals enrolled in the first year. The candidates first have to submit an application form, which is considered by an academic committee, and a decision is then made. No advice or guidance is currently given to the candidates to help them make their choices.

The first set of application forms has been analysed and the results are reported here. It is clear that in many cases the applicants' main interest is to increase their knowledge, particularly of professional information, rather than to be awarded an academic degree.

The application form

The application has five fields to be filled by the candidates: identification of the candidate; the disciplines they wish to follow (up to a maximum of four); their academic background; their motivation; and their professional situation.

Disciplines can be chosen at all levels: undergraduate and postgraduate (including the masters level). The main motivations given for wishing to undertake a course were:

- To update professional skills (in the same area as their initial education);
- To acquire professionally relevant, complementary skills;
- To experience the pleasure of learning; and
- To renew or retain contact with academic life.

The main professional situations of the candidates were: professionally active, retired, unemployed and student.

Analysis of the applications

The number of applications (20) is too small to make a useful statistical analysis but a qualitative description can be given.

Age and academic background

All the candidates were over 24 years of age. The majority of them fall in the 26- to 36-year-old range and three-quarters of them have a university degree. Among those without a degree, the youngest was 27 years old.

The results seem to confirm that earlier education provides the basis for further education since the majority of the candidates already had university experience. This also answers positively the questions 'Do people really need or want more education?' It was noted that some adults are keen to undertake more education even though they do not receive an academic qualification, they do not have a utilitarian purpose, and regardless of whether the times of the courses are appropriate.

An interesting feature here is the lack of 18–24-year-old candidates. This suggests that higher education is not yet attractive for the younger adult public. We have no data to explain this phenomenon but one can speculate that at least two factors may contribute here: one is the engrained idea in society that university study is only for students who have completed their secondary schooling and who are 18–19 years old; those who do not fit these two categories should go to work. The second factor is that young adults are often more concerned with their professional and family lives at this stage. Other perspectives may open for them later.

Gender and family life

The majority of the candidates, about two-thirds, are women and also two-thirds are single. Roughly half of the women candidates are single and half of the youngest candidates are also single. These results suggest that family life does not hinder the willingness of younger candidates to engage in higher education but that it does present a barrier later. It is worth noting that the majority of the candidates are women even though they carry the greater responsibility for supporting traditional family life. (Branco, no date; APFN, 2003).

The professional situation and the distance factor

Two-thirds of the candidates are professionally active. Two-thirds of them also live near Aveiro but applications were received from up to two hundred kilometres away.

The results indicate that it is mainly professionally active people who look for more education, in spite of the fact that the teaching takes place during the day. Most of the candidates live near Aveiro, suggesting that distance is an important factor for people wishing to follow university courses. Information and communication technology (ICT) should help to overcome this problem.

Motivation

Three-fifths of the candidates expressed their wish to acquire complementary skills which were professionally relevant. In this they were not looking to renew their initial skills but to learn skills in related areas. The second most common reason given for applying, suggested by one-fifth of the applicants, was simply the pleasure of learning. The results mostly agree with the previous section: most of the candidates were professionally active and they looked for higher education that complemented their existing skills.

Profile of a typical candidate and its consequences

The above analysis can help us to draw a picture of a typical candidate, although it is emphasised that this is based in only a small number of cases: they are adults, mostly women, who had finished their university studies a few years earlier, living near a university and looking for new skills to complement their performance at work.

This picture raises important issues for AE in universities that need to be explored if the number of candidates is to increase. Distance learning, either by ICT or outreach initiatives, must be developed if people living well away from the university are to be reached. In addition, evening programmes should be introduced and asynchronous learning (using ICT) should be increased. Typical candidates have sufficient initial knowledge to be able to follow higher education courses without additional support.

On the other hand, this picture also raises some problems with no clear solutions: how can younger adults, in the 18–24 year age range, who probably have different educational backgrounds, be reached?; how can older adults, over the age of 40, be reached who probably feel far removed from academic life?; Is the university offering suitable programmes for them?; Should the university develop a consistent scheme for the accreditation of prior learning (APL) allowing people to enter higher education and providing guidance and support while they do so? In our view, it is desirable to have answers soon to these questions because they imply different perspectives for the role of the university in society. They require an in-depth internal analysis and debate as well as the necessary political recognition by the State.

Adult education in Portugal

In spite of the lack of legislation on AE in Portugal, universities play an important role in its provision. Portuguese universities each have their own policies, with different levels of priority for AE from one to another, and with their own specific structures and organisation.

A picture of AE in Portugal, from the view of public universities, is presented here. Based on the assumption that one of the purposes of universities is to provide services to the community, in this case to offer learning opportunities to adults, a very open questionnaire was designed and sent to a range of institutions. This looked for the existence of institutional policies and provision by analysing the nature, organisation and development of structures related to AE. Different approaches are currently being developed at several universities and these are reported here.

Portuguese adult education framework

An overview of the responses to the questionnaire reveals that all the institutions agree that it is necessary to define policies dealing with:

- The education at the undergraduate level of adults who, in the past, had no opportunity to follow higher education;
- The education of those who had interrupted their formal education and who now wish to undertake short courses;

- The education of those who are looking for longer-term formal education, such as postgraduate studies;
- The aspirations of people who are looking for advanced knowledge without a research dimension but with recognition of their learning by the university;
- Appropriate programmes targeting people not at work, particularly retired people; and
- The development of DL, closely related to the potential of ICT.

It is clear that any attempt to shape AE is a complex task, taking into account the diversity of the social, cultural and professional needs of citizens living in the information society.

A detailed analysis of the questionnaire reveals that:

Organisation of adult education

In some universities, Adult Education Units are working in collaboration with Centres of Continuing Education with two main aims: to develop a systematic education and training strategy and to carry out research in this area.

Collaborative work is at the heart of many projects, in an attempt to increase their learners' sense of responsibility and their autonomy towards their learning. Networks linking universities to institutions and companies where learners work are also desirable and need to be developed. With these in place, it is easier to identify educational needs and to agree the appropriate strategies to meet them.

A number of constraints, arising from the nature of the Portuguese education system and from economic and social issues, are responsible for another form of AE organisation adopted by a few universities. Their Centres for Teacher Training are separate from those responsible for professional development. (This is, for example, the case with CIFOP at UA, mentioned earlier.) The FOCO courses are located in these units and they are also responsible for the undergraduate programmes for teachers who have not yet qualified through the In-service Teachers Training Programme.

Professional training in some universities is provided using a different approach in order to maintain the link with society in general. Here, independent non-profit-making units have been established to provide specific AE courses.

Different approaches

The two different approaches to the provision of CPD courses have already been mentioned: it can be provided by traditional short courses; and by DL. In the first case, the courses are included in an annual programme widely advertised to the general public; or they can be tailor-made and delivered for a specific organisation, as done by UNAVE, described earlier.

The provision of DL based on the Internet has already been described in the section on UNAVE. Communication by e-mail is another medium very much used in these courses, developing and improving the interaction between tutors and students and among students themselves. Using the Internet, the provision of learning materials is straightforward and, using one of the standard educational Internet programmes available, students can discuss these materials with one another at specified times using the chatrooms or forums available.

Attendees' profiles

Potential candidates for AE courses can be classified into three groups:

- Practitioners who seek, voluntarily, to gain new perspectives, new trends and refresher courses to benefit their careers and develop new competences;
- Practitioners who have to achieve a particular number of credits in order to be promoted in their careers. Some of these people want to receive a certificate rather than to develop professionally because they believe that 'they already know everything'; and

- People who, for the pleasure of learning, wish to develop their knowledge more broadly. They can be professionals, unemployed, retired people … or whoever.

The response of the universities to this diverse group of adult students is to offer undergraduate and postgraduate courses and uncertificated specialised courses.

It should be stressed that all the universities are making an important investment both at the undergraduate and postgraduate levels. The emphasis on other specialised courses is strongly related to the policies for AE defined by each institution.

All the institutions make great efforts to advertise the courses in a wide variety of ways. A significant number of applicants receive the information via the Internet. As mentioned earlier, however, it is now generally recognised that traditional advertising channels such as newspapers, magazines or the radio, are less effective.

The results of this first questionnaire should be seen as very positive, taking into account that all the universities answering it emphasised that the rate of enrolment for their courses was high.

Features of the curriculum

The AE provision in universities requires modifications to be made to the procedures used for full-time courses. Flexibility of delivery is a defining characteristic of AE, planning the organisation of short courses at times that suit the learners (in particular, outside working hours), and providing them with a range of modules from which they can choose what to study.

The characteristics of the courses, and of the candidates, influence the way that the curriculum is designed. For the most part, the institutions attempt to design a flexible model fitting the needs of the public. Within this, it is sensible to provide a curriculum which can be negotiated between those responsible for its implementation and the students themselves.

The data collected so far indicate that this model works successfully. There are several examples of adult students who were forced to start a course and who, by the end, were sufficiently motivated to choose for themselves to continue their training by enrolling for another.

Implementation of programmes

Several of the institutions concerned here have adopted decentralised policies for their AE. This means that some courses, or at least parts of them such as the seminars and discussions, take place outside the universities. This facilitates, both for geographical and for professional reasons, the participation of learners in the sessions and allows the universities to develop valuable professional, social and cultural links with local institutions, schools, private companies and voluntary associations with a wide variety of purposes. This interactive process is being developed in some institutions by forming a network to include all the participants with the aim of improving the effectiveness of the courses.

The future of AE in Portugal can be predicted with a reasonable level of confidence. To summarise the present social context, we have: increasing life expectancy; increasing demands for vocational courses; and decreasing numbers of university applicants coming from the usual social and cultural background. The concept of AE matches well with these strong social currents. It would be surprising if the development of AE was not taking place both in Portugal and elsewhere.

Acknowledgements

We wish to thank the following collaborators: Alberto Eduardo da Silva e Melo, Professor, University of Algarve; Maria José Ferro Tavares, Rector of the Open University of Lisbon; and Paulo Dias, Associate Professor, University of Minho, Maria do Rosário Pires, UNAVE.

References

APFN, 2003. *Portugueses sem tempo para os filhos.* (Portuguese people without time for their children.) Portugal Diário, 19 Março, 2003 (in Portuguese).

Branco, A., no date. *O posicionamento da mulher na Sociedade Portuguesa.* (The position of women in Portuguese society.) Available at: http://www.ipv.pt/forumediz/f2_idei1.htm

Costa, N., Alarcão, I. and Frade, J., 2001. Rethinking Post Graduate Education: The Case of the University of Aveiro, Portugal. Conference on Postgraduate Education in Europe: past, present and future, 3–5 May 2001. Linkoping, Sweden.

Neves R., 1998. *A Supervisão na Conceptualização do Projecto de Formação e Acção Pedagógica* (PFAP). (Supervision in the Conception of the Education and Pedagogical Action Project.) Actas do I Congresso Nacional de Supervisão. (First National Congress on Supervision Proceedings.) Universidade de Aveiro, CD-ROM (in Portuguese).

Soares, T., 1998. *Supervisão e Profissionalização em Serviço – Operacionalização crítico-evolutiva na Universidade de Aveiro.* (Supervision and in-service training – A field action in the University of Aveiro based on an analysis-and-evolution process.) Actas do I Congresso Nacional de Supervisão. Universidade de Aveiro, CD-ROM (in Portuguese).

ION OLTEANU AND VALENTIN OPREA

17: Adults in Romanian Higher Education

Introduction

Adult education in Romania, which can be traced back to the second half of the nineteenth century, arose from the initiatives of a number of distinguished Romanian figures and a range of cultural, scientific and artistic organisations. Many of the early programmes focused not only on culture but also on the eradication of illiteracy, especially in rural communities, where this problem was most serious. Among the most significant early providers of adult education were the Transylvanian Association for Romanian Literature and the Culture of the Romanian People (ASTRA, *Asociația Transilvană pentru Literatura Română și Cultura Poporului Român*) established in Sibiu in 1861, which founded numerous schools and libraries in Transylvanian villages, and the Society for the Learning of the Romanian People (*Societatea pentru învățătura poporului român*) which set up the first schools for adults in 1867.

The reform programme initiated by Spiru Haret just before the turn of the century also played an important role in the development of adult education. The education law of 1896, revised in 1899 to follow Haret's proposals, regulated the system of adult education in Romania for the first time and a regulation for adult schools was adopted in 1904. The first folk university was founded in 1908 in Vălenii de Munte by Nicolae Iorga, while in Bucharest a folk university was founded in 1910 by the Association of the Folk University of the Romanian Capital (*Asociația Universității Populare din Capitala României*). Folk universities were also founded in Constanța (around 1912), Galați (1913) and Craiova (1922) (Itu, 1981).

The period between the two world wars was one of increasing activity and of theoretical studies. The importance of adult education increased during this time and it gained even wider recognition once the main Romanian universities began taking a research interest in the subject. They undertook field studies, investigating the social conditions and the specific educational needs of rural communities and a number of solutions to the problems of the time were proposed. Some providers that had been active before the First World War expanded their activities to the national level and new ones also appeared. One of the most important during these years was the Cultural Foundation '*Principele Carol*', which set up 'houses of culture' in urban and rural localities. These became the cultural and educational centres of their communities.

After the Second World War, the social and political events had a strong impact on the evolution of adult education. After an initial stage of preoccupation with science and international cooperation, the end of the communist period was marked by stagnation from the point of view of developing theory and research. Although the number of adult education institutions and programmes increased greatly, these became strongly politicised. Folk universities were created in the most important towns and villages but the funding they received was insufficient for up-to-date logistic supplies or for development. Frequently, they also lacked qualified personnel, as the institutions dealing with folk education were regarded by the communist officials as of secondary importance. As a result, the folk universities gradually became marginalised and their prestige fell (Schifirneț, 1997).

It is important to note the strong emphasis put on continuing professional development (CPD) during this time. Inspired by French legislation, a Law (2/1971) strengthening the national system for the improvement of vocational training was adopted in 1971. In addition to the refreshment and enrichment of vocational knowledge and the acquisition of modern methods, this Law introduced the concepts of 'multi-qualification' (the acquisition of a new qualification, in addition to a basic qualification) and 'requalification' (the change of qualification, in cases when the basic qualification no longer meets the necessary requirements). This law stipulated that 'the socialist units must enable every worker to attend vocational training programmes periodically'. At the same time, however, it was part of an over-centralised system within a hierarchical structure, stretching from the basic units at the bottom to the ministries and other central organisations at the top. Also, the individuals were obliged to attend vocational training programmes, as this was 'the permanent obligation of every worker' (Bârzea, 1998).

After the fall of communism in 1989, the reorganisation of the adult education system took place only slowly, due to the inherent difficulties during a period of transition. The legislative disarray, together with the changing priorities, the social reform and the consequent need for overall reorganisation, had a strong impact on the institutions involved. As a result, interest in adult education declined and many folk universities were closed while others were forced to change to providing vocational training programmes, which were in much greater demand. In this period of high unemployment, the vocational training market grew, while the cultural aspects of adult education played a decreasing role. Many of the legislative instruments introduced during these years favoured the creation of programmes leading to qualifications.

More recently, the strengthening international contacts and Romania's participation in European Union (EU) programmes have offered important opportunities for the regrowth of adult education. Starting in 1993, the International Cooperation Institute of the German Association for Adult Education (IIZ/DVV) initiated a large programme to support the development of adult education in Romania, offering financial support and assistance to the folk universities and the houses of culture. The Institute also supported the foundation of the National Association of the Folk Universities (*ANUP, Asociația Națională a Universităților Populare*) (Sava and Mitrache, 2003). The projects that developed at the same time within the EU's Tempus, Socrates and Leonardo di Vinci programmes enabled the exchange of experience, particularly on curriculum development and evaluation standards, and the creation of new institutional structures, especially in the universities. International events, such as the UNESCO Conference on Adult Education in 1997 and the publication of the EU's Memorandum on Lifelong Learning (European Commission, 2000) had a strong impact in Romania (Bârzea, 2001a).

The Law of Education, adopted in 1995, which contained general provisions for adult education, was revised in 1997 when the National

Council for Continuing Training and Education (*Consiliul Național pentru Formare și Educație Continuă*) was created. In addition, the role of the Ministry of Education in evaluating, accrediting and financing vocational training programmes was clarified. The Council for Occupational Standards and Testing (*COSA, Consiliul pentru Standarde Ocupaționale și Evaluare*) was created in 1999 and in 2000 the Government issued an ordinance (129/2000) regulating adult vocational training. Intense activity followed in the area of research on adult education in the universities, the Institute of Educational Sciences and the Ministry of Education. Seminars and conferences on the subject were organised and studies were carried out at the national level. Since 2000, with the support of IIZ/DVV, the National Association of Folk Universities has organised (in collaboration with the appropriate government ministries, the National Council for the Vocational Training of Adults, the National Agency for Employment, and the National Association of Adult Education Centres), an annual fair to promote the continuing education on offer in Bucharest and other major cities.

Legislation

At the time of writing, Romania does not have a specific law for adult education to ensure a coherent approach and a common framework at the national level. Though such a project was considered in the early 2000s, it never reached the stage of being discussed in Parliament. Within Romania's vast body of legislation, the key acts which currently address adult education are the:

- Education Act 84/1995, with later amendments, which includes a chapter dedicated to adult education;
- Government Ordinance 102/1998, regarding the organisation and functioning of the system of continuing education within educational institutions;

- Government Ordinance 129/2000, relating to continuing vocational training, sanctioned by Act 375/2002;
- Act 145/1998, regarding the foundation and functioning of the National Agency for Employment;
- Act 132/1999, relating to the foundation, organisation and functioning of the National Council for Adult Vocational Training; and
- Act 53/2003, the Labour Code, which includes a chapter on vocational training.

Many other acts also refer to adult training related to their subjects.

According to the Education Act, the main purpose of adult education is to provide access to scientific and cultural knowledge for all citizens to help them adapt to the major changes that have occurred, and which are likely to continue, in society. The system of adult education is coordinated by the Ministry of Education, which collaborates with the Ministry of Culture and other interested ministries, as well as the media, religious groups, folk universities, cultural foundations and other institutions. The Ministry of Education, through its various units, also offers consultancy to the adult education providers.

According to the law, continuing education delivered as part of the formal educational system has the following objectives:

- The completion of participants' basic education;
- The provision of continuing vocational training;
- The provision of civic education; and
- Education to enhance the skills and interests of individuals.

Adult education programmes are organised by a wide range of educational institutions including vocational training centres, folk schools of art, folk universities, houses of culture, libraries, museums, and non-governmental and professional organisations.

The most regulated sector of adult education is vocational training which provides a valuable response to the serious threat of unemployment (Bârzea, 2001b). From the point of view of vocational training, adults are defined as people who have reached the legal age to work (and who can then participate in vocational training programmes). In this respect, a distinction is made: initial vocational training provides the training required to gain the competences needed to obtain a job; continuing vocational training occurs after the initial training and make possible either the development of vocational competences already acquired or the acquisition of new ones. An important provision of the law regulating adult vocational training is the parity that it gives to non-formal and informal training, bringing them in line with formal training to lead to vocational competence. Professional competencies are defined by the levels of skill, specified in the occupational standards, that are required to carry them out.

A report carried out for the National Council for Adult Vocational Training (Ghinaru, 2001) made a series of recommendations for adult education on the:

- Need to encourage organisations and employers who wish to invest in vocational training and to stimulate the providers formulating and implementing human resource policies regarding the training of trainers;
- Abolition of privileges for public providers. This included the introduction of the same accreditation requirements for all training providers and the elimination of all financial subsidies for this work;
- Accreditation criteria shaped for programmes to stimulate the modularisation of training programmes and to raise their quality;
- Professional, independent and periodic accreditation, based on national auditing standards;
- Need to encourage the auditing organisms, as a self-regulating factor for the vocational training market;
- Reorganisation of the vocational training programmes for 'at risk' groups, using a voucher system, which would allow them to choose the provider and would stimulate competition; and
- Implementation of a set of standards for adult vocational training.

Institutions participating in adult education

Institutions with a regulatory role

The *Ministry of Education* and the *Ministry of Labour* are both responsible for the formulation of national policies concerning human resource development. These include the vocational training of adults, setting up certification systems for professional competencies within a CPD framework, defining the methodology and criteria for validating providers of CPD programmes and building a National Registry of Professional Qualifications.

The *Ministry of Culture*, on the other hand, is responsible for the methodologies and criteria required to endorse institutions involved in the field of adult education within the education system.

Institutions with a coordinating role

The institutions below are concerned with all the providers of training of adults, including the higher education institutions.

The *National Council for Adult Vocational Training* (CNFPA, *Consiliul Național pentru Formarea Profesională a Adulților*) is an autonomous administrative authority with a consultative role in promoting the policies and strategies concerning vocational training for adults. It supports the process of adult vocational training by providing the elements necessary to implement the policies and strategies adopted in this area. In addition, it coordinates the accreditation of vocational training providers and the maintenance of a national register of these providers.

The *Council for Occupational Standards and Testing* (COSA, *Consiliul pentru Standarde Ocupaționale şi Evaluare*) is an autonomous non-governmental body whose purpose is to develop a system of evaluation and certification based on occupational standards.

The *National Agency for Employment* (ANOFM, *Agenția Națională pentru Ocuparea Forței de Muncă*) organises and coordinates vocational training for job seekers at a national level. It also submits project proposals to the Ministry of Labour regarding employment and vocational training.

Institutions providing adult education programmes

A wide array of providers in Romania offer adult education programmes: many public and private institutions, associations, foundations and centres for vocational training are active in this sector. Most of them offer a broad range of adult education activities, often collaborating with other educational, social and cultural providers.

Providers active within the Ministry of Education's network

Within the Ministry of Education, the General Directorate for Continuing Education and Teacher Training (*Direcţia Generală pentru Educaţie Continuă şi Formarea şi Perfecţionarea Personalului Didactic*) is responsible for determining national policies and strategies concerning the development of human resources. This includes vocational training for adults, the organisation of certification frameworks for professional competencies within the CPD system, the implementation of adult education programmes with a view to developing the professionalisation of different categories of occupation and the creation of a consistent legislative framework for adult education.

Also part of the Ministry of Education are the National Centre for the Training of Personnel for Pre-university Education (*Centrul Naţional de Formare a Personalului din Învăţământul Preuniversitar*), which is responsible for ensuring the quality of training programmes for teachers and managers, and the National Centre for Continuing, Open and Distance Education (*Centrul Naţional pentru Educaţie Continuă şi Învăţământ Deschis la Distanţă*), responsible for organising, coordinating and monitoring continuing education and open and distance learning activities in higher education.

Guided by the government's policy, universities have developed adult education programmes alongside their existing postgraduate teaching. These have expanded and diversified and recently some universities have created adult education departments offering courses. Some of these were established with international support, arising from EU projects such as Phare and Tempus. Among the most relevant ones, it is worth mentioning the Romanian Institute for Adult Education founded by the University of the West, Timişoara, which mainly conducts research on the subject (Sava and Mitrache, 2003). The University of Craiova has also more recently set up a Centre for Complementary Education with the task of coordinating the adult vocational training courses organised by the university.

Throughout Romania, the 'houses of teachers' provide training courses geared to the needs of a wide range of education professionals (teachers, managers and inspectors). At the same time, they support the organisation of scientific, methodological and cultural training activities and work closely with university teacher training departments.

Providers active within the Ministry of Culture's network

The *General Directorate for Public Reading, Lifelong Education and Traditional Civilisation* (*Direcţia Generală Lectură Publică, Educaţie Permanentă şi Civilizaţie Tradiţională*) is responsible for developing and coordinating cultural education strategies. The houses of culture, which exist in more than 200 urban centres and more than 2000 of the largest rural communities, carry out cultural and artistic programmes. In every district, including Bucharest, there are also folk schools of art which offer theoretical and applied courses. The folk universities are organised as cultural institutions, offering programmes in all subject areas, ranging from the humanities, culture, civilisation and foreign languages to health education and vocational training courses. In Romania, there are about 150 folk universities. These generally work within the houses of culture, although a few are registered independently (Sava and Mitrache, 2003).

Providers working within other ministries' networks

The *Ministry of Youth and Sports*, offers youth educational programmes through its district subsidies, on topics such as leadership, project management, entrepreneurship, ecology and tourism education. It also supports the creation of similar programmes by youth organisations.

The *Ministry of Health*, through hospitals and district health authorities, organises programmes of health education. Continuing training of medical doctors is organised by those universities that have medical faculties. This is carried out in cooperation with the Ministry of Health.

The *Ministry of the Interior*, the *Ministry of Justice* and the *Ministry of Defence*, through their subsidiary institutions, organise training programmes for their own personnel on civic education and also literacy for convicts and for recruits to the armed services.

Other agencies and organisations

The *district agencies for employment*, as subsidiaries of the National Agency for Employment, offer employment services and they also finance vocational training programmes.

The *Regional Centres for Adult Education Training*, established in 2000 by the National Agency for Employment, provide a large range of services, including vocational training programmes, entrepreneurial programmes and general education modules. The centres are working in five major cities: Călăraşi, Cluj-Napoca, Craiova, Râmnicu Vâlcea and Turnu Măgurele. (For more information see: www.crfpa.anofm.ro)

The Chambers of Commerce and Industry founded the *Romanian School of Business* in 1992 with 32 satellite centres and with its headquarters in Bucharest. The courses provided include entrepreneurial education programmes for company managers and vocational training programmes for employees. The annual enrolment for training in the Romanian School of Business increased from 1,500 in 1992 to 13,200 in 2000. (For more information: www.cci.ro)

The *social partners* (the employers' associations and the trades unions) organise adult education programmes through their own networks. These are chiefly directed to their own members, although some are also open to the public. The trades unions also organise a large variety of cultural and artistic activities (Sava and Mitrache, 2003).

Non-governmental organisations, such as student or youth organisations, foundations and societies, have programmes in all areas of adult education, some of which benefit from financial support from international organisations. Among the most active are the Soros Foundation for an Open Society, the Foundation for the Development of the Civil Society, the International Foundation for Management and the ProWaldorf Foundation (Modrescu, 1999).

Vocational training centres also offer training and conversion courses. These are private companies which provide vocational qualifications, often in collaboration with education institutions.

Currently there is no national database listing these centres or the programmes that they organise and legislation has recently been passed requiring that a national registry of training providers should be created.

Education programmes for adults

The objectives of adult education programmes are determined by the needs of the groups for which the courses are intended. These in turn determine the content of the education on offer, the teaching and evaluation methods used, the length of the teaching and whether certification is offered.

Admission criteria vary from one programme to the other. These may refer to the minimum age for participants (generally the age of graduation from the compulsory educational sector or the minimum age for starting work) or educational background (usually graduation from the secondary school or high-school, while a university degree is requested for university postgraduate programmes). In addition, only unemployed people can apply for requalification and conversion courses financed by the National Agency for Employment using social security funds. (It is a legal requirement that those receiving unemployment benefits must participate in the courses organised by their district employment agencies.) Some vocational training also requires diagnostic testing as a prerequisite. Finally, as an obvious but important point, participation in self-financing courses is necessarily limited to those who are able to pay (Modrescu, 1999).

The curriculum is determined by the organising institutions, depending on the nature and needs of the group for which they are designed. In the case of training courses organised by vocational training centres, the curricula and syllabi are authorised and evaluated by the CNFPA.

The teaching and assessment use a combination of traditional and modern adult education methods. Assessments usually consist of oral and written examinations together with on-going tests. Most adult education institutions do not have well-developed human resource development strategies and many trainers come from the formal education system and work as associated teachers. Only a small proportion of the teachers are full-time employees of their adult education institutions. The official classification of occupations in Romania does not include a specific category for adult educators and training organisations usually categorise them as 'lecturers' or 'trainers'.

Not every adult education programme offers qualifications but the most likely to offer nationally recognised certificates are vocational training courses where the provider is authorised by the CNFPA. Foreign language courses also offer a variety of certificates, some of which are recognised internationally.

University continuing education

Lifelong learning programmes are offered by universities in a variety of forms. The CPD of teachers working in the pre-university sector has been a well-developed sector since the communist era. It is provided by universities, within teacher training departments. Alongside traditional programmes, like the CPD of teachers and medical doctors, or postgraduate courses organised to meet well-defined social and economic needs, the universities gradually adapted to the new demands, focussing on lifelong learning programmes. The higher education institutions introduced and developed flexible lifelong learning programmes for most of the study areas, either postgraduate programmes, short vocational courses and informal courses with a wider appeal. The fields with the most developed adult education programmes are business and management, information and communication technology, engineering and foreign languages (Bârzea, 1998).

Foreign language courses

Since 1990, the demand for language courses has increased dramatically reflecting Romania's increasing international contacts. The establishment of subsidiaries of international companies in Romania, the increasing access to many products and services originating in other countries and the wider opportunities to study and work abroad, have all been important factors in this respect. Language courses are organised by educational institutions, folk universities, specialist centres and by the subsidiaries of international organisations. The range of courses on offer is vast, from the formal to non-formal and also including distance learning programmes. Their curricula and lengths vary, depending on the level of study and the type of organisation and they range from short intensive courses, lasting for up to several months, to extensive courses, lasting for three years or more. The main languages in demand are English, French, Spanish, German and Italian, together with Greek, Arabic, Bulgarian and Polish. Courses on Latin and Esperanto are also run. Generally, the Romanian providers of foreign language courses offer either attendance or graduation certificates and only a few of these are nationally recognised. On the other hand, international institutions often offer internationally recognised certificates on successful completion of their programmes (Modrescu, 1999).

Courses in art and culture

All folk universities, houses of culture, folk schools of art and student clubs offer programmes in fine arts, performance and interpretive arts, music, philosophy, religion, ethnology and other subjects. Literary circles, festivals, exhibitions, workshops, lectures and conferences are also organised. These are open to anyone who wishes to attend.

Civic education courses

This category includes courses organised by the district subsidies of the Ministry of Youth, non-governmental organisations and others. They run programmes mainly on civic culture, education for democracy, ecology, health, moral education and active citizenship. These are usually short-term programmes and are offered to all.

Vocational education

The largest category of beneficiaries from adult education programmes are people seeking work. As explained previously, they are offered requalification and conversion courses, organised either by the district employment agencies, private training providers or by their employers. Since 1990, when a market economy began to develop, Romania has experienced a number of employment problems. The social and economic changes, together with the introduction of the new technologies, have created a more demanding labour market. The requirement for higher-level competencies, including computing skills, has increased while the demand for other qualifications has dropped. The formal educational system has adapted relatively slowly and many private providers of vocational training have appeared as a result (Sava, 2001). A Government Ordinance sets the following objectives for vocational training:

- To facilitate the social integration of the participants in accordance with their vocational aspirations and the needs of the labour market;
- To raise the competitiveness of the work force;
- To update their knowledge and to improve the vocational training for the basic occupations;
- To provide the new qualifications required, reflecting the economic restructuring, increasing social mobility and the reducing number of jobs on offer; and
- To provide the advanced knowledge and new skills required to enable trainees to carry out their work effectively.

The vocational training is provided either through courses organised by suppliers, employers, internships or specialised stages. The training is financed by:

- Employers;
- The social security budget;
- Sponsorship and donations; or
- Participants' fees.

The training programmes finish with an evaluation, including theoretical, and sometimes practical, tests. Depending on the type of programme, the trainees may get on completion:

- A certificate of vocational qualification, for qualification or requalification courses; or
- A graduation certificate for initiation courses or for improvement or specialisation stages.

The certificates issued by suppliers authorised by CNFPA are nationally recognised.

Vocational training is still delivered to a narrow market which is dominated by individual consumers influenced by cost rather than quality. Few companies have the resources to invest in training at present. Consequently, the training process in Romania currently has a weak structure and most of the programmes are ad hoc, targeting short-term goals rather than long-term development strategies (Ghinaru, 2001).

Literacy courses

Communism, in its last decade, declared illiteracy officially eradicated. After 1990, however, the Institute of Educational Sciences revealed the existence of 'at risk populations', especially among the gypsy communities and those in isolated communities. The first literacy courses were organised by schools with the support of organisations dealing with gypsy matters. These courses currently take place in special or evening classes and there are also home teaching programmes, for those unable to travel to school, second chance programmes and concentrated courses. Adult literacy programmes can be funded by the State, by local budgets, contributions from charitable foundations, or through international programmes. Non-governmental organisations, including the church and local authorities, also play an important part in this. As mentioned earlier, programmes are also organised by the Ministry of Defence for soldiers who are found to be illiterate and by the Ministry of Justice for prisoners (Modrescu, 1999).

Conclusion

Adult education in Romania, in spite of its long tradition, currently has a relatively low status within the national education system. Lack of resources, outdated ideologies left over from the communist era and other major social concerns have created obstacles to its development. The initiatives of the last few years have been encouraging, however; the legislation supporting adult education has been strengthened, several important adult education agencies have been created, and increasing numbers of institutions are now offering adult education programmes. Attitudes are also changing, greatly influenced by the nationwide fair, which began in 2000, that presents the continuing education on offer each year.

Education generally in Romania is a national priority. The specific measures put in place by the government for the development of adult education include adequate support for the educational system, a legislative framework for adult education and the diversification of the adult education provision. Education and training are now seen as necessary components of all development programmes. There is institutional coordination of the main actors of the educational processes and the system has been coordinated with the internationally funded programmes to avoid overlaps and gaps within the system and excessive dependence on external funding sources.

These elements form the basis for the future development of the adult education system in Romania, working within the broader framework set up by the EU to create a European Area of Learning and Knowledge.

References

Bârzea, C., *et al.*, 1998. *Dezvoltarea educației permanente în România* (The development of lifelong learning in Romania). Bucharest: National Council for Financing, Alternative Publishing House.

Bârzea, C., *et al.*, 2001a. *Învățarea permanentă – prioritate a politicii educaționale din România* (Lifelong learning – priority for the educational policy of Romania). Bucharest: Institute of Educational Sciences.

Bârzea, C., *et al.*, 2001b. *Impactul social al formării profesionale în România* (The social impact of vocational training in Romania). Bucharest: Observatorul Național Român.

European Commission, 2000a. *Memorandum on Lifelong Learning*. Brussels: Commission of the European Communities. Available at: http://www.bologna-berlin2003.de/pdf/MemorandumEng.pdf

Ghinaru, C., *et al.*, 2001. *Cercetare explorativă privind formarea profesională a adulţilor – Rezumat al Raportului final* (Exploratory research on adult vocational training – Abstract of the final report). Bucharest: National Council for Adult Vocational Training and GOPA RAG.

Itu, M., 1981. *Forme instituţionalizate de educaţie populară în Romania 1859 – 1918* (Institutionalised forms of folk education in Romania). Bucharest: Scientific and Encyclopaedic Publishing House.

Modrescu, C., *et al.*, 1999. *Sistemul educaţional în România. Descriere a responsabilităţilor, structurilor şi acţiunilor de politică educaţională* (The educational system in Romania. Description of the educational policy responsibilities, structures and actions). Bucharest: Trei Publishing House.

Sava, S., ed., 2001. *Educaţia adulţilor în Româmia – Politici educaţionale, culturale şi sociale* (Adult education in Romania – educational, cultural and social policies). Proceedings of the First Conference on Adult Education. Timişoara: Almanahul Banatului Publishing House.

Sava, S. and Mitrache, M., *et al.*, 2003. *Portret al educaţiei adulţilor în România* (Portrait of adult education in Romania). Bucharest: IREA and IIZ/DVV.

Schifirneţ, C., 1997. *Educaţia adulţilor în schimbare* (Adult education shifting). Bucharest: ANUP and Fiat Lux Publishing House.

JÁN PORVAZNÍK AND MARÍNA HUČKOVÁ

18: Adults in Slovakian Higher Education

Definitions and terms

The terms 'further education' (*ďalšie vzdelávanie*), 'continuing education' (*kontinuálne vzdelávanie*) and 'lifelong education' (*celoživotné vzdelávanie*) are all used to refer to adult education in Slovakia. The term 'further education' was introduced in 1997 to replace 'adult education' (Porvazník and Hučková, 2000). As the term 'adult education' is more widely used for this form of education elsewhere in Europe, however, this will be used in the rest of this chapter.

In 1997, the National Council of the Slovak Republic (*Národná rada Slovenskej republiky*) adopted the Further Education Act (No. 386/1997) (*Zákon o ďalšom vzdelávaní*). This law is unclear about the age at which people are considered as adults. It does, however, recognise the problem of determining an appropriate age for classifying an adult and 14, 16, 18 and '20 plus' have all been considered. The age of completion of compulsory school attendance has also been suggested. The factors adopted to define adult education were that:

- It occurred after the completion of compulsory school attendance and followed an interruption of one or more years; and
- When participants continue in part-time education, they should normally be employed.

The Further Education Act (No. 386/1997) states that adult education enables participants to:

- Widen, deepen or replenish their knowledge and proficiency. (Participants are usually awarded a certificate accredited by the Ministry of Education when they complete their courses successfully.);

- Be retrained (usually leading to a certificate);
- Satisfy their own needs and interests whether civil, cultural or other (when a certificate of attendance is provided); and
- Obtain an academic qualification either from the school or higher education (HE) system (for example, a certificate of primary or secondary education or an academic degree or diploma).

The Further Education Act was changed in 2001 to indicate that a masters course or other postgraduate study could not be considered as adult education. Other educational activities, however, which universities organise for graduates (either from their own or from other universities) or for those who have completed their secondary education, are considered to be adult education.

Adult education is organised in specific institutions, including universities, taking the form of both short and long-term programmes and using a variety of teaching methods. The courses take various forms (e.g. part-time study, short retraining courses and programmes of the University of Third Age). The teaching includes both traditional and new methods. For example, some courses use a multimedia approach, videoconferencing or distance learning using correspondence education or the Internet. Detailed information about the adult education provided in all the HE institutions in Slovakia is given in the Appendix.

The current involvement of adults in Slovak universities

Adults can undertake learning either in:

- The faculties of universities that organise education in the form of daily and part-time study sometimes called 'external study' (*externé diaľkové, kombinované štúdium*) or 'study alongside employment' (*štúdium popri zamestnaní*). The aim of these courses is to lead to a university degree or diploma. Unlike many European countries, however, the part-time courses in Slovak universities are not considered to be part of adult education: they are regulated by the Universities Act (No. 131/2002, *Zákon o vysokých školách*) rather than the Further Education Act (No. 386/1997); or
- Adult education centres which organise courses aimed at widening and deepening learners' knowledge. These also provide retraining opportunities and special-interest education for graduates and secondary school leavers on a commercial basis. In this case, participants can be awarded a certificate which can be accredited. To get an accredited certificate, participants have to pass examinations and defend their projects at the end of the course. For employers the accredited certificates are more valuable.

Diploma courses offer their graduates a university qualification while other courses offer certificates of attendance. The Slovak Ministry of Education accredits courses, which are equivalent to those at universities, provided by other adult educational institutions. A course is eligible for accreditation if, according to Further Education Act, No. 386/1997:

- The activity is defined as educational;
- There is appropriate course documentation on the activities outlining the teaching methods and other educational issues;
- It has suitable staff to deliver the course; and

- It has the appropriate learning resources and technical support.

The Ministry approves courses for a five-year period. On the successful completion of an approved course, an accredited certificate with nationwide validity is awarded. The competition between public and private providers of adult education means that the programmes are of high quality. Each course must have appropriate content, study materials, suitable lecturers and an appropriate learning environment, for example suitable accommodation.

Who provides adult education?

At the time of writing (2003) there are twenty-three HE institutions in Slovakia: three State universities, one private university and nineteen public HE institutions. These contain 92 faculties in total.

In the academic year 2001/02, there were about 144,000 students studying in Slovak universities of whom about 97,000 studied full-time and 47,000 part-time. Foreign students numbered 1635.

Table 1: Total numbers of HE institutions, faculties and students

Numbers	1999	2000	2001
HE Institutions	18	20	20
Faculties	86	89	89
Total number of HE students	118,848	125,896	133,664

Table 2: Total numbers of adult students

Numbers	1999	2000	2001
Adult students in all institutions	270,265	283,906	390,254
Adult students in HE institutions	11,778 (4.4%)	15,102 (5.3%)	18,754 (4.8%)
Of whom the number of women is	5,968 (2.2%)	8,028 (2.8%)	8,503 (2.2%)

These figures come from a survey of the whole Slovak education system (Ministry of Education, 2003). The information is compiled from data provided from a sample of about 10% of the 3,000 or so institutions in the country.

Further details of the adult education provided in each Slovak HE institution is given in the Appendix at the end of this chapter.

Problems experienced by adults wishing to take a university diploma course

The motivation for many adults wishing to study at university is the need to improve their qualifications at work, often to achieve career enhancement or because of a long-term interest in a particular subject. An investment in career development often leads to wider job opportunities and this in turn brings a higher salary.

Many adults, however, have problems studying at the HE level following a break after their school education. To help them overcome this, some HE institutions provide preparatory courses to assist adults returning to study at the HE level. (Courses are also available in some university adult education centres to prepare applicants for university entrance examinations.) A further problem is the scarcity of places, particularly in the subjects of law and economics, preventing applicants, including adults, from obtaining places in the subjects that they wish to study.

The number of applicants for university studies is always higher than the number of students who can be accepted (Ministry of Education, 2000b). Therefore requirements for the entrance examinations in some cases exceed the knowledge gained in the schools. The access courses provided by lifelong learning institutes prepare the applicants to manage this situation. They are focussed on subjects tested in the entrance examination. For example, for the University of Economics the applicants are trained in Economics, Mathematics, German and English language and have the possibility of choosing one of five different arrangements of the courses: two-term evening course, two-term Saturday course, one-term evening course, short term evening course or daily intensive course.

As university entrance examinations are based on the secondary school curriculum, there are problems in determining the level of knowledge and skills needed. These may be overcome by proposals which are currently under discussion for a national school leaving examination. The results of the leaving examination provide an initial indication of students' suitability for study at the HE level. If a national examination is adopted, it will be possible to set standardised requirements for university entrance (as is already the case in some countries, including the USA).

Some entrants also experience problems once they have taken their places as part-time students: the demands of studying, and the length of time since some of these students have studied previously, pose particular problems. The universities have responded to this by providing additional courses to help adults who are returning to study to develop the necessary study skills quickly.

Problems experienced by adults wishing to undertake higher education certificate courses

Adults have had fewer problems studying at the certificate level. These courses are organised on a commercial basis and are often seen by the institutions as a good way of supplementing their incomes.

Some restrictions exist, however, if universities teach their courses in a foreign language because the course participants need to speak the language in which the teaching is carried out. This is a problem, for example, for some Master of Business Administration (MBA) and Master of Public Administration courses, which are taught in German or English.

The fees for these courses are paid either by the participants or by their companies. In either case, there are some restrictions with this. For individuals in Slovakia, the salaries are generally low. It is also true that many firms are either not willing to invest in the education of their employees or they have very limited resources to do so.

The State sometimes provides financial support for certified university courses that provide retraining for the unemployed. Where this happens, funding is normally limited to courses offering a restricted range of subjects such as computer skills, business start-up courses, work in small- and medium-size enterprises (SMEs), management accounting, and the organisation and management of businesses.

The universities are also involved in providing courses for older adults (through the University of the Third Age) and the handicapped. The University of the Third Age has a good reputation. Here older people can attend courses in, for example, Fruit and Flower Growing, Gardening and Managing Money as well as computing and foreign languages. Older adults pay a minimal fee for these courses, which can last for up to three years.

The Romany and Hungarian minorities in Slovakia are particularly disadvantaged as far as study at universities is concerned, both at the diploma and certificate levels. Their problems stem mainly from an insufficient knowledge of the Slovak language. Many of the

Romany people have not attended either primary or secondary schools and they do not speak the Slovak language. Although the Hungarian minority have their own schools, they rarely take the opportunity to learn the Slovak language. As a result, members of both minorities are not usually able to pass the entrance examinations for diploma study and they are under-represented on courses leading to qualifications.

Good practice in university adult education in Slovakia

There are many examples of good practice in Slovak university adult education. The following example is taken from the Centre for Advanced Studies of the University of Economics in Bratislava (UEB). This Centre is one of the outstanding university adult education centres in Slovakia. It is an expert educational and research body and it also provides counselling and consulting. Although it was only established in 1990, it has already successfully completed a number of research projects funded both by the Slovak Grant Agency and by a number of international bodies. The Centre has also carried out European Union-funded projects on the management of change, with partners in England and France, and on the education and requalification of adults, in cooperation with partners in the Netherlands and Ireland. It has also participated in EU-TEMPUS projects.

The Centre organises a wide range of courses for varying age groups. It organises preparatory courses for the entrance examinations for the students who wish to study at UEB. In collaboration with other faculties, it also provides courses on a wide range of university subjects. The credits that students earn on these courses are recognised by the University if they enrol for a degree. These courses are provided on a commercial basis. The fees are paid either by the students' companies, by the Labour Office (if they are unemployed), or by the individual students.

The courses in greatest demand are those on marketing, management and economics disciplines. Of these, the most sought after subjects are: the New Economics; Liquidation; Receivership; the Evaluation of Property; preparatory courses for the State examinations for auditors and tax consultants; training for middle and senior managers; and the MBA. The Centre also delivers these courses within the framework of the University of the Third Age.

The Centre for Advanced Studies in UEB has served as a model for other universities when they have established similar units. In the year 1999/2000, the following centres were set up at other Slovak universities:

- The Centre for Further Education and Lifelong Learning at the Comenius University in Bratislava;
- The Institute of Lifelong Learning at the Technical University in Kosice;
- The Centre for Lifelong Learning at the Slovak Technical University in Bratislava; and
- The Institute for Lifelong Learning at the University of Zilina.

Besides these institutes, other universities have also established independent units to provide adult education and new institutes for lifelong learning are being established every year. Through these, universities are developing their cooperation with practice and are receiving additional financial resources in return. Appeals for lifelong education and keeping in contact with graduates are nowadays parts of the presentations of the majority of university chancellors. Improving the quality of the education and research is a major challenge for the development of activities in adult education.

Case Study: A programme for adults – Economics for Everyone

Who is the project designed for?

Economics for Everyone is designed for those who:

- Are already working in marketing, management or financial posts and who lack the necessary knowledge in these fields or who are interested in updating or widening their knowledge;
- Wish to change their professions and who would like to work in marketing, management or financial positions; or
- Are entrepreneurs, including the owners of SMEs.

The aim of the project

The project aims to provide up-to-date knowledge from:

- Marketing, in which the participants learn how to use the concepts of marketing in their businesses and more widely in their professional careers;
- General management, where they learn how to put management structures in place and how to operate these; and
- Finance, where they learn how to manage financial matters efficiently and economically.

The structure of the project

The course contains the following modules:

1. Management in work and business
2. Legal forms of enterprise organisations
3. Entrepreneurial legislation
4. Basics of marketing
5. Personnel management
6. Corporate finance
7. Accountancy

8. Insurance
9. Banking
10. Taxes and taxing
11. Financial analyses
12. Costing and pricing
13. Budgeting
14. Purchasing and stock control
15. Exporting and importing.

Entrance requirements

The only entrance requirement is to have completed secondary school education. Applicants can enrol for all the modules or for a selection of these according to their needs.

Accreditation and assessment

At the end of their study, the participants are required to take a written examination and also to defend a report on a project that they have carried out on an approved topic. Successful students are awarded a certificate that has national recognition. The project is accredited by the Ministry of Education of the Slovak Republic.

Forms of study

Study in the project is organised in different forms:

- 108 hours – e-learning study. (Only three modules are available in the e-learning mode at the moment. The twelve other e-learning modules are in the course of preparation.);
- 128 hours – one term, weekend study;
- 180 hours – distance study, in correspondence form; or
- 240 hours – two-terms evening study (twice a week) and retraining study for the unemployed in daily form (six hours per day).

The number of hours matches the initial knowledge of the participants.

Study materials

Students are issued at the beginning of their course with the following study materials:

- Study texts for the fifteen modules (about 2,200 pages);
- Notes for each lecture session (about 200 pages);
- Materials for e-learning study (about 420 pages, for three modules).

Updating study materials

The basic study literature is updated every three years. (The materials are presently in their Third Edition.) The notes for the lecture sessions are updated at the beginning of each course.

Interest in the project

Between 1993 and 2003, 850 students graduated from this course. The course currently enrols between 100 and 150 students a year but not all of these graduate and are awarded certificates.

References

Further Education Act, No. 386/1997. *Zákon o ďalšom vzdelávaní.*

Ministry of Education, 1999. *Ďalšie vzdelávanie na Slovensku: inštitúcie ďalšieho vzdelávania a ich programy ďalšieho vzdelávania.* (Further education in Slovakia: educational institutions and their programmes of further education). Bratislava: Ministry of Education of the Slovak Republic.

Ministry of Education, 2000a. *Ďalšie vzdelávanie na Slovensku: inštitúcie ďalšieho vzdelávania a ich programy ďalšieho vzdelávania.* (Further education in Slovakia: educational institutions and their programmes of further education). Bratislava: Ministry of Education of the Slovak Republic.

Ministry of Education, 2000b. *Štatistické údaje.* (Statistical data). Bratislava: Ministry of Education of the Slovak Republic.

Ministry of Education, 2003. *Ústav informácií a prognóz školstva.* (The Institute of Information and Predictions of the Education System). Bratislava: Ministry of Education of the Slovak Republic.

Osborne, M. and Thomas, E., eds., 2003. *Lifelong learning in a changing continent: Continuing education in the universities of Europe.* Chapter 28. Leicester: National Institute of Adult Continuing Education.

Porvazník, J. and Hučková, M., 2000. *National Report on Adult Education in Slovakia.* Bratislava: Centre for Advanced Studies, University of Economics. Prepared for the SOCRATES – Alpine Programme.

Universities Act. No. 131/2002. *Zákon o vysokých školách.*

Appendix: Educational activities offered for adults in Slovak universities

This information is based on: Ministry of Education, 1999, Ministry of Education, 2000a, Osborne and Thomas, 2003)

Name of University	*Departments/ Centres/ Institutes providing continuing education*	*Year of foundation*	*Educational activities offered*	*Web addresses*
University of Economics in Bratislava	Faculties		language courses, information technology (IT) courses, preparatory courses for entrance examinations.	www.euba.sk
	Centre for Advanced Studies	1990	financial management, management of SMEs, business strategy and development planning, MBA. New Economics: marketing, finance and management, accountancy, entrepreneurial skills development, legislative and tax code, enterprise liquidation, assets administration, enterprise assets valuation, computing and language courses, UEB admission and induction courses, soft-skills training: self and time management. Bachelor's studies, correspondence studies, University of the Third Age.	http://cdv.euba.sk
	Centre of European Studies	1998	educational programmes for experts, integration of the Slovak Republic into the European Union (EU).	

Name of University	*Departments/ Centres/ Institutes providing continuing education*	*Year of foundation*	*Educational activities offered*	*Web addresses*
Slovak University of Technology in Bratislava	Faculties		short courses and study programmes: management, marketing, IT, languages, production quality, supplementary teaching courses for graduates and university students, summer schools.	www.stuba.sk
	Institute of Lifelong Learning – departments: Continuing Education Centre, Intensive Education Centre, Language Centre, French Centre, Local Centre of Distance Education, University of Third Age	1994	language courses (French Centre and Language Centre), architecture, food and health, IT (University of Third Age), specialised and retraining courses, industrial ecology, electrotechnical competence, safety at work for managers and entrepreneurs (Continuing Education Centre), new educational and technological possibilities available for the provision of distance education at the Slovak University of Technology, Bratislava, educational courses for the general public on request: IT, computing related to distance education (Intensive Education Centre, former National Centre for Distance Education), development of cooperation between faculties, universities and international partners for the implementation of projects (Intensive Education Centre). Distance education courses: Preparation for university studies: mathematics, physics, chemistry, ICT, management, pedagogy, multimedia, Internet/Intranet, English for professional communication (Local Centre of Distance Education).	www.stuba.sk/svk/studium/index.html www.kar.elf.stuba.sk/lsdv

Name of University	*Departments/ Centres/ Institutes providing continuing education*	*Year of foundation*	*Educational activities offered*	*Web addresses*
	Institute of Industrial Management		management and economics courses for university graduates.	
Slovak University of Agriculture in Nitra	Faculties		teacher training for university and secondary school graduates, course on university teaching. Three-year specialised study: environmental management, language courses, and summer schools.	www.spu.sk
	Centre for Lifelong Education		distance education: biodiversity conservation and sustainable development in agro-environments, other short courses (Local Centre of Distance Education).	http:/www.fern.uniag.sk/dv
	University of the Third Age		horticulture, viniculture, nourishment and health, agricultural tourism, accountancy, economics, management.	
Technical University Košice	Faculties			www.tuke.sk
	Institute of Lifelong Learning Departments: Local Centre of Distance Education, Centre for Continuing Education, University of the Third Age	1996	educational programmes: MBA, strategic management, environmental management, electrical engineering, human resources, risk management, quality management. Distance education: banking, retraining courses, the new economics and entrepreneurship, personnel management. Short courses: IT, languages, communication skills, project management, mathematics. Internet distance education programmes: dealing with problematic people, on-line courses (Local Centre of Distance Education), environ-	www.tuke.sk/icv/

Name of University	*Departments/ Centres/ Institutes providing continuing education*	*Year of foundation*	*Educational activities offered*	*Web addresses*
			mental management courses, IT, human resource development. Summer schools: Ecology (Centre for Continuing Education), University of the Third Age, teacher training.	
Technical University Zvolen	Faculties		retraining courses, short courses.	www.tuzvo.sk
	Local Centre of Distance Education (independent from the University)	1994	corporate management, finance and banking, environmental education, waste treatment, landscaping and land surveying, computing, on-line courses. University of the Third Age.	http://alpha.tuzvo.sk/~simakova/
Comenius University in Bratislava	Faculties		supplementary teaching skills courses, teaching the mentally ill and handicapped, school speech therapy, teaching in kindergartens, special pedagogy for governesses/tutors, teaching in primary and secondary schools, translation (Faculty of Education). Distance education course: biodiversity, conservation and sustainable development (Faculty of Natural Sciences).	www.uniba.sk
	Centre for Further Education and Lifelong Learning	2000	short-term courses: effective communication, development of business skills, communication in managing people, communication with clients, diplomatic protocol, managing stress, time management, handwriting expertise, journalism, environmental studies. Long-term courses: theory and practice in journalism, the Slovak economy, publicity, marketing, communication management,	www.uniba.sk/cdcv/index.htm

Name of University	*Departments/ Centres/ Institutes providing continuing education*	*Year of foundation*	*Educational activities offered*	*Web addresses*
			lecturers' certificate course, education management, social management, psychology of management, effective management of human resources, modern personnel management, language courses.	
	University of the Third Age	1990	archaeology, economics, history of fine art, history of religions, philosophy, gerontology, Slovak history, general history, environmental science, Japanese culture, yoga, regeneration of the strength of seniors, ethnology, social work, medicine, pharmacy, psychology, computers and information, legal journalism, horticulture and gardening, astronomy.	www.uniba.sk /webuk/www/ sucasti_uk/ UTV/index. htm
Matej Bel University in Banská Bystrica	Faculties		supplementary teaching skills study: Slovak language and literature for tutors and university graduates.	www.rekt. umb.sk
	University of the Third Age	1992	nourishment and unconventional forms of medicine, natural medicine, the healthy way of life in old age, gerontology, getting older successfully, horticulture, law, philosophy and art, travelling, formal and diplomatic protocol, languages.	
	Methodical Centre of the Matej Bel University for Slovaks living abroad	1993	social sciences, natural sciences (taught in Slovak).	

Name of University	*Departments/ Centres/ Institutes providing continuing education*	*Year of foundation*	*Educational activities offered*	*Web addresses*
	Centre of Lifelong Learning		European studies. Special English language courses: First Certificate in English, Certificate of Advanced English preparation and effective presentations in English.	
University of Žilina	Faculties		supplementary pedagogical study, supplementary courses of teacher training for students and graduates. Specialised courses for members of the Armed Forces: defence and security, technical protection of railways and the conveyance of material in emergency situations, forensic engineering.	www.utc.sk
	Institute of Lifelong Learning Departments: Local Centre of Distance Education, French – Slovak Centre for Education, University School of Languages, Centre for Language Preparation of Foreign Students	1997	distance education: banking, logistics, company management, sales management and marketing, environmental politics, tunnels, road quality, computer courses, Internet, Course for Webmasters (Local Centre of Distance Education). Languages (French – Slovak Centre for Education, University School of Languages). Additional Pedagogical Study (Department of Professional Development). University of the Third Age.	www.utc.sk/ lsdv/default. htm
University of Trnava	Faculties		lifelong study: organisational management (in English), pastoral theology (in Polish), social legislation and social doctrine of the Catholic Church, supplementary courses.	www.truni.sk

Name of University	*Departments/ Centres/ Institutes providing continuing education*	*Year of foundation*	*Educational activities offered*	*Web addresses*
Prešov University	Faculties		supplementary teacher training study. Three term course: basics of teaching adults for directors of academies of education. Two year study: translation, teaching the mentally ill and socially disturbed.	www.unipo.sk
University of Trenčín	Faculties		teaching skills study (for the staff of UT), IT, languages, University of the Third Age.	www.tnuni.sk
Catholic University in Ružomberok	Faculties		supplementary teaching skills courses.	www.ku.sk
The University of Sts. Cyril and Methodius in Trnava	Faculties		mass media study programme, supplementary teaching skills courses for university graduates.	www.ucm.sk
Constantine the Philosopher University in Nitra	Faculties		retraining teachers, doctoral study, languages, and additional study for Foiskolai (Hungarian) graduates, and preparation of distance learning, University of the Third Age.	www.ukf.sk
Pavol Joseph Šafárik University in Košice	Faculties		extended teaching skills. Supplementary teaching skills study: biology, physics, geography, chemistry, mathematics, IT, tailor-made courses. University of the Third Age.	www.upjs.sk www.science.upjs.sk
University of Veterinary Medicine, Košice	Faculties		specialised study for practising veterinary surgeons, postgraduate study.	www.uvm.sk
Academy of Fine Arts and Design, Bratislava	Faculties		supplementary study for university students, supplementary teaching skills.	www.afad.sk

Name of University	*Departments/ Centres/ Institutes providing continuing education*	*Year of foundation*	*Educational activities offered*	*Web addresses*
Military Academy in Liptovský Mikuláš	Faculties		short specialised courses, additional teaching skills, languages, retraining courses for retired soldiers.	www.valm.sk
Academy of Music and Dramatic Arts, Bratislava	Faculties		teaching skills (teachers, public), study visits. Short courses: film art, film history, projection, specialised language courses for the art industry, management courses for cultural institution staff.	www.vsmu.sk
The Air Force Academy of GMRS in Košice	Faculties		courses for students and graduates.	www.vlake.sk
Art Academy in Banská Bystrica	Faculties		summer courses, seminars.	www.aku.sk
Military Police Academy in Bratislava	Institute for Lifelong Learning		one term supplementary courses: police services, languages.	http://apz.minv.sk
City University			courses for the general public: general English, business English, preparation for TOEFL (Teaching of English as a Foreign Language) examinations.	www.vsm.sk/

MARGERITA ZAGMAJSTER

19: Adults in Slovenian Higher Education

Introduction

Higher education (HE) for adults in Slovenia has been defined by Mihevc *et al.* (1995) as:

> [...] different modes of education provided by HE institutions for those who did not continue with education immediately after completing their secondary schooling, irrespective of the content, the level, or the methods used. It includes formal education for the acquisition of education (part-time studies, post-graduate studies) and also shorter programmes which have been adapted to the needs of adults.

In this paper we will present the general structure of the HE sector in Slovenia, the statistical data on different types of provision for adult education, the problems adults are facing in the field of part-time adult HE, endeavours for improvements of part-time studies at the University of Ljubljana and within the National Programme for HE. At the end of the paper, an example of good practice in the field of HE for adults is given.

Higher Education in Slovenia

In Slovenia, HE institutions provide a range of educational programmes specifically for adults together with programmes where adults are the main constituent group, though not exclusively so.

The HE sector in Slovenia is composed of three public universities and a number of other independent HE establishments. One of the three public universities is situated in the capital, Ljubljana, another in the second largest town, Maribor and the third in the main city of the Slovenian coast, Koper. The University of Ljubljana is made up of 22 faculties, three art academies and one professional college. In addition, one professional college has associate status within the University. The University of Maribor has eleven faculties and one professional college. The University of Primorska was established recently (in 2003) and consists of three faculties and two professional colleges. There are also seven private HE institutions, independent HE establishments (*Visoko šolstvo*, 2004).

Continuing education broadly in Slovenia's universities has already been recently described (Zagmajster, 2003). The universities and other HE institutions also provide other types of provision outside the university sector involving adults. The provision of different types of adult provision within Slovenian HE is decentralised and there are no separate units providing education for adults at the university level.

Some HE institutions have departments which offer short courses, for example the Faculty of Arts, University of Ljubljana has the Centre for Pedagogical Education and the Faculty of Economics, University of Ljubljana has a Centre for Management Development and Training.

Part-time studies are also offered in many different locations in Slovenia, usually in centres for continuing education.[1] The delivery of HE programmes depends on the demand for education and this varies from place to place. The opportunity to study at home has also provided greater access to education for particular target groups, particularly adults, and has especially helped to stimulate regional development.

1 These are independent institutions with legal status and their main role is to provide education and training broadly for adults in the region.

Modes of Provision

Adult education is provided in different forms and at different levels. These include:

- Part-time studies at the undergraduate level (organized both as university-type programmes and as professional-type programmes);
- Postgraduate studies;
- Short continuing education courses; and
- Various methods of university outreach.

Part-time HE studies for adults is usually organised separately from full-time studies and the organisation and scheduling of lectures and seminars is normally adapted to meet the specific needs of adults. The lectures are usually organized at weekends (on Friday afternoons and Saturdays). The number of lecturing hours in part-time studies is lower than in full-time studies. The number of lecturing hours depends on the specific requirements of each course and on the experience of how demanding the course is. The courses are usually delivered one after another; within full-time studies the courses are usually delivered simultaneously. The examinations follow some days after the end of the course delivery and they take place in the premises of the study centre if the part-time study programme has been delivered there.

Funding of adult higher education

HE institutions are financed from the national budget[2] to deliver full-time, but not part-time, studies. Full-time students at public HE institutions are not required to pay tuition fees while part-time students are (Higher Education Act, 1998). In some cases, however, the fees for

2 They also receive other funding, for example from tuition fees and payments for other services.

the latter are paid by their employers. The level of the fees differs from one institution to another and also for different types of programme.

There are currently no reliable statistics on how many adults in total take part in the various forms of adult education in Slovenian HE. However, data for the academic year 2002/03 show that most, but not all, HE establishments invited applications for part-time study in HE programmes.[3] More than 75% of the HE institutions in Slovenia, however, offered at least one programme to be delivered part-time.

In Table 1 the number and structure of the undergraduate student body is shown by mode of study.

Table 1: Undergraduate students in Slovene HE by mode of study. Source: (Prijave *[...], 2002/03)*

	2002/03
Undergraduate students (absolute numbers)[4]	
– full-time	49,818
– part-time	22,526
TOTAL	72,344
Undergraduate students (percentages)	100.0%
– full-time	68.9
– part-time	31.1

Table 1 shows that during 2002/03 part-time students numbered 31%. Most part-time students study in the fields of business administration, management, economics, public administration, organisational sci-

3 In the call for applications for study in 2002/03 the opportunity to study part-time is available in 44% of the undergraduate full-time study programmes (*Razpis* [...], 2002).

4 These numbers exclude those who still have the formal status of students but who have not yet finished their studies completely. A period of 12 months is given at the end of formal study in Slovenia during which time students have the opportunity to complete their study obligations and to prepare their theses.

ences, maritime studies, law and education. These subjects reflect the needs of the job market.

In some HE institutions, the number of part-time students outstrips the full-time student number. This is partly explained by the fact that about half the part-time students are unemployed and have previously been rejected as full-time students because of the *numerus clausus*[5] or are not entitled to enrol in HE because of other limitations concerning enrolment in full-time study.

The number of part-time students increased from 5,791 in the academic year 1990/91 (*Statistični letopis* [...], 2003) to 22,526 in 2002/03 and is growing faster than the number of full-time students.[6]

Postgraduate studies are designed mainly for adult learners. In 2002/03 there were 5,606 students enrolled on postgraduate studies (of whom 668 were at the specialist level and 4,938 enrolled for masters degree programmes). 52.3% of postgraduate students are women (*Statistične informacije* [...], 2003). No data are available on the number of adults who have enrolled for doctoral study.

Postgraduate studies have been partially financed from the national budget since 1998/99. HE institutions are therefore able to obtain some funding to support those postgraduate programmes that meet the required criteria.

Some HE institutions deliver short programmes or courses aimed at updating the knowledge of past students or other target groups. The Centre for Management Development and Training in the Faculty of Economics, University of Ljubljana (CISEF) offers courses in the fields of marketing, banking, finance, general management, economics and organisation, business communication, accounting, human resource management and foreign languages (CISEF, 2003) to about 2000 managers, executives and professionals from companies, banks and other organisations annually. The Centre for Pedagogical

5 The percentage of part-time students who were unemployed differs by year of study. In 2001/02, in the first study year 40.2% of the part-time students were employed, in the second year 52.3%, in the third year 73.9% and in fourth year 75.6%. In total, 56.5% of the part-time students were employed.

6 The number of part-time students grew by 389% and the number of full-time students by 260% if we compare the numbers of students enrolled in the years 1990/91 and 2002/03.

Education within the Faculty of Arts, University of Ljubljana offers a wide range of programmes which can be clustered in three main groups:

- Programmes for permanent professional training (in topics such as andragogy, foreign languages and librarianship);
- Programmes for training in the fields of pedagogy, andragogy, library science, philosophy, geography, classical languages, musicology, pedagogy, psychology, sociology, art history, history, including interdisciplinary programmes (philosophy, culturology, sociology); and
- Different programmes (including summer schools) in the field of HE didactics (*Center* [...], 2003).

The programmes are mostly aimed at the training or updating of schoolteachers.

These types of programmes provide HE institutions with additional resources. Participants are required to pay the full fees (although in many cases these are reimbursed by their employers).

Some HE institutions also organise lectures and discussion programmes for the general public with the aim of meeting the needs of the wider community. These are not aimed at the business sector and no charge is made. For example the Faculty of Law of the University of Ljubljana organises international forums on different topics such as the enlargement of Europe and EU law delivered by prominent personalities, including politicians, from other countries.

Issues in involving adults in higher education

The change from a socialist economic system to a market-oriented economy, which began in 1991, has led to many changes in Slovenia. The transition period of the nineties, moving towards the new economic, social and political structures, led to a new demand for further and higher education. Even though the number of part-time[7] and post-graduate students has constantly risen over this period, adult students have faced a number of obstacles inhibiting them from participating in HE.

Adults interested in higher adult education face different types of barriers which have been widely reported in the international adult education literature (Rubenson, 1986). These barriers are classified as situational (for example, lack of time and money), institutional (for example, HE programmes not adapted for the needs of adults) and dispositional (such as negative attitudes towards the education of adults).

Adults in Slovenia who wish to participate in higher adult education face all three of these types of barriers. Earlier research by Mihevc *et al.* (1995) showed that a number of problems exist in Slovenia in the field of part-time adult HE. These can be summarised as follows:

- Entry requirements for HE programmes are the same for full-time and part-time students (in general this is the completion of secondary schooling);[8]
- Accreditation of prior experiential learning (APEL) is not yet possible within the HE sector;
- The curriculum is the same for young full-time students and for adults and is not adapted to the working experience of adults;

7 Interest in part-time study rose, mirroring the rising ambitions of young people, high rates of unemployment, the increase in the number of places available for study, and the establishment of new HE institutions (Kump *et al.*, 1998). The growing interest in part-time study in recent years has arisen, at least in part, because of the new regulations concerning part-time studies in the Higher Education Act. Before this Act came into force, a prerequisite for enrolment in part-time studies was that the candidate had to be employed. From 1994 onwards, unemployed adults have also had the right to enrol.

8 The candidates for part-time studies have to register for HE programmes using the same procedure as the candidates for full-time studies. The conditions for enrolment are the same for both groups (*Razpis* [...], 2002).

- The delivery mode in higher adult education is in most cases based on traditional education which is not sufficiently flexible (except in one case);[9]
- The teaching methods are not adapted to the different characteristics, experience and problems of adults;
- Most part-time students have to pay their own fees in order to study;[10]
- Some HE programmes are still offered only to full-time students;
- The possibility of studying part-time is limited as the number of applicants outstrips the number of places available for part-time study in some HE institutions;
- Guidance before enrolment on study for part-time students has not been adapted to the specific needs of adults;
- There is a lack of short updating programmes for adults who graduated some years ago and who are looking for additional knowledge in some professional areas;
- There is a lack of systematic training for teachers in the teaching methods appropriate for adults, in the use of ICT in education and in e-learning;
- The financing of higher adult education is mostly left to the market and resources from the Government for financing higher adult education are very limited;
- Part-time students were often lower achievers at their secondary schools and they lack the skills for studying independently; and
- There is a lack of systematic support for research in the field of adult HE.

9 The Business School in the Faculty of Economics of the University of Ljubljana has delivered distance education programmes since 1995. This example of good practice is presented at the end of this chapter.

10 Part-time students are not able to obtain credit for their study except from commercial banks. In addition, for some HE programmes the payment of fees by instalment is not permitted.

While the solution of all these issues is relevant to encouraging adults to participate in HE, there is a need for further testing through local research programmes to define more precisely what the problems are and how they might be solved.

An attempt has recently been made to improve the delivery of part-time studies at the University of Ljubljana. In the academic year 2000/01, the particular problems experienced by academic staff working with adult students studying part-time were considered by the senior management of the University. Within this survey, a number of criticisms of part-time studies arose centred on their lower efficiency (for example, lower progression rates from one year to the next and lower average marks). It was also suggested that the main aim of some HE institutions in offering these courses was opportunistic: that they were developing this form of provision just to obtain additional resources rather than to provide students with high quality education.

Members of the University of Ljubljana were asked to comment on the delivery of part-time studies in their own departments and also to write a self-evaluation report for 2000/01. In the draft paper on quality which was prepared on the basis of these reports, it was revealed that efficiency was usually lower in part-time than in full-time studies. Problems which were found to inhibit the further expansion of part-time studies included the lack of adequate financial support for students and the shortage of classroom space (Mihevc, 2001). The University of Ljubljana has recently recommended limiting the number of part-time students, particularly those who had not succeeded in getting a full-time place and who had subsequently enrolled on a part-time programme and, in particular, those who were unemployed. It was also recommended that the number of part-time students should not outstrip the number of full-time students at individual faculties. A further problem which was recognised was that the teachers delivering courses to adults were the same teachers who delivered courses to full-time students; they do not have any special training on how to teach adult students or on how to manage their particular needs.

Adults in higher education: new possibilities

There is currently no specific policy at either the national or university level aimed at lowering the barriers for the education of adults within the HE sector. In February 2002, a National Programme for Higher Education (*Nacionalni* […], 2002) was approved by the Slovene Parliament. One of the main objectives of this programme is to widen access to HE both at the undergraduate and postgraduate levels. The overall aim is to increase the level of education of the Slovene population. The programme states that the resources for financing HE from the government will increase in the coming years. The following proposals concerning adults were made:

- The further development of higher adult education should be stimulated with shorter programmes at a higher level, especially to update the knowledge of graduates;
- Part-time studies should be aimed largely at those students who cannot enrol in full-time studies for employment or other personal reasons. At the same time the numbers of places for full-time studies should be increased to ease the pressure on part-time places;
- Some financial support for part-time studies should be provided from the national budget in line with the increase in the numbers of part-time students;
- HE institutions are responsible for assuring the same quality of provision for both groups of students (full-time and part-time); and
- The development of distance education (DE) programmes should be accelerated because of the success already achieved (*Nacionalni* [...], 2002).

Case Study: Distance education involving adults in the Faculty of Economics, University of Ljubljana

An example of good practice in the HE of adults is the DE programme of the Faculty of Economics at Ljubljana, which seeks to provide better access to learning for adults. This project uses innovative approaches by replacing part-time face-to-face studies with DE.

The Faculty of Economics is the largest faculty in the University of Ljubljana; the total number of students enrolled in the academic year 2000/01 exceeded 10,000. In the early nineties the proportion of part-time students in the Faculty increased substantially. While part-time study became a considerable source of income for the Faculty, questions concerning its overall efficiency began to be raised. The dropout rate on the part-time programme was much higher than on the full-time programme and the delivery of part-time studies required much more input by staff, who had to travel each week to outreach centres scattered around Slovenia.[11] This was in addition to an already high full-time teaching load.

As a result it was decided to develop DE programmes to:

- Increase educational opportunities in Slovenia;
- Provide greater flexibility in the implementation of study programmes; and
- Provide better access to education for those adults whose opportunities are restricted within the traditional mode of delivery, such as the handicapped and people who are unable to attend classes due to work restrictions (Bregar, 1995).

The problems associated with the existing provision led the management of the Faculty to conclude that DE would be a better tool for improving teaching and learning for adults. A DE project was therefore developed by the Business School within the Faculty. This commenced in 1994 and the first DE students enrolled in late 1995. In

11 One of the Faculty's programmes was delivered to part-time students in nine study centres at different locations in Slovenia.

the first year, this programme was organised in three study centres, with a total of 200 students enrolling.[12] Since then, the programme has developed a second, third and fourth year of study. After a successful start, the number of students has increased. In 2002 there were more than 1,600 students enrolled in eleven study centres.

The University of Ljubljana is at present the only HE institution in Slovenia delivering a fully accredited degree programme by DE. The diploma obtained from this programme is equivalent to the taught course diploma obtained through full- or part-time study.

Admission requirements are the same for all three categories of undergraduate students in the Business School: full-time, part-time and DE students. Everyone who has successfully completed his or her secondary schooling and has passed the final secondary school examination is eligible to enrol.

Most DE students are adults. The majority are economically active, either in paid employment, self-employment or occasional employment (Bregar, 1997). For many of them, the DE study mode offers the only possible way of obtaining a degree because of family, job or financial circumstances. DE is especially suited to those who work in shifts or whose working hours are split into two parts during the day, for those living in remote geographical areas or with poor access to formal education centres, for women with small children and for the handicapped. Since the DE programme is delivered in study centres throughout Slovenia, the students do not have to reside in Ljubljana or to come there.

This programme might be better described as guided self-study. The classical face-to face lectures no longer exist. Instead the students are provided with a package of study materials[13] developed mainly in

12 The development of this DE programme was part of the EU-funded Phare Multi-country Programme for Distance Education. The Phare Programme lasted from 1995 to 1999 and Slovenia was one of 13 Central and Eastern European countries which took part.

13 Printed DE study materials are still the most common although, for certain courses (e.g. foreign languages), audiotapes are available. For some courses (especially statistics), students are provided with diskettes with self-assessment activities, CD-roms or interactive on-line study materials with links to outside data and courses.

the Faculty. For most of their time, the students study independently at home. In addition, however, different forms of student support, organised by tutors and academic staff, are available within the study centres.

The effect of the introduction of DE within the Faculty has been to improve the quality, especially of the study materials and of the educational process generally. DE was the impetus for the development of higher quality study materials coupled with the introduction of modern media into the educational process. Not only DE students benefited from this change but also the full-time and part-time students. The routine teaching workload of professors became smaller (with less need to deliver the same lecture to several student groups) and this has made it possible for them to focus on more creative professional work. In this process, the teaching and support staff have also acquired additional knowledge of their subjects and new skills in the use of information technology.

The programme has considerable potential for economic, social and cultural development across Slovenia and it has also had a positive impact on widening access to HE. It is creating new opportunities for education and is also reducing pressure on the HE system from students who would otherwise have had to enrol as full-time studies.

A recent examination of the efficiency of the programme has shown that the programme delivered in the DE mode can be more efficient than part-time study and in some respects even outstrips full-time study. The main results of the investigation are summarized in the table below.

Table 2: Results of the survey on study efficiency in the Economics Faculty of the University of Ljubljana for students who enrolled in the academic year 1995/96 (Balon, 2000).

Performance Indicators	Distance education	Traditional education	
		Part-time study	Full-time study
Number of students in the survey	115	340	437
Percentage of students progressing from the first to the second academic year of study	47.0	38.5	49.1
Average first year score of students enrolled in 1995/96	7.04[14]	6.82	6.91
Average first year score of students enrolled in 1999/2000	7.85	7.28	7.47

The development and introduction of DE into Slovenian HE has brought benefits to students (especially adults) and to the members of the academic staff. It has also promoted access to education for adults from all over Slovenia.

Conclusion

The rapid changes in society are beginning to impact on HE and the universities are starting to look at the issue of how to provide for the needs of lifelong learners. How Slovene HE as a whole will cope with this challenge has yet to be seen. While there are many problems

14 The maximum score in the Slovenian higher education assessment system is ten, with six as the minimum score to pass the examination.

ahead, however, the new national programme may well provide the incentive that is needed to meet these demands.

References

Balon, A., 2000. *Izkušnje in dosežki Ekonomske fakultete pri uvajanju študija na daljavo.* (Experiences and Results in DE Development in the Faculty of Economics). Proceedings of the Conference on the Quality of Adult Education. Portorož, Slovenia, 16–17 May 2000.

Bregar, L., ed., 1995. *Študij na daljavo – nove priložnosti za izobraževanje.* (Distance Education – New Educational Opportunities). Ljubljana: Ekonomska fakulteta. Univerza v Ljubljani.

Bregar, L., 1997. *The Introduction of Distance Education – The Accelerator of Innovation at a Traditional University.* 18th ICDE World Conference 'The New Learning Environment: A Global Perspective', Pennsylvania.

Center za pedagoško izobraževanje, 2003. Available at: http://www.ff.uni-lj.si/rsz/cpi2.html

CISEF. 2003. Available at: http://www.cis.ef.uni-lj.si/english/contents/prva.asp

Higher Education Act. In: *Higher Education in Slovenia*, 1998. Ljubljana: Ministry of Education and Sport.

Kump, S., Vrečko, D. and Podmenik, D., 1998. Slovenia: System of Higher Education. In: Husen, T., Postlethwighte, N., Clark, B.R. and Neave, G. eds., *Education: The Complete Encyclopedia.* Oxford: Elsevier Science.

Mihevc, B. *et al.*, 1995. *Visokošolsko izobraževanje odraslih.* (Higher Adult Education). Ljubljana: Andragoški Center Republike Slovenije.

Mihevc, B., 2001. *Izboljševanje kakovosti univerze – naša stalna skrb.* (Improving the Quality of the University – Our Permanent

Concern). *Ugotovitve in predlogi iz poročil članic Univerze v Ljubljani, študijsko leto 2000/2001. Delovno gradivo*. Ljubljana: Univerza v Ljubljani.

Nacionalni program visokega šolstva v Republiki Sloveniji. 2002. (National Programme of Higher Education in Republic of Slovenia). Ljubljana: Uradni list Republike Slovenije št.20/2002.

Prijave za vpis v prvi letnik, študijsko leto 2002/03. (Applications for Enrolment in First Year of Study, Academic Year 2002/2003). Visokošolska prijavno-informacijska služba. 2003. Available at: http://www.vpis.uni-lj.si

Razpis Univerze v Ljubljani, Univerze v Mariboru in samostojnih visokošolskih zavodov za vpis v študijskem letu 2002/2003, 2002. (Call for Applications for the University of Ljubljana, the University of Maribor and for free-standing higher education institutions). Ljubljana: Ministrstvo za šolstvo in šport. Republika Slovenija.

Rubenson, K., 1986. Distance Education for Adults: Old and New Barriers for Participation. In*: Distance Higher Education and the Adult Learner. Occasional Papers of the Dutch Open University. Vol. 1*. Heerlen: Dutch Open University.

Statistični letopis Republike Slovenije 2001 (Statistical Yearbook of the Republic of Slovenia 2001). Vol. XL. Ljubljana: Statistični urad Republike Slovenije.

Statistične informacije št. 136 (Rapid Reports No.136). Statistical Office of the Republic of Slovenia, June 2003.

Visoko šolstvo. Ministrstvo za šolstvo, znanost in šport, 2004. Available at: http://www.mszs.si/slo/solstvo/visoko/visoko.asp

Zagmajster, M., 2003. University continuing education in Slovenia. In: M. Osborne and E. Thomas, eds., *Lifelong Learning in a Changing Continent: continuing education in the universities of Europe*. Leicester: National Institute of Adult Continuing Education, pp.422–34.

EBBA OSSIANNILSSON

20: Adults in Swedish Higher Education

Introduction

Adult education (*vuxenutbildning*) is extensive in Sweden and has a long tradition. It ranges from higher education (HE) to non-formal popular education and, in subject matter, from vocational training to competence development for life. Although rich in the variety of its subjects and delivered through a large number of organisations, some common principles can be found. Swedish adult education is highly decentralised and autonomous. Responsibility for this work is carried by institutions, municipalities and local organisations. As a general principle, adult education is free of charge to the learner and is financed by the public purse (although a few organisations can charge fees). Students and learners are offered financial assistance in the form of grants and loans in order to facilitate their studies (Sweden, 2003a). Just over one million people are currently enrolled in adult education programmes, including the Adult Education Initiative (*Kunskapslyftet*) and popular adult education.

The Swedish Government has responded to the recommendations and demands for initiatives on lifelong learning and e-learning, both from the OECD (1998; 2002) and the European Commission (European Community, 2000; 2001a; 2001b; 2001c; European Community, 2002a; 2002b; Collis and Wende, 2002; Holmes, 2001; and elearning-europa, 2003). In 2001, the Open University Bill (*Den Öppna Högskolan*, 2001/02, p.15) was passed. This provides directives and guidelines for all higher education institutions (HEIs) which are regulated by the National Agency of Higher Education (*Högskoleverket*, 2003). The Swedish perspective, mainly since 2000, together with some specific examples of good practice, are summarised in this chapter.

The Swedish Government is making heavy demands on universities to provide high quality lifelong learning (SUHF, 2001; *Högskoleverkets årsrapport*, 2001; *Budgetpropositionen*, 2002; *Den Öppna Högskolan*, 2002). Society is changing rapidly at the moment; working life is becoming ever more complex, requiring high levels of competence and knowledge and new ways of updating work-based competences are needed. Research into different forms of university continuing education (UCE) is already extensive and is increasing. The Swedish system currently offers opportunities for continuing education, in-service training and reskilling. The system is open to everyone with the necessary entrance qualifications, irrespective of age or social background, and it also provides an entitlement to financial support for study.

Swedish adult education and its context

Some facts and figures are necessary here to give a clear picture of the environment within which Swedish adult education has developed. Higher education in Sweden is delivered through 13 State universities and 37 university colleges (of which 23 are State run). The student population is 300,000 per semester, of whom 18,000 are enrolled in training for research. This service is provided by 20,000 staff, working as teachers and as researchers. The total annual budget amounts to SEK 44 billion (4.8 billion euros). Municipal adult education, which is provided by 419 schools in 280 municipalities, has 300,000 students per year. In addition, liberal adult education is delivered both through 147 folk high schools to 100,000 participants per semester and through 11 national study associations with 900 local units. This provides education for 1.5 to 2 million participants per year in study circles and has a budget of SEK 2.5 billion (272 million euros). Finally, Advanced Vocational Education (AVE) is provided by 180 educational providers offering 330 courses to 11,000 participants, with a total budget of SEK 55 million (6 million euros) (Andersson, 2002; Sweden, 2003a).

Sweden is a large country with long distances, a comparatively small population[1] and a severe winter climate. The official language is Swedish but the recognised minority languages are Sami (Lapp), Finnish, Meänkieli (Tornedalen Finnish), Yiddish and Romani Chib (a gypsy language). In the last century, during Sweden's rapid transformation from a backward agrarian country into one of the world's strongest and most advanced industrial nations, there were heavy demands for the development of the infrastructure, transportation, communications and technological development. This accounts for Sweden's sophisticated infrastructure and high degree of technological maturity today. This is reflected in everything from the roads, railways and other transportation systems to the IT systems. In this latter area, Sweden is sometimes regarded as the most developed nation in the world.

One of the many indications of Sweden's internationally recognised reputation for its speed in adopting new technology is that, in 1900, Stockholm had more telephones than London, Paris or Berlin. The Swedish people have become famous for their openness to new technology and to new trends and patterns of behaviour and consumption. For this reason, the country has increasingly come to be used as a test market by multinational corporations in the development of new products and services. Sweden continues to hold its IT leadership position and was rated as the world's leading information economy by the 2003 IDC/World Times Information Society Index (ISI). For the fourth year in a row, the ISI index has ranked Sweden as the country in the strongest position to benefit from the Information Revolution. (Sweden, 2003a; Sverige.se, 2003; SIKA, 2003; elearningeuropa.info, 2003).

In March 2003 the Ministry of Education commissioned a report to make suggestions for change to the rules for access to HE. The aims

1 Sweden's 9 million inhabitants live in the third largest country in Western Europe, an area of some 450,000 km^2. Its land consists of forests: 53%, mountains: 17%, cultivated land: 8%, and lakes and rivers 9%. Its longest North-South distance is 1,574 km; and its longest East-West distance is 499 km.

are to increase direct access from high schools (*gymnasium*) to HE, to encourage students' achievements in high schools, to decrease competition for completion, e.g. for students who have already passed some grades and who then complete their grade requirements at *Komvux* (see below), and finally to promote widening access to HE. One aim is to have 50% of school leavers entering HE direct from school (Sweden, 2003b; 2003c; 2003d; 2003e). Specific initiatives include improving mathematical knowledge and foreign language skills for specific target groups such as pupils, students teachers, researchers and parents from kindergartens, adult education, HE and adult education (Sweden, 2003f).

The national organisation of Adult Education

Municipal Adult Education (Skolverket)[2]

Municipal Adult Education (*Komvux*), one form of adult education administered by local authorities, was established in 1968 to provide courses for people who want to upgrade their education, allowing them access to higher education if they wish. It is possible to study single subjects or full programmes and get the equivalent of nine years of compulsory school (*grundskola*) or high school. Supplementary courses are also available, as are full programmes at the university level, mainly Internet-based, run in collaboration with the universities. Programmes are available both in the daytime and the evenings and all are free of charge. It is also possible to get help with study techniques and also to use the services of the local study centres. For both types of education provided by *Komvux*, all the studies are individually based and a tutor is available for one-to-one tuition.

Since 1996, the *Kunskapslyftet* (Knowledge Increase) initiative has seen the largest concentration of adult education in Sweden. *Kunskapslyftet* has three aims: to increase skills and competence; to

2 See http://www.skolutveckling.se/vux/index.html

reform adult education; and to decrease unemployment. This project ended in December 2002 but, from January 2003, special support from the Government has been available for the municipalities, adding around 47,000 full-time study places (*årsstudieplatser*).

College Education

College education offers an introduction to university studies, in co-operation with the universities and with *Komvux*. This provision is part of the strategy for recruiting different groups and additional students to universities. The education is structured with 30 credits at the high school level and 30 credits at the university level. (These latter are equivalent to the credits in the European Credit Transfer Scheme, ECTS.) Several universities in Sweden, for example Lund University, organize these courses. In the pilot phase 2002/03, 15,000 students were enrolled totally on the introductory course and a further 1000 students enrolled later in the year. The college semester will be useful both for students who are not yet eligible for university studies and also for those who already have the necessary qualifications but who, for some reason, need to undertake further study before they can enter the course of their choice. (*Den Öppna Högskolan*, 2001).

*Advanced Vocational Education (*Kvalificerad yrkesutbildning*)*[3]

During the period 1996–2001, a pilot project involving AVE was carried out in Sweden. Advanced vocational education is a new form of post-secondary education in which one third of the time is spent in the application of theoretical knowledge in a workplace. What this entails is not the traditional traineeship period but active learning and problem solving in a workplace context. The courses are based on close cooperation between companies and the course providers (higher education, upper secondary schools, municipal adult education and companies). They are intended to meet the real needs in the labour

3 See http://www.ky.se/engelskainfo.html

market for workers with new skills such as flexibility, social skills, problem solving and a capacity to see both the overall picture and the individual processes throughout the company. There are no restrictions to the sectors where AVE can be provided. The courses are open both to individuals coming directly from upper secondary schools and to people who are already employed and who wish to develop their skills within a defined area (*Myndigheten för kvalificerad yrkesutbildning*, 2002). Successful results from the pilot scheme led the Swedish Parliament (*Riksdag*) to decide that, from 2002, AVE will be included in the regular educational system in Sweden. The Swedish Agency for Advanced Vocational Education has been made responsible by Parliament for the supervision of AVE at the national level. This is the Agency that approves the applications and makes the grants.

The Swedish Agency for Flexible Learning

Flexible learning involves a form of teaching in which the student's own wishes and needs are paramount. Flexible learning gives students the opportunity to choose the time, place, pace and structure of their studies. Teaching is student-centred and organisations have to adapt their course structures and techniques to meet the needs of their students. Given these major changes in the world of education, the Swedish Government launched the Swedish Agency for Flexible Learning (*Myndigheten för Flexibelt Lärande*, CFL)[4] in January 2002 to meet the needs of those who organise training for skills development and advice. The CFL promotes the development and use of flexible learning in municipal adult education, liberal adult education and in the workplace.

The Agency's responsibilities can be summarised as follows:

- To develop and provide adult education, primarily at the upper secondary level, in the form of distance education;

4 See http://www.cfl.se/english/index.htm

- To allocate funding and otherwise support projects in the fields of general education and adult education, with a view to developing distance education and flexible learning;
- To develop and disseminate knowledge on methods and ways of working when using various media, and providing descriptive information on the current range of Internet-based software which can be used in the field, and to act as a networked information agency for IT-supported distance education;
- To provide further training for teachers, head teachers, administrators and study circle leaders;
- To monitor and provide information on research and development work relating to distance education and flexible learning in other countries; and
- To develop support for mature students who have sign language as their first language, working in cooperation with the Swedish Institute for Special Needs Education (*Specialpedagogiska institutet*).

The Swedish National Council of Adult Education

The Swedish National Council of Adult Education (*Folkbildning*)[5] distributes grants to the study associations and to folk high schools, submits budget and fiscal reports, follows up and evaluates popular education activities, and administers the Popular Education Net, a digital platform for learning and conferences. The Council was founded in 1991 as a non-profit organisation with three members: the National Federation of Study Associations, the Federation of County Councils, and the Interest Organisation for Popular Movement Folk High Schools.

5 See http://www.folkbildning.se/page/59/Translations%20/%20Översättningar

Adult Education par excellence: the Swedish experience

For more than a hundred years, people in Sweden have come together to study on their own terms, to listen to lectures, to take part in cultural projects and so on. People meet to learn together, to increase their opportunities to influence their personal situation in life and often to change their social conditions more broadly. These activities are wide-ranging. Around 75% of Swedes, ranging from the ages of 18 to 75, have at some time taken part in these events; around 40% have taken part in at least one course over the last three years; 13% percent have taken a short folk high school course; and 8% have taken a long course. The *folkbildning* provides a popular non-formal and voluntary education system for people of all ages.

Study circles

The most typical form of liberal adult education in Sweden is the 'study circle'. These take place though study associations (*studieförbund*). There are 11 of these, each supported by Government funding, which conduct around 350,000 study circles every year, with about 3 million participants.

Every study association has a number of local units; there are around 900 in total. They also have their own more or less clear-cut profiles, depending upon the popular movements and other organisations which are members of the association. In total, the study associations have more than 270 associated member organisations. In addition, they cooperate locally with a range of different associations.

The study circle is the most common study format found in Sweden and it provides learning opportunities in a very wide range of subjects chosen by the participants. Since many people take part in more than one circle per year, the actual number of participants is estimated to be 1.5–2 million per annum. They also arrange more than 200,000 cultural events such as concerts, theatre performances and exhibitions, which have about 15 million participants in all.

Many study associations and folk high schools also conduct other learning activities for councils and organisations. A small group of people meet regularly for a period of time, most often one night a week, to study a subject or theme or to take part in a cultural activity. The circle consists of five to twelve participants, of whom one is the leader. The study circles are characterised by democratic values and are based upon the participants taking responsibility for their work. Together they plan their studies, based on their own needs and interests. An important part of study circle methodology is the exchange of experiences and ideas between the participants and their own analysis of the subject studied. A major part of liberal adult education, both in study associations and the folk high schools, is carried out in close cooperation with other organisations which are either members of the study associations or are responsible for folk high schools.[6]

Folk high schools

These are the other main providers of liberal adult education in Sweden. The first folk high school (*folkhögskolor*) was founded in 1868 and today there are a total of 147 schools, spread throughout the country. Most of these are run by independent organisations, though some are run by regional governments or local councils. Folk high schools are intended mainly for adults who have received only basic schooling. The freedom given to these schools allows each of them to create courses according to the particular needs of their adult students and to the objectives of the school. This in turn gives course participants ample opportunities to influence the aims and contents of their programme, determined by their current knowledge, interests, and needs. Here, theme studies and project work are often used as teaching methods and the participants' experiences from work and social life are seen as great assets. Folk high schools offer courses at different levels and with differing aims and objectives. Every school has long-term courses which will qualify for university entrance. There are also

6 See http://www.folkbildning.se

large numbers of special courses: for example, studies in music, media, theatre, and health. The long courses last from a term to one or more years; the short courses last from one day to around two weeks.

All tuition in the folk high schools is free of charge. The total number of participants in the long courses in each semester is around 20,000 and in the short courses about 80,000. Folk high schools have their own information service which is part of the Council of Adult Education. This distributes information about all folk high school courses.[7]

Finance

Perhaps the most significant aspect of Swedish liberal adult education is that it is largely financed by grants from national and regional governments and local councils.[8] Parliament has laid down the aims and conditions for granting government support to liberal adult education: the participants must be given the opportunity to influence their situation in life and to take part in social development; democracy must be strengthened and developed; interest in culture must be broadened; and individual participation and creativity must be furthered. Liberal adult education is expected to give priority to activities that bridge educational gaps and that are geared towards the people who are educationally, socially or culturally disadvantaged. Particularly important target groups for this form of education are people of foreign descent, those with physical or learning disabilities and those who are unemployed.

7 See http://www.folkbildning.se/page/9/Folkhögskolor.htm

8 The Swedish Association of Local Authorities (*Svenska kommunförbundet*), founded in 1908, represents all the municipal authorities in Sweden (289 primary local authorities). Its main aims are: to support and develop the system of local self-government; to defend local authorities' interests; to promote co-operation between local authorities; and to assist local authorities through service and expert advice. (Swedish Association of Local Authorities, 2003).

Strengthening democracy is a fundamental principle underpinning the Government's support for liberal adult education. A Government Bill in 1998 stated, amongst other things:[9]

> The role of liberal adult education today is also a matter of defending, vitalising, and developing democracy. The instability of democracy is obvious when seen in an international perspective. There is the risk of weak popular support and alienation between the elected and the electors; there is a feeling of impotence in the face of social development that we do not seem able to influence. Through our membership of the European Union, the Swedish decision-making process has extended beyond our national borders. A series of new rights and obligations has also taken effect for the individual. This situation demands new knowledge. The survival and vitality of democracy must build on a culture of democracy with dialogue, discussions and participation as important elements. It must also comprise knowledge about values, conditions and institutions necessary to democracy. Giving liberal adult education the opportunity to grow is – in its essence – just this: strengthening democratic culture, and filling gaps of knowledge and information in society. Liberal adult education has a key role in this process. It can help create meeting-places for change and bridge the gaps between groups of people and between humans and technology.

Since 1996 there have been several experimental projects to introduce IT support to liberal adult education in order to increase its breadth through distance learning.[10] Moreover the teaching resources on the Liberal Adult Education Net have been created as a database for popular education.[11] It is possible here to look for pedagogical Internet links, project reports and study materials suitable for popular education in various subjects. These databases are constantly being updated.

9 See http://www.folkbildning.se/page/40/Styrdokument#fordning

10 The experiences from the first years of those experiments in folk high schools and study associations is collected and presented in the 1999 report, 'Popular Education as Distance Learning?' (*Folkbildningsrådet*, 1999). In August 2001 the Swedish National Council of Adult Education published a book on distance learning within liberal adult education (*folkbildning.net*, 2001). Later, in January 2002, the book was published in English and can be ordered from the Swedish National Council of Adult Education.

11 Accessible on http://www.folkbildning.net

Widening adult participation and adult education in universities: the Government Bill

The Government Bill (*Den Öppna Högskolan*, 2001) mentioned earlier aims to widen participation in education for adults as summarised below:

- Special regulations are contained in the Act concerning the universities' duty to promote and widen their recruitment, with the recommendation that each university should create a special commission responsible for promoting wider recruitment and that each should agree an action plan set to achieve this wider recruitment;
- It also supports college education, together with the adult education provided by local authorities;
- The Government also promotes a new role for universities: to stimulate lifelong learning (*validering*) by developing methods to accredit prior (experiential) learning, in addition to the formal education system;
- The promotion of Commissioned Education (see below) confirms the universities' role in lifelong learning;
- Doctoral students are able to study part-time and students with licentiate degrees can also be enrolled on research programmes;
- The Government also commits itself to the importance of teaching in higher education, as well as the need for organisational and structural changes in this area. All higher education lecturers should also have a formal training in teaching, including in the use of information and communication technology (ICT) methods;
- The Swedish Net University was established in March 2002. The Internet courses from all of the Swedish universities are now coordinated by the Net University;
- From 2002, a new organization, CFL (already mentioned) was made responsible for the coordination, stimulation and

promotion of all flexible learning. The Government stipulated that the new forms of distributed learning and alternatives to traditional education should stimulate lifelong learning;

- The Government also anticipated greater concentration on courses for immigrants, particularly for those with foreign higher education qualifications; and
- The wider perspective of internationalisation is also expected to affect recruitment to higher education and to increase the recruitment of foreign students including those from outside Europe.

Examples of good practice

Introduction

Adult students in Sweden have always had access to university programmes, including university single subject courses. The new challenge today is to develop structural arrangements for this provision (Askling *et al.*, 2001). These authors have identified the components that have to be considered, namely the means of access to higher education, the supply of courses and programmes, the selection and structure of knowledge and competences, the teaching and learning methods, and finally the accreditation of students' results and the recognition of their competences. Other official sources confirm the need to address these issues, especially adult student recruitment and learning and teaching styles (Wigforss, 2000; *Högskoleverket*, 2001; Lundgren and Liljevall, 2001; SUHF, 2001; Söderberg and Anderberg, 2001).

Internet courses offer one efficient method (*Den Öppna Högskolan*, 2001) for students to be able to study wherever they want and more or less whenever they wish: 'just in time, just in the right place'. For this reason special local study centres (*lokala studiecenter*) have been set up to give easy access to computers, with tutors available at specific times, for those without access at home.

Scientific seminars during the daytime and in the evenings are also frequently organised by HEIs. This very basic format sometimes attracts people to further continuing education: these seminars allow the participants to 'taste' the possibilities for themselves and to make more informed decisions for their futures.

There is a high demand from students with disabilities requiring specific arrangements to suit their needs. For these student groups, it is found that Internet courses are a challenge as well as an opportunity. Nevertheless, for some, the Internet courses offer their only possible access to higher education (Anderberg, 1999; Söderberg and Anderberg, 2001).

It is also possible for each individual university to allocate 10% of its intake as a 'free quota' outside the regulatory system. This free quota can be used to help groups disadvantaged by, for example, gender, age, equality, or disabilities.

The Swedish Net University[12]

The Government has recently taken the initiative in creating the Swedish Net University, a consortium of universities with a common interest in providing education for adults through distance learning. The role of distributed distance learning for adults will no doubt become increasingly important in the coming years. The use of ICT will also bring the traditional full-time courses closer to the non-traditional ones. The Net University, which was launched in March 2002, is likely to be a crucial step in the future development of ICT in Sweden. (European Commission, 2001a; Holmes, 2001; *Myndigheten för Sveriges Nätuniversitet*, 2001; and 2002; Björk, 2002).

12 See http://www.netuniversity.se

Commissioned Education

Commissioned education (*uppdragsutbildning*) is seen by the Government as an important instrument to strengthen the role of the universities in the lifelong learning process. Universities have to be more active in their work to provide commissioned education (*Den Öppna Högskolan*, 2001; SUHF, 2001). This form of adult education consists of courses offered on demand to private companies, municipalities and government institutions. To provide this, Lund University, for example, set up a University-owned enterprise in 2000, Lund University Education AB (2001). The aim of this enterprise is to commission courses from university departments and to sell them to companies and authorities to meet their in-service continuing professional development (CPD) needs. The same idea has been developed at the Karolinska Institute in Stockholm with the formation of Karolinska Education AB (2001).

The Folk University (Folkuniversitetet)[13]

Folkuniversitetet is an adult education association that offers a wide range of adult education all over Sweden. It is an association of five providers: the extra-mural departments attached to the Universities of Stockholm, Uppsala, Göteborg, Lund and Umeå. Their links to the universities allow them to provide, through lectures, study circles and seminars, information about the latest developments in research. They also engage academic staff in offering university-level courses in a wide range of subjects. *Folkuniversitetet* is independent of all political, religious and trade union interests. (*Folkuniversitetet*, 2003)

13 See http://www.folkuniversitetet.se

Validation: the recognition of prior experiential leaning

The validation of students' competence offers a further way of recruiting new students to the universities (*Den Öppna Högskolan*, 2001; Sweden, 2003c; 2003d; 2003e). According to a Ministry of Education communication (Sweden, 2003c), the Government intends to appoint a commission to carry out this validation starting in 2004.

Education for adults in Lund University

The Government stated in 1999 that universities should declare their policy for the education of adults. This had already been done in 1995 by Lund University, with the creation of the Office for Continuing and Distance Education (OCDE). In 2000 the University Board put forward a policy document (Lund University, 2000) to define the aims and support structure for the education of adults. So far this initiative has been successful, particularly in the early use of ICT in distance education. The OCDE (Wigforss and Badersten, 2000; Wigforss, 2000; Lund University-OCDE, 2001) provides teachers and students in UCE and support for course development. This policy document has now been used as a model for other universities and is described in SUHF (2001).

The policy states (Lund University, 2000):

> UCE, and distributed learning, will be an area of high priority; quality assurance for UCE is of the same importance as for [full-time] undergraduate and postgraduate studies; UCE will be part of the ordinary tasks of lecturers and will contribute to the quality development of courses in general at the university. In addition to their academic qualifications, applicants' engagement in UCE will be a qualification when making appointments to posts and in the determination of their salaries; for service and actions concerning commissioned education there will be a special University-owned enterprise. (Lund University, 2000; SUHF, 2001; Björk, 2002; Borg, 2002).

Lund University has recently developed a strategic plan for 2002–2006 (Lund University, 2002), which follows the European Commission's recommendations on lifelong and distributed learning mentioned earlier. The University has also developed agreements with the largest trade union in Sweden, the Union for Local Government Workers, which has over 600,000 members, and whose action plan clearly states their members' right to higher education. The University is also involved with the Swedish Industries Union and the Employers Association.

The University has also taken advantage of the concept of Individual Competence Assurance (ICA). In Sweden many companies have established ICA, in which traditional university courses or tailor-made CPD programmes form a large part of companies' regular training programmes. Individual competence assurance can be used for different learning situations in the lifelong learning process according to Lundgren and Liljevalls (2001). In this activity, Lund University has cooperated with some of Sweden's largest companies, including Skandia. Most large firms throughout the country are involved in the ICA scheme through UCE.

Lund University is also involved in several regional development projects concerning lifelong learning and the learning regions, for example:

- The R3L Initiatives, through CoLabs (see http://www.CoLabs.eu), which are based on Triple Helix Alliances;
- The Baltic Sea Virtual University (BSVC), which provides and support lifelong learning online. (See http://www.bsvc.org);
- *Öresundsuniversitetet*. (See http://www.uni.oresund.org);
- eLearning Öresund. (See http://www.elearningoresund.net/eloen/publikationer/kompetenskluster.asp); and
- eCompete, a project with SMEs. (See http://www.ecompete.net).

Conclusion

The following are among the factors that are successfully bringing adult learners to HE in Sweden:

- Liberal education and its long tradition in the country;
- *Kunskapslyftet*;
- The long history of 'education for all' and of including adults in universities at every level;
- The IT portal on adult education;
- The infrastructure for adult education in the country;
- The Government Bill (*Den Öppna högskolan*, 2001) including the Swedish Net University;
- Validation;
- The wide recruitment, accessibility and support for disadvantaged groups;
- The strong support from the government and the different initiatives it has taken over the years;
- The financial support allocated to education at all levels. All education is free of charge for individuals in Sweden and this is undoubtedly important; and
- The cooperation among the stakeholders at the different levels.

A number of obstacles can be recognised to expanding adult education: some adults lack time, money and interest. On the part of the providers, there is difficulty in responding to the inquiries and there are limits to the courses that can be offered.

The support of democratic values for sustainable development is a general objective of Swedish Government policy. Initiatives that are likely to be seen in the coming years are:

- Further support for the IT portal;
- Further development on adults learning and validation;
- An overhaul of the rules for admission to HE;
- The delegation of validation for national equivalence;
- Extra resources for the Swedish Net University;
- The strengthening of the Fifth Generation of eLearning;
- Progress towards the European Higher Education Area;
- The further extension of the concept of the third mission of universities;
- The development of learning regions, work with SMEs, commissioned education and learning communities. (See http://www.regeringen.se).

References

Askling, B., Christiansson, U. and Foss Fridlizius, R., 2001. *Livslångt lärande som idé och praktik i högskolan.* (Lifelong Learning as ideology and practice in higher education). Rapport 2001:1R, *Högskoleverket: Utbildningsdepartementet.*

Anderberg, P., 1999. *Internetlärande för alla. Om insatser för de första fullvärdiga studiemöjligheterna för människor med funktionshinder.* (Internet learning for everyone. On the achievements of the first satisfactory study possibilities for people with disabilities). Licentiate dissertation. Lund University. Department for Industrial Design, Centre for Rehabilitation Engineering Research.

Andersson M., ed., 2002. *Made in Sweden*. Stockholm: HA.

Björck, I., 2002. *Tänk om. Om–och nytänk kring distansutbildning vid tre högskolor*. (Rethinking distance education). *Distum Distansutbildningsmyndigheten*, Rapport 3:2002.

Borg, C., ed., 2002. *Vetenskaparnas visioner. Elva samtal om framtidens studier och undervisning i högskolan.* (The science visions). *Distum Distansutbildningsmyndigheten*, Rapport 4:2002.

Budgetpropositionen för 2002, 2002. *Regeringens proposition.* (Government Bill). 2001/2002, p.19.

CFL, *Centrum för Flexibelt Lärande*, 2003. (Centre for Flexible Learning). Available at: http://www.cfl.se/english/index.htm

Collis, B. and van der Wende, M., 2002. Models of Technology and Change in Higher Education. Cheps: Toegepaste Onderwijskunde. Available at: http://www.utwente.nl/cheps/publications/new_publications/

Den Öppna Högskolan, 2001. *Regeringens proposition* 2001/02, p.15. (The Open University. The Government Bill). In Swedish.

ELearningEuropa, 2003. Available at: http://www.elearningeuropa.info

European Commission, 2000. *Memorandum on Lifelong Learning.* Commission Staff Working Papers. 30.10.2000. SEK (2000) 1832. Brussels.

European Commission, 2001a. *e-Learning – Designing tomorrow's education. What's new in e-Learning, 2001.* Brussels 25.5.2000, KIM (2000) 318 COM (01), final. Available at: http://europa.eu.int/comm./education/elearning/wn2001_05/

European Commission, 2001b. *Making a European Area of Lifelong Learning a Reality.* Available at: http://europa.eu.int/comm/education/policies/lll/life/index_en.html

European Commission, 2001c. *European e-Learning Summit Declaration.* COM (01) 18/5/2001, final. Available at: http://europa.eu.int/comm/education/programmes/elearning/summit.pdf

European Commission, 2002a. *European report on Quality Indicators for Lifelong Learning*, Brussels, June 2002.

European Commission, 2002b. *e-Learning Action Plan.* Available at: http://europa.eu.int/eur-lex/en/com/cnc/2001/com2001_0172en01.pdf

Folkuniversitetet, 2003. *Facts about Folkuniversitetet.* Available at: http://www.folkuniversitetet.se/templates/Page.aspx?id=3460

Folkbildningsrådet, 1999. *Popular Education as Distance Learning.* Available at: http://www.folkbildning.se

Folkbildning.net, 2001. Available at: http://www.folkbildning.net

Folkbildningsrådet, 2003. Available at: http://www.folkbildning.se

Holmes, B., 2001. e-Learning: Designing Tomorrow's Education. What's new? In: *Proceedings of the European Conference on e-Learning in a Lifelong Learning Perspective, 2nd WBLE Conference, 24–26 October 2001*. L. Badersten and E. Ossian-nilsson, eds. Lund University.

Högskoleverket, 2001. *Universitet och högskolor 2001. Högskoleverkets årsrapport 2001*. (HEI Annual Report from the National Agency). *Sveriges Officiella Statistik.*

Högskoleverket, 2003. (National Agency for Higher Education). Available at: http://wwweng.hsv.se/en/iwt/startpage/startpage_en.jsp?home=location

Karolinska Education AB, 2001. Available at: http://www.karolinskaeducation.ki.se/index_en.html

Lundgren and Liljevall, 2001. Distansundervisning som stöd för livslångt lärande i arbetslivet. *Arbetslivsinstitutet*. In: *SUHF, Hur skall högskolan öka uppdrags-utbildningen?'-reflexioner och förslag av en arbetsgrupp inom SUHF. Sveriges universitets och högskoleförbund.* (Distance Education as a Support for Lifelong Learning in Working Life.) October 2001.

Lund University, 2000. Policy document. Lund University, June 2000. Available at: http://www.lu.se, www.fov.lu.se

Lund University, 2002. *Strategic plan, Lund University 2002–2006.* Available at: http://www.lu.se/info/strategiskplan

Lund University Education, 2003. Available at: www.education.lu.se

Lund University-OCDE, 2001. Available at: http://www.fov.lu.se

Myndigheten för Sveriges Nätuniversitet, 2001. *Kommittédirektiv. Myndigheten för Sveriges nätuniversitet*, 2001. (Authority for the Swedish Net University). Dir 2001, p.91.

Myndigheten för Sveriges Nätuniversitet, 2002. *Regeringen. Utbildnings departementet 2002*. (Authority for the Swedish Net University). Available at: http://www.netuniversity.se

Myndigheten för Kvalificerad Yrkesutbildning, 2002. (Swedish Agency for Advanced Vocational Education). Available at: http://www.ky.se/engelskainfo.html

Myndigheten för Skolutveckling, 2003. (Authority for School Development). Available at: http://www.skolutveckling.se/vux/index.html

OECD, 1998. Education. *OECD*. Available at: www.oecd.org

OECD, 2002. Education. *OECD*. Available at: www.oecd.org

SIKA, 2003. *Fakta om informationsteknologi i Sverige*. (Facts about Information Technology in Sweden). Available at: http://www.sika-institute.se/english_fr.html

Söderberg, A. and Anderberg, P., 2001. *Funktionshinder och distansutbildning*. (Disabled people and distance education). *Distum Distansutbildningsmyndigheten*, Rapport 2:2001.

SUHF, 2001. *'Hur skall högskolan öka uppdragsutbildningen?' – reflexioner och förslag av en arbetsgrupp inom SUHF*. (How will HEIs increase commissioned education?). *Sveriges universitets och högskoleförbund*. October 2001.

Svenska Institutet, 2003. (Swedish Institute). Available at: www.si.se

Sverige.se, 2003. *The Official Gateway to Sweden*. Available at: www.sverige.se

Sweden, 2001a. *Regeringskansliet*. Ministry of Education and Science. *The Debate on the Commission's Memorandum on Lifelong learning 2001*. Working Group for Lifelong Learning, 6-12-2001.

Sweden, 2001b. *Regeringskansliet*. Ministry of Education and Science. *Detaljerat arbetsprogram för uppföljningen av målen för utbildningssystemen i Europa. 5828/02 EDUC 17,* Förslag nr.: 11762/01 EDUC 102 – KOM(2001) 501 slutlig. (Detailed work programme following up the goals of the education system.) Available at: http://register.consilium.eu.int/pdf/su/02/st06/06365s2.pdf

Sweden, 2003a. *Regeringens skrivelse*, 2001/02. *Utbildning för kunskap och jämlikhet-regeringens utvecklingsplan för kvalitetsarbetet i förskola, skola och vuxenutbildning*. 2001/02:188. (Education for knowledge and equality.)

Sweden. *Regeringskansliet*. Ministry of Industry, Employment and Communication. Available at: http://naring.regeringen.se/inenglish/index.htm

Sweden. *Regeringskansliet*, 2003b. *Utbildningsdepartementet. Vuxen-utbildning och folkbildning.* (Adult education and liberal education). Available at: http://utbildning.regeringen.se/ansvarsomr/vuxfolk/

Sweden, 2003c. *Regeringskansliet. Validering mm-fortsatt utveckling av vuxnas lärande,* DS 2003:23. (Validation for continuing development of adult learning). Available at: http://utbildning.regeringen.se/propositionermm/ds/2003/ds_2003_23.pdf

Sweden, 2003d. *Regeringskanlsiet. Översyn av reglerna för tillträde till grundläggande högskoleutbildning.* Dir.2003:38 (2003-03-27). (An overhaul of the regulation for access to HE). Available at: http://rixlex.riksdagen.se/htbin/thw?%24%7BHTML%7D=DIR_LST&%24%7BOO

Sweden, 2003e. *Regeringskansliet. Pressmeddelande 030608. Fortsatt utveckling av vuxnas lärande – idag presenteras ny skrivelse om validering mm (Departement skrivelse, Ds).* (Continuing development of adult education). Available at: http://www.regeringen.se/galactica/service=irnews/action=obj_show?c_obj_id=50290

Sweden, 2003f. *Regeringskansliet.* Ministry of Education. *Löpsedel.* Available at: http://utbildning.regeringen.se/index.htm

Swedish Association of Local Authorities, 2003. *About SK.* Available at: http://www.svekom.se/skvad/indexeng.htm

Wigforss, E., 2000. *Utveckling och kvalitetssäkring av nätburen distansutbildning.* (Development and Quality Assurance of Internet-based Distance Education). FoV rapport, Lunds Universitet.

Wigforss, E. and Badersten, L., 2000. Indicators of Best Practice for the Delivery of Online Learning. In: European ODL Liaison Committee. A Trinidad, ed. *Proceedings of the European Conference: ODL Networking for Quality Learning, Lisbon, June 19–21, 2000.* Lisbon: Universidade Aberta.

MICHAEL OSBORNE

Chapter 21: Adults in British Higher Education[1]

Introduction

The tradition of providing opportunities for adults to enter higher education institutions (HEIs) in the United Kingdom is longstanding and can be traced back to the late nineteenth century. From this time until late in the twentieth century the dominant form of such provision was of short non-credit courses variously known as 'liberal adult education' or 'extra-mural courses'. The genesis of this work is described in a range of texts including notably Kelly (1992), Newman (1994), Stock (1996) and Fieldhouse (1997). In previous work I have detailed the nature of the range of traditional provision in UCE (Osborne, 1997), and have also more recently outlined the reasons for its demise in the United Kingdom and for the ascent of provision concerned with widening access to mainstream undergraduate education (Osborne, 2003a). From the 1970s until now there has been a steady, and latterly spectacular, increase in student numbers in higher education (HE), and certainly in the first two decades of that expansion, it was adults rather than younger people whose rates of participation grew most rapidly.

The issue of widening access to HE for all groups has been a prominent driver for national policy within the United Kingdom during recent years and, very explicitly, the period since the election of a Labour government in 1997 has been linked closely to wider

1 Some sections of this chapter are based on the introduction to a report recently produced by the author and colleagues for the Scottish Executive (Murphy *et al.*, 2002), updated to include more recent policy developments. I am grateful for the work of my colleagues Mark Murphy, Brenda Morgan-Klein and Jim Gallacher who all contributed to that report. I am also grateful for the helpful comments from Ted Thomas and Rob Mark on this chapter.

concerns about social justice and inclusion. However, as in other HE systems in Europe, Britain's provision is under considerable financial stress, having suffered almost continuous reductions in funding per student over the past two decades (European University Association, 2003). The questions of affordability and the relative roles of governments and individuals in funding participation are therefore prominent within the current public debate.

The ideology underpinning recent policies and practices are best understood within the context of the government's vision of a learning society described in the Green Papers published in 1998 (Department For Education and Employment, 1998; Scottish Office Education and Industry Department, 1998; Welsh Office, 1998). These were influenced to a large extent by the European White Paper *Teaching and Learning* (European Commission, 1995). However widening participation, whilst the target of certain directed funding, has been paralleled by the declining investment per student and a consequent drop in support for university infrastructure and maintenance. In recognition of what is now little short of a crisis, in the White Paper *The Future of Higher Education*, the government has signalled that the English HE sector faces some 'hard choices on funding, quality and management' (DfES, 2003a, p.4). In this White Paper, whilst a commitment to expanding the HE system and to broadening the social class range amongst those entering the system remains, the proposal to allow universities to charge partial fees (known as 'top-up' fees) has been controversial. This has been seen by a number of commentators as antithetical to improving access. Nonetheless the United Kingdom government is adamant that the only way for the HE system to receive further funding is through increasing contributions from individuals who it deems can afford to pay, with part of this funding used to support those who cannot afford it through a means-tested bursary system. Although this strategy is the favoured solution (DfES, 2003b), it has been strongly opposed by a number of parliamentarians in the ruling Labour party, so much so that the government obtained a majority of only five for the first reading of its proposed HE bill in January 2004.

Parallel policies have since been developed in Scotland in *Opportunities for Everyone, a strategic framework for Further Education*

(Scottish Executive, 1999) and in *Scotland, a Learning Nation* (Scottish Executive, 2000), though significant differences have emerged, coming from the devolved government there. Most notably in Scotland, no fees are charged to students at the undergraduate level and there is little prospect of universities being given the right to charge 'top-up' fees. Recently the Scottish Parliament (2002) review of lifelong learning made radical recommendations, the most prominent of which is the idea of a Lifelong Learning Entitlement of five full-time equivalent years of study after the age of 16. In such a system an individual would be able to 'spend' this entitlement flexibly throughout their lifetime. Subsequently the Scottish Executive has stated that 'the overarching framework and priorities within which HE operates are those for lifelong learning' (Scottish Executive, 2003a and b).

The range of provision for adults in United Kingdom universities

Although the main focus in this chapter will be on access to mainstream undergraduate qualifications, as indicated above, a range of provision still exists in the United Kingdom, although most of the longstanding short courses in the liberal adult education tradition are no longer offered. In broad terms, provision can be described as being on the one hand concerned with personal and social development and on the other on continuing professional development, though such distinctions are always difficult since individual participants generally have multiple motivations.

Historically many of the courses for adults in universities in the liberal tradition have been made available by specialist units variously known as 'extra-mural', 'adult education' or 'continuing education' departments or centres. More recently such units more frequently use the nomenclature of 'lifelong learning' or 'widening participation', reflecting the change of emphasis to improving access to wider constituencies of the population. Although these specialist departments have also had much wider responsibilities, other academic units in universities and traditional academic departments also play direct and indirect roles especially in providing structural flexibility and in CPD. Thus numerous examples exist of academic departments, often in collaboration with the specialist units, offering flexibility in time, mode and location of their undergraduate and postgraduate courses to suit the needs of adult students.

Since the mid-1990s many more credit-bearing programmes for adults have arisen at the sub-degree level, which generically can be described as Certificates and Diplomas in Continuing Education. These have emerged as a result of protectionist measures taken by departments to sustain historic funding arrangements (see Osborne, 2003b, p.467), and normally carry credits equivalent to the first or second year of undergraduate degrees. Despite reservations about the transferability of this credit in many instances, these courses have had success in bringing university courses to disadvantaged communities, for example through the use of outreach centres within both urban and rural settings. Courses on offer are diverse including those related to personal development, active citizenship and community development as well as those that are work-related and work-based.

There are also many special initiatives directed toward particular groups to be found in universities funded by the United Kingdom government, the Scottish Executive and the Welsh Assembly, by the Higher Education Funding Councils of the countries making up the United Kingdom and by the European Union. A range of such activities has been listed (Osborne, 1997). Currently there is a diverse range of activities for groups such as ethnic minorities, non-native speakers of English, women, excluded men, prisoners, asylum seekers, disabled students and people with mental health problems. A fuller picture of this range of provision can be found by navigation through the sites of the two major networks for continuing education in the United Kingdom, the Universities Association for Continuing Education (UACE) and the Forum for the Advancement of Continuing Education (FACE).[2]

2 Universities Association for Continuing Education (UACE) website is at http://www.uace.org.uk and has links directly to many of the continuing education

National policy on widening participation

The following discussion reviews recent developments in national policy relevant to the issue of widening access, particularly for adults, to British universities and the context within which these policies have emerged.

It is important to note here that the issue of widening access, or more generally of educational inequality, did not suddenly appear in the 1990s. There is a long history of institutional, governmental and extra-mural initiatives designed to increase participation in post-compulsory education for the socially excluded. These have been usefully reviewed elsewhere.[3] Within the United Kingdom, there have

departments of the United Kingdom. The Forum for the Advancement of Continuing Education (FACE) website is at http://www.f-a-c-e.org.uk

3 A discrete journal in the United Kingdom, the *Journal of Access Studies* (now *Journal of Access and Credit Studies*) has existed since the mid-1980s, reflecting interest in this area. It contains a number of overviews of the field. An article by Parry (1996) gives a particular good historical account of the English position. Davies (1995) and Woodrow (2000) contextualise perspectives on widening participation from a number of countries and include United Kingdom perspectives. The development of policy and practice on access in Scotland prior to 1998 has been usefully documented elsewhere (Osborne and Gallacher, 1995). Of particular note are the national initiatives designed to increase the proportion of entrants from non-traditional backgrounds, whether they are adults, working-class students, women, members of ethnic minorities or people with disabilities. These initiatives included the Scottish Wider Access Programme (SWAP), the Scottish Vocational Education Council (SCOTVEC) (now Scottish Qualifications Authority (SQA)) qualifications and the Scottish Credit Accumulation and Transfer Scheme (SCOTCAT) scheme. The SQA (and formerly one of its predecessor organisations SCOTVEC) is the body responsible for the development and validation of Higher National Certificates and Diplomas and has a major emphasis on progression routes via such awards onto degree programmes (Osborne and Gallacher, 1995, p.239). SCOTCAT, established in 1991, provided a formal agreement between all the main institutions of HE recognising a framework for credit accumulation toward a degree. These early developments illustrate the recurring themes of progression and flexibility in both policy developments and the debate over access. It is now the SQCF (Scottish Qualifications and Credit Framework) that provides the template for credit accumulation and transfer.

historically been comparable practices of widening participation within each of the constituent countries (i.e. England, Wales, Scotland and Northern Ireland). It was in England and in Northern Ireland that some of the most significant early developments occurred of what would now be described as widening participation.

Access courses for adults seeking to enter HE in the United Kingdom were first developed in Northern Ireland in the early 1970s. These were set up as a response to the growing concern about social and political injustices in Northern Ireland, particularly in the City of Londonderry. Following the escalation of street violence in the city in the early 1970s, courses were established at Magee College, Londonderry (an outreach college of Trinity College Dublin (TCD)), mainly for the training of the clergy. It was transferred to the University of Ulster in 1972. These courses were set up as a response to the failure of the then Northern Ireland government (abolished in 1972 under direct rule from Britain) to create HE opportunities in the North Western part of the region. The City of Londonderry was at that time one of the most deprived areas in Western Europe, the region having the highest level of unemployment in the European Community when Britain joined the European Union (EU) in 1972.

Adults in this region were until this time effectively excluded from HE due to the distance from the nearest HE establishments in Belfast and Coleraine. The high levels of social deprivation in Londonderry, coupled with distance from other HE establishments, meant that few adults had the opportunity to participate. These access courses were fully funded (with full- and part-time places) by the Department of Education for Northern Ireland (DENI). The initial Magee College courses served as a model for the development of other types of access courses from the 1970s onwards through franchising arrangements with further education (FE) colleges and they are still running. It is clear that the courses developed in Northern Ireland were a very early response to the particular problem of exclusion from political, social and education structures which led to widespread alienation and which brought about street violence. The response in Northern Ireland was partly a result of the failure of local structures but was also a response to the international movement for greater democratisation and involvement of citizens that had taken hold in Europe and North America in the 1960s. The full impact of this exclusion was not realised in the other parts of the United Kingdom until later.

The 'adult access movement' in England developed from the late 1970s onwards, and was originally conceived as a means of combating another form of exclusion. It was concerned with attracting mature students, particularly from ethnic minority groups into certain professions where they were under-represented, including teaching, social work and law. Access courses were for some time the subject of criticism from those concerned with the supposed dilution of standards since they admitted students to universities without traditional qualifications (DES, 1985). They were, however, eventually accepted as a 'third route' into HE (Davies and Parry, 1993). A variety of concerns at the national and institutional levels related to factors including economic competitiveness, demographic change and institutional survival from the late 1980s onwards, have seen widening participation coming to the forefront of HE policy.

The focus in this chapter is on very recent change and reflects the fact that the problems of access and participation have been constructed differently in terms of their causes and solutions by successive generations. Therefore the discussion here focuses on the recent explosion of policy on lifelong learning, the restructuring of HE and the development of the subsequent critical debate on the subject.

The precursor of the current debate, the European White Paper, *Teaching and learning: Towards the learning society*, (EC, 1995), identified a number of challenges for education and training. These include:

- The impact of the information society;
- The impact of internationalisation; and
- The impact of the scientific world.

These challenges were to be met by emphasising the merits of a broad base of knowledge and by building up employability. The focus in the White Paper on both economic challenge and the need for both a socially cohesive and socially inclusive society are echoed in a variety of British policy documents on post-compulsory education and training. These include the Dearing and Garrick reports (NCIHE, 1997), and the Kennedy report (FEFC, 1997). The problem of social exclusion was considered particularly in the report on the Scottish University for Industry (Scottish Office, 1998). The Dearing report offers an inclusive vision of a learning society which embraces people at all levels of achievement, envisaging the expansion of the HE provision with particular emphasis on the sub-degree level and it reiterated the need to address the under-representation in HE of particular social groups. Garrick echoed these concerns recommending, for example, enhanced access routes into degree programmes for students in FE colleges, the diversification of provision and a new Scottish Qualifications Framework. The Kennedy report *Learning Works* (FEFC, 1997) argues that the Further Education (FE)[4] sector is the key to widening participation given its diversity and the potential progression opportunities it can offer.

In England,[5] at the institutional level HE institutions have been variously rewarded through specially earmarked funding (HEFCE, 1995) and later, as Davies *et al.* (2002) report, by a 'combination of funding approaches: through mainstream formula funding, the allocation of additional student numbers, a special funding programme', with the balance of funds available lying 'more towards mainstream

4 In the United Kingdom, almost uniquely in Europe, there has been a strong impetus to link the vocational education and training (VET) sector to universities though a system of credit accumulation and transfer. The nearest equivalents in Europe are the Regional Technical Colleges in Ireland and the recently developed polytechnic sector in Finland. It is further afield, however, in parts of Australia (primarily in the State of Victoria), and in the Community Colleges of Canada and the USA that close approximations of this model are found. In a recently commissioned report for the Review of Higher Education in Scotland (Scottish Executive, 2003b), Osborne *et al.* deal with the role of FE in the context of short cycle HE, and include descriptions of a range of international models.

5 As is becoming evident, the United Kingdom's position is complex. Only the position in England and Scotland is described here. Policy in Northern Ireland is essentially the same as in England and Welsh policy has differed in only one significant respect. Universities in Wales have, unlike in the rest of the United Kingdom, been funded for the direct provision of Access Courses rather than solely for their development (HEFCW, 2000).

formula funding rather than special funding' (HEFCE, 1999, p.3). Mainstream funding mechanisms involve an adjustment in the block grant for teaching given to HE institutions, essentially offering them extra funds for recruiting students from particular target groups: these include the disabled, part-time students, mature students, and those from areas with below average participation. Special funding of a developmental nature for 'widening provision' was initiated in 1995 following the removal of the historic funding streams for non-accredited liberal adult education in universities.[6] This has led to the development of a range of institutional practices for widening participation (UACE, 1997). Many of these, as Field (2002) has suggested, build upon initiatives already started in the early 1990s. However, it is significant to see that, as in other parts of the United Kingdom, a shift in emphasis from adult students to school pupils is evident. (In terms of initiatives, this has meant *inter alia* the development of a range of strategies to raise awareness of HE amongst poorer school pupils as young as 12 and the creation of Access Summer Schools to give second chances to pupils who narrowly fail to achieve the examination grades needed for entry to university.)

The government has also supported a number of structural initiatives, notably the introduction of foundation degrees. These are two-year HE qualifications offered by partnerships of FE colleges, HE institutions and employers. They most closely resemble associate degrees in the United States offered by community colleges. The emphasis on offering short-cycle HE is also reflected in the efforts being put into encouraging FE colleges more generally to play a stronger role in widening participation. In the most recent policy documents produced by HEFCE (2001), the focus has shifted further towards partnership between FE colleges, schools and HE institutions to meet the target of achieving 50% participation of the school-leaving cohort in HE by 2010. This was set out in the 1998 Green Paper (DfEE, 1998). The aim of this policy is to raise attainment at National Vocational Qualification levels 2 and 3 and to encourage more and better-prepared students to stay on in education at age 16 and continue to HE. Indeed there is little prospect of this target being met otherwise

6 These funding changes have been described in some detail in Osborne (1997).

(although it is not clear why 50%, rather than any other figure, is being obsessively pursued by the government).

At an individual level, the thrust for widening participation has received some setbacks due to the changes in the ways in which students are being financially supported in HE. The introduction, for the first time, of fees for full-time undergraduate HE and the replacement of student grants with loans in the late 1990s has provided some evidence of individuals being discouraged from applying to HE throughout the United Kingdom. This has particularly been the case for mature students (Davies *et al.*, 2002). The present call for deregulation of fees and the introduction of top-up fees[7] presents a particular threat to the thrust for increased access and equity.

In the Scottish context, the publication of *Opportunity Scotland* (SOEID, 1998) was a significant policy document that outlined a number of key changes, such as the introduction of *Higher Still* (a new framework for the education of 16–18-year-olds) and a ten-point action plan, including the launch of the University of the Highlands and Islands Project, to address the perennial problem in Scotland of geographical remoteness. Recent changes have also included the funding of a number of additional places in FE and HE, with resources being targeted particularly at groups traditionally under-represented within both sectors. In Scotland the aim was for an additional 40,000 FE and 2,000 HE students by 2002 (SOEID, 1998).[8] Key themes in *Opportunity Scotland* are familiar ones and include the economic imperatives created by global competition, technological change and

7 After considerable speculation, the English White Paper, *The Future of Higher Education* (DfES, 2003a) has proposed the introduction of top-up fees. In this case, a course fee of up to £3,000 per year can be levied by universities at their discretion. It will be payable once graduates have gained employment through the taxation system once their salary has reached the threshold for payment of £15,000. The scheme currently proposed is predicated on safety nets being provided for poorer students, including the reintroduction of a grant of £1,000 and the continuance of the payment of current fees of £1,100 for those eligible on grounds of low income.

8 The numbers in FE increased by 25% in the period 1999–2002. A 40,000 increase necessitated only a 10% increase (Scottish Further Education Funding Council (SFEFC, 2003)). In same period, first degree numbers in HE increased by 6,256 and sub-degree numbers by 3,187 (Scottish Executive 2003c).

the challenge of the knowledge economy, individual responsibility and self-improvement, employability, flexibility of institutions and individuals, social inclusion and citizenship.

A number of specific policy initiatives were launched following publication of *Opportunity Scotland*. Those of particular relevance to FE and HE are: the funds (Widening Access Development Grants) allocated since 2000 to both sectors by the Scottish Higher Education Funding Council and the Scottish Further Education Funding Council. These funds have been allocated to promote wider access initiatives (including widening access through part-time study). Other important initiatives include the encouragement of new forms of partnerships between educational providers, advice agencies and employers through the aegis of LearnDirect Scotland (launched in 2001) using information and communications technology (ICT) as an important vehicle to do so; and the establishment of a national qualifications framework based on the Higher Still and SCOTCAT frameworks.

In addition to these initiatives, a number of student support measures have either been announced or initiated by the Scottish Executive. Funds were initially made available to support part-time students on low incomes. In its response to the Cubie report[9] (Scottish Executive, 2000), the Scottish Executive states clearly that the main aim of FE and HE in Scotland is now to widen access. The consultation document makes a number of recommendations designed to target resources on the socially excluded. The Executive has already committed itself to a number of initiatives in response to Cubie, including funding for childcare support worth £8 million over two years (targeted at FE students); means tested bursaries of up to £2,000 with a further £500 available in loans for poorer students (estimated at 30% of the total student population) and £10 million of funding to support mature students, £2 million of which is 'new' money (again

9 The Cubie Inquiry into student finance was established following the Scottish elections. The Labour and Liberal Democrat coalition created considerable pressure for reform of student finance since the Liberal Democrats had promised to waive the student contribution to tuition fees.

estimated as helping up to 30% of the student population);[10] and the waiving of the student contribution to tuition fees. More recently the Scottish Executive has announced plans to provide universities with £750 per head for students from poorer backgrounds

The Wider Access Development Grant provided by the Scottish Higher Education Funding Council is comprised of four strands, including the development of the FE/HE interface, institutional development and coordination, regional forums of providers from different sectors (primarily FE and HE) and selective funding. These grants have been used to fund a variety of institutional and supra-institutional developments, including the establishment of four regional access forums and the Scottish Network for Access and Participation (SNAP), the work of which spans both the further and higher sectors. A number of policy documents (Scottish Executive, 1999; Scottish Executive, 2000) emphasise inter-institutional collaboration within and between sectors and the most recent Higher Education Review (Scottish Executive, 2003b) puts particular stress on links between FE and HE. The Scottish Higher Education Funding Council is about to offer an incentive for collaborative provision within its funding model.

Access: a Critical Debate

In parallel with these developments, a public and academic debate has emerged over the issue of widening access. A key focus of this debate has been the issue of fiscal policy in relation to HE. The rapid expansion of HE in the 1990s, particularly in the FE sector, led to an intense debate over the affordability of HE both for the state and the individual. Public disquiet over the imposition of tuition fees has in turn been fuelled by intense media interest in perceived injustices as when a seemingly well-qualified state school pupil, Laura Spence, was

10 The Framework Document (Scottish Executive, 2000) indicated £10 million for the Mature Student Bursary Fund and an £8 million reduction in current access funds (from £14 million to £6 million).

rejected by an Oxford college in 2000. The government's decision to highlight both the issues of social justice and access in policy (DfEE, 1998; Scottish Executive, 2000; SOEID, 1998) whilst simultaneously reforming student funding, has certainly been politically difficult. The fiscal controversies surrounding HE, and student funding in particular, have been further amplified by the divergence of policy in the United Kingdom following Scottish devolution (Independent Committee of Inquiry into Student Finance, 1999; Scottish Executive, 2000).[11]

This crisis of affordability for individuals and the state has unfolded at a time when HE in the United Kingdom has been comprehensively restructured. The creation of new universities in 1992 from the old polytechnics (called 'central institutions' in Scotland) resulted in a more unified system of HE institutions. The emphasis on flexibility and accessibility in the former polytechnic sector had the potential to stimulate change across what became a new university sector as these institutions participated in the same policy forums. In the same year, the FE colleges in the United Kingdom were freed from local authority management. This, together with their links with the new universities, allowed them to increase their HE provision, often involving franchising and other links with the new universities (Osborne and Gallacher, 1995). These changes helped trigger the proliferation of institutional developments traditionally associated with greater accessibility including credit accumulation and transfer schemes, modularisation of courses, semesterisation, accreditation of prior learning, the growth of open and distance learning initiatives and inter-institutional access arrangements.

Despite these considerable changes in provision, there remains concern in the United Kingdom as a whole that the increase in participation in the 1990s has in fact done little to widen access. Instead it has given rise to what has been called a 'crowded traditional system' (Robertson, quoted in Watson and Taylor, 1998). Sargant *et al.* (1997)

11 In Scotland the newly imposed tuition fees were quickly replaced by a graduate endowment which waived the student contribution to tuition fees. This created a situation where English students at Scottish universities were required to pay fees while their Scottish counterparts (and students from elsewhere in the EU) were not.

reported that in the United Kingdom twice as many people from the highest social classes A and B (as measured by employment status) participate in HE than do those from lowest classes D and E and this is confirmed in a more recent report (National Audit Office, 2002a). Similar patterns of participation are, of course, apparent elsewhere in Europe (for example, see Parjanen and Tuomi, 2002). Within the United Kingdom, it is in Northern Ireland that students from poorer backgrounds particpate in the highest proportions (Field, 1997).

A key characteristic of the recent expansion that has repeatedly been emphasised in research is the continued differentiation: the older universities continue to prove less accessible than the new (Schuller *et al.*, 1998; Bourgeois *et al.*, 1999; CVCP, 1998). Indeed the differential between the pre- and post-1992 universities in terms of non-traditional enrolments raises the possibility that increasing differentiation in recruitment terms is now underway with low-income students increasingly concentrated within newer universities (CVCP, 1998). Certainly, research suggests that some institutions are more involved in widening access than others, with some institutions providing fewer alternatives to the normal access route (Bourgeois *et al.*, 1999, p.53). One consequence of this is differential access by students from poorer backgrounds to certain elite professional areas such as medicine, dentistry and veterinary science, which are almost exclusively located in older universities (Field, 2002).

At the newer end of the institutional scale, research indicates that a crucial factor in widening access provision is competition between institutions for students. The need to recruit students, and the marketing strategies required to achieve this recruitment, are confusing the initiatives to widen access. The effect has been to ensure that access provision has become an issue in some, but not all, institutions. In terms of overall growth, patterns of provision and the widening of access, much will depend upon the market strength of each institution (Smith and Saunders, 1991, p.11).

Alongside these changes, national policy on lifelong learning is increasingly challenged in the academic literature and the concept has been subject to a number of criticisms. The focus on employability in lifelong learning policy is criticised as a form of social control (Coffield, 1999) and as a clumsy educational answer to the changing imperatives of business (Murphy, 2000). The model of social inclusion underlying current policies has also been criticised for its individualistic focus on non-participants possessing personal deficiencies rather than on factors in the external environment (Preece, 2000). Meanwhile, the current emphasis on access has stimulated a debate of a different kind concerned primarily with the question of effectiveness (as defined by the Funding Councils and the policies of the institutions). Unfortunately these two debates on access and social justice in HE have proceeded in parallel; each one has largely failed to inform the other. In particular, the debate over the purpose of lifelong learning policy has largely ignored the questions of purpose and motivation in practice and in policy implementation. This means that the institutional policy context has often been disregarded. Given the increasing differentiation between universities and the targeting of resources designed to widen access to institutions, this is a serious omission. Discussions of the 'what works' variety, on the other hand, sometime ignore questions of purpose, offering only normative accounts of access practices which do not facilitate a greater understanding of motivations and purpose in practice or the development of analytical categories for understanding access in action.

An overview of access initiatives

It is increasingly difficult, due to the proliferation and diversity of the provision, to provide an overview of the field of access initiatives in the United Kingdom. The issue is not so much related to the quantity of work taking place (although it is becoming increasingly difficult to identify this due to the vast number of organisations involved). The issue is more qualitative. First of all, how are access initiatives defined? For instance, could extra-mural or liberal adult education be considered an access route into HE? Extra-mural courses are designed to facilitate access to the HE curriculum for those who have an interest in academic knowledge. Their purpose is not directly related to facilitating access to HE qualifications but extra-mural provision can act as an informal 'first step' for many mature students, either by allowing them to 'test the water' in HE or by increasing their interest in progression (Inglis and Murphy, 1999).

The second qualitative issue is how best to conceptualise and categorise access initiatives to make them more amenable to further analysis. A recent report (Universities Scotland, 2001) on access in Scottish HE institutions is useful in this regard. Institutional developments are described in terms of how they address three issues affecting access and retention: academic (raising entry qualifications); cultural (raising awareness); and internal (changing institutional structures). For instance, Summer Schools are viewed as a means of addressing the academic issue of raising students' qualifications prior to entry, while credit accumulation and transfer address the internal issue of facilitating a wider range of possibilities for progression through institutions.

A distinction between the different forms of access available, provided by Toyne (1990, pp.63–5), is useful. He suggested that there are two broad types of access initiative: those that focus on people 'getting in' to HE; and those that emphasise 'getting out' to the people who are under-represented in HE. Access courses for adults and summer schools are concerned with people 'getting in' to HE via non-standard means. Partnerships with schools, communities and employers, on the other hand, are much more involved with FE and HE institutions 'getting out' to under-represented groups and the socially excluded. For the purposes of this chapter, these two types are defined as 'in-reach' and 'out-reach' respectively.

Toyne does not allow room in his distinction for the crucial category indicated by Universities Scotland as addressing internal issues affecting access and retention. Alongside in-reach and out-reach, a number of initiatives cannot be categorised primarily either as in- or out-reach, and have more to do with transformations and adjustments to the structure, administration and delivery of HE programmes. They include part-time provision, open and distance learning and links between FE and HE institutions. We have previously referred to these broadly as 'flexible' access initiatives. This three-part map of access is illustrated in Figure 1. In work on Scotland (Murphy *et al.*, 2002), it has been demonstrated that these different types of initiative are affected by issues of supply and demand and also by institutional policy responses.

Within this typology it would be invidious to single out particular institutions to demonstrate particularly good practice. Many universities now have a history of 20 years or more of directly providing adult access programmes with considerable success. The in-reach provision of summer schools, on the other hand, does not have an exclusively adult clientele but is a well-established form of offer and a network of 'Access Summer Schools' exists throughout the United Kingdom with even the most elite institutions involved.

There is a less comprehensive coverage of institutions when outreach and flexibility are considered. Certainly there is concern that, if new demand is to be stimulated, then direct links should be made with communities and workplaces. Despite the considerable emphasis on workplace learning in the 1990s, there has been relatively little progress in this area at the access level (see Reeve *et al.*, 1995). Similarly, there are few community-based initiatives although the 'Open Road' programme run by the Open University in Dumfries and Galloway provides a useful example of the approach.

Flexibility is best demonstrated by the large number of universities that have now established links with FE colleges. In what might be described as the strongest of such models, some universities are moving to complete unification to create single institutions. An example of this is the network involving the University of Bradford and a number of colleges in its region. However, the linkages between the United Kingdom's Vocational Education and Training (VET) sector (i.e. the FE colleges) and the universities is rather patchy with clear skewing of links towards the post-1992 institutions (Osborne *et al.*, 2002). There is danger here of a 'ghetto effect' with less wealthy (though not necessarily less able) students progressing to less elite institutions.

The use of open and distance approaches is shown most obviously by the United Kingdom's Open University, which provides a very high proportion of the undergraduate education at a distance for adults in the country. A number of other universities have also, to an extent, tried to incorporate some provision through teaching at a distance in their programmes, principally using ICT. The recently established University of the Highlands and Islands Millennium project, located in the remotest part of the United Kingdom and based around a network of colleges, is reliant on ICT to provide education to geographically isolated areas. Part-time provision in the traditional face-to-face mode has a relatively low priority in many universities and, although there are some examples of well-integrated modular provision with the possibility of multiple modes of study, these are relatively rare.

The move towards the greater use of ICT reflects the wider European policy spelt out within the Memorandum on Lifelong Learning (EC, 2001). Its 'Key message 6: Bringing learning closer to home' is relevant and contains the following objective:

> Developing innovative teaching and learning methods in which ICT-based technology is an integral part. [...] To provide lifelong learning opportunities as close to learners as possible, in their communities and supported through ICT-based facilities wherever appropriate.

Such statements typify approaches that see ICT as a solution to overcome barriers to participation and difficulties caused by geographical isolation and immobility.[12] Barajas and Sancho (2000) argue that contemporary society cannot afford the exclusion of certain sections of society for reasons of health, family, economic or professional situations. It is therefore obliged to maximise the potential of human resources for economic, technological, scientific and cultural development. Similar sentiments are expressed at the national level and manifest themselves in a range of forms of initiatives linked to the provision of continuing education and lifelong learning. In Scotland, for example, one of the Scottish University for Industry's roles will be to break down 'barriers to learning by using new technology to make learning easier and more convenient' (Scottish Office, 1998).

A final element of flexibility is the availability of part-time opportunities shaped to the lifestyles of many potential entrants, particular those in work. It could, of course, be argued that most under-

12 See for instance the survey by CEDEFOP (2001).

graduates in today's universal HE system in Britain are part-time given the financial necessity of combining study and work. Most are still formally full-time however, and complete their undergraduate degrees in three or four years. Furthermore, despite the emphasis on semesterisation and modularisation, the system as a whole has done relatively little to improve flexibility with regard to its mode of delivery.

Figure 1: A Map of Access Initiatives

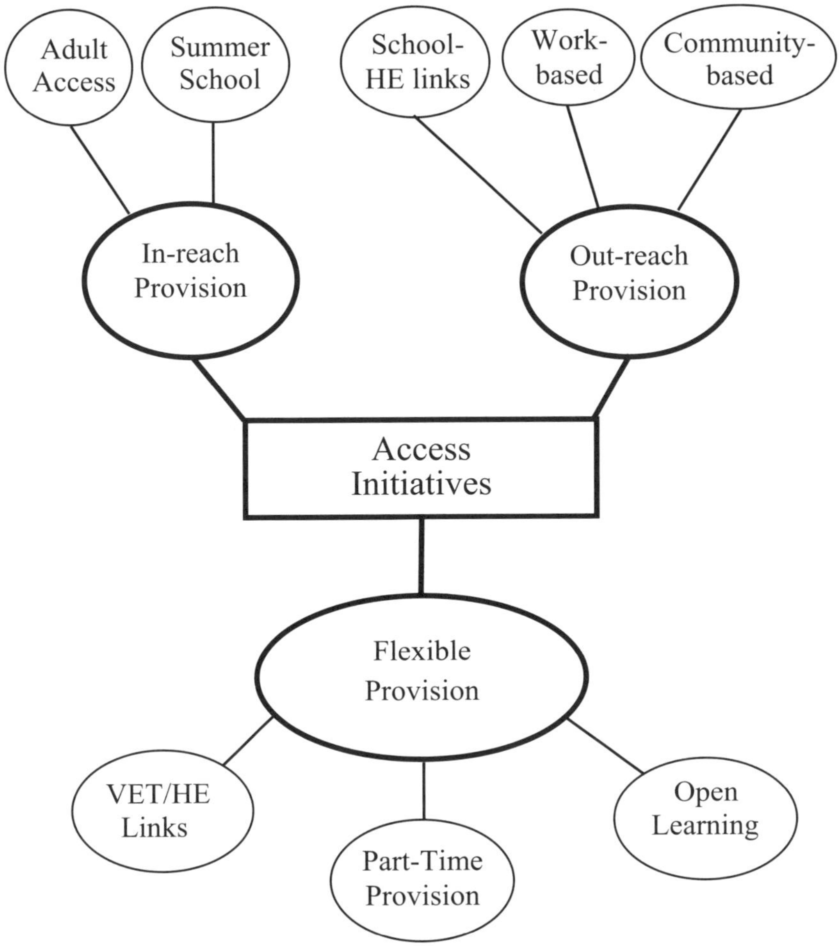

The experience of university

Although the United Kingdom has high levels of student retention,[13] by the standards of the Organisation for Economic Cooperation and Development (OECD) at around 80%, there is considerable variation by institution and, with widening participation, there are anxieties that this figure will decrease. A recent report (National Audit Office, 2002b) has shown that mature students are more likely to drop out than those who are under the age of 21 at entry. A recent report on student retention (Universities UK, 2001) has already highlighted a number of problems that are experienced by undergraduate students. First, and most crucially, there are increased financial constraints associated with study: as a consequence more students are now working during term time than ever before and the anti-social nature of some of their working hours is having deleterious effects upon their studies (Independent Committee of Inquiry into Student Finance, 1999).[14] Perceptions of debt certainly have been, and remain, critical to mature students' decisions to enter, and remain, in HE. This is particularly true for those from poorer backgrounds (DfEE, 2000; CVCP, 1998 and 2000). Callender and Kempson (2000) found that students from classes A and B receive the most in terms of parental contributions and gifts. Mature students have the highest levels of spending on essential items, not the least of which is childcare (Davies *et al.*, 2002;

13 For more detail of completion rates in HE see OECD, 2003, p.49–54. In Europe for Tertiary A type HE, the United Kingdom, together with Ireland and Turkey, there are survival rates of over 80%. By comparison, in Austria, France, Italy and Sweden these rates are below 60%. However strict comparison is difficult because of the varied duration of provision. Tertiary level A education requires a minimum cumulative theoretical duration of 3 years' full-time equivalent study, normally are 4 years equivalent in duration, though may be longer. By comparison Type B programmes focus on practical, technical and occupational skills leading to direct entry to the labour market, though may contain some theoretical components, and are of a minimum of 2 years equivalent in duration. No obvious differences in retention are evident for type B.

14 See also Barke *et al.*, 2000; Brennan, 1999; Kember, 1999; Mills and Shah, 1999 on the effects of paid work during termtime.

Osborne *et al.*, 2001), and are most likely to take out student loans to meet these essential needs. This suggests a financial divide between relatively rich traditional age students and relatively poor mature students.

Second, although in many institutions there is considerable flexibility in time, place and mode of study, many universities still offer a traditional curriculum structure that does not match the needs of mature students (McGivney, 1996). Third, even where elements of flexibility do exist, these are not generally complemented by appropriate student support provision. Such unsupported flexibility can have detrimental effects upon students with no prior family history of university attendance.

In terms of the learning experience of adults as undergraduates, class background appears to be a crucial factor. To working class mature students, the expectations of life improvements are high (Davies *et al.*, 2002; Osborne *et al.*, 2001). At the same time, however, the phenomenological notion of being a 'student' and the idea of a 'university education' are concepts which remain mysterious to the outsider, especially those from working class backgrounds (Merrill, 1999). Moreover, many adults may have had unsatisfactory personal experiences of schooling which need to be overcome before they can learn effectively (Carter, 1998). As well as this, there exists the fear in the minds of many potential mature students that the university is an alien environment and that they will struggle to fit in (Osborne *et al.*, 2001). Gender also appears to be a crucial factor, since female mature students are often better able to bring life experience to seminar discussions than males, who remain, for the most part, silent. By contrast, women are more likely to be stressed and to feel guilty if they experience difficulty in juggling their time to meet the commitments of academic and family life.

In this area of retention, there is now increasing concern that greater attention should be given to comprehensive support to mature entrants at all phases of their university careers from the pre-entry stage onwards. A good example of collaborative and holistic action in this domain is provided by Bolam and Dodgson (2002) who describe and analyse procedures that have been adopted by the universities of the North-East of England.

Conclusion

It is clear that the field of widening university participation is of central importance in United Kingdom educational policy. In a recent article concerning this topic within a European domain the following observations were made:

> […] the purposes of initiatives to widening participation were associated with economic instrumentalism, social justice, and pragmatism and expediency (Gallacher *et al.*, 1996). Little has changed in the intervening years with respect to these objectives, though the extent, scope and forms of widening participation policy and practice has diversified considerably. The three themes can still be clearly identified within the wide European domain. To a greater or lesser degree massification is economically-driven; struggles for social justice have intentionally led to certain gains for historically excluded groups, though the resultant changes in HE practice are differentially distributed according to institutional history, tradition and form. Much change is undoubtedly pragmatic and, rather than a response to genuine commitment to provide greater equity, is a short-term response to decreases in demand from traditional entrants. Much done in the name of widening participation by institutions is probably a necessity to meet growing quantitative targets and *in extremis* to secure institutional survival in the light of falling birth rates, and the resultant shifts in profile are inevitable rather than planned. (Osborne, 2003a)

These remarks have particular resonance in the United Kingdom where much activity in this field of endeavour has been undertaken, with a range of intentions and outcomes. There can be no doubt that access to HE has improved for groups that had previously been marginalised. However, the gains that they have made may be relatively small. Much of the broadening of participation has been to non-elite institutions and, as a consequence, access to 'high status knowledge areas' (Bourgeois and Merrill, 2001) such as medicine and veterinary science, to name but two fields, remains poor. Furthermore, simply gaining access is not enough as exemplified by the relatively poor retention figures for many institutions. In order for the gains of the past few years to be built upon, attention in the next decade must be given to supporting the heterogeneity of the universal system that is modern British HE.

References

Barajas, M. and Sancho, J.M., 2000. *The Implementation of Virtual Environments in Education and Training.* Final report of IVETTE Thematic Network Project – TSER Programme, Contract No SOE2-CT98-2037.

Barke M., Braidford P., Houston M., Hunt A., Lincoln I., Morphet C., Stone I. and Walker A., 2000. *Students in the Labour Market: Nature, Extent and Implications of Term-Time Employment Among University of Northumbria Undergraduates.* DfEE Research Report 215.

Bolam, H. and Dodgson, R., 2002. Retaining and Supporting Mature Students in Higher Education. *Journal of Adult and Continuing Education*, 8(2), 179–94.

Bourgeois, E., Duke, C., Guyot and Merrill, B., 1999. *The adult university.* Buckingham: SRHE/OU Press.

Bourgeois, E. and Merrill, B., 2001. Learning in Universities: Impacting on private and public lives. In: *Proceedings of ESREA 2001 Wider Benefits of Learning*, Lisbon, 13–16 September 2001.

Brennan J., 1999. *Part-time Students and Employment: report of a survey of students, graduates and diplomates.* London Open University, Quality Support Centre.

CEDEFOP, 2001. *Technology will improve access to learning for people with disabilities.* Available at: http://www2.trainingvillage.gr/etv/elearning/surveys/surmain.asp

Callendar C. and Kempson E., 2000. *Changing Student Finances: Income, Expenditure and Take-Up of Student Loans Among Full- and Part-Time Students 1998–9.* Sudbury: DfEE.

Carter N., 1998. Divergent Paths: helping adult learners to negotiate their school histories. *Language Issues*, 10(2), 4–7.

Coffield, F., 1999. Breaking the consensus: Lifelong learning as social control. *British Educational Research Journal*, 25(4), 479–99.

CVCP (Committee of Vice-Chancellors and Principals), 1998. *From elitism to inclusion: Good practice in widening access to higher education*. London: CVCP.

CVCP (Committee of Vice-Chancellors and Principals), 2000. *Discussion Paper from the Funding Options Review Group*. London: CVCP.

Davies P. and Parry, G., 1993. *Recognising Access. The Formation and Implementation of the National Framework for the Recognition of Access Courses*. Leicester: NIACE.

Davies, P., 2002. England. In: M. Murphy *et al. Widening Participation to Higher Education*. Glasgow: Scottish Executive.

Davies, P., Osborne, M. and Williams, J., 2002. *For me or not for me? – Mature Student Decision-making and Higher Education*. DfES Research Report 297. London: DfES.

DES (Department for Education and Science), 1985. *Academic Validation in Public Sector Higher Education: the Report of the Committee of Enquiry into the Academic Validation of Degree Courses in Public Sector Higher Education*. Cmnd 9501 London: HMSO.

DfEE (Department for Education and Employment), 1998. *The Learning Age*. London: HMSO.

DfEE (Department for Education and Employment), 2000. *Changing Student Finances: Income, Expenditure and Take-up of Loans Among Full-time and Part-time Higher Education Students*. London: DfEE.

DfES (Department for Education and Skills), 2003a. *The Future of Higher Education*. London: DfES.

DfES (Department for Education and Skills), 2003b. *Admissions to Higher Education. Review website*. Available at: http://www.admissions-review.org.uk/

EC (European Commission), 1995. *Teaching and learning: Towards the learning society*. Luxembourg: Office for the Official Publications of the European Communities.

EC (European Commission), 2001. *The Memorandum on Lifelong Learning*. Available at: http://www.europa.eu.int/comm/education/life/index.html

EUA (European University Association), 2003. *Trends 2003 – Progress towards the European Higher Education Area*. Geneva: EUA.

Field, J., 1997. Access or Equity? Adults in higher education in Northern Ireland. *Journal of Access Studies,* 12(2), 139–52.

Field, J., 2002. Further and Higher Education Links in England. In: M. Osborne *et al. A Research Review of FE/HE Links*. Glasgow: Scottish Executive.

FEFC (Further Education Funding Council), 1997. *Learning Works.* Kennedy Report. Coventry: FEFC.

Fieldhouse, R., 1997. *A History of Modern British Adult Education.* Leicester: NIACE.

Gallacher, J., Osborne, M. and Postle, G., 1996. Increasing and widening access to higher education: A comparative study of policy and provision in Scotland and Australia. *International Journal of Lifelong Education*, 15(6), 418–37.

HEFCE (Higher Education Funding Council for England), 1995. *Non-Award Bearing Continuing Education Funding – The Outcome.* Circular C16/95. Bristol, HEFCE.

HEFCE (Higher Education Funding Council for England), 1999. *Widening participation in higher education. Funding decisions.* Circular C99/24. Bristol: HEFCE.

HEFCE (Higher Education Funding Council for England), 2001. *Partnerships for Progression.* Consultation 01/73. Bristol: HEFCE.

HEFCW (Higher Education Funding Council for Wales), 2000. *Non-award bearing non-vocational continuing education: an evaluation*. Circular W00/27HE. Cardiff: HEFCW.

Independent Committee of Inquiry into Student Finance, 1999. *Student finance: Fairness for the future* (Cubie Report). Edinburgh: HMSO.

Inglis, T. and Murphy, M., 1999. *No room for adults? A study of mature students in University College Dublin*. Report prepared for the Higher Education Authority. Dublin: Social Science Research Centre/Adult Education Office, University College Dublin.

Kelly, T., 1992. *A History of Adult Education in Great Britain (2nd ed)*. Liverpool: Liverpool University Press.

Kember, D., 1999. Integrating Part-time Study with Family, Work and Social Obligations. *Studies in Higher Education*, 24(1) 109–24.

McGivney, V., 1996. *Staying or Leaving the Course: Non-Completion and Retention of Mature Students in Further and Higher Education*. Leicester: NIACE.

Merrill, B., 1999. *Gender, Change and Identity: mature women in universities*. Aldershot: Ashgate.

Mills, J. and Shah, T., 1999. Part Time Students and Employment. *Higher Education Digest*, Autumn, pp.1–8 of supplement.

Murphy, M., 2000. Adult education, lifelong learning and the end of political economy. *Studies in the Education of Adults*, 32(2), 166–80.

Murphy, M., Morgan-Klein, B., Osborne, M. and Gallacher, J., 2002. *Widening Participation to Higher Education*. Glasgow: Scottish Executive.

National Audit Office, 2002a. *Widening Participation in Higher Education in England*, Stationery Office, London.

National Audit Office, 2002b. *Improving Student Achievement in English Higher Education*. HC 486 Session 2001–2002, 18th January.

NCIHE (National Committee of Inquiry into Higher Education), 1997. *Higher education in the learning society* (Dearing Report). London: National Committee of Inquiry into Higher Education.

Newman, M., 1994 *Defining the Enemy: adult education in social action*. Sydney: Stewart Victor.

Organisation for Economic Cooperation and Development (OECD), 2003. *Education at a Glance*. Paris: OECD.

Osborne, M., 1997. *Continuing education in the UK*. In: Thematic Network in Continuing Education – 1st year report. Liège: EUCEN.

Osborne, M., Brink, B., Cloonan, M., Davies, P., Marks, A., Turner, E. and Williams, J., 2001. *For me or not for me in Scotland? That is the Question: A report of mature student participation in higher education*. Stirling: Centre for Research in Lifelong Learning.

Osborne, M., Gallacher, J. and Murphy, M., 2002. *A Research Review of FE/HE Links*. Glasgow: Scottish Executive.

Osborne, M., 2003a. A European Comparative Analysis of Policy and Practice in Widening Participation to Lifelong Learning. *European Journal of Education*, 38(1), 5–24.

Osborne, M., 2003b. University Continuing Education in the UK. In: M. Osborne and E. Thomas, eds., *Lifelong learning in a changing continent: Continuing education in the universities of Europe*. Leicester: National Institute of Adult Continuing Education.

Parjanen, M. and Tuomi, O., 2002. Finland. In: M. Murphy *et al., Widening Participation to Higher Education*. Glasgow: Scottish Executive.

Parry, G., 1996. Access education in England and Wales, 1973–1994: From second chance to third wave. *Journal of Access Studies*, 11(1), 10–33.

Preece, J., 2000. Challenging the discourses of inclusion and exclusion with off limits curricula. *Paper prepared for OU/University of East London Colloquium on lifelong learning.*

Reeve, F., Gallacher, J., Sharp, N., Osborne, M., Land, R., Whittaker, R., Dockrell, R. and Neal, P., 1995. *Developing Employment-based Access to Learning (DEAL) – Final Report*. Glasgow: Glasgow Caledonian University/University of Stirling/Napier University.

Sargant, N., Field, J., Francis, H., Schuller, T. and Tuckett, A., 1997. *A study of participation in adult learning in the United Kingdom*. Leicester: NIACE.

Schuller, T., Raffe, D., Morgan-Klein, B. and Clark, I., 1998. *Part-time higher education: Policy, practice and experience*. London: Jessica Kingsley.

Scottish Executive, 1999. *Opportunities for Everyone, a strategic framework for FE*. Edinburgh: Scottish Executive.

Scottish Executive, 2000. *Scotland: A learning nation*. Edinburgh: Stationery Office.

Scottish Executive, 2003a. *Life Through Learning; Learning Through Life*. Edinburgh: Stationery Office.

Scottish Executive, 2003b. *A Framework for Higher Education in Scotland. Higher education Review; Phase 2*. Edinburgh: Stationery Office.

Scottish Further Education Funding Council (SFEF), 2003. FE student numbers surpass targets. Media Release PRFE/03/03, 7 February 2003.

Scottish Office, 1998. *Scottish University for Industry*. Edinburgh: Scottish Office.

Scottish Parliament, 2002. *Final Report on Lifelong Learning*. Edinburgh: Scottish Parliament. Available at: http://www.scottish.parliament.uk/official_report/cttee/enter-02/elr02-09-01.htm

Smith, D. and Saunders, M., 1991. *Other routes: Part-time higher education policy*. Buckingham: SRHE/OU Press.

SOEID (Scottish Office Education and Industry Department), 1998. *Opportunity Scotland: A paper on lifelong learning*. Edinburgh: Stationery Office.

Stock, A., 1996. Lifelong Learning: thirty years of educational change. In: P. Raggart *et al*., eds., *The Learning Society – Challenges and Trends*. London: Routledge.

Toyne, P., 1990. Achieving wider access. In: G. Parry and B. Wake, eds., *Access and alternative futures for higher education*. London: Hodder and Stoughton.

UACE (Universities Association for Continuing Education), 1997. *Proceedings of Beyond the Boundaries – UACE Educational Equality Network Conference*. 6/7 January 1997, University of Lancaster.

Universities Scotland, 2001. *Access to Achievement: A guide to how the Scottish higher education sector is promoting social exclusion*. Edinburgh: Universities Scotland.

Universities UK, 2001. *Select Committee Evidence – Higher Education: Student Retention*. Available at: http://www.UniversitiesUK.ac.uk/

Watson, D. and Taylor, R., 1998. *Lifelong learning and higher education: A post-Dearing agenda*. London: Falmer Press.

Welsh Office, 1998. *Learning is for everyone*. Cardiff: Welsh Office.

Woodrow, M., 2000. European experience and good practice in widening access to young people from disadvantaged backgrounds. In: R. Osborne and H. Leith. *Evaluation of the targeted initiative on widening access for young people from socio-economically disadvantaged backgrounds*. Dublin: Higher Education Authority.

Overview

MIREILLE POUGET

22: New Opportunities and Challenges

In the introduction to this book, Robin Mark highlights the diversity of the adult education provision at the higher education (HE) level in Europe and the problems in presenting a coherent picture of the structural and institutional responses to widening access for adult learners. Moreover, he points to some of the intrinsic conflicts underpinning the European discourse on social inclusion through lifelong learning. These tensions reside in conflicting objectives. On the one hand, the focus is on adult education for the labour market with an emphasis on short-term, market-led vocational training while, on the other, the emphasis is on equality of opportunity and social justice for every citizen. As mentioned by Martin Beyersdorf, strong elements of this latter liberal adult education philosophy still remain in Germany.

One purpose of this book is to identify the barriers that adults might face in entering HE, particularly those facing individuals and groups who are socially and culturally disadvantaged within society. This chapter is directed specifically at universities rather than HE institutions more broadly. Higher education is now provided in many non-university institutions including colleges of further education, polytechnics and institutes of HE across Europe. These institutions are often more flexible than traditional universities in their entrance requirements and curriculum organisation. The focus of this chapter is on the barriers that adults encounter when seeking entry to universities. The picture which emerges is rather mixed; some universities are still formal and inflexible, presenting many barriers for adults.

The meaning of widening access to HE for adults has many complexities. In the United Kingdom, Michael Osborne cautions that increased participation is not the same as widening access, and refers to a 'crowded traditional system' where increased access is brought about by increasing numbers from socio-economic groups that are already well-represented in HE. Robin Mark, in his introductory chapter, refers to a number of research studies which support this position. So, instead of widening the social base of the student population, access policies in the United Kingdom could be accused of failing to reach those adults traditionally under-represented in HE.

What then are the barriers which adults learners face when entering universities? In the first chapter, Robin Mark refers to Cross's (1981) and McGivney's (1990) categories of barriers: personal, situational, institutional and informational. This model has been loosely used to highlight the difficulties adults face in accessing HE. In this chapter, two of these categories, situational and institutional barriers, will be discussed.

The situational barriers faced by mature learners were clearly identified in a recent study by Davies *et al.* (2002) and range from financial considerations, domestic situation and location, educational background, experience and qualifications, occupational status, perception of labour market opportunities and the value of HE qualifications, career aspirations and support from employers (Osborne, 2003, p.11).

Situational barriers arise from the social, cultural and economic contexts in which people live and they have a bearing on other personal factors such as self-esteem, health, perception of the value of HE and financial autonomy, thus blurring the distinction between personal and situational barriers. Conflating the two categories together avoids the pitfall of a 'personal deficit model', mentioned by Michael Osborne, where the cause and effect of social exclusion are seen as an individual's problem rather than a common societal problem.

Situational barriers are also linked to the concept of the social exclusion of groups who traditionally do not go to a university or any other HE institution. Social exclusion is a complex concept, allied to poverty. According to Clasen *et al.* (1998, p. 96) 'poverty may be both a pre-cursor of social exclusion and a consequence of it […].' Social exclusion

> is caused by a range of factors including unemployment or low income, lack of educational qualifications and marketable skills, poor housing, poor health and

> other forms of social disadvantage. These factors interact with each other: a key characteristic of social exclusion is that it arises from multiple layers of disadvantage and can be aggravated by discrimination. (Powery *et al.*, 2000, p.12).

The second main category to be examined is institutional barriers (which include the effects of governments' policies). Here the overall lack of institutional adaptability and flexibility in responding to the needs of the new adult student population, including the lack of information and guidance systems and learning support for adults, will be examined.

Situational barriers

The cost of higher education

The financial burden of the cost of study for mature students should not be underestimated. Michael Osborne reports that, in the United Kingdom, the fear of debt is a critical factor for those from a poor background in their engagement with HE. The current controversy surrounding the United Kingdom government's decision to introduce 'top-up' fees in English universities illustrates the institutional and governmental role in determining participation to HE.

In many countries, it appears that increasing adult participation and the deregulation of HE has been accompanied by the introduction of fees, particularly for short professional development courses and part-time undergraduate programmes. Thus, while part-time provision is noticeably increasing (for example, in Slovenia over 75% of universities offer at least one part-time programme) the effect has been counterbalanced by the introduction of fees. Here, Margerita Zagmajster notes that part-time students are more likely to be charged a fee than full-time students in public HE institutions. It also appears that, in some institutions, payment by instalment is not permitted and this administrative inflexibility can adversely affect adult student recruitment.

In Poland, the tremendous expansion of HE has been created by the establishment of private universities, now representing 64% of the sector. The figures provided by Dimitcho Tourdanov show that the flexibility of provision offered by the private universities (who offer courses in the evenings and at weekends), attracts many adults aged over twenty-five. He also points out that, in a country where 35% of the population lives in rural areas, such provision provides a greater opportunity for adults to take vocationally oriented programmes. However, this provision is provided at a price. Providers charge substantial fees with the cost per semester often amounting to more than double the average monthly Polish salary. This in turn introduces a barrier for some sections of Polish society.

In Latvia, Ineta Kristovska provides figures for 2001 which show that all the part-time students, and a substantial proportion of the full-time undergraduate students, are self-funded. In Slovakia, Ján Porvaznik and Marína Hučkova also report that students enrolling on HE certificate courses are charged a fee and that employers are reluctant to contribute to their staff's professional development and training. Even in Finland, where education is heavily subsidised, the Open University charges between 20 and 100 euros for each course.

In Estonia, 53% of all students, mainly full-time, are state financed. Others pay their own tuition fees or are sponsored by their employers, (except for unqualified teachers whose part-time studies are paid by the State). Aune Valk's report on the survey of students attending the University of Tartu's Open University shows that 45% of adults have their fees paid by their employer, while 30% are fully self-financing. However, she points out that since 1996 the figures show a decrease in contributions from employers, since new tax laws treat these contributions as taxable benefits.

The Estonian survey also shows that adults, although embracing Web-based opportunities, are sensitive to the cost of telephone lines for Internet use and many consider lack of financial support a major obstacle to participation.

The question of employers' contributions to staff training and professional development is mentioned in most reports. This represents a major issue for policy makers. Working people often wish to continue their professional development and they sometimes have no choice but to engage in learning if they want to remain in employment.

However, many small employers, seeing training as a cost, rather than an investment, do not fund sufficient training and this increases the financial burden on the individual. This issue is reported from Germany, Portugal and Hungary.

Barriers due to cultural and socio-economic disadvantage: the case of ethnic minorities

Among the rich description of new developments in adult education within the HE sector across Europe, a striking feature is the apparent lack of involvement of universities with socially excluded minorities.

The disfranchisement of ethnic minorities from society as a whole is suggested in several reports. Aniko Kálmán remarks that, in the case of Hungary, the gypsies' unemployment rates are worse now than they were under the old regime. It would appear from these reports that the burden of intervention in providing any kind of lifelong learning provisions for such communities is not seen to be the responsibility of HE institutions, even from a research point of view.

Margrit Wetter reports that in Italy non-formal adult education is offered by various cultural associations which, with local authority support, facilitates better integration for immigrant workers by offering Italian language courses combined with information on the Italian legal and administrative frameworks as well as Italian customs. Ján Porvaznik and Martina Hučková also report on how illiteracy in Slovakia affects Romany and Hungarian minorities, exacerbating their social exclusion through their inability to speak the Slovak language, let alone being able to participate in any form of learning. Ion Olteanu and Valentin Oprea mention that in Romania, school-based literacy programmes are offered to 'at risk' populations such as gypsies and isolated communities, with funding provided by public, charitable and European sources, but with no apparent input from the HE sector.

An exception can be found in Greece where Athina Sipitanou reports that universities have implemented a number of programmes of in-service training of primary and secondary teachers which include the education of immigrants and Muslim and Romany children.

The apparent absence of higher education involvement with such socially-excluded groups, either directly or in partnership with the non-formal sector providers, presents another major policy challenge for European policy makers. Without action, we are in danger of institutionalising divisions between those who have access to a network of educational facilities and those who remain at the margins of the knowledge-based economy.

Institutional barriers

Entry requirements, lack of specific preparation for entry and learning support for adults

One of the first hurdles faced by adults wishing to return to education via a university is the entrance requirement. Rossica Betcheva states that in Bulgaria the criteria for university admission for adults are the same as for younger entrants: a secondary school diploma and the university entrance examination. In theory, therefore, everyone has an equal chance of access. As Straw (1989) and Rees (1998) have demonstrated, however, equal access does not necessarily represent equality of opportunity, fairness and redress of disadvantage. Adults who find themselves in competition with school leavers are at an obvious disadvantage.

Competition for places on full-time programmes, illustrated for example by the competition for places in medical schools in Bulgaria, is a common occurrence. In Slovakia too, competition for university places is such that entrance examinations are set at a very high level, making it more difficult for adults to succeed. In the case of Slovenia, as Margerita Zagmajster explains, the imposition of restrictions on full-time places paradoxically boosts the numbers of part-time entrants. In some Slovenian institutions, their numbers have increased significantly (to constitute 31% of the total student population in 2002/03) since they were unable to join full-time programmes because of the restrictions imposed.

In the case of Bulgaria, Rossica Betcheva also highlights the problems which adults face when they are competing for places on courses such as computing studies. Here, a lack of the necessary mathematical skills and of extra preparatory support create significant problems for mature students. In the Czech Republic, Miloslava Chovancová and Andras Chernel refer to the concept of equality of access to HE institutions: here everyone who has completed their secondary education has the right to apply to any HE institution and to take the entrance examinations. However, the disadvantaged position of these mature entrants, once they have started their courses, may be deduced from the figures provided. Although 5.6 % of the HE entrants are over the age of 30, their success rate in completing their studies is only 27% compared to 48% for the newly qualified secondary students.

In Estonia, Aune Valk comments on the lack of confidence of adults who have not engaged in any form of education. This adds to the other obvious situational obstacles such as family and work commitments. The survey, already mentioned, of the University of Tartu's Open University students, showed that on average they had not engaged in formal study for eight years, highlighting the issues adults have to overcome to gain the appropriate study skills to become autonomous learners. Margerita Zagmajster from Slovenia also points out that part-time students were often lower achievers at the secondary school level and may have never had the skills for independent study.

The difficulties adults face before they have entered HE have been addressed in some chapters. A number of universities do offer flexible preparatory programmes for adults, based on the subjects tested in the entrance examination. In Slovakia, additional learning support courses are in some cases available to returning students and, in the Czech Republic, some universities offer preparatory courses for university entrance.

Other countries, like France, have created specific entry routes, such as special examinations. These are for adults who do not have the traditional school-leaving qualifications. They are preceded by a structured preparatory programme, which can sometimes be taken through distance learning. However, as Osborne points out, these special examinations are often modelled on the traditional school-leaving examination and may not be 'attuned to the needs of adult aspirants' (Osborne, 2003, p.15).

Flexibility of delivery: part-time versus full-time programmes

It is useful to get an overall sense of the proportion of adults involved in HE and whether the HE institutions are more flexible in accommodating a student population that is increasingly employed. Writers such as Patricia-Anne Moore from Ireland, highlight the fact that the boundary between part-time and full-time students is decreasing as more full-time students work to fund their studies.

Margrit Wetter explains that in Italy the numbers of working students has risen with a 20% increase in students who are over 22 years of age. In Slovenia, as seen already, 31.9% of students studied part-time in 2002/03 and of these 56.5% are in employment. Margerita Zagmajster also specifies that 44% of the mainstream undergraduate full-time programmes can be taken part-time, an unusually high percentage. In Slovakia, adults represented 4.8% of the undergraduate student population in 2001 but, as 51% of the undergraduates are studying part-time, this alerts us to the fact that part-time study and education for adults are not always interchangeable. Jiri Manninen and Tina Engblom on the other hand talk about an 'adultification' of HE in Finland with an example from the Åbo Akademi University. There adults made up 40% of the student population in 2001. In contrast, 5.6% of students who register in Czech universities are over the age of 30, while in Hungary, applicants over the age of 18 formed 16% of university applications in 2001. In polytechnics in Finland, Jyri Manninen and Tina Engblom explain that 57% of the students are over the age of 25. In Estonia, 13% of the adult population engage in some form of short course study according to government research. From the Polish report, we know that 54.7% of undergraduates study part-time. These figures give us the most detailed figures of adults studying in a flexible mode; altogether nearly 75% of adults over the age of 21 are studying on evening courses and 84.5% study at weekends.

What does this rapid overview of the figures provided by the reports tell us? First, it implies there is a need for a comprehensive survey and analysis of adult participation in all forms of HE across Europe. Information should be collected on the mode of participation, such as access to undergraduate programmes or study on a part-time or distance learning basis.[1] Equally important are the figures showing the success rates of adults and the levels of the qualifications obtained. Such data would be useful in shaping policies towards increasing adult participation in HE.

It appears from the country chapters that the provision available to many adults consist mainly of short professional development courses, such as those described for Portugal, Hungary and Romania. Here undergraduate programmes are not always available part-time, thus limiting the choices adults can make.

The picture which emerges from this limited survey is that there is a very varied response from the HE sector to adults' demands for undergraduate studies and for professional development. This depends on the nature of the institutions: the more traditional universities are generally less flexible than the newer institutions such as the polytechnics and the private universities.

Teachers' professional development for lifelong learning

A lack of institutional flexibility in responding to adults' needs is reflected in the difficulty experienced by existing academic staff in universities in adapting to new teaching methods and to a new professionalism that encompasses not only the use of information and communications technology (ICT) but also addresses a new student

1 The 2005 Adult Education Survey proposed by the European Commission and the survey of learning in enterprise (European Community, 2001) may well provide some of the qualitative and quantitative indicators needed here.

population whose needs and expectations are markedly different from those of school leavers.

This theme recurs in many of the chapters. Aune Valk from Estonia writes about the reluctance or inability of university lecturers to take into account adult students' needs. This adds to the lack of self-confidence that many adults already have in their learning ability.

It is also reported that in Slovenia there is a lack of training available for teachers of adults, in particular in the use of ICT and e-learning. For Latvia, Ineta Kristovska reports that although some university departments offer weekend and evening tutorials and examinations close to students' homes, there is a marked lack of motivation on the part of university teachers to participate in adult education provisions. She cites the lack of a centralised system for the development of adult education within the universities for this situation. This would also facilitate administrative and organisational aspects of adult provision such as publicity, registration, quality assurance and accreditation.

A lack of specific training or qualifications in Romania for the teachers of adults in the various adult education institutions is also reported. This is in spite of a well-developed structure for adult vocational training (through the National Council for Adult Vocational Training, for example, and the Regional Centres for Adult Education and Training). Ion Olteanu and Valentin Oprea make the point that most teachers of adults come from the formal education system and use traditional methods of teaching and assessment. Other writers similarly remark on the inappropriateness of the traditional teaching and assessment methods for adult education purposes.

Ineta Kristovska from Latvia highlights the need not only for development planning for adults but also for effective support systems for students and teaching staff. She gives the example of the development of a programme in Baltic studies, a mixed-mode distance learning programme using Web-based learning and written material, audio-conferencing and face-to-face tutorials. This was developed in partnership with the Universities of Tartu (Estonia), Vilnius (Lithuania) and Turku (Finland). This programme highlighted the need to develop teachers' expertise in computer skills, in student-centred learning methods including ICT and in developing appropriate study materials. Regarding the use of ICT, the Estonian survey also reminds us of mature students' fear of losing face-to-face contacts with teachers and fellow students, considering Web-based learning as an additional tool rather than as a substitute for face-to-face teaching.

Several writers, including those from Lithuania and Latvia have highlighted the need for evaluation and quality assurance procedures for distance learning and for designing high quality e-learning products. This issue is echoed by Osborne and Oberski (2004, p.4) who emphasise the problem of relying 'on the importation of pedagogical approaches from traditional HE practice that is often poorly conceived in its source environment let alone within the online mode'.

Guidance and learning support and responding to learners' needs

In Ireland, Patricia-Anne Moore raises the issue of appropriate and relevant adult information, guidance and counselling, which she considers necessary to accompany any development in adult participation. This point is also made elsewhere.

Lack of information or advice regarding opportunities for training and professional development courses appears to be a common problem for many employees. Yet simultaneously policies emphasise the need for training or re-skilling the workforce for the new knowledge-based economy. Employees do not necessarily feel that the training provided corresponds to what they perceive their professional development needs to be. For example, in Lithuania, Daiva Dumčiuvienė, Marius Mikulėnas and Danguolė Rutkauskienė report on a survey which shows that employees did not feel that their learning was appropriate; only 33.3% were completely satisfied.

In Portugal, Nilza Costa, Pedro Mantas and Luis Marques present the work of a non-profit making unit delivering continuing professional development to the private sector. This highlights similar issues where some private-sector employees either do not choose to undertake the training provided or do not see its relevance and where their own perceived needs may not match the corporate view. Similar findings were reported in a study (Brink *et al.*, 2003) regarding the importance of providing learning that helps people to do their jobs more effectively.

On the issue of adult information and guidance practice for prospective students, the University of Aveiro also reminds us that, although people can participate freely in what the authors call 'detached disciplines' (equivalent to auditing), its advantages are limited if people do not have access to advice on choosing the most appropriate subjects to take.

Margerita Zagmajster also identifies a lack of adequate guidance for mature part-time students prior to enrolment as one of the key issues that needs to be addressed if greater participation of adults in HE is to be achieved.

Partnerships, progression, credit transfer and recognition of prior non-formal and informal learning

Some solutions have been found to resolve the unsuitability of rigid full-time programmes for adults with working and family commitments, for example, through distance learning. Such programmes are often delivered in collaboration with other institutions, such as the creative 'multiform studies' in Finland. Jiri Manninen and Tina Engblom report that the Open University there operates local study groups in collaboration with adult education centres. This collaboration creates progression routes between what Osborne (2003) calls a binary system of education involving intermediate institutions such as colleges of further education in the United Kingdom, polytechnics in Finland and colleges which work in collaboration with the *Komvux* (municipal adult education) and the universities in Sweden. Michael Osborne reports on the development in England of foundation degrees, delivered by colleges and universities working together.

The real question for adults is how much these routes provide a seamless path into HE. There is evidence in the chapters in this book which suggests that some are either not credited or that the credits awarded do not count for entry into a university course. Entry may also be limited to a very small number of these students. In Bulgaria, for example, transfer to a university course for college graduates can only be achieved by the top 5% of students.

The situation is particularly acute regarding informal learning. The example of Romania, with its rich adult education structure, and the recent creation of a National Association of Folk Universities, indicates the need for the informal learning that takes place to be given credit. This was recognised in the recommendations made in 2001 by the Romanian National Council for Adult Vocational Training.

In Lithuania, non-formal education certificates (part of personal and social development), developed following the 1998 Non-Formal Adult Education Legislation, are recognised by employers but not by the State. In French-speaking Belgium, it is reported that continuing education courses provided by universities cannot lead to an academic diploma.

Opportunities for widening adult participation: emerging issues

The development of systems for credit transfer, recognition and accreditation of prior learning in formal, non-formal and informal contexts

The question of what counts towards HE in the form of credit transfer is one that many countries recognise as a priority to be addressed, especially in the light of the Bologna Declaration (1999). This will lead to a common frame of reference for qualifications which will provide flexibility and variation in different countries and different subject areas. Here the length of the study undertaken is expressed not as a total number of years but as the number of academic credits that must be successfully completed.

The Bologna Declaration identifies lifelong learning as a key element of the European HE area it seeks to promote. It affirms that lifelong learning strategies are necessary to face challenges of economic competitiveness and the importance of the use of new technologies to improve social cohesion, equal opportunities and the quality of life.

The European Commission's Memorandum of Lifelong Learning (European Commission, 2000) emphasises the importance of recognising non-formal and informal learning. This suggests the need to find new forms of assessment and to identify learning and the development of an innovative pedagogy designed to address the 'shift from knowledge acquisition to competence development' (European Commission, 2001, p.5).

The problem of how to determine what counts for credit is not addressed in these policy documents and the need to promote accreditation of prior and experiential learning (APEL) as a tool for social inclusion is not backed up from research findings (Cleary *et al.*, 2002). The official texts do not address the question of 'the significance of institutions and stakeholders in arbitrating what constitutes worthwhile knowledge, skills and understanding' (Edwards, 1997, p.135). The judgements that institutions make about 'worthwhile' credits may continue selective and exclusive practices rather than genuinely enhance wider participation.

Edwards (1997, p.136) points out 'the ambiguity of credit frameworks and systems within an increasingly consumer-oriented provision of learning opportunities may well result, therefore, in differential consequences, with certain providers adopting a "pile it high, sell it cheap" approach and others an approach of "excellence, quality and value-added"'.

Equally, one has to ask whether only learning that can be counted and measured will be valued. Those engaged in informal learning, with no desire to gain credits for it, may find themselves, or their subjects, undervalued in the learning market. Already the British example shows how funding support in universities for non-accredited continuing education courses has been withdrawn.

Many countries are beginning to introduce credit transfer systems. The Belgian chapter from Anne-Marie André and Geneviève Cochez demonstrates how the Flemish community and the social partners can work together to develop an educational framework which will enable greater modularisation and certification of non-formal learning, as well as the possibility of accrediting informal educational processes and experiences. In Ireland too a new qualification framework is being developed, while in Italy it is possible for adults to have their professional experience recognised, and given credits, through the creation of outreach centres.

We have seen how, in Sweden, through effective collaboration between informal and non-formal adult education within the *Komvux*, the colleges and universities create an effective credit system for adults returning to study, facilitating wider participation from different groups. In Finland, the polytechnics' open university courses are not only open to all, irrespective of age and qualifications, but they do also carry credits which enable transfer to a traditional university via the Open University Channel.

Perhaps the most notable development in the recognition of prior learning (RPL) comes from France, where the 2002 Law on Social Modernisation, includes the recognition of experiential learning (*Validation des Acquis de l'Expérience*, VAE). Guy Arquembourg and Arnaud Haeringer explain that the new law gives French citizens the right to have their experience, professional or otherwise, recognised and accredited, provided that the qualification that is the subject of the VAE application is registered in the national qualifications register which has been introduced by the legislation. (For further information on the development of the VAE see Pouget and Osborne, 2004). The greatest difference between the French VAE and other accreditation frameworks is that the VAE provides an evaluation of competences rather than simply an assessment of prior learning mapped against specific units and qualifications (Blachère, 2002). This reflects the shift in emphasis from knowledge acquisition to competence development mentioned earlier. The 2002 legislation on VAE has put into place one of the main priorities for action identified in the European Commission's Memorandum recommendations (European Commission, 2001). This has been done through the engagement of French universities on a national scale in the implementation of measures aimed at the assessment and recognition of formal, non-formal and informal learning.

The RPL measures and credit transfer processes are facilitated not only through the formalisation of national credit systems but also by a partnership approach to lifelong learning. An example of this is found in Belgium's Walloon Skills Centres where public-private partnerships, including partners from the universities, provide professional training in local centres.

In Estonia, three universities have regional colleges where students can study locally for mainstream degrees and for Open University or continuing education courses, with tutor and Web-based support. In Finland, Open University 'multiform studies', mentioned earlier, guarantee access and flexibility in remote parts of the country. In the German chapter, Martin Beyersdorf speaks about the new German model of 'life-accompanying learning' as part of a national programme of 'learning regions', focussing on developing local and institutional learning concepts for well-defined groups in local communities.

The development of the Distance Education Project in Lithuania, involving thirteen universities and colleges and creating an infrastructure for distance learning, provides an impressive model of co-operation between different types of institutions for the benefit of a wide range of learners.

These examples of partnerships echo the determination at the European policy level to promote 'local level partnerships' (European Commission, 2001, p.11) which bring together key stake-holders from the public, private and voluntary sectors in a new approach to valuing learning and building bridges between different learning contexts.

The response to the Memorandum on Lifelong Learning consultation (European Commission, 2001) also stresses the need to develop instruments for valuing learning, aiming to facilitate the transfer of qualifications and competences anywhere in Europe in a transparent way.

The role of adult guidance

The Memorandum on Lifelong Learning highlights the importance of recognising that information, guidance and counselling services act as 'the interface between learning needs and the learning on offer'. This helps learners to 'find their place in increasingly complex learning systems' (European Commission, 2001, p.13) and emphasises the role of partnerships in the informal learning and voluntary sector. The Walloon region of Belgium which created ten training and information centres (*carrefours de formation*, crossroad training centres) is a good example of such an infrastructure. In Ireland the setting up a National Centre for Guidance in Education has recognised the importance of guidance while in Poland information and guidance is now part of the government's strategy for developing adult and continuing education.

Innovative pedagogy and research in lifelong learning

Many of the national reports in this book highlight the importance given to the role of the teacher in adult learning, and the importance of professional development in building new knowledge and skills for a competitive economy. Many also highlight governmental resolutions to promote research into lifelong learning and adult pedagogy.

The following is a summary of some of the key developments which are currently taking place across Europe:

- In Estonia, 3% of the budget for teachers' salaries is devoted to teachers' professional development; the Tallinn Pedagogic University has focused on teacher training; new programmes are being offered in adult education at the bachelors, masters and doctoral levels in three HE institutions;
- In Hungary, professional development for teachers, including mentoring programmes, is now being offered. For example, a Lifelong Learning Centre has been established in the University of Debrecen to carry out research into lifelong learning and adult teaching;
- In the Czech Republic, the largest numbers of adult education programmes in professional development are in Pedagogy, Teaching and Social Care;
- In Greece, emphasis has been given to the retraining of primary and secondary teachers to provide continuing and professional development programmes and engage in

research on lifelong learning and developmental activities through the Institutes of Lifelong Learning in universities;
- In Romania, 'houses of teachers' are found in every part of the country and these provide training courses for a wide range of education professionals;
- In Germany, the provision of training for university staff involved in continuing education has been encouraged;
- In Belgium, lifelong learning policy in Flanders has emphasised the need for innovation in teaching and learning for adults and a focus on research on lifelong learning; and
- In Lithuania, the Government has provided state funding for research on the educational needs of adults.

It was noted earlier that traditional universities now have to consider new challenges to adapt their provision to meet the needs of adult learners by providing appropriate learning environments and technologies. Academics and institutions must adapt to the fact that the 'student' has now become the 'learner', which is 'consistent with a discourse of lifelong learning, [which] foregrounds the fact that people learn not only from institutions but in various and diverse life settings and can adopt a learning approach to life' (Edwards, 1997, p.130). Moreover

> while still considered as the guardian of academic knowledge, institutions and academic staff are challenged by the fact that individuals, as learners, are given greater opportunity to negotiate their own ways through the range of learning opportunities available to them, invest their own meanings within the learning process and negotiate the relationship between learning and other activities (Edward, 1997, p.130).

In the face of the changing student identity, some academic staff members find it difficult to reconceptualise the teacher-student relationship and adapt to a new order where the availability of choice even questions the existence of academic disciplines.

The Memorandum on Lifelong Learning emphasises that the shift from teaching to learning demands new approaches requiring the acquisition of new skills and 'multi-cultural competences for teachers which ensure that they are ready and motivated to face new challenges, and therefore to promote tolerance and democratic values' (European Commission, 2001, p.24). In all of this, the role for HE is increasingly seen as to increase research and training in the field of lifelong learning.

'Third Age' adult education

United Nations' figures (United Nations, 1999) show that Europe will be the area of the world most affected by ageing, with the proportion of older persons increasing from

> 20% in 1998 to 35% in 2050. By then, one in every three persons will be 60 years or older. By 2050, the 'oldest country' in the world will be Spain closely followed by Italy, with 3.6 and 3.4 persons aged 60 or above for each person below 15 years of age, respectively [...]

Facilitating access to learning opportunities for senior citizens and older workers (often called 'third age' learning) also features, albeit rather fleetingly, in the Memorandum on Lifelong Learning (European Commission, 2001, p.13). Opportunities for older learners are mentioned in a number of the chapters in this book, often related to the University of the Third Age. For example, Miloslava Chovancová and Andras Chernel from the Czech Republic point to successful third age activities organised in fifteen public universities, covering a wide range of arts, social science and scientific subjects.

In Finland, 9,500 retired people took part in OU programmes in 2002. The German chapter shows that in 2001, 50 universities had established branches of the University of the Third Age with 25,000 participants in total over the age of 55 attending programmes ranging from study skills and learning support to research methodology. In Slovakia, universities are also involved in providing courses for older adults through the University of the Third Age, charging a minimal fee for older adults for a period of up to three years.

It would seem that current preoccupations relating to an ageing Europe centred around the fact that older people are at a greater risk of social exclusion (Older People's Forum, no date). Still more attention should be paid to the lifelong learning needs and aspirations of older learners at all levels, as their numbers are set to increase substantially in the future.

Who are we widening participation for?

At the moment, it is difficult to judge to what extent the recent policies (on new credit systems, the recognition of informal and non-formal learning or the greater flexibility in the delivery of programmes for adults) are succeeding in widening participation.

While there has been a substantial increase in adult participation, especially in the vocational areas, what is less clear is whether the increase in mature students in universities represents a widening of the socio-economic background of adults participating in HE. As Edwards (1997) notes, high levels of participation are not increasing differentiation by factors such as social class.

More specific data are required if we are to analyse the backgrounds of learners accessing the new pathways to HE and to know if we are targeting groups which have traditionally been excluded with appropriate courses and methodologies.

In the United Kingdom, data on HE participation clearly shows that, where universities have increased participation, it is often for groups who have benefited previously (such as those with previous qualifications and various professional groups). There is continuing under-representation from the skilled non-manual, skilled manual and the partly skilled/unskilled social classes (HEFCE, 1996, p.23, in McGivney, 1999).

There are some indications of gender differences in participation in the chapters of this book. For example, women constitute 76% of the students attending Open University programmes in Finland, in courses that traditionally attract women (such as the social sciences), and they make up 70% of the University of Tartu's Open University students. McGivney (1999) points to differing patterns of participation in post-compulsory education between the sexes in the white population, with women over the age of 25 tending to choose more flexible, part-time or access programmes and more likely to enter HE as mature students. In the more informal adult education sector, while women participate in larger numbers, choosing self-development or general education courses, men tend to restrict their choices to more vocational courses such as computing or management training. Figures also show that, across the European Union, more women over the age of 50 than men engage in general education programmes, while a larger number of older men enrol on courses leading to qualifications (European Commission, 1997).

Conclusion

This chapter has attempted to analyse the barriers that adults face when entering HE across Europe. The main thrust of the reports focused on the provision of adult education rather than on the learners themselves. Adults are constrained by their life situations, as workers, parents, or as members of ethnic minority groups. The cost of lifelong learning does not always appear to be a major deterrent, for example when the increased participation in fee-paying programmes in Poland is considered. In the United Kingdom on the other hand, the fear of debt is very real for both adult and young students and increasing tuition costs have been shown to be a factor in non-participation or drop-out rates among adult learners.

Governments and employers are seen to contribute to some extent to the cost of retraining and professional development, in the form of tax rebates, by paid study leave, or through a fee contribution. Employers decide which courses they will fund, thus limiting the learners' choice. As a result, learners may feel that their perceived learning needs remain unmet.

In examining adult learners' needs, we often stumble across the notion of institutional flexibility, especially regarding the flexibility of course delivery to complement adults' working commitments. Many of the reports in this book convey a sense of optimism about Web-based learning, and many countries are developing a technological infrastructure to reach isolated or rural populations. Some examples of effective collaboration in this process are given, in particular where universities, colleges and the informal learning sector collaborate at the local level to deliver varied and flexible programmes, as in Finland and Sweden. Some reports express the learners' wish for personal contacts with tutors and other learners and the need to develop adults' and teaching staffs' competences in the use of ICT. Collaboration between institutions provides better credit transfer mechanisms and enables students to progress between different levels and modes of provisions. Breaking down barriers between these institutions, for example in the acceptance of each other's academic credit, is one of the most effective ways of widening access to HE. It provides an incremental pathway which can be followed at a pace chosen by the learners themselves.

As well as learners' attitudes to learning, the reluctance of some staff in the university to shift from teaching to learning and to engage with a lifelong learning agenda and interdisciplinary curricula constitutes an obstacle to change which many government policies are seeking to address.

The commitment of national governments, as expressed in many reports, to implement policies designed to facilitate the recognition of prior learning acquired outside formal education, while laudable, is fraught with many difficulties, starting with the concepts of knowledge and competence.

There is no doubt that all the countries considered in this book are working towards achieving the aims of the Bologna Declaration, which supports the creation of a European area of HE. This will promote citizens' mobility and employability, through the development of flexible frames of reference for qualifications, aided by robust quality assurance, evaluation and accreditation mechanisms across Europe.

Universities could nevertheless engage more fully with the lifelong learning challenges, for example by opening up their mainstream provisions to adults, through making available more part-time and flexible provision and by providing greater information, guidance and support for learning at the pre-entry level. Support for learning could also be offered more frequently and systematically to mature students during their studies and this would increase retention and success rates. Unsupported flexibility can work against students with no prior family history of university attendance.

The content of this chapter has been encapsulated by Scott (2002, p.151), who wrote, following an illuminating analysis on the reform of the HE systems in Central and Eastern Europe:

> [...] the challenges facing HE in Central and Eastern Europe appear [...] as part of a wider enterprise to reorient the whole of European HE by reaching out beyond the élites, old and new, cultural or technical, into the diverse communities that constitute modern Europe, and by and by realising the potential of the new synergies between knowledge and society and the economy, identity, and culture. It is not Central and Eastern European HE that is in transition; it is all HE.

References

Blachère, M., 2002. La VAE entre dans le code du travail. *Actualité de la formation permanente*, 177 (mars–avril). Paris: Centre INFFO.

Bologna Declaration, 1999. *Joint declaration of the European Ministers of Education. Bologna, 19 June 1999.* Available at: http://www.eua.be/eua/jsp/en/upload/OFFDOC_BP_bologna_declaration.1068714825768.pdf

Brink, B., Munro, J. and Osborne, M., 2002. *Using on-line technology in an SME work-based setting. Educational Technology and Society.* Available at: http://ifets.ieee.org/periodical/vol_2_2002/v_2_2002.html

Clasen, J., Gould A. and Vincent J., 1998. *Voices within and without. Responses to long-term unemployment in Germany, Sweden and Britain.* Bristol: The Policy Press.

Cleary, P., *et al.*, 2002. *Social Inclusion through APEL: the Learners' Perspective*. Available at: http://crll.gcal.ac.uk/SOCRATESSite/ComparativeReport.pdf

Cross, K.P., 1981. *Adults as Learners: Increasing Participation and Facilitating Learning*. San Francisco: Jossey-Bass.

Davies, P., Osborne, M. and Williams, J., 2002. *For Me or Not for Me – Mature Students' Participation in HE*. London: Department for Education and Science, Research Report 297.

Edwards, R., 1997. *Changing Places? Flexibility, Lifelong Learning and a Learning Society*. London: Routledge.

European Commission, 1997. *Age becomes her: older women in the EU*. Women of Europe, dossier 45, May–July, European Commission. In: V. McGivney, 1999. *Excluded Men. Men who are Missing from Education and Training*. Leicester: National Institute of Adult Continuing Education.

European Commission, 2000. *Memorandum on Lifelong Learning*. Brussels: Commission Staff Working Paper. Available at: http://europa.eu.int/comm/education/policies/lll/life/memoen.pdf

European Commission, 2001. *Making a European Area of Lifelong Learning*. Communication from the Commission. Available at: http://europa.eu.int/comm/education/policies/lll/life/communication/com_en.pdf

HEFCE, 1996. Widening access to HE: a report by the HEFCE advisory groups on access and participation. Higher Education Funding Council for England. In: V. McGivney, 1999. *Excluded Men. Men who are Missing from Education and Training*. Leicester: NIACE.

McGivney, V., 1990. *Education's for Other People: Access to Education for Non- Participant Adults*. Leicester: National Institute of Adult Continuing Education.

McGivney, V., 1999. *Excluded Men. Men who are missing from Education and Training*. Leicester: National Institute of Adult Continuing Education.

Older People's Forum, no date. Available at: http://www.age-platform.org/EN/B-Policy/C-Older.htm

Osborne, M., 2003. Increasing or Widening Participation in Higher Education? – a European overview. *European Journal of Education*, 3(1), 5–24.

Osborne, M. and Oberski, I., 2004. University Continuing Education – the role of Communications and Informational Technology. *Journal of European Industrial Training*, Vol. 28 (in press).

Pouget, M. and Osborne, M., 2004. Accreditation or *validation* of prior experiential learning: knowledge and *savoirs* in France – a different perspective? *Studies in Continuing Education,* 26(1), 45–65.

Powery, J., McPake, J., Edwards, L. and Hamilton, S., 2000. *Gender inequalities and lifelong learning in Scotland. Research Series.* The Scottish Council for Research in Education. Equal Opportunities Commission.

Rees, T., 1998. *Mainstreaming Equality in the European Union. Education, Training and Labour Market Policies*. London: Routledge.

Scott, P., 2002. Reflections on the Reform of Higher Education in Central and Eastern Europe. *Higher Education in Europe*, XXVII (1–2), 137–52.

Straw, J., 1989. *Equal Opportunities. The Way Ahead.* London: Institute of Personnel Management.

United Nations, 1999. *Towards a Society for all Ages. International year of the older person. Demographics of older persons*. United Nations Department of Public Information, DPI/1964/G, September 1999. Available at: http://www.un.org/NewLinks/older/99/older.htm

EDWARD THOMAS

23: European Higher Education for Adults, an Overview

It is clear from the preceding country chapters that we live in a world where international contacts and influences are increasing rapidly, where major technological developments are affecting essentially all our lives and where access to information is continually widening. The world is changing for all of us. We have to change with it. How can we cope?

The answer is clear. If we need particular information, we must learn it. If we need new skills, we must develop them. To be able to do this efficiently, we need the opportunity to learn whatever is necessary when we need it, where we need it. Perhaps more importantly, before we can do this each of us has to be able to recognise our own education and training needs as they arise and to know how to go about satisfying them. The economic benefits that come to us as a result of doing this, as individuals as well as to our nations' economies, are obvious. What is less clear, although it is equally true, is that our additional learning also provides social benefits, to us as individuals and to society. Adult education, for that is what is being referred to here, is clearly linked to the European Union's aim (European Council, 2000) that Europe should have 'the world's most dynamic and competitive knowledge-based economy' by the year 2010. The European Union (EU) and many national governments clearly expect adult education to contribute greatly to the achievement of this aim. Certainly it can. In addition to this economic benefit, adult education can also help Europe to become the most dynamic and vibrant society as well.

This book contains a great deal of information (much of it based on considerable experience) concerning the education of adults. It has concerned not the school leavers who start their higher education courses at the age of 18 or 19 but those who have taken a break from education after finishing school or a first university course before returning to study. This latter group is more mature, more experienced, almost always more motivated than the school leavers. It is this latter group that is referred to as 'adults' throughout this book.

The information presented here comes from higher education providers and has been collected from twenty countries, ten drawn from central Europe (Bulgaria, the Czech Republic, Estonia, Hungary, Latvia, Lithuania, Poland, Romania, Slovakia and Slovenia) and ten from western Europe (Belgium, Finland, France, Germany, Greece, Ireland, Italy, Portugal, Sweden and the United Kingdom).

To summarise the information contained in these chapters is a formidable task. This chapter starts by surveying the existing provision for adults in European higher education. It then considers in less detail (since this has already been addressed to some extent in the previous chapter), the barriers that hold back adults from participating in education across Europe. Finally, it examines the many ways in which higher education providers are successfully breaking these barriers down.

The organisation of adult higher education in Europe

One striking feature of the descriptions of the provision for teaching adults described in the previous chapters is the wide variation between them. Martin Beyersdorf's description of the adult education that is taking place in Germany, for example, focuses particularly on the seminar courses in the universities which provide liberal adult education for the adult public. In Poland, on the other hand, Dimtcho Tourdanov concentrates mainly on the provision of part-time degree and diploma courses for adults. An outline of the application of management methods to adult education, together with a large number of case studies illustrating good practice in the use of these techniques taken from across Europe, and incidentally confirming these differences, has been given by Mitchell (2002).

In a number of countries, national laws govern the adult education that takes place. In the Dutch-speaking part of Belgium, Anne-Marie André and Genèvieve Cochez have pointed out that the policy of the Flemish Education Ministry (2003) for learning at all ages, including the education of adults:

- Guarantees universal and continuing access to learning for everyone, allowing them to gain or renew the skills that they need for sustained participation in the knowledge society;
- Raises the level of investment in human resource 'in order to give priority to Europe's most important resource, its people'; and
- Encourages innovation in teaching and learning for adults.

As an example from central Europe, Ion Olteanu and Valentin Oprea have pointed out that in Romania education for adults that is delivered as part of the formal education system has, amongst its objectives, the provision of:

- Continuing vocational education;
- Civic education; and
- Education to extend the interest of individuals.

An important provision of the Romanian law is that non-formal (i.e. with classes but no assessment) and informal (i.e. without even classes) training are also recognised and these are given parity with formal training when determining adults' vocational competences. This is also the position in the Dutch-speaking part of Belgium.

As a further policy example, Guy Arquembourg and Arnaud Haeringer have reported three goals that have been identified in France for the *Diplôme d'Accès aux Etudes Universitaires* courses for young adults and job seekers:

- To reduce social exclusion;
- To update the competences of salaried workers to improve business competition; and
- To enable all active members of society to improve their social positions.

The laws relating to university continuing education across Europe as a whole have recently been summarised elsewhere (Osborne and Thomas, 2003, pp. 522–5). We can, therefore, concentrate here more on the other forms of decision making that affect the education of adults.

In addition to the laws, regulations applying to specific groups are also likely to affect adult education. In Estonia, for example, which is well provided with legal support for the development of education for adults, Aune Valk has noted that adult demand for vocational education (i.e. education planned to enable the learner to get a job, keep a job, or get a better job) is influenced by the detailed regulations set for particular occupations. Medical doctors in Estonia, for example, have to continue with their training to maintain their right to practise. In the case of Estonian schoolteachers, it is a government requirement that 3% of their total salary bill should be spent by local school authorities on teachers' professional updating. A requirement to undertake continuing updating is also in place in Portugal for schoolteachers who wish to progress within their professions. Regulations of this sort clearly increase the demand for continuing education and training in specific subject areas from those who are employed.

Important policy decisions can also be made within higher education institutions themselves. For example, the Dutch Open University, which has established study centres in the northern part of Belgium as well as in the Netherlands, has chosen to give priority on some of its recent training courses to handicapped adults.

People can benefit from the education that they receive from universities in many ways. In addition to education for vocational purposes, Michael Osborne has noted that some providers in the United Kingdom have set out to meet the needs of particular under-privileged groups in society, for example prisoners, the unemployed and the disabled, to help them overcome their problems by raising their education and skills levels. It often appears to be more difficult to obtain information about (and therefore more easy to ignore) education with social motives. The provision of all these forms of adult education will be considered later in this chapter.

Wide variations are seen in the numbers of universities across Europe that offer education for adults. In Estonia, for example, all the universities offer learning opportunities for professionals such as schoolteachers, doctors, engineers and civil servants, providing both short courses and opportunities for part-time study leading to graduation, either by face-to-face teaching or by distance learning. Some universities have large numbers of adult students. In Tallinn Pedagogical University, for example, the number of short course students (about 11,500) and adult students taking degrees (about 1,800) easily exceeded the number of full-time students (almost 6,000) in 2003. In the University of Tartu, its 9,000 short course adult students and 4,500 distance learning students equals the number of full-time students (about 13,500). Poland also has about 940,000 evening and weekend students in its universities, most of whom are likely to be adults, from a total student number of about 1.7 million (*Szkoły wyższe i ich finanse*, 2002). Here most of the adult students are likely to be in one of the 200 or more private universities that have been created in Poland since 1990.

The numbers of adult students are reported to be growing rapidly in some parts of central Europe. In the Czech Republic, for example, Miloslava Chovancová and Andras Chernel have reported that, in 2002/03, 29,838 adult students were recruited. This compares with 17,099 adults in 2000/01, i.e. an increase of 74% in two years. Here the largest number of programmes is found in the teaching and social care disciplines. These subjects are closely linked to the changing aims of Czech education and the related changes in Czech society more generally.

The forms of higher education for adults in Europe

Vocational education

The importance of vocational higher education is clear from the previous chapters; it appears that every country offers vocational courses at a higher education level; equally well, the higher education institutions in some countries appear to offer nothing but vocational education to adults. In Bulgaria, for example, Rossica Betcheva has reported that the choice of courses by adults is largely influenced either by the needs of the labour market at home or by the prospect of getting a job abroad. The importance of vocational courses is seen particularly where unemployment is high and vocational training is undoubtedly a valuable response to this problem in all these countries. As in other countries, many of the vocational courses on offer relate to computing, finance, languages and management.

One particular form of vocational education that is mentioned by authors in a number of countries, including Athina Sipitanou in Greece and Nilza Costa, Pedro Mantas and Luis Marques in Portugal, is in-service training courses for teachers. These courses frequently contain material on specific subject areas, such as mathematics or history, together with information on teaching the subject. Courses can also consider topics such as vocational guidance or counselling in schools or the teaching of immigrants or Muslim or Romany children. In some universities, for example in the University of Aveiro in Portugal, adult students are able to accumulate credits from these courses to achieve a masters degree in education if they wish.

In a related area, it has been reported from a number of countries, including Germany and Latvia, that since the 1980s training to develop the professional skills of the university staff themselves, both academic and administrative, has been a responsibility of the adult education departments in some universities.

Higher education institutions in all the countries reviewed in this book provide short vocational courses and these appear to follow a fairly similar pattern, often negotiated with companies or public administrations, as reported from France (Jallade, 2000). When considering longer vocational courses, however, a surprisingly wide range of approaches is taken. In Finland, for example, Jyri Manninen and Tina Engblom have reported that, in addition to the face-to-face teaching for longer courses, Web-based provision is also common. Mixed format teaching, combining distance learning with face-to-face meetings, is also available to those students who want to have the benefits of distance learning but who also wish to retain some personal contact with their teachers.

In France, some vocational training also has the purpose of reducing the possibility of social exclusion for the adults taking part and of facilitating their social mobility. These courses can lead to diplomas offered by individual universities or, more recently, by the French state. The courses are usually provided in response to the demand for qualifications from private or public employers, from job seekers or from adults who wish to have their experience recognised and accredited (Feutrie, 1998).

Vocational courses can be offered by universities as part of wider projects such as the Hungarian 'Training for the World of Work' Project in which the University of Debrecen was a partner from 2002 to 2004. Aniko Kálmán has described how education and training was used to help meet the need in the Great Plain region of eastern Hungary for increased numbers of well-qualified and effective managers. This project was carried out within the culture of a government centralised in Budapest, at the far end of the country, and with many of the existing training organisations still reluctant to accept the need for economic and social change in the region. Within this project, the University played a considerable role in the training of agricultural experts and, in doing so, made a substantial contribution to the region's economic development.

In the countries of central Europe the economic, as well as the political, changes have been particularly large since the early 1990s. In Latvia, for example, in addition to short updating courses, Ineta Kristovska has reported that programmes leading to re-qualification have been provided for those whose former qualifications are no longer needed, providing them with the skills needed to cope with their new social and economic situations. There was a particular need to retrain government and municipal officials and, to meet this, a Local Government and Project Management State Training Centre was set up within the University of Latvia. Together with partners from Germany, this Centre has developed a considerable body of training material and currently offers about 60 courses which have already been attended by several thousand local and national government officials.

It has already been mentioned that in Poland the private universities provide most of the higher education for adults. The majority of their courses are part-time and they are usually held in the evenings or at weekends. All these universities offer vocational courses at the first degree and diploma levels in subjects (for example education, management and finance) reflecting the urgent need in Poland at the moment for more professionals in these subjects. About a quarter of the new universities also offer postgraduate courses in these subjects. These universities receive little or no financial support from the Polish Government and necessarily have to charge relatively high fees for their courses. They are, however, able to compete with the established state universities (whose fees are low or zero) because of their flexibility: the new universities offer the right courses in the right places at the right times. In doing so, they have, in little more than a decade, already provided university opportunities for many thousands of Polish adults.

Finally, in this brief review of the rich and dynamic provision of vocational education for adults by Europe's higher education institutions, an interesting form of adult vocational education (AVE), described by Ebba Ossiannilsson, has been developed in Sweden. In order to ensure that trainees gain not only their specialist knowledge but also the broader skills that they need to work effectively (such as flexibility, social skills and problem solving), one-third of the time of trainees in the AVE system is spent in the workplace applying the theoretical knowledge they have gained in the classroom. This provides them with opportunities to reinforce their classroom learning as well, incidentally, as enabling them to develop their wider skills. Following the successful conclusion of a five-year pilot project on this learning system, the Swedish Parliament decided in 2002 that AVE should be included in Sweden's regular educational provision and funding is now made available for this. Here the universities provide the theoretical training when the subjects are appropriate; this can, however, also come from other providers when they are more able to do so.

Personal and community development

This category is less well defined but contains courses on, for example, citizenship and social improvement. Some courses on this latter topic may also have vocational objectives; vocational courses in France, for example, with the secondary aim of social promotion, have already been mentioned. Not all of these latter courses fall into the vocational category, however.

Despite the reduction that has taken place in the universities' provision of education for adults in the United Kingdom in the 1990s, some courses with a social purpose still remain. In particular, credit-bearing courses developed for adults at the sub-degree level have sometimes had the effect of bringing university teaching to disadvantaged communities, often through outreach centres both in urban and rural areas. The courses on offer there are diverse, some relating to personal development, others to active citizenship and to community development (as well as others on more work-related topics). There are also many social initiatives directed towards particular groups in the United Kingdom (Osborne, 1997). Recent examples include courses for ethnic minorities, non-native speakers of English, excluded men and women, prisoners, asylum seekers, disabled students and people with mental health problems. The courses provided by the Open Universities, in Britain and elsewhere, can also often be accessed by some members of these groups.

In the Dutch-speaking part of Belgium an organisation, Education for Social Promotion, has been set up to support this form of education for adults. This aims to support adults in three target groups: those aiming at a basic qualification; those specialising in certain areas; and those attending courses to increase their social integration or citizenship skills.

The University of Latvia has taken a different approach to help people achieve their personal aims. In this case adults learn language and computer skills in addition to general information about the country. It is found that the language and computer skills incidentally help people to adjust more easily to the new society, for example by making them more prepared to take risks and to make decisions.

Liberal adult education

Liberal adult education (LAE) is education that adults undertake simply for their love of the subject with no vocational intent; it is education for their personal development. This was the major form of education provided for adults provided by universities in a number of European countries, including Germany, Sweden and the United Kingdom, for many years. Today, however, only the Swedish LAE, particularly that offered in the 'study circles' and the 'folk high schools', continues to flourish.

In Germany LAE courses, which covered a very wide range of subjects, developed in Lower Saxony in the late 1940s and spread throughout the country, reaching their peak between 1960 and 1980. The format of these courses was to present the results of academic research and then to pose questions to the adults taking part. Here entry was open, regardless of the participants' previous educational levels (Schneider, 1999, p.16). In the 1990s, however, the numbers of these courses began to decline as a shift towards vocational subjects took place and also as financial support for LAE began to be withdrawn by the German regional governments. At its peak, courses related to topics such as nuclear energy, ecology, the consequences of the new technologies and the women's movement were in considerable demand. These have now greatly diminished, however, and only about 5% of the programmes that remain deal explicitly with these types of social issues.

The decline in the United Kingdom was somewhat similar: LAE was by far the most common form of education provided for adults by British universities in the second half of the twentieth century. In the 1990s, however, the government decided that financial support should be given only for those LAE courses that led to academic credit. Departments providing LAE were generally unable to find sufficient numbers of adults wishing to undertake these credit-bearing courses. This was particularly the case in universities where the credits on offer were not recognised by the universities themselves for their own full-time degrees. In this situation, the financial support for LAE fell away following the decrease in adult enrolments. Some of the credit-bearing courses leading to degrees have managed to establish themselves, however, and LAE continues to be provided by some British universities. Many of the short-course programmes of earlier years have disappeared, however. A detailed account of the demise of LAE courses in the United Kingdom has been given by Osborne (2003).

Some 'interest-related education' is reported from elsewhere and it is likely that a number of the courses offered for other reasons are taken by some adults for personal interest only. The one other area of LAE that is clearly flourishing is that provided for retired adults, much of which is LAE. This is reported from the Czech Republic, Finland, France and Germany and is also provided by some universities in Poland. In each of these cases, the provision is made under the supportive umbrella of the University of the Third Age.

Access courses

Courses to enable adults to access traditional higher education courses first developed in France in the late 1960s. This started with the introduction of an examination for university entry especially for those who had failed, or simply not taken, the school leaving certificate and who had at least two years of work experience. At first the success rate in this examination was low but, in addition to short courses, programmes lasting two or three years were soon created to prepare adults who wished to enter a university. These courses, which required the development of specialist teaching materials and teacher training, have become an important tool for social advancement in France. In 1994, it was decided that they should lead to a national diploma for access to university studies. The great majority of the students on these courses now move on to higher education once they have been awarded their access diplomas.

In the United Kingdom, adult access courses began to develop for different reasons and in a rather different way. Originally they were set up in response to a growing concern about social inequality in Northern Ireland. Later their aim was changed to attract mature students from across the whole country, particularly from ethnic minority groups, into a number of specific professions (including teaching, social work and law) where they were under-represented. This range of occupations has since been extended greatly. Because of the diversity of the courses that have developed, it has now become difficult to review this work. Looking back at the effects of these access initiatives over the past two decades, it is clear that access to higher education has improved for at least some of the groups for whom university entry had previously been difficult. Some British universities, however, still apply the principles and approaches of flexible learning much less than others. As a consequence, adult entry to some subjects, for example medicine and veterinary studies, still remains very limited (Bourgeois and Merrill, 2001).

Although access courses are provided on a large scale in France and the United Kingdom, it appears that this form of provision for adults has not yet developed, at least on a large scale, in most other countries in Europe.

Organisation

It is clear from the previous chapters that the organisational structures chosen to provide education for adults clearly vary greatly from one country to another: in Poland, for example, formal 'adult education universities' have in effect been established; in Sweden on the other hand AVE, one of the forms of education that is currently being developed, aims to provide individual adult students with almost complete control over what, when and how they learn.

The private university system which developed in Poland following the passing of the Higher Education Act in 1990, (*Ustawa*..., 1990) made it possible for private institutions to be established. As already mentioned, within a decade over 200 of these had been formed. These universities are flexible and open and they are structured particularly to meet the needs of those aged 25 years and over. Many of these universities have been established in smaller cities where there is no public university. Even though students have to pay fees in the private universities, as mentioned earlier, many choose to study privately partly because this cost can often be more than offset by the saving on the cost of the travel and accommodation that would otherwise be necessary.

A more common form of adult education organisation is that found in Slovakia, reported by Ján Porvazník and Marína Hučková, where individual faculties organise part-time study for adults alongside their full-time courses. This arrangement has the advantage of closely integrating the courses for adults with the other teaching of the faculties. One result of this is that these courses, because of their closeness to the other teaching of the university, are more likely to lead to a degree or diploma.

A development of this arrangement is seen in the Special Departments of Adult Education that have been established in the individual faculties of the University of Debrecen in Hungary. There, in addition to these departments, a central Lifelong Learning Centre has also been established which runs its own courses, particularly on adult education as a subject. The Centre also keeps a record of the courses for adults that are run elsewhere in the University, as well as carrying out research on the subject.

A further development of this model is found, for example, in the University of Tartu in Estonia. Here the management of all the University's non-traditional teaching activities is centralised in one place. This centre, known as the 'Open University', is responsible for the coordination of the degree-level education for adults, short courses, computer-based teaching and the regional activities of the University. This centralisation supports the effective planning of the adult education provision and allows the University to use its intellectual and material resources more efficiently as a result. It also enables adult students to move easily from short courses to degree courses and vice versa. In addition, this arrangement facilitates the recording of the credit points that are being accumulated by adult students towards the award of a degree. Centralised adult education units, although not usually with such wide ranges of responsibilities, are also commonly found in British, French and German universities.

In the case of the University of Tartu, learning opportunities are made available to many more adults by offering courses run in local colleges. The University has representatives in each region who can negotiate contracts on its behalf with their district authorities for the provision of information exchange, training and retraining, research and consultancy services, and cultural activities. In addition, the University has recently broadened its adult education provision even further by the introduction of Internet-based courses. These have seen rapid growth since their introduction.

In a few centres across Europe, education for adults is provided by independent organisations established by universities. This is the case, for example, in the University of Aveiro which set up its Association for Research and Professional Development (UNAVE) in 1998. This centre provides professional development courses and is established as a private non-profit making association. This arrangement gives it great flexibility so that, for example, if there is no appropriate member of the academic staff in the University to teach an element of a course that is required, UNAVE is able to contract an expert from outside. A significant disadvantage of this arrangement, however, is that the independence separates the centre from the university so that, for example, UNAVE is not able to award academic credit.

The most flexible form of educational provision is that in which the students' own wishes are paramount. Fully flexible learning would give students the opportunity to choose for themselves the time, place, pace and structure of their studies. This form of teaching is student-centred and providers that adopt it have to adapt their course structures and teaching techniques significantly to meet their students' needs. To support the attainment of this form of provision, the Swedish Government set up an Agency for Flexible Learning in 2002. This aims to advise and support those who organise all forms of education and training (including, but not restricted to, university providers) helping them to increase the flexibility of their teaching. The development of the work of this Agency will undoubtedly be followed with close interest in the other countries of Europe.

A more detailed review of the organisational structures available for use in the provision of higher adult education has been given by Michael Brennan in chapter 4 of the *Manager's Handbook* (Mitchell, 2002).

The barriers which prevent adults from participating in higher education

The barriers to participation in higher education generally have been considered in detail (Cross, 1981; McGivney, 1991) and have already been referred to in Chapters 1 and 22 by Robin Mark and Mireille Pouget respectively. Four broad categories were identified there: the *personal* barriers created by the students themselves; the barriers arising from students' *situations*; the barriers set up by the *institutions*; and the *informational* barriers. These four areas will be used to provide a framework to examine in more detail the difficulties experienced by adults wishing to enter higher education in the European countries surveyed in the book. The situational and institutional barriers have already been considered in detail in Chapter 22 and will therefore be considered more briefly here.

In addition to the barriers that adults may experience on entry, we are reminded from a number of countries that adult students can also experience difficulties once they have taken up their student places. As seen by the education providers, these are problems of student retention. They too are important and they will also be considered in the section that follows.

Personal barriers

These are the barriers created by the adult students themselves, arising from their attitudes, perceptions or expectations.

As reported from the United Kingdom, some adults carry with them unsatisfactory experiences of their times at school. The negative expectations that these experiences generate need to be overcome, at least to some extent, even before people decide to apply for university entry.

From Estonia, research (*Elukestva…*, 2002) has shown that there are two major personal obstacles to adult participation: the feeling either that they are too old; or that they do not need more education. It is also mentioned from the United Kingdom that the notions of being a 'student' and of having a 'university education' may appear mysterious to people who are not familiar with the university system, particularly to those from working class backgrounds whose immediate family and friends are also unlikely to have any higher education experience (Merrill, 1999). In the minds of some potential mature students, the university itself can be seen as an alien environment where they will have to struggle to fit in (Osborne *et al.*, 2001). These attitudes may arise because the adults in question have low aspirations generally or because they lack self-esteem.

Situational barriers

These are the barriers that relate to the students' personal situations. This can be lack of time or lack of money to pay the course fees (and, in some cases, the associated costs of travel and accommodation). These two problems appeared in the research mentioned earlier to be by far the most important situational barriers holding adults back from further study (*Elukestva…*, 2002).

Lack of time and money

Lack of time is a familiar problem for many adults, particularly for those who combine jobs with family responsibilities. Lack of money is by no means unfamiliar either and the cost of study is often high in European universities. In the case of the Polish private universities, for example, the cost per semester is more than double the average monthly Polish wage. High course fees can be a problem even in relatively affluent countries. The problem is correspondingly greater in those countries where the salaries are relatively low, such as Slovakia. In this latter case even firms have difficulty in investing in the education and training of their employees and they often have very limited resources available for this purpose.

It was reported from a number of countries that, with relatively few exceptions, national governments will only pay the fees of full-time students. Patricia-Anne Moore has pointed out that some countries, including Ireland, allow adults who are studying part-time to claim back the tax on the fees that they have paid. Generally however, as reported from Slovenia by Margerita Zagmajster, the financing of higher adult education is left mainly to the market and financial help from governments is very limited. The irony of this situation, which exists across much of Europe, is that adult learners (who in most cases are tax payers whose contributions help to support full-time students, whose fees are often paid in full) are unable to reclaim the tax paid on fees for themselves. In effect, these adults are paying their fees twice. This is an inequitable situation.

Lack of study skills, knowledge and language issues

In the University of Tartu, the Open University students have, on average, not engaged in any systematic study for the previous eight years. This means that they are likely not only to lack the skills to start their study but also to have forgotten (or possibly never had) the additional skills and habits necessary to function effectively as independent learners once they have started. From both Bulgaria and Slovakia it is mentioned that, after a break, adult students may no longer have enough knowledge to pass the university entrance examination. This problem arises particularly for adults who wish to enter popular courses. In Bulgaria, for example, entry to computer science courses is very competitive. These require a high initial level of mathematical knowledge and this is a major barrier for many adults wishing to enter.

An extreme example of these problems is reported from Slovakia where both the Romany and Hungarian minorities are particularly disadvantaged as far as study in universities is concerned. Their problems stem mainly from an insufficient knowledge of the Slovak language. Many of the Romany people have not attended either primary or secondary schools and they do not speak Slovak. Although the Hungarian minority has its own schools, they rarely take the opportunity to learn the language. As a result, members of both groups are not usually able to pass the university entrance examinations and they are under-represented on the courses.

One specific problem of adult participation in university education in small countries is the language of the study material. In Estonia, for example, the number of Estonian speakers (approximately one million of the 1.4 million inhabitants of the country) does not warrant the publication of up-to-date university textbooks in Estonian. This forces students to use other languages for learning. At present it is mainly English, and in some subjects German, that is used. For younger students this does not cause a major problem since they are likely to have learnt these languages at school. Older people, however, speak Russian as their first, and often only, foreign language (since the previous political regime imposed the use of Russian and limited contacts with the rest of the world). Most of the current subjects on offer are based on textbooks and research articles in English and many older adult students in Estonia encounter problems as a result.

Restrictions obviously exist in those universities that have chosen to offer their courses in a foreign language. This is the case in Slovakia, for example, where some universities teach their Master of Business Administration (MBA) and Master of Public Administration courses in English or German. Only those adults with a good knowledge of the appropriate language can even consider applying for places in this case.

Lack of suitable entrance qualifications

Adults often lack the appropriate entrance qualifications, resulting in some cases from the fact that they were the weaker students at school. This puts them at a disadvantage when the number of places available is less than the number of applicants. This is often the case with popular courses and, in this situation, adults are often unable to find a suitable place. On the other hand, the subjects of those courses where places are available are usually less attractive (often because the salaries of their graduates are lower).

Distance from educational providers

One barrier that is sometimes predicted for adult students is the distance that they have to travel from their homes to the places of study. This problem was mentioned relatively infrequently in the country chapters, however, and it may well be that many universities have already found ways of overcoming this barrier. In Poland, for example, where many adults who wished to study at a public university would in the past have had to travel to a medium-sized or large city, this difficulty has been greatly reduced, as already mentioned, by the emergence of the private universities; many of these have branches in the smaller towns and cities. In Estonia too, which is in any case a relatively small country, the three largest public universities have all established regional colleges where students, including adults, can study for degrees without leaving home. It may be that this combination of developments has significantly removed the need for long-distance travel to courses for many adults in Europe. With the rapidly increasing availability of distance learning, particularly through Web-based e-learning, this barrier is likely to become even less important in the future.

Institutional barriers

These are the barriers created by the policies adopted by higher education providers and by the attitudes and decisions of their staff.

Institutional policies

We have already seen that the European Union and a number of national governments have adopted policies that support the development of adult education and these are echoed in the policies of many individual higher education institutions. We have been reminded in Chapter 1, however, that policies can raise barriers for wider groups of students as well as lower them. There can be conflicting political agendas at all levels.

In a number of European countries, the traditional concept of a university is still dominant. In the Czech Republic, for example, it is reported that universities are still generally regarded as institutions with dual missions: to provide courses for full-time students; and to conduct research and development activities associated with this. This may well have met the needs of society in the nineteenth century when this tradition became widely established; it is unlikely, however, to meet the needs of society in the twenty-first century.

Policies that, perhaps inadvertently, hinder adult student entry have been reported from a number of countries. These apparently arbitrary regulations are often directed towards part-time courses rather than to adult students *per se.* Since adult students are most likely to enrol on part-time courses, however, they are the ones most likely to be affected by these restrictions. For example, the University of Ljubljana in Slovenia (which is a university whose Business School in the Economics Faculty offers a very successful distance learning course) has recommended that the number of places for part-time students should be limited, particularly for those who had not succeeded in getting a full-time place and who had subsequently enrolled on a part-time programme. It was also proposed that limits should be placed on the number of students who were unemployed and that the number of part-time students should not be allowed to exceed the number of full-time students in any individual faculty. It is not known why these proposals were put forward but clearly none of them are in the interest of adult students.

The decisions may have been taken because of the view in some universities that part-time courses have a 'lower efficiency' than full-time courses. It is found that students' progression rates from one year to the next are often lower for part-time courses and, particularly, that part-time students often have lower average marks. This latter certainly need not be the case as the experience from the distance learning course in the University of Ljubljana, mentioned earlier, shows. Following the reorganisation of this course, the average student marks for the whole of the first year cohort in the Economics Faculty in 1999/2000 were: distance education 7.85; traditional part-time 7.28; traditional full-time 7.47 (Balon, 2000). (In this case, the maximum score was 10 and the pass mark 6.0.) It is clear, at least for this course, that when the course structure has been adapted to meet the needs of all the students taking it, they can all perform well academically. Not surprisingly, this course is very popular: in 2002 more than 1,600 students were enrolled in 11 study centres. This is in a country with a population of about two million people.

In Finland, it is reported that university continuing education is usually targeted towards university graduates. This seems unnecessarily limiting and, as far as is known, this policy is not followed in any other European country.

Policies can also hinder the entry of adults to higher education by omission. From the Czech Republic, it is reported that there are insufficient links between the universities and the vocationally-oriented higher education colleges, presumably because no explicit policy exists to foster them. Relatively few students move on from these colleges to the universities as a result. In some countries, a number of universities have set out to develop college/university links and pre-university access courses are being run successfully, for example in the United Kingdom. Both the colleges and the universities benefit as a result. More importantly, these links are also of considerable advantage to those students who, starting in the colleges, are able to progress to a degree course. From Latvia comes another example of hindrance by omission. Here the lack of a policy to encourage staff to participate in adult education, for example by setting up suitable funding arrangements within universities to pay them for their extra work, acts as a considerable disincentive to them to become involved.

Academic staff

One of the problems that adults can face when they enter a university is the unhelpful attitudes of some lecturers towards adult students and their unwillingness to take account of their different needs. Many university teachers still have no training in teaching and learning (and, particularly, none in teaching adults) and this is likely to be one cause of their inflexibility.

Systematic training for academic staff in the teaching of adults is lacking in many countries. The effect of this is seen especially clearly in the lack of knowledge of most staff when they are faced for the first time with teaching a distance learning course or writing e-learning materials. It is not surprising that the teaching approaches used by many higher education staff (mentioned in the case of Slovenia but likely to be true for most, if not all, other European countries as well) are still based on traditional university teaching methods. These are often not sufficiently flexible and they need to be adapted to meet adults' different characteristics and experience.

With this lack of training, it is not surprising either that (as reported from Latvia but again almost certainly the position in many other countries) there is no general understanding amongst university staff of the education of adults and some members are not yet prepared to participate in the development of adult teaching.

As seen from the viewpoint of the adult students, these staff attitudes all create unnecessary barriers both to their entry to higher education and to their remaining on the courses once they have entered.

Limited course formats

Some courses are still offered only in the full-time mode and this automatically excludes many adult students who have other major demands on their time. The experience in a number of countries is that, when courses have been adapted for adult students, their contents are still based closely upon the contents of the full-time courses rather than taking into account adults' greater experience of the subject. One result of this is that the courses are likely to last for several years and this causes problems for some adult learners (and for their employers, and perhaps their families too).

One concern of academic staff is that changing the format of a course to make it suitable for adult students may lower its academic level. This is an important concern and it is the responsibility of the academic staff concerned to ensure that it does not happen. Certainly a lowering of standards is not inevitable and none of the changes that are advocated, either in this chapter or elsewhere in this book, imply a reduction. Indeed, since adult students are often more experienced in the subject and more highly motivated than school leavers, the changes can, if anything, provide the opportunity to raise the academic standards of the course if this is required.

The curricula of courses intended for adults are at present often the same as those for young full-time students; they are not adapted to take into account the working experience which many adults bring with them. In addition, the detailed content of vocational courses does not always reflect the changes that are currently taking place within the profession or the changing needs of societies more broadly. The subjects of the courses also do not always meet the needs or interests of adults, particularly at the postgraduate level. The Czech Republic, for example, is reported to lack courses in the humanities and law. A shortage of courses in law and economics for part-time students is also reported from Slovakia. The numbers of good applicants to all these courses are higher than the numbers that can be accepted.

The range of subjects on offer can also limit the types of students who enrol. It is reported from Finland, for example, that the majority of their Open University students are women. This reflects the content of the course provision which is biased towards the behavioural and educational sciences; these are subjects that appeal less to men.

Organisational problems

Many of the institutional barriers encountered by adults wishing to enter universities arise because their organisational systems lack appropriate structures. It is reported from many universities that one or more of the necessary elements of the systems needed to support adult students are missing. A list of these, drawn widely from across the Continent, is:

- No guidance system adapted to meet adults' specific needs is available before enrolment;
- The entry requirements are identical for full- and part-time students and these often relate to the completion of secondary schooling. If they take this approach, universities ignore the broader academic experiences that adults are likely to bring with them and they discriminate against their adult applicants as a result;
- No centralised student registration system appropriate for adults is in place;
- There is a lack of flexibility within the university system once the students have entered, preventing them from changing from one course to another if they need to do so;
- Even when a flexible university system does exist, this is not generally complemented by appropriate student support. Unsupported flexibility can have a detrimental effect on students;
- At the time of writing, in some universities no academic credit accumulation system is in place. This in turn hinders the establishment of the accreditation of prior learning or prior experiential learning (APL or APEL). Even in those universities where a credit system does exist, the status of the credit points for adult education courses has not always been satisfactorily defined. (This position should, however, change in all European universities before 2010 when, as one consequence of the Bologna Agreement, it has been agreed that a uniform and comprehensive credit accumu-

lation system will be established throughout central and western Europe and beyond.); and
- No university-wide quality assurance system for part-time and short courses exists.

It is not likely that all of these flaws will exist in a single university. Certainly, however, a good many of them can be found in some.

Another organisational barrier that is sometimes predicted for adult students is the lack of additional student support facilities, for example for disabled students or for students with young children. Undoubtedly these demands have existed. The fact that they have not been emphasised in the country chapters in this book may indicate that the problems are now generally recognised within universities and that these needs are being met, at least to an acceptable extent.

Informational barriers

These are the barriers that arise because of the difficulties that adult learners face in accessing information about the educational provision available.

In this book, it will be seen that only in the Czech Republic has the problem of the lack of information on the contents and outcomes of specific courses been mentioned. This has undoubtedly been an appreciable problem for adults in the past and is by no means easy to solve completely. The fact that it is not mentioned more strongly, however, may indicate that higher education institutions are now largely aware of this issue and that strenuous efforts have been made to solve it. The need for good information is certainly not lost, particularly on those institutions that have more places available in some subjects than they have applicants to fill them.

The universities' efforts to publicise their courses will undoubtedly have been assisted by the rapidly increasing accessibility of the Internet. By now, every university in Europe must have its own Website and some of these are quite sophisticated. This increased access to information is also supported by the fact that the number of adults in

Europe with the skills needed to access information efficiently from the Web is rapidly increasing.

Research on adult education and the barriers to access

The final underlying barrier to successful adult recruitment and teaching has been mentioned in the chapter from Slovenia: it is the lack of systematic support for research in the field of adult higher education and the lack of detailed information that comes from this. While it is possible to extract a considerable amount of information on the subject from the previous chapters, it is also clear that in the countries surveyed here (and this undoubtedly applies to all the other countries of Europe), there is still a great deal to be learned. This is an unsatisfactory situation and finding a remedy for it should be a first priority for action. It is from this research, and the sharing of good practice, that ways of lowering most, if not all, of the barriers to participation included here are likely to be found.

Overcoming the barriers to widening participation

There can be no doubt that many barriers exist to widening participation in higher education. In reading the country chapters, however, mention of the barriers is usually followed by descriptions of tried and tested ways of overcoming them. The tone of all the chapters is positive; they concentrate on the solutions, not the problems. One approach to a discussion of widening participation would be to address each barrier in turn and consider how to overcome it. To some extent the last section, at least by implication, has already started to do this.

An alternative way to consider overcoming these barriers is to use as a framework the model for improving access proposed by Toyne (1990, pp.63–5) and extended by Universities Scotland (see Chapter 21). Toyne suggested that there are two broad types of access initiative: *in-reach* methods, that concentrate on bringing people into higher education; and *out-reach* methods that aim to take the institutions out to the under-represented groups. Here, access courses and summer schools are suggested as examples of in-reach, bringing potential students into universities; partnerships between universities and further education colleges or employers, taking the universities outside, are given as out-reach. This two-pronged categorisation will be used here. Universities Scotland proposed a third category, which they called *flexibility*, to describe the changes in the structure and organisation of institutions to help widen access. The introduction of part-time courses and distance learning methods are given as examples in this case. However, the introduction of part-time courses undoubtedly increases the number of students who can come into an institution, i.e. in-reach, while distance learning takes courses outside the institution's walls, i.e. out-reach. This third category, therefore, will not be used in this chapter.

Achieving access to a course is only the start of a student's learning experience. To be successful in the course overall, non-traditional students may well need non-traditional support and guidance services while they are studying. Looking at the students from the point of view of the institution, they need to be 'retained'.

Within the ALPINE Project, as mentioned in the Preface, a Web-based Manual of Good Practice has been created. (See http://www.qub.ac.uk/alpine) This has identified a number of key areas where improvements can be made. Of these, two are concerned with increasing access:

- Community outreach, ICT and adult learning; and
- Action on participation.

The others, in the way in which they are considered in the Manual, are concerned with student retention:

- The curriculum in adult education;
- Teaching, learning and adults;
- Languages and adult education; and
- Student support and adult guidance.

Each of these areas is discussed in detail on the Website and a number of examples of good practice are described for each.

In-reach methods

These forms of access focus on bringing new groups of adult students into higher education. Attracting students is by no means an unfamiliar task for adult educators and a great deal is known about marketing adult education generally. From Portugal, for example, we are reminded that traditional advertising channels, such as newspapers, magazines or radio are usually not effective for adult education. It is interesting that a significant number of entrants now receive their information from the Internet. (For further information on marketing adult education, including a number of case studies describing good practice in the area, see Mitchell, 2002, Chapter 6.)

Experienced adult educators also know that it is important to make it as easy as possible for adults to undertake the course of their choice. A good example of this comes from Slovakia where the successful Economics for Everyone programme in the University of Economics in Bratislava is offered in a very wide range of course formats: one term, weekend study; two term, evening study; a daytime course (providing retraining for the unemployed); by distance education, in correspondence form; and, for three of the 15 course modules, by e-learning.

Access and special entry courses

Many adults who wish to return to study at the higher education level following a break after their school education, find that neither their knowledge nor their study skills are any longer sufficient. To help them overcome these problems, some preparatory courses are offered. These are particularly necessary in those countries, such as Slovakia, where it is necessary for university entrants to pass an examination. In this case, the courses are offered by lifelong learning institutes. These focus on the subjects of the examination itself; for entrance to the University of Economics, for example, applicants receive teaching in economics, mathematics, English and German. Again a wide range of course formats is offered: two term, evening course; two term, Saturday course; one term, evening course; short evening course; and a daytime intensive course. From Bulgaria, it is mentioned that the improved job opportunities and salary prospects that are likely to result for students who complete their courses successfully are both strong motivators for adult access to universities.

Many European universities over the past 20 years have built up considerable experience of providing access courses, either in the forms above or as summer schools. A network of access summer schools exists, for example, throughout the United Kingdom. These courses are well established and, while they are at least partly intended for adults, their enrolment is by no means entirely limited to them. There is evidence that special entry programmes of this sort are of particular value to those who take part. Studies have shown that students who enter under these special admission procedures do as well both academically and in their subsequent careers as those who enter through the conventional routes to the same institutions (Bowen and Bok, 1998).

Partnerships

Partnerships can contribute both to out-reach and in-reach methods of aiding access depending on how they are operated. In this section, partnerships that bring adult students into higher education institutions will be considered. The unemployed cannot generally afford to pay course fees and they do not usually have other means of financial support. In their case, however, a number of organisations, notably the European Union, can provide funds, as reported from Germany, to pay for courses on topics such as Key Skills for Managers, Marketing for Women, and Transnational Quality Management.

Retired adults form a much more varied cross-section of society but in their case there is an organisation in many countries, the University of the Third Age (U3A), that represents their interests. As mentioned earlier, universities in a number of European countries work closely with the U3A and many courses are provided for them. Individual U3A groups not only offer courses on specific subjects but they also provide opportunities to carry out other learning activities such as assembling the learning biographies of individual group members and using these to indicate the further learning projects that the member might undertake as a result. These groups also put into practice the knowledge that they have acquired in order to promote their own regions, for example by offering consultancy on environmental issues, such as energy saving, or cultural or social self-help topics. This form of education is likely to become more significant in the coming years as the number of older people in Europe increases.

Trades unions sometimes also have an interest in linking with universities to provide courses of value to their members. Lund University, for example, as reported by Ebba Ossiannilsson, has developed agreements with the largest trade union in Sweden, the Union for Local Government Workers, (which has over 600,000 members), and the Swedish Industrial Union. The University also has links with the Swedish Employers' Association.

There are also possibilities of developing links with industrial companies to identify potential students. In Sweden again, many companies have adopted the approach of 'individual competence assurance' for their employees. University courses, either of the traditional variety or tailor-made programmes, can form a significant part of a company's regular training programme. Lund University has cooperated with a number of Sweden's largest companies, including Scandia, in this way. Links with professional bodies and accrediting groups can also be valuable in attracting appropriate student groups and these have been reported from Ireland.

These new approaches can also lead to international partnerships. One result of these has been the development in the University of Hamburg, in partnership with a Japanese university, of an academic 'feng shui' certificate and also a course on Buddhism. Much valuable collaboration has also been reported between universities in different European countries, often made possible initially using European Union funding.

The attitudes of employers (and also of universities) vary from one country to another on the subject of collaboration. Employer-university relations can, however, be very good. A survey amongst Estonian adults (*Elukestva…*, 2002) and another among graduates of the University of Tartu (*Tartu...*, 2003) have shown that Estonian employers generally take a positive attitude towards employee training. 90% support their employees' university studies, for example by giving time off to allow regular participation in study sessions. They consider that investment in the education of their employees is useful to the company. More than 80% of employers find that part-time university study undertaken while their employees continue to work is better related to the company's activities than full-time studies. Taking into account all the forms of education and training, provided not only by universities but also by all the other training providers, it was found that 45% of employees' participation was paid for wholly by their employers and that a further 30% was financed by the employers and employees together. The remainder was financed by the employees or from other Estonian or European sources.

National governments can also support increased participation: the Estonian Adult Education Law (*Täiskasvanute...*, 1993), for example, specifies that public service employers can take up to 79 days of part-paid leave for learning. In addition, Estonian, Hungarian and Irish tax laws permit the refund of the income tax paid by individuals for their own education. For some groups the government chooses to pay the whole of the fee itself. This is so in Estonia for teachers who are working in schools but who do not yet have a university qualification or for those whose qualification is in a subject that is no longer needed. In this case, the fees for a part-time degree or for a re-qualification programme taken by distance learning, are paid in full by the State.

National governments, if they choose, can also make available direct funding for adult education. It is reported from Ireland, for example, that substantial funds have been made available to universities to develop initiatives to support specific student groups: for example 2.49 million euros in 2000/01 rising to 7.49 million euros in 2001/02 for students from socio-economically deprived backgrounds; and 1.57 million euros in 2000/01 and 2.17 million euros in 2001/02 to support students with disabilities.

Universities themselves can also make their contributions to help adults enter universities in a variety of ways. Following the university reforms carried out by the Italian government in the late 1990s, the universities there were no longer required, amongst other things, to charge large amounts when students returned from breaks in their studies: these students previously had to pay the fees for the whole intervening period when they came back, together with a penalty for late payment. Now each university is free to set its own fee when a student returns. Many universities have decided to encourage students who have not completed their degrees to come back and, in some cases, the charge is a token amount. In the case of the University of Venice Ca' Foscari, for example, the charge for absence is around 10 euros per year.

Out-reach methods

Teaching courses outside the institution

Out-reach methods take university teaching outside the walls to new adult student groups. These activities were commonly used, and well developed, in both Germany and the United Kingdom from the 1950s until they were severely curtailed by the cuts in government funding for adult education in both countries in the 1990s. Traditional out-reach of this sort is valuable since it provides flexibility and openness to universities. As mentioned earlier, a number of Estonian universities have recently begun to offer not only learning opportunities but also cultural activities, together with research and consultancy services, to local communities via the colleges in their areas.

Distance learning

Greater flexibility can be achieved, and a much wider audience addressed, using distance learning methods. These have been developed over a decade and more in a number of European countries including Estonia, Finland, France, Germany, Greece, Italy, Portugal, Spain and the United Kingdom. They were initially developed by producing printed learning materials that were then delivered to students by post. The students respond by submitting their assignments, again by post (or, more recently, by e-mail) and are given written feedback on their work, supported by telephone and occasional face-to-face contact. This can be regarded as the conventional distance learning approach and, despite a number of obvious limitations, it greatly increases the availability of study programmes and also provides access for large numbers of people who are not able to take part in traditional face-to-face teaching, such as the disabled or those who cannot attend because of the demands of their work (Bregar, 1995).

These developments are widening rapidly at the moment with the increasing opportunities to replace printed materials and the use of the post by the Internet and e-mail. This is e-learning. The use of this method is likely to increase rapidly as the availability of the Internet grows. These changes require large-scale developments in universities and are taking place in centres in almost all European countries. Distance learning is particularly well developed in the Baltic region.

The major impact of e-learning comes from its flexibility, making it available to a much larger (and still rapidly increasing) population. As expressed in Germany, the Internet makes learning available to the 'global learning village'. National boundaries are now of much less consequence. The Environmental Engineering Institute of Kaunas Technical University, for example, reported in the chapter for Lithuania by Marius Mikulėnas, Daiva Dumčiuvienė and Danguole Rutkauskiene, in cooperation with the University's Distance Education Centre, is delivering training in Zimbabwe.

When a distance learning course is offered, students can enrol in large numbers. Research carried out in the University of Tartu has shown that there are many reasons for their choice of this form of learning. It appears, however, that the three factors that are of paramount importance in this choice are:

- This form of study is suitable for adults who are in full-time employment;
- The quality of the teaching is high; and
- So is the prestige of the provider.

Despite the obvious attractions of distance learning, particularly in the e-learning mode, its introduction (as with any new development) can have problems. From the point of view of the students, inevitably, some of them do not welcome the change since:

- Most welcome the face-to-face meetings with both staff and the other students that lectures bring;
- Some students positively enjoy lectures;
- Some lack the computing skills needed to use e-learning methods;
- Many more lack experience of using ICT methods of learning;
- Some lack computer access; and
- The cost of the telephone line for access to the appropriate Website is a major disincentive for some (Valk and Pilt, 2001).

In summary, most students are eager to participate in Internet-based courses but they are not keen to substitute them totally for their face-to-face learning.

The problem of lack of personal contact for the students has been recognised, and addressed, for some time in Finland. Here a system of 'multiform studies' has been developed in which a variety of teaching methods is used. These involve a combination of local study groups with a tutor, distance learning methods, and lectures at a distance using video- and teleconferencing. The study groups can, in principle, also provide support in both computing and e-learning skills and Internet access for those who need it as well as instruction in the subject of study. This system provides the necessary personal contact together with a very flexible study system; it also enables adults from all parts of the country to participate in the programmes.

Not surprisingly, it is also found that some academic staff do not welcome the change of teaching medium. Many have little experience of distance learning at the moment and some have no wish to change.

Finally the organisational hurdles to surmount in introducing the use of an e-learning system are significant. If e-learning is introduced on a large scale, a considerable investment in time, money and skills is required.

Help for academic staff who are beginning to work with the new teaching media can be provided centrally within universities. In Lund University, for example, the Office for Continuing and Distance Education is responsible for providing support for both the staff who are developing e-learning materials and for the students who subsequently use them

Higher education institutions that are intending to become e-learning providers have a number of important decisions to make, particularly at the beginning. To help it with this, Kaunas Technical University, which at the time of writing is in the process of establishing its own e-learning facility, has set up an E-studies Council to set the policy for the change and to monitor its implementation. The most important tasks of this Council are:

- To determine the priorities for e-studies at the University;
- To identify and prioritise the potential consumer groups;
- To create a database of technical and other information on e-learning as a subject;
- To create an approval and certification system for e-study;
- To ensure the quality of the e-study educational material together with overall quality assurance;
- To ensure that there is career progression for the programmers;
- To establish mechanisms to enable the work of e-study organizers and teachers to be recognised;
- To develop a system to encourage academic staff to contribute to the development of e-learning courses; and
- To carry out research into e-learning as a subject.

The four priority areas in the University's e-learning provision are expected to be:

- Infrastructure and equipment;
- E-learning and support;

- Quality of service; and
- Opportunities for European cooperation.

This facility makes available both degree courses and short courses for continuing professional development.

The scale of an e-learning development is such that the resources needed are sometimes well beyond those that can be provided by a single higher education institution. To overcome this problem, in France the Ministry of Education has developed the concept of the Digital Campus. Here a number of university networks have been created, and part-funded, by the government to increase the use of ICT in adult education. In addition to helping students to use the new teaching methodologies, the staffs of these centres have been involved in andragogical and methodological research as well as in the production of e-learning materials.

In Estonia the six higher education institutions, together with the Ministry of Education and Research and the Estonian Information Technology Foundation, have set up the Estonian E-University. This should enable the available resources to be used effectively and also enhance the quality of the e-learning that is provided. This initiative includes not only the state-funded universities and the applied higher education institutions but also a number of partners from private universities and government organisations. One of the main aims of this initiative is to make access to university education easier for adults, including those from 'non-traditional' groups.

A larger-scale example of inter-university cooperation in the use of ICT is the Finnish Virtual Open University, which was formed in 1997. Almost all Finnish universities already offer some e-learning courses in the Open University. (The details of the e-learning service of the Open University can be seen at: http://www.avoinyliopisto.fi/english/index.html) By the year 2000, 3000 students had already enrolled on these courses. It is anticipated that both the need for, and the provision of, Web-based courses will rise rapidly in the near future. In Finland, they are currently especially popular amongst middle-aged adults and those in white-collar positions (Mannisenmäki and Manninen, 2004).

The largest university distance learning network in Europe at the moment, described by Margrit Wetter, is provided by NETTUNO. This is a consortium of 38 Italian universities which is offering an alternative to traditional classroom teaching. Its courses are disseminated by two satellite television channels and via the Internet. In addition, students can keep in contact with their tutors not only by e-mail but also by audio and video means. Already 20,000 hours of video lessons and 20,000 exercises are available on the Internet. In addition to diploma and short courses, 25 complete degree courses have been available since 2003 covering a wide range of subject areas and nearly 500 students graduated in the first year.

E-learning materials are generally created for use by adults outside the universities (and possibly outside the country of origin of the materials as well). Once these courses for part-time students have been fully developed and tested, they are also likely to have a major effect on the teaching of full-time higher education students as well.

Details of the management methods used for distance education in European universities have recently been discussed by Frank Moe in chapter 5 of the *Managers' Handbook* (Mitchell, 2002).

Student retention

Remaining as students on longer courses (those lasting for several months or more) can be a considerable problem for a minority of the adult students in any cohort. Their problems generally arise because of the responsibilities that they necessarily bear. (This is one of the features that distinguishes adults from most younger students, whose responsibilities have usually not yet appeared.)

How can adults be helped to remain on courses when problems arise? Many possible approaches have been put forward in the previous country chapters, starting by anticipating their problems and trying to solve them before they appear. Bearing in mind the strong vocational motivation of many of the adults who undertake longer courses, it is important that the course they enter should be able to meet their needs. To ensure that this is as far as possible the case, particular care is taken with the support provided for adult students at the entry stage in French universities. Here, in addition to the details of the course itself, careers advice centres provide potential students with detailed information on the possible careers that should be open to them afterwards. Once the career is chosen, advisers are available to help students as individuals to design development plans for themselves that are relevant to their vocational goals, choosing courses that will allow them to take up their new career following successful completion of their courses. At the Centre for Languages and Self-directed Training (CLAM) in the University of Haute Alsace, which is mainly concerned with language training, computer tools are also available to allow students to assess themselves while they are studying. This in turn allows them to define their further learning needs and a staff member can then help them to select the appropriate units to meet these.

A number of university continuing education centres in France have also been funded by the Ministry of Education to provide ICT facilities for teaching and learning for adults. Some of these departments, including the Department of Continuing Education of the University of Lille 3, have developed classrooms and facilities for the development of multi-media learning programmes. These include e-learning materials leading to specific university diplomas. The negotiation by adult students of their curricula with academic staff is also possible for some courses in Portugal and Finland.

It is common that the study skills, even of adults who have been successful students earlier, need to be refreshed when they resume their study. From Slovakia, it is reported that courses are offered to returning students to help them regain these skills quickly; it is certainly good practice to build an element on study skills into the introduction of most (if not all) longer courses for returning adults.

Even after the careful choice of a course by the student, a few find soon after the start that it does not meet their needs (or occasionally they have realized by then that their needs are different). In this case, it is desirable that the student should change to another course. This can usually be done relatively easily if the course programmes run within a credit accumulation framework. The existence of a credit system also allows students to shorten a course or to take a break from their studies if necessary and return at the start of the following semester or year.

Adults cannot usually predict when problems will arise and, even at the end of a course, a sudden family problem, for example, may appear unexpectedly. It is reported from Poland that universities there have responded to these situations by making special arrangements for students to sit examinations at times that are appropriate for them.

The underlying reality concerning student retention is that adults, because of the stage of life that they have reached, are necessarily less flexible at times. If universities wish to retain them as students, and it is usually in the interest of both the student and the university that the university should do so, then the latter must become more flexible to compensate.

Pointers for the future

Just as this chapter has tried to distil the main points made in the earlier chapters of the book into a relatively few pages, this final section seeks to present the pointers leading on from these for the continuing development of adult higher education in the coming decade and more.

There can be few universities in Europe that have not experienced major changes since the beginning of the 1990s. These changes have been particularly marked in the countries of central Europe. In Estonia, for example, two higher education reforms have taken place during this time. Until 1992, courses for their initial qualification, the higher education diploma, lasted for five years, followed by studies for the Candidate of Science and leading, usually after decades of research, to the Doctor of Science degree. In 1992 a new system was introduced: bachelors degree, four years; masters degree, two years; doctorate, four years. In this situation the old diploma was regarded as the equivalent of the new bachelors degree while Candidates of Science and Doctors of Science were taken to be equivalent to the new doctorates. In 2001 a second reform began with the move to the course arrangements specified in the Bologna Agreement: bachelors degree, three years; masters degree, two years. The need for APL during changes such as these is inescapable.

In addition, while these changes were taking place, the language of the textbooks used in the Estonian universities changed (from Russian to English). While these local changes were taking place, Estonia was not shielded from the other major changes taking place across Europe as a whole: the recognition of the need for continuing education by the universities; and the application of the emerging ICT opportunities to university teaching. As an additional pressure, the established universities in some central European countries saw the formation of private institutions able to compete with them for students. If the older universities refused to make the changes that were required, there could be no doubt that the new universities would. Institutions that have coped with all this may well not welcome further change. There can be no doubt, however, that they are able to cope with it if they need to do so.

A common approach to adult education

It is for national governments and individual institutions to decide for themselves the most appropriate aims for the provision of their adult education (and for the adult students themselves to decide on which courses they will enrol). Whatever decisions are taken, however, it is likely that the policies will include the general principles for adult education put forward by Beresnevičienė (1997):

- Openness to society;
- Equality in education: learning opportunities should be accessible to adults at all levels;
- Permanent lifetime learning: flexible and available both at work and in the individual's free time; and
- Oriented towards the needs of the individual.

Moving closer to the adult learners

One theme that emerges from a number of the country chapters is the need for higher education providers to learn more about their potential students. The more they know about them the more they will be able to understand their educational needs and the more likely they will be able to meet them. Universities, often with government support, have set out to do this in a number of different ways and three of these are outlined here.

To support the development of lifelong learning in Germany, the Ministry of Education has initiated a programme of 'learning regions'. The first fifty-four of these were established in 2001 with funding of 118 million euros, of which 51 million euros came from the European Social Fund, for the period 2001/06. Each region is linked with an educational institution (not necessarily concerned with higher education). Their purpose is to develop learning for well-defined local target groups. This should ensure that the courses on offer are relevant and that the most appropriate learning materials are used. (See: http://www.bmbf.de/de/411.php)

The Swedish government has put forward the concept of 'commissioned education' to encourage universities to be more active in providing vocational continuing education (SUHF, 2001). The universities are required to provide courses commissioned by private companies, municipalities and government organizations. In order to do this, some universities have established wholly university-owned but separate organizations. The Karolinska Institute, for example, the largest medical university in Sweden, has set up Karolinska Education AB with the overall aim of making its scientific knowledge available to organizations and companies. In this case, the organisation commissions courses from the Institute's academic departments and then sells places on these to organizations to meet their in-service continuing professional development needs. (See: http://www.karolinska education.ki.se/index_en.html)

In Greece, the government decided (Law No. 2525/1997) that a number of Institutes of Lifelong Learning (ILLs) should be established, each one linked to a higher education institution. At the time of writing, it is expected that these will begin operation very soon. Their function is to broaden the educational and vocational opportunities available to adults (in this case defined as people over 25 years of age) who have at least completed their standard secondary schooling. These institutes will enable them either to update their knowledge and skills or to undertake an academic higher education course. The ILLs' courses will be run in parallel with the courses of the sister higher education institution and be provided at times suitable for adults or by distance learning. The ILLs will have their own teaching and support staffs and they will offer their own Certificates of Further Training or Continuing Education. The ILL staffs will also undertake research on lifelong learning and develop innovative activities to support its growth and improve its quality generally.

If these initiatives, and similar ones taking place elsewhere, are successful in determining the needs of their potential students accurately, the demand for adult education is likely to grow considerably.

The accreditation of educational and personal experience

The accreditation of adults' prior learning has taken place for a decade or two but the decisions so far have often been taken at the level of individual academic departments or of their admissions officers in an *ad hoc* manner. It has already been mentioned that the need for APL is likely to increase greatly in the years running up to 2010 when essentially all the universities across Europe bring their course systems into line with the Bologna proposals and the equivalence of the degrees and diplomas taken before and after these changes will need to be agreed.

If the numbers of adult students entering universities rise, as expected, then the demand for the accreditation of prior experiential learning (APEL) is also likely to grow. This is a more difficult task for universities to undertake but fortunately we can look to the French experience for help with this. The accreditation of French higher education began in 1985 and the process has been refined, and the range of courses to which it can be applied has been greatly widened, since that time. Legislation for APEL (*Validation des Acquis de l'Expérience*. VAE) was introduced in 2002 and gives all French citizens the right to have their experience accredited to count towards the award of any diplomas or professional qualifications approved by the State (Blachère, 2002). The way that the credit is awarded in this case is that a committee, set up by the university, considers each application individually. Its decision is then passed to the appropriate Board of Examiners and the credit put towards the student's qualification. Blachère (*ibid.*, p.101) has pointed out that this marks a shift of principle. Before the new law, the knowledge and experience of the candidate was compared to the content of a course examination; since the law, it has been compared to the knowledge and skills profile required by the holder of the particular professional qualification. The award of credit for experiential learning is a large-scale activity in French universities. More than 800 applicants are expected in 2003/04 in the Nord-Pas-de-Calais region alone.

Major developments for the future

Distilling the major requirements for the continuing development of adult education from the information that has gone before, five pointers are proposed:

- *Provide more support for academic staff*
  New and quite different demands are now being made on university teachers: some are being required to tutor distance learning courses, for example, or to write e-learning materials. Staff are more likely to be prepared to take part in these activities if they are confident that they have the skills required to undertake them. Universities should have more training available for staff on these and other topics and staff themselves should accept that this is needed;
- *Provide realistic government funding for part-time student teaching*
  The two greatest barriers to adult entry to higher education in Europe are lack of time and money. Some institutions have already done a great deal to help potential students to

overcome the problem of lack of time and a good deal has also been done to reduce the cost of learning, for example by taking the courses to the students to reduce their travel and accommodation costs. There is, however, an irreducible minimum fee that the universities have to charge. National governments need to accept that they also have to make their contribution. This can be done partly by removing the financial disincentives to students, for example stopping the additional taxation of employees in Estonia when their degree courses are funded by their employers. Following this, governments must also accept that if they want more graduates, they have to provide more money to the institutions to fund them;

- *Increase collaboration between and outside higher education institutions*
  We have seen that some of the changes taking place require large-scale developments and these can be beyond the resources of a single institution. In the case of the introduction of e-learning, the problem is being overcome through collaboration with other organisations. These collaborations need to take place not only between universities but also, possibly more importantly, with other non-university organisations which have different skills and information at their disposal;
- *Increase the amount of information available on adult education*
  Despite the large amount of information presented in this book, it is clear that much more needs to be known. The lack of statistics, both at the national and the European levels, concerning adults in higher education remains a fundamental block to understanding how higher education institutions as a whole are coping with the changing demands upon them. The need for research on issues specific to adult education has been referred to in the chapters. Some research is developing. The 'digital campuses' in France, for example, have adult education research as part of their responsibility and research is also one of the tasks

listed for the proposed ILLs in Greece. At the moment, however, many more questions can be asked than answers given; and

- *Disseminate widely the information produced*
  The importance of these research results needs to be much more widely recognized and they need much wider dissemination. Despite the many initiatives to overcome the barriers to participation, for example, relatively few reports have been published on their success or failure. Publication of these results in journals and books, through presentations at seminars and at national and international conferences, can all play an important part in this.

It is clear from the previous chapters that the higher education institutions are already providing a good deal of education for adults in Europe. It is equally clear that they could do a great deal more. If they do so (European Commission, 2000), Europeans will:

- Increase their capacity to play a full and active role in society; and
- Improve their employability by acquiring and updating their skills.

This book has indicated many ways in which the institutions can increase and improve their adult education provision and it has also indicated where more information is needed. It is now up to the universities, with the support of the other major stakeholders, to put these ideas into practice. Adult learners and, through them, Europe as a whole will benefit if they do.

References

Balon, A., 2000. *Izkušnje in dosežki Ekonomske fakultete pri uvajanju študija na daljavo.* (Experiences and results in the development of distance education in the Faculty of Economics). Proceedings of the Conference 'Quality of Adult Education'. Portorož, Slovenia, 16–17 May 2000.

Beresnevičienė D., 1997. Adult Education in Lithuania: The Context of Central and Eastern Europe. *Adult Education Research Exchange*. Bulletin for Central and Eastern European and the Baltic Countries, 2, 11–12.

Blachère, M., 2002. La VAE entre dans le code du travail. *Actualité de la formation permanente*, 177 (mars–avril), Centre INFFO.

Bourgeois, E. and Merrill, B., 2001. Learning in Universities: Impacting on private and public lives. *Proceedings of ESREA, 2001. Wider Benefits of Learning*. Lisbon, 13–16 September 2001.

Bowen, W. and Bok, D., 1998. *The Shape of the River: Long-term consequences of considering race in colleges and university admissions*. New York: Cambridge University Press.

Bregar, L., 1997. *The Introduction of Distance Education – The Accelerator of Innovation at a Traditional University*. 18th ICDE World Conference 'The New Learning Environment: A Global Perspective', Pennsylvania.

Cross, K., 1981. *Adults as Learners: Increasing Participation and Facilitating Learning*. San Francisco: Jossey-Bass.

Elukestva õppe vajaduste analüüs, 2002. ETKA, Andras. (Analysis of lifelong learning needs. Estonian Adult Education Association, Andras).

European Commission, 2000. *GRUNDTVIG: Adult education and other educational pathways*. Available at: http://europa.eu.int/comm/education/socrates/adult/home.html

European Council, 2000. *Meeting in Lisbon, March, 2000*. Available at: http://europa.eu.int/comm/education/policies/2010/et_2010_en.html

Feutrie, M., 1998. *University Continuing Education in France*. Available at: http://www.fe.up.pt/nuce/FRA.html

Flemish Education Ministry, 2003. *Actieplan een leven lang leren in goede banen,* 7/72000. Report to the European Commission.

Greek Law No. 2527/1997. Unified secondary schools. Student access to higher education.

Jallade, J.-P., 2000. Lifelong Learning in French Universities: the State of the Art. *European Journal of Education*, 35(3), 301–15.

Mannisenmäki, E. and Manninen, J., 2004. *Avoimen yliopiston verkko-opiskelijan muotokuva*. (The portrait of Open University Web-students). Helsinki: Palmenia-kustannus.

McGivney, V., 1991. *Access to Education for Non-Participant Adults*. Leicester: National Institute of Adult Continuing Education.

Merrill, B., 1999. *Gender, Change and Identity: mature women in universities*. Aldershot: Ashgate.

Mitchell, V. ed., 2002. *European University Continuing Education: the Managers' Handbook*. Available at: http://distance.ktu.lt/thenuce/ebook/fcoursecard.html

Osborne, M., 1997. *Continuing education in the UK*. In: Thematic Network in Continuing Education: 1st year report. Liège: EUCEN.

Osborne, M., Brink, B., Cloonan, M., Davies, P., Marks, A., Turner, E. and Williams, J., 2001. *For me or not for me in Scotland? That is the Question: A report of mature student participation in higher education*. Stirling: Centre for Research in Lifelong Learning.

Osborne, M., 2003. A European Comparative Analysis of Policy and Practice in Widening Participation to Lifelong Learning. *European Journal of Education*, 38(1) 5–24.

Osborne, M. and Thomas, E., eds., 2003. *Lifelong Learning in a Changing Continent: Continuing education in the universities of Europe*. Leicester: National Institute of Adult Continuing Education.

Schneider, W., 1999. Der Anfang. In: M. Beyersdorf, ed., *Zur Zukunft der – wissenschaftlichen – Weiterbildung*. Hanover: Schriftenreihe der ZEW.

SUHF, 2001. *'Hur skall högskolan öka uppdragsutbildningen?'. Reflexioner och förslag av en arbetsgrupp inom SUHF*. (How will higher education institutions increase commissioned education?). Sveriges universitets och högskoleförbund, oktober 2001.

Szkoły wyższe i ich finanse, 2002. Warsaw: GUS. (Higher Schools and their Finances. Warsaw: Central Statistical Office of Poland).

Täiskasvanute koolituse seadus (RT I 1993, 74, 1054; 1999, 10, 150; 60, 617) 10.11.1993. (Estonian Adult Education Law).

Tartu Ülikooli lõpetanute uuringute, 2003. Career Centre of the University of Tartu. Available at: http://www.ut.ee/career/Tooandjatekysitlus2003.pdf

Toyne, P., 1990. Achieving wider access. In: G. Parry and B. Wake, eds., *Access and alternative futures for higher education*. London: Hodder and Stoughton.

Ustawa z dnia 12.9.1990 o szkolnictwie wyższym. (Act on the Schools of Higher Education, 12 September 1990).

Valk, A. and Pilt, L., 2001. *Virtuaalõppe väljakutsed õppijale ja õppejõule*. In: L. Pilt, ed., Elukestev Õpe Eestis. Tartu: Tartu Ülikooli Kirjastus. (Challenges of virtual learning for students and teachers).

Useful Websites

ALPINE Project E-manual: www.qub.ac.uk/alpine

Finnish Open University: http://www.avoinyliopisto.fi/english/index.html

German Ministry of Education: www.bmbf.de

German Learning Regions: www.bmbf.de/de/411.php

Karolinska Education AB: www.karolinskaeducation.ki.se/index_en.html

Index